MEMORY, MEANING & METHOD

A View of Language Teaching

Second Edition

NEWBURY HOUSE
PROFESSIONAL TITLES

MEMORY, MEANING & METHOD

A View of Language Teaching

Second Edition

Earl W. Stevick

HEINLE & HEINLE PUBLISHERS
I(T)P *An International Thomson Publishing Company*
Boston, Massachusetts 02116 U.S.A.

New York • London • Bonn • Boston • Detroit • Madrid • Melbourne • Mexico City • Paris •
Singapore • Tokyo • Toronto • Washington • Albany, NY • Belmont, CA • Cincinnati, OH

The publication of *Memory, Meaning & Method: A View of Language Teaching, Second Edition* was directed by the members of the Global Innovations Publishing Team at Heinle & Heinle:

David C. Lee, Editorial Director
Lisa McLaughlin, Senior Production Services Coordinator
John F. McHugh, Market Development Director

Also participating in the publication of this program were:

Publisher: Stanley J. Galek
Director of Production: Elizabeth Holthaus
Senior Assistant Editor: Kenneth Mattsson
Production Editor: Maryellen Eschmann
Manufacturing Coordinator: Mary Beth Hennebury

Heinle & Heinle Publishers
An International Thomson Publishing Company
Boston, Massachusetts 02116 U.S.A.

Manufactured in the United States of America

ISBN: 0-8384-5569-7

10   9   8   7   6   5   4   3   2   1

To Betty Rae

sine qua non!

TABLE OF CONTENTS

Preface to the Second Edition   *xv*

PART I   MEMORY

Chapter 1   What We Remember   **3**
Questions I Asked Myself   3
Introduction   3
Contents of Memory   4
  The "Five Senses"   5
  Emotion   6
  Purposes   7
    Academic Motivations   8
    Life Motivations   8
    Classifying Purposes   10
  Operating Characteristics   11
  Cognitive Operations   11
  Metacognition   12
  Language   12
  Time   13
General Attributes   13
  Size   13
  Abstractness   14
Schemas   16
Some Answers I Reached   17
Further Questions   17
Notes   17

Chapter 2   "Kinds" of "Memory"   **23**
Questions I Asked Myself   23
Introduction   23
Sensory Persistence   23
Short-Term Memory and Long-Term Memory   24
Working Memory, Holding Memory and Permanent Memory   26
  Working Memory   27
  Holding Memory and Permanent Memory   29

Comparison of Working Memory and Long-Term Memory 29
"Chunking" 31
Declarative Memory and Procedural Memory 32
Recall, Recognition and Identification 36
Episodic Memory and Semantic Memory 37
Decision on Familiarity 38
Explicit Memory and Implicit Memory 39
Tasks Experimental and Pedagogical 39
Decision on Familiarity 39
Identification 40
Free Recall of Words 40
Cued Recall through Paired Associates 41
Recognition 41
Some Answers I Reached 41
Further Questions 42
Notes 42

Chapter 3   Memory at Work: Basic Processes 48
Questions I Asked Myself 48
Introduction 48
Two Preliminary Models 48
The Dual Coding Model 48
The ISM Model 49
An Aside on Visual Images 50
Networks 52
What I Mean by "Networks" 52
Language Data and the Network Concept 55
Activity within Networks 57
Two-Way Traffic between the Worktable and the Files 58
Priming 59
Output from the Networks 60
A Pair of Diagrams 60
Figure A 60
Figure B: An Incidental Guess 63
Coterminous Pathways 65
Aural Comprehension 67
Production 68
Connectionism 69

Some Answers I Reached   71
Further Questions   72
Notes   72

Chapter 4   Processes of Memory: What Happens within the Files   78
Questions I Asked Myself   78
Introduction   78
How Long-Term Memory Changes   78
    Evidence from the Repetition Effect   79
    Evidence from Judgments of Learning   80
    Evidence from the Value of Retrieval   82
    Rapid Complex Simulation   84
    The "Din in the Head"   86
Examples of Comparison   91
    "What's Different?"   91
    "Who Do I Sound Like?"   91
    "Did I Say What I Meant?"   93
    "Am I Making Myself Clear?"   93
    "Am I Saying It Correctly?"   94
Memory as Construction from Fragments   94
    The "Worse than Average" Illusion   95
    The Flaggenheisch Incident   96
    "The Name's Right Here on the Tip of My Tongue"   97
Emotions   98
Reasoning   100
Some Answers I Reached   102
Further Questions   103
Notes   103

Chapter 5   Managing Memory: The Mechanical Side   107
Questions I Asked Myself   107
Introduction   107
Concentrated Learning versus Diffused Learning   107
    Concentrated Learning   107
    Diffused Learning   108
    Three Approaches to Managing Memory   108
Effects of Time   109
    How Long Things Stay in Working Memory   109

The Primacy Effect 110
Timing 111
Spacing 112
Pacing 113
Crowding 113
Effects of Activity 114
An Effect of Free Recall 114
The Worktable and Subjective Organizing 114
Experimental Evidence 115
Depth of Processing 116
Clinical Evidence 117
Classroom Evidence 118
The Generation Effect 119
"Mnemonics" 122
Some Answers I Reached 124
Further Questions 125
Notes 125

Chapter 6   Memory and the Whole Person   128
Questions I Asked Myself 128
Introduction 128
Communication and "Communication" 128
The Dimension of "Depth" 129
Total Physical Response 132
The Effects of Personal Significance 132
"Depth" and Memory 134
"Depth" and Communication 136
Some Answers I Reached 137
Further Questions 137
Notes 138

PART II   MEANING

Chapter 7   The Meaning of Speaking   141
Questions I Asked Myself 141
Introduction 141
The Meaning of How We Speak 142
Some Psychodynamic Meanings of Pronunciation 142

The Social Significance of Subtleties 142
The Guiora Studies 143
What We Can Expect 145
Meaning and Memory 146
Example 1: Pronunciations of "Stevick" 148
Example 2: Degrees of Foreign Accent among Adult Language Learners 150
Example 3: Use of Varying Styles or Accents within the Native Language 151
The Meaning of Ease in Speaking 152
Willingness to Use the Language 153
Restriction in Range of Speaking 154
The Importance of Ease in Speaking 155
Some Answers I Reached 156
Further Questions 156
Notes 157

Chapter 8 Interpersonal Meanings **159**
Questions I Asked Myself 159
Introduction 159
Two Sets of Conclusions 159
Arcadian Conclusions 159
Utopian Conclusions 160
Contrasting Techniques for Doing the Same Thing 161
A Utopian Technique 162
An Arcadian Technique 162
Comparison of These Two Techniques 163
Transactional Analysis and the Language Classroom 165
Ego States Described 165
Ego States in Language Study 167
A Simple Example: Classical Drills 168
Choosing Our Meanings 172
Some Answers I Reached 172
Further Questions 173
Notes 173

Chapter 9 The Language Class as a Small Group **175**
Questions I Asked Myself 175
Introduction 175

The Teacher   175
   Inside the Teacher   175
   A Hypothetical Questionnaire   177
Authority Structures   180
Interpersonal Trust   183
A Goal: "Voice in Community"   185
Some Answers I Reached   187
Further Questions   187
Notes   187

PART III   METHOD

Chapter 10   Three Views of Method   **193**
A Question I Asked Myself   193
Introduction: The Riddle of the Right Method   193
A View from Inside the Learner   194
   Performance: Self-Started or Reflective?   194
   Learning: Defensive or Receptive?   195
   The Role of the Learner   199
Mitchell's Principles for the Communicative Approach   199
Bridges   201
   The Bridge Format   201
   The DO Phase   202
   The OBSERVATION Phase   203
   The SPAN Phase   203
   Samples of the Bridge Format   204
   A Culvert   204
   A Larger Bridge   205
   Adding Spans   205
   Summary of the Bridge Format   208
Some Answers I Reached   208
Further Questions   209
Notes   209

Chapter 11   Six Methods   **211**
Questions I Asked Myself   211
Introduction   211
On Various Methods   211

Grammar-Translation   211
The Reading Method   214
Audiolingualism   216
The Silent Way   219
Community Language Learning   223
The Natural Approach   226
An Aside on Feedback   229
Some Answers I Reached   231
Further Questions   232
Notes   232

Chapter 12   Tradition, Diversity and Oakley's Thesis   235
Questions I Asked Myself   235
Introduction   235
Diversity and Tradition   235
Tradition   236
    A Poetic Illustration   236
    Investment   237
Oakley's Thesis: A Source of Diversity   238
    Ann   239
    Bert   240
    Carla   240
    Derek   241
Results of the First Questionnaire   241
The Second Questionnaire   243
Thoughts about the Questionnaires   246
Dealing with Diversity and Tradition   247
My Own Position   248
Summary: What I Hope for in a Classroom   249
Some Answers I Reached   251
Further Questions   251
Notes   251

Afterword   253
References   255
Index   273

PREFACE TO THE
SECOND EDITION

As our Model A Ford reached the end of its years, my father used to say that the only satisfactory way to repair it would be to jack up the radiator cap and put a new car underneath. The invitation to prepare a revised edition of *Memory, Meaning & Method* left me with very much the same feeling.

The need for "something new underneath the title" was obvious in the section on memory. Experimental research and theoretical developments of the past 20 years have made obsolete much of what I said on that subject in 1976. The section on method was even more in need of replacement, both because the alternative approaches to which I gave most attention then are no longer new, and because my understanding of them has in any case increased with experience. That section has been completely replaced. I have also made changes in the chapters on meaning.

Rewriting has required me to look carefully at what the first edition was trying to do, and at what it was not trying to do. Here is what I saw:

□ *In its coverage of existing literature, the book was selective.* (To have undertaken a comprehensive survey of fields outside my own would have been foolhardy.)

□ *In its assessment of the literature, it looked for practical implications.* It did not pretend to settle the issues that were occupying the theoreticians. (To have attempted to do so would have been presumptuous.)

□ *Reports of what the experts had* thought *were accompanied by accounts of what they had* done. (To have omitted the illustrations would have allowed for more content, but at the expense of clarity.)

□ *Language was kept as nontechnical as possible.* (The aim was to be intelligible more than to establish a new position.)

In this second edition, I have endeavored to preserve those four features of the original. At the same time, however, I have drastically modified my treatment of some concepts, such as the short-term versus long-term dichotomy in memory, and the overly simple treatment of the role of "depth."

This brings me to a second favorite quotation, the Swahili proverb "The country rooster doesn't crow in the city." In working on this revised edition, I have often felt like a country rooster, and that for four reasons. Most serious, no doubt, is the fact that I am not and never have been an academician. By that I mean I have not spent my years with ready access either to well-stocked libraries or to well-informed, theory-oriented colleagues. My employment always required at least 40 hours a week of getting things done in ongoing language programs, with flesh-and-blood students. Reading and thinking has been done in spare hours as a hobby.

A second reason for diffidence is that the professional experiences out of which I write have been unlike those of nearly all my readers. Even the languages with which I have spent most of my time have been ones that most readers will have heard of, but will have never actually heard spoken. Moreover, except for 10 years in English as a Second Language, I have never taught conventional academic courses either in secondary schools or in universities or in commercially operated facilities, which is where most language teachers work. On the other hand, what I have done as a teacher, learner, consultant, and course supervisor has allowed me to observe closely some aspects of the language-learning process that lie outside the experience of most of my colleagues. In addition, over the years I have achieved at least temporary conversational ability in eight quite diverse languages—Armenian, French, German, Portuguese, Shona, Spanish, Swahili, and Turkish—and ability to do something or other in a few others—(Arabic, Chewa, Hebrew, Japanese, Swedish)—not including reading ability in Anglo-Saxon, Gothic, and Latin. I also had four semesters of academically successful but linguistically fruitless college Russian. More important than the number of languages I have studied myself is the wide diversity of language-teaching methodologies I have experienced as a learner.

A third reason why I am a country rooster is point of view. I prepared the original version of *Memory, Meaning & Method* as a teacher and learner of languages who was trying to help other teachers to better understand certain parts of what was going on with their learners. In so doing I assumed that what is remembered is generally created out of interactions among people, but that it is registered and retained inside the nervous systems of individuals. I also assumed that learning (the building and shaping of memories) is a "total human experience"—one that is emotional and purposeful as well as mental and muscular. And I assumed that while some of the roles and responsibilities of the teacher can be shared by their learners, others probably should not be. Now 20 years later, some may find these assumptions to be either obvious or outmoded.

In this sense, although most of the details in this second edition are new, the book is no newer than its title, for it has been written largely from the same point of view as its predecessor. It is "the same book with mostly (78%, actually, counting kilobytes) different facts and words." If one believes (as I do not) that the human race is becoming better or wiser as the years pass, then assumptions I made so many years ago can no longer be of interest. If, on the other hand, one believes (as I also do not) that the human race is progressively going downhill, then such a point of view is of less value than those that went before it. What I do believe is that goodness and wisdom, where they exist, come into our lives only as creations both delicate and ephemeral. If we can create these qualities at all, or if we can be receptive to them when they are offered to us, we must constantly look clearly through our own eyes, but we can profit also from seeing as much as we can through the eyes of those from other places, other professional settings, and other times.

Finally, there is the matter of personality type. A few years ago I took a multiple-choice test, the results of which I suspect were largely accurate. It indicated that I am equally at home in looking for possibilities and relationships, and in working with known facts. So far so good. But it further told me that I value flexibility and spontaneity more than order, careful planning, and certainty, and that I am likely to base my judgments more on personal values than on impersonal logic. My impression has been that most books for language teachers are written by people who are temperamentally more devoted to order, certainty, and logic than I am. And so this edition, like its predecessor, is not so much a survey of the state of the art, and not so much an essay in theory building, as it is a personal memoir: an attempt to make sense of half a century of learning and teaching languages, and to share the results with colleagues. Each chapter begins with a short list of questions that had been facing me, and ends with a summary of answers that the chapter points me to, plus further questions it has raised in my mind.

Another Swahili proverb is *Hakuchi, hakuchi, kumekucha,* "It isn't dawning, it isn't dawning, it has dawned." This revision has been long in coming, but now here it is. I would like to thank those who have helped to make it possible. James E. Alatis, Mark Clarke and Ron Schwartz have been dependable sources of support and encouragement for many years, each in his own special way. John Hubbard, M.D., a psychiatrist, and J. Gordon Burch, M.D., my neurologist, have verified the plausibility of certain points within their respective fields of professional competence. Special thanks go to James R. Frith, long my dean at the Foreign Service Institute, for giving me freedom to explore new ways. My students at the University of Maryland in Baltimore County and at the TESOL Summer Institute in Barcelona (especially Seamus Haughey and Gerry Sweeney) bore patiently with my early reexplorations of memory. I am grateful to the Georgetown University Round Table in Languages and Linguistics, the Japan Association of Language Teachers, New York State TESOL, and the Conference on the Role of the Imagination in Second Language Acquisition, for allowing me to draw on materials first prepared for them and published by them. The students and staff of the Master of Arts in Teaching program at the School for International Training in Brattleboro, Vermont, have been unfailingly helpful and refreshing for decades now. Diane Larsen-Freeman, Lee Rawley, and Ken Schmidt gave thoughtful written reactions to an early partial draft. Most recently, Donald Freeman, David Nunan, Tom Scovel, and H. Stephen Straight have provided me with excellent detailed criticisms and suggestions for the entire manuscript. I have deeply appreciated their contributions even though circumstances have required me to suspend work before I could act on all of them. Responsibility for errors and other shortcomings of course remains entirely with me.

Part I
Memory

Chapter 1

What We Remember

Questions I Asked Myself
- [ ] What is "memory"?
- [ ] What is "in" my students' memory?

INTRODUCTION

With language we design great bridges and fight wars, we express our deep feelings and our spiritual aspirations, and even set forth our most subtle linguistic theories. We can talk, we can talk about talk, we can talk about talk about talk, and so on forever. Language is the special treasure of our human race. It is a mystery linking one entire person to other entire persons over space and time. To learn a second language is to move from one mystery to another. To teach a second language is to watch and guide that movement.[1] This is a book for language teachers.

But language, mystery that it is, rides on a deeper, broader mystery called "memory." In this human life at least, the self each of us knows—the self that speaks and reads and responds to language—is made of memories. And this word "memory," whether used in folk speech or in the writings of cognitive scientists, has four meanings. At times it refers to the sum of all changes that are left in our minds as a result of what has happened to us: metaphorically, this is "what" we remember, memory as *product* ("I have a very clear memory of the whole incident").[2,3] This kind of memory will be the subject of Chapter 1. In a second metaphor, "memory" often sounds as if it were a *place* ("How can I fix their names in my memory?").[4] "Memory" can also stand for the properties of our nervous system that give us that product. This is memory as a *power* ("Three Weeks to a More Powerful Memory!!!"). Chapter 2 will list and describe some of the powers of memory, and the "kinds" of memory "in" which information is said to be stored: "short-term memory," "episodic memory," and the like. In other contexts, "memory" is pictured as doing something—as going through a series of steps. Here it is treated as an action, or even almost as an actor. This is memory as *process*,[5] treated in Chapters 3 and 4. Chapter 5 on the management of memory and Chapter 6 on memory and the whole person will complete Part I of this book. Part II will go on to explore "meaning"—not dictionary definitions of words, but what differences the using and learning of language may

3

make in the life of the learner. Finally, Part III will consider how what we have found out about memory and meaning may be applied to how we teach.

In any of the four senses I have just mentioned, memory in turn rests on "mind." We can think of the working of the mind as a vast forest—a forest spread out over broad and uneven terrain, a forest whose lush growth, sometimes seemingly impenetrable, reveals no simple organization. Each set of observed facts about the mind is then a clearing in the forest. The theories of cognitive scientists are maps suggesting how best to get from one clearing to another—how to connect one research finding with others. Teachers, as practitioners, are primarily movers within that forest. We need to know our way around it so as to better accomplish numerous practical tasks for ourselves and for our students.[6]

I see my own role in the chapters on memory as that of an outrider—of one who does not live in the territory, but who has scouted this part of the created order,[7] bringing word back to the main body of troops. Or it is the role of cicerone, who does not own the palace but can still point out many of its treasures. My purpose will be not to inform fully, but instead to give readers an overview of what they may find if they look at the literature; not to establish terminology, but to clarify how certain words have been used; not to settle issues, but to prepare readers to consider them.

CONTENTS OF MEMORY

"To remember" is more than to bring back to mind some kind of replica of what we saw or heard in the past. The slogan "Remember the Maine!"[8] was not just a request that hearers restore to consciousness a mental picture of a particular sunken battleship. It urged citizens to support a war either by enlisting in the armed forces, or by paying taxes, or both. Similarly "Remember now thy Creator in the days of thy youth"[9] is an admonition not only to bring to mind a theological concept, but also to show corresponding evidence of humility and confidence, as well as to demonstrate ethical behavior in one's relations with other people. Even "I can't for the life of me remember her name!"[10] implies a desire not only to bring the forgotten name to mind, but also to have it available for use at an appropriate time, and for definite purposes. So "remembering" involves not just "memories," but also what we might do with those memories, and how they affect us.

Each of these three quotations is telling us the same thing about "remembering": that whatever we learn about memory, we must infer from people's behavior, whether in everyday life or in the laboratory. We then attribute to memory whatever *changes* in behavior seem to show a correlation with something in past events. What is "remembered" consists of events and parts of events—or more precisely, it consists of *information from* events and parts of events. In this sense, evidence for "learning" comes from observation of changes in behavior, and "learning" itself consists of changing what has been "remembered"—in modifications of the bases for action that are provided by memory.

Scientists who have studied these connections between past events and future behavior have made observations that are both numerous and often quite different from one another. It would of course be possible for the scientists simply to summarize their observations and stop there. But what we all really want from the scientists is some set of statements—statements that will not only summarize what has already been observed, but also predict what may happen under new circumstances.

There is however a price to be paid for these statements. In order to put them together, one must use at least a few nouns. And here is where things can get tricky, because language allows us to use a noun as a convenient tag for any set of observations. Yet we all too easily assume that every noun is, in the words of the classic definition, the name either of a person (an actor), or of a place, or of a thing. Then if we meet a tag-for-observations noun and treat it as though it stood for a thing, we are reifying it[11,12]; if we take it as standing for something that acts, we are personifying it—turning it into a "homunculus"; if we see the noun as standing for a place, we will draw simple maps.[13] Yet memory, like language but unlike mathematics or surveying, is inherently messy.[14] Ellis[15] hints that at least part of the "vagueness and confusion" in the metalanguage we use in talking about that messiness comes from abstraction. Accordingly, I shall endeavor to provide a relatively large amount of concrete narrative background about the experimentation that lies behind the concepts I introduce.[16]

Moreover, it has long seemed to me that even now, over 900 years after the Norman Conquest, imprecise thinking expressed in English is still hardest to spot when the lexical items come from Greek (e.g., "psychodynamics" or "autonoetic"), easier to spot when the vocabulary is derived from Latin ("inter- and intrapersonal actions" or "recollection"), and easiest of all when a writer sticks to the old word stock that has come down to us from Anglo-Saxon ("what goes on inside and between folks" or "knowing what was in our head at the same time as something else").[17] In this book, therefore, I will try to give prominence first to the observations (to what the researchers have seen and heard), to bring in terminology only later, and to define concepts in everyday phraseology.

In this first chapter, we will look briefly at memory as *product*, that is, at some of the many kinds of information that get stored from events.

□ THE "FIVE SENSES"

In talking about the contents of memory, most people would probably think first of sensory information. In the folk view, there are exactly five "senses": visual, auditory, olfactory, gustatory, and kinesthetic—in plain English, sight, hearing, smell, taste, and feel. This is of course an oversimplification. Sight includes many kinds of data: color, location, size, and distance, to name only the most obvious. Color in turn includes both hue and intensity, and location is expressed in terms of three-dimensional space. Hearing includes pitch, harmonic structure, loudness, and so on. The term "kinesthetic" is particularly tricky, since it is often left to account for whatever the other four don't: everything from temperature, to texture, to muscular resistance, to weight, to hunger, to vertigo, to a whole range of pains from puncture wounds to pleurisy, and much more.[18] So one inventory,[19] in use since 1909, lists seven major sensory modalities: visual, auditory, cutaneous, kinesthetic, gustatory, olfactory, and organic. But there are other, less obvious kinds of information, some of which are also extremely important for the overall working of memory.

□ EMOTION

One of those additional kinds of memory content is information about what is loosely called "emotion." Writers have sometimes provided lists of semantic features—features that are either present or absent for any given word—with the idea that definitions consist of combinations of those features. There is certainly truth in this hypothesis. But Zurif and Caramazza have put forward an alternative view. They suggest that the way word meanings relate to one another in the mind relies heavily on an undefined "residuum of meaning," which for any given word is made up of idiosyncratic details associated with its meaning, and that some of those details are affective.[20] They further report that adults who have partially lost the power of speech are more likely to retain affective features than they are to retain meaningful and grammatical features.[21]

The mutual independence of the affective and the lexical/grammatical features of speech is illustrated dramatically in neurologist Oliver Sacks's account of patients who were listening together to a speech by a well-known politician.[22] Most of these patients suffered from receptive aphasia. These patients were unable to understand words as such, but were unimpaired in their ability to respond to extraverbal cues: tone of voice, gestures, and the like. Their reaction to the speaker was derisive laughter. Another patient had tonal agnosia, which left her with just the opposite symptoms. She could respond normally to the speaker's words, but was unable to pick up on the nonverbal sides of an utterance. Her reaction to the same speaker was highly critical: "Either he is brain-damaged, or he has something to conceal."

Bogoch[23] cited a considerable body of evidence to support the conclusion that information is rarely, if ever, stored in the human nervous system without "affective coding." A quarter of a century later, writing about language acquisition in particular, Pulvermüller and Schumann echo Bogoch when they say, "A 'learned' [cortico-striato-thalamic] assembly with amygdala-midbrain associations represents *not only a linguistic element with its somatosensory and motor associations, but also an emotional state associated with that element*" [emphasis added].[24] Similarly Brierly[25] stated that "what is important and emotionally charged tends to be more rapidly [ensconced in memory] than that which is emotionally neutral or unimportant." More recently, Schumann has listed "emotional appraisal" of incoming stimuli as an integral part of cognition.[26] The key role of emotion in all personal functioning including learning also stands out clearly in H. D. Brown's summary of the work of Carl Rogers. Pulvermüller and Schumann cite a range of clinical evidence for the importance of emotional involvement in the perception and acquisition of language, the significance of emotional factors in language processing, and the value of emotional factors in testing or therapy with aphasics.[27] Just how these emotional factors influence the processes of memory is still the subject of some discussion.[28] Overall, however, I believe that the power and the pervasive role of emotional factors should not be underestimated. Nor should it be oversimplified into some ill-defined metaphor such as an "affective filter." I will have more to say on this subject in Chapters 2 and 4 when we examine how memory works.

□ PURPOSES

If what we are after, and the ways we go after it, and what we expect to find on the way, begin to show any consistencies and predictabilities among themselves, then they are likely to become parts of interrelated conceptual structures. Like other kinds of conceptual structures, these may in turn become associated with more conventionally "semantic" material in memory.[29] These purposive structures may indeed play a central role in how things fit together. As long ago as 1956, Klein[30] observed that "the perceptual system acts as if it picks up a great deal, concerns itself with a little, and acts upon still less." Klein pointed out that only some of what has been picked up is relevant to conscious intentions. He said, however, that even information irrelevant to these intentions may prove to be a means for fulfilling motives that are not the ones we are primarily focused on, but that are still active. He went on to speculate that coordination with fringe motives *is perhaps what gives permanence or persistence* to many things that have come in through the senses.

Richter[31] put it more clearly when he said that "more than 99% of the sensory information reaching the brain is quickly forgotten. The small fraction selected for retention is not passively recorded, but is grasped as an active process by the living organism because of its apparent relevance to the *basic drives,* for possible use at some future date" [emphasis added]. Schank[32] speculated that "goals are the basis of memory organization. We remember an event primarily in terms of the *goals* to which it pertains" [emphasis added]. Pulvermüller and Schumann cite evidence that "aphasia therapy that guarantees communication relevant to the patient's *goals and needs* sometimes leads to unexpected improvement."[33] Weinstein and Mayer report that "the *purposes* for which notes are taken and later used can have a large impact on the underlying [memory] processes used and [on] the learning outcomes produced."[34] Surely this principle is valid for activities other than note taking.

A stimulating restatement of the central importance of what I have been calling "purposes," "motives," and "intentions" is found in Snyder's discussion of "mood" and its relation to learning. He uses this word in a special way, to stand not for a momentary feeling, but for "the overall meaning of a person's existence at a particular time."[35] He goes on to say:

> Whether we are concerned with abstract thought or [with] sensori-motor skills, learning is [the] progressive adoption of the mood concerning that which is to be learned. Learning refers to a future, and to use of that which is to be learned. That is, *the function [in the individual's future existence in the world] of what is to be learned* is the key to grasping the mood of learning [emphasis added].[36]

In the language classroom, it may be useful to think of our students' "goals," "basic drives," "purposes," "needs," and "motivations"[37] in terms of two categories: academic motivations and life motivations.[38]

Academic Motivations

Language teachers generally place high value on the "communicative" use of language. True communication "involves active interchange with someone, and has elements of drama, hope and challenge in it."[39] Yet all too often we find that psychologically, "speaking [the FL] in the classroom lacks [EWS: even relatively simple kinds of] communicative purpose[s, and that this lack renders] it less effective as practice."[40] Instead, we find a set of three characteristic *academic motivations*: (1) to get the right answer, (2) to keep the teacher happy, and (3) to enhance one's standing in the class.[41] Unfortunately, most students seem to have only a limited supply of these academic motivations.

Life Motivations

on the other hand, are virtually inexhaustible. I have sometimes heard teachers discussing how best they might "motivate" their students. A better question, I think, would be how to identify our students' particular combinations of existing "life motivations," and how to harness those motivations for the work at hand.

One list of *deeper, more general* needs, abridged and adapted from Abraham Maslow,[42] includes three levels. Most fundamental, according to Maslow, is the need for security, and a fundamental component of security is predictability. The opposite of predictability is disorientation, *anomie*. For some of our students, predictability includes very physical questions: "Where will my next meal come from?" "Where will I sleep tonight?" or even "Will I still be alive a month from now?" For many, concern for predictability includes "If I follow this unfamiliar method, will I learn as fast and as much as I would by a more familiar method?" and "How might success with this method or this language change me as a person?" For all students, at least to some extent, it includes making sense out of what is going on around them at the moment: "What am I supposed to do in this class, anyway?" or "How does Japanese form the past tense?," and so on.

The second level of life motivation mentioned by Maslow is social: "Am I accepted as a member of a social group that I can depend on to support me?" Ahsen[43] has observed that this is true also for the relationship between teacher and student: "Children, especially while growing up, need confirmation of what they have observed before they can be introduced to harder challenges." This concern for the social side of motivation is particularly conspicuous in our profession, for language learners are necessarily operating between two cultures. My old way of expressing myself was not only a means of conveying information: it was also a way of expressing solidarity with those around me. The society that speaks this new language is different from the society that gave me birth, that nurtured me and taught me to speak, and both are different from the microsociety of my classmates. The relationships among these various societies may even have been marked by conflict or contempt.

A third level of need—of life motivation—is for ability to do those things that will maintain and improve one's standing in the group. These range all the way from earning money, to making reliable judgments in some area of common interest, to demonstrating superior performance in cooking or carpentry or correctness of grammar.[44]

As Maslow saw these needs, they form a hierarchy. That is to say, it is generally difficult to be motivated by needs on a higher level until one's needs on the level before it have been tolerably met. And the choices one makes in meeting a more fundamental need limit the choices one will have available for meeting a less fundamental need later on. If a "purpose" is an attempt to meet some need, and if needs are indeed hierarchical, then it is urgently important for us to be aware of our students' motivations on each of these three "deeper" levels.

There are also other needs, such as for getting up and moving around, or for satisfying curiosity, or for having fun, or for experiencing pleasurable colors or sounds or textures. Ahsen[45] asks, "Can a child remain involved for a long period of time in something which is basically ungratifying? We know well that the natural perception in the child involves pleasure and appreciation of beauty. . . . In order to remain involved with [a] picture, the child's interactions with the details must therefore . . . involve such acts as appreciation, touching and caressing beautiful details in the photograph." These "life motivations," which Bruner[46] called "intrinsic," do not fit easily into Maslow's hierarchy as I have interpreted it. Language teachers will however recognize them as belonging to the "inexhaustible" category. Sadow[47] comments that intrinsic motivations can be both causes and effects of language study.

Murphey[48] tells about meeting a Japanese woman whose English was so good that he asked her how many years she had spent abroad. She replied that she had never been abroad at all, but had simply exposed herself to the language at every opportunity, and replayed it in her mind between exposures. "You may not control the external environment as much as you would like," she told Murphey, "but you are in control of the internal one. You can tune your own brain in to any channel you want, at any time." Murphey summarized her account by saying she was "English-hungry."[49]

This story is probably an example of the powerful role purpose and emotion play in the process of learning a language. Apparently any activity, external or internal, that fed this woman's extraordinary "English-hunger" was rewarded by positive emotions, and by awareness of having partially realized a driving purpose. Of course, we still can only guess why her "English-hunger" was so much stronger than most people's.

The relatively good and long-lasting results of my own exposure to German may have had a similar basis. I remember that as I headed back to college for the Composition and Conversation course, I exclaimed to my brother, "Just think! At the end of the summer I'll be able to speak a foreign language!" I smile now at the naive optimism of that assumption. Notice, though, that I said "speak a *foreign langage*," and not "speak German." Since this conversation took place in June of 1942, we can be fairly certain I was not driven by some "integrative" motivation toward German-speaking society.

Classifying Purposes

Some purposes have to do with conveying mostly *cognitive information*: requesting an object or an action, commenting on an object or an action, answering, acknowledging, and the like. These sorts of categories sometimes appear in works on second language acquisition.[50] Longer lists of "functions" have been provided by Finocchiaro, van Ek, Wilkins, and others.[51] We may wonder how often the criteria for inclusion in such lists include ease of identification, and occurrence in a setting that the investigator can control.[52]

In none of the above senses is it possible to make *neat, nonoverlapping lists of "purposes" or "motivations" or "needs" or "functions."*[53] There are three reasons why this is so:

- □ Some purposes are *included* in other purposes: "to please the teacher" includes "to get the right answer," and is itself included in "to enhance one's academic standing."
- □ Many acts are intended to promote two or more purposes *at the same time.*[54] Thus an indirect complaint (e.g., "They never have what you need in this library!") may at the same time vent feelings, elicit help, open the way for further conversation, and contribute toward building a relationship.[55] Or figuring out a new predictability ("rule") in how the FL works may or may not be at the same time a means toward enhancing one's standing in the class.
- □ Similarly, Oxford and Shearin point out that many overall motivations for choosing to study a language—receiving intellectual stimulation, showing off to friends, pursuing a fascination with an exotic writing system, or having a parent-proof code, for example—fail to fit into either of the familiar "integrative" and "instrumental" categories[56]; and Clément, Dörnyei, and Noels hope to see an early end to what they consider the overly simple use of the integrative-instrumental dichotomy.[57]

□ OPERATING CHARACTERISTICS

Closely related to "purpose" in learning or using an item is information about what that item can do, or what can be done with it. A nonlinguistic illustration comes from research with the game of chess. In one experiment, between 20 and 25 chess pieces were placed on a board, and subjects whose chess skills ranged from average to the grand-master level were allowed to look at the arrangement for 5 to 10 seconds. Then they were asked to reproduce the arrangement they had seen. If the pieces had been placed on the board in a purely random fashion, then all subjects tended to put about 6 pieces in the right positions. But if the arrangement had come from an actual game, grand masters and masters were generally able to reproduce it almost without error. Ordinary players did no better with the actual game configurations than with the random arrangements.[58] The grand masters and masters apparently "saw" not only the pieces themselves, but also what might have brought the pieces into that particular configuration, and what might happen during the next several moves.

The same kind of thing happens with language. As they learn their first language children constantly notice countless details about words. They notice which words occur in which kinds of sequences with elements such as forms that mark tense or other grammatical categories. In so doing, they gradually learn which of those semantic-distributional patterns frequently co-occur. By the time they reach school age, children can use this accumulated information in order to identify the category a particular word is in. This in turn enables them to predict many other patterns in which the word will appear.[59]

We find a simple linguistic example in the words "sometimes" and "never." Students very early learn the lexical difference between them. But advanced learners and native speakers also know that at the beginning of a statement the two words call for different word order:

"Sometimes I wonder . . ."
"Never do I wonder . . ."

and this requires information about "operating characteristics."[60] This sort of information both about linguistic entities and about outside-world entities is essential to living and communicating.

□ COGNITIVE OPERATIONS

A little-noted "other" kind of information that gets stored in connection with everything else has to do with the cognitive operations through which one went in order to accomplish a certain task. Rabinowitz conducted a series of experiments in which subjects either studied whole words (e.g., ALCOHOL), or generated the words from fragments (e.g., AL_OH_L). The results of her research supported an idea already advanced by others, that "records of cognitive operations are stored as part of the memory trace of the stimulus event" and contribute to subsequent performance.[61]

This sort of information is no doubt of much more importance in the laboratory environment where it was identified than it is in everyday living. But there is a second situation where memory for cognitive operations may also be quite important: in producing or in comprehending the inflected forms of a new language. One can either simply memorize the fact that the whole word "ten-e-mos" in Spanish means "we have," or one can know what each of its three pieces is doing there, and put it together (in production) or take it apart (in comprehension). Learners differ, sometimes dramatically, in which of these routes they find more congenial or even possible.[62]

□ METACOGNITION

"Metacognition" is a Greco-Latin word that stands for what a person knows about his or her own knowing:

□ We know what kinds of knowledge we *have or lack*: "I know that I don't know the French word for souffle"; "I know that I know how to screw in a light bulb unhesitatingly with my right hand, but that I must stop and think if I try to do it with my left hand"[63]; "I know that I have a way of figuring it out."

□ To a large extent, we know when our attempts to use our knowledge are *succeeding or failing*: "For some reason, the bulb isn't tightening." "This new way of going at the untangling of German sentences has been working very well."

□ We know something about how we *control or use* our knowledge: "When I hear a new surname, I try to repeat it in my head and tie it in with some familiar word." "In screwing in a bulb with my wrong hand or from an unusual angle, I need to stop first and visualize which way the bulb will go."[64]

□ LANGUAGE

A very special kind of stored information has to do with language. Language is a means for both intake and output of information. It is the channel through which we receive much of the other information that we remember, but it is also one conspicuous vehicle through which the effects of that information are expressed and measured. Anyone who has learned a first language has already picked up a great deal of knowledge about language in general.[65]

As we learn any language, we hold onto pieces of various sizes. Some are single words: *come, round, ever*. Others are meaningful parts of words: *kindness* has two parts; *beneath* is probably an indivisible unit for many speakers, while for others it consists of two parts: *be-* as in *before,* and *behind,* and *neath* as in *nether*. Still other units of linguistic information—and these should not be overlooked—are the countless total utterances that have been met in connection with total contexts: *She was my aunt*, *It's on Nelson Street*, etc. These longer stored pieces of language are sometimes called "routines."[66]

Our memory of any specific piece of language may include information about (among others):

- Articulation: the physical acts of tongue, jaw, and the like that are needed in order to produce a spoken form.
- The physical acts[67] needed for the performance of writing.
- Audible sounds, whether coming in from outside, or generated internally.
- Sequences of individual letters that stand for words, whether coming in from outside, or generated internally.
- The overall appearance of a written form.
- Phonetic, syntactic, and semantic features of words.[68]
- Linguistic relationships and structures.[69]

□ TIME

A final type of information has to do with what we call "time." Within this category are *remoteness* ("How long ago did I experience this?"), *duration* ("How long did it last?"), and *frequency* ("How often have I met this feature or combination of features?"). By combining answers to these questions, we are able to answer two more questions that are essential to learning. The first is "Did these two (or more) features occur at the same time?" Answers to this question are essential to what is called "episodic memory." (p. 37) The second question is "How consistently do these two (or more) features occur together?" This information is especially important for nondeliberate learning. (p. 93) It is related to the formation and modification of what in Chapter 3 I will call "networks."

GENERAL ATTRIBUTES

All the kinds of data listed above can vary in two general ways: in their size and in their degree of concreteness or abstractness.

□ SIZE

The items in memory differ in their size and complexity: a face consists of complexion, features, and so forth; a sentence contains words, and words are represented by sounds or by some form of written characters. From a very early age, children show a surprising ability to divide sentences, words, and syllables into successively smaller parts.[70] Even single letters are complex: research on the perception of printed capital roman letters has shown a hierarchy of distinctions. The most fundamental distinction is clearly whether a letter does or does not include any curved lines (P, C, etc. vs. A, L, etc.). Within this contrast there are finer distinctions, such as that between curved letters with intersections (P, B, etc.) and those without (C, S, etc.), or between curved letters that do or do not have closure (S, J vs. Q, D).[71,72] Similarly, word meanings are not indivisible entities, but are acquired one component at a time,[73] and may have their own electrophysiological correlates in the activity of the brain.[74]

In general, then, we can think of the events that get recorded in memory at a microlevel, such as individual list items, or at a macrolevel, such as the entire instructional or experimental episode.[75] Spolsky expresses the conviction that some of the memory items we are accustomed to working with are only "gross, approximate ways of dealing with the outcomes of processes" made up of items so small and so subtle that we are unable to talk about them in ordinary language.[76]

□   ABSTRACTNESS

These same items of memory vary not only in their size, but also in their abstractness. We are accustomed to thinking of abstraction in classical logic: "If all A is B, and C is a member of A, then C is B."[77] Even imprecise logic provides plentiful examples: "Most men's voices are deeper than most women's voices. The person on the phone has a deep voice. Therefore the person on the phone is probably a man."

But abstraction is also of fundamental importance even in sensory and motor experience. Thus certain skills in swimming have been shown to be transferable from back to front.[78] Another nonlinguistic example is "looming."[79] As a human face comes closer, the amount of the visual field it occupies increases, and the angles from the center to the edges become greater. But the features themselves, and their *relative* locations, remain constant. If the face is then rotated 10° in any direction, the proportions will change, but they will change according to a constant ratio. A child very early learns to make these abstractions.

A linguistic example may be drawn from the perception of vowel sounds. The audible difference between one vowel and another lies in the location of two or three bands of acoustic energy, particularly in the range of 60–3000 Hz. For a particular vowel sound, the locations of the bands remain fairly constant for any one speaker, but they vary greatly between speakers. What does remain constant from one speaker to another is again the *relative* locations of the bands of energy.[80,81]

A little experiment I once conducted casts light on how abstractions of linguistic *form* may be absorbed unconsciously. The subjects were 25 language teachers, none of whom had ever been formally exposed either to any Scandinavian language, or to Turkish, or to any language that like Turkish has borrowed heavily from Arabic vocabulary.

The experiment consisted of two parts. In the first, I presented the class with five pairs of words. In each pair, one word was from Turkish, the other from Swedish. I asked the class to vote on which was which:

tanke	mahsus
förestods	kapak
imar	tiden
böyle	början
vidare	sezmek

All of the majority votes turned out to be correct. Since it was very unlikley that any of the subjects had ever actually run across any of these individual words, they were evidently responding on the basis of features they had picked up over the years in casual contact with names or other isolated words from Scandinavia or the Middle East. After each vote I told the class which word was from which language.

The second part was like the first except that now the subjects had to vote on individual words, whether each was from Swedish or from Turkish:

ledning
ljusbild
imdat
fri
olgun
hizmet
aldrig
mindre
isim
var

Again the subjects voted, and again I announced the right answers. As we went along, the correct majorities grew generally larger, word by word, *until the very last item*. For *var* there was obvious uncertainty. This was just what I had hoped for, since a word spelled that way means "there is/are" in Turkish, and "our" in Swedish!

I encountered abstractness of linguistic *meaning* the very first time I had occasion to try to use a language I had studied. We were alone in my teacher's living room—a former czarist general and I—and for openers he asked me in Russian, "How old are you?" I looked at my watch. All I had picked up from the general's utterance was that it was a question, and that it had something to do with time.

SCHEMAS

In the recent literature of language learning, as well as in the literature of cognitive psychology in general, we find frequent references to "schemas" (or "schemata" or "frames"). The term "schema" goes back at least to 1932, to a classic work by Bartlett,[82] where it referred to a "mental organization or framework based on cultural experience into which new facts are fitted."[83,84,85] We have different schemas for different words or concepts or activities: for horses, for houses, for changing residences, for auto accidents, and so forth.[86,87]

These complex structures called schemas may contain information of all the types mentioned earlier in this chapter, some of it relatively concrete. Many of the components of a schema, however, are quite abstract, consisting of categories that may be filled by any number of variables.[88] A schema includes information about what conditions must be met before a given situation can qualify as an example of a concept,[89] whether of a restaurant or of a gracious act or of an indirect question. But in addition to the knowledge itself, a schema also contains information about how this knowledge is to be used.[90]

A nonlinguistic schema is mentioned by the psychologist and professional flautist Thomas Wolf:

> It should . . . be apparent to the pian[o accompan]ist sight-reader . . . that the first important unit, represented by the flute solo, is four measures in length. Since it is a Baroque convention to build a movement out of thematic blocks of music which are of equal duration, the pianist knows that his most concerted attention will be required at the beginning of each new four-measure unit.[91]

In addition to catching a glimpse of the content of this musical schema, we see what the schema is good for: for giving the pianist some general information in advance, and thus enabling him[92] to devote more of his cognitive resources to the details.

Neisser, though not a language professional, applies the schema concept to foreign language study:

> Let us suppose that instead of acquiring a set of isolated responses, students of Spanish discover a structured system of relationships. Their knowledge of vocabulary, their ability to recognize idioms and to state rules of grammar, and especially their ability to understand Spanish text depend on their mastery of that system. Bartlett might have said that they acquire a *schema* for Spanish.[93]

Obviously this particular schema is a very broad one, with countless subschemas,[94] subsubschemas, and so on.[95]

Finally, we must keep in mind that such entities are not related to one another only as a series of successive branchings, like the trunk, limbs, and twigs of a tree. They may also overlap each other, with a single ([sub]sub)schema sharing items with other ([sub]sub)schemas: one and the same person may be the waitress of one person, the wife of another, and a creditor of yet another; a well-chosen word in a poem may be part of a formal schema that specifies rhyme and rhythm, and at the same time stand for an attribute of the subject of the poem.

Sadow[96] provides a helpful and well-illustrated thumbnail sketch of how schemas can figure in language study.

■ ■ ■ Some Answers I Reached

"Memory" itself is just a word. It refers in general to the fact that what has happened to us or in us in the past changes how we are able to act, or are likely to act, in the future. "Learning" consists in modifying these inner resources.

Our students' memory contains more than just the sounds, words, and structures of language plus their meanings. In addition to data from the "five senses," students retain information about time, about their past emotions and purposes, about what things can do in the world, and about what they themselves have done within their own minds. They even remember that they know certain things about their own knowing. All of this information is organized not only into hierarchies of size and hierarchies of abstractness, but also into configurations of things that have been found together in the past.

In this opening chapter we have been concerned with the metaphor of memory as object or product. In the chapters that follow, we will look at where and how this information gets used.

■ ■ ■ Further Questions

- □ Which kinds of data in the memory of students are we teachers most often conscious of? Which do we often in practice ignore?
- □ What would "memory" be like if it lacked visual data? Auditory data? Data about time? Data about emotions and purposes?

Notes

1. Hatch, Shirai & Fantuzzi (1990:705) put the matter very simply: "[We] believe that language learning must include an important role for teaching as influencing internal processing."

2. "Thanks for the memories!" (L. Townes). "Consciousness can raise to the level of awareness . . . an incredible number of engrams [memories]" (Granit 1977:75).

3. "There are some persons whose erudition so much outweighs their observation, and have read so much, but reflected so little, that they will not hazard the

most familiar truism, or commonplace allegation, without bolstering up their ricketty judgments in the swaddling bands of antiquity, their doting nurse and preceptress. Thus, they will not be satisfied to say that content is a blessing, that time is a treasure, or that self-knowledge is to be desired, without quoting Aristotle, Thales, or Cleobulus" (Caleb C. Colton, quoted by Allibone in his section on pedantry).

4. "In the darkest recesses of memory . . ." (Folk saying). "Ideas are imprinted on the memory . . ." (John Locke). "When this strategy works, listeners are saved from searching memory any further" (Clark & Clark 1977:65).

5. "Episodic memory acquires new information and keeps it available for some time" (Kliegl & Lindenberger 1993:617).

6. I very much agree with McLaughlin (1990:631) that cognitive psychology is not "the only way to truth" in understanding language learning; and with Block (1990) that we should neither ignore cognitive science nor accept it uncritically, but that we may do well to take into account the work being done by these researchers. Compare also Hosenfeld (1992:235).

7. Wolters 1985.

8. Slogan from the Spanish-American War, 1898.

9. Ecclesiastes 12:1.

10. Folk saying.

11. Salthouse et al. (1989:508) express a similar concern: "[One] problem is that the specific nature of [processing resources] has seldom been discussed. Instead, researchers have employed a variety of synonyms such as *effort, energy* or *capacity* without ever specifying exactly what is meant by those terms. Adjectives are occasionally added with the apparent intent of specifying exactly what is meant by these terms, e.g., *cognitive effort . . .* , but these elaborations have not been accompanied by more explicit descriptions that would remove the ambiguity inherent in the resources construct." The same could be said about the use of most other technical terminology.

12. Comments on the dangers of reification are plentiful (Neisser 1984:32; Gregg 1989:16; Casey 1976:xv). Of course, those of us who warn against it sometimes do it ourselves, but that doesn't make it any the less pernicious.

13. Hatch, Shirai & Fantuzzi (1990:702) summarize the pros and cons of simple maps: "To make *our research* feasible, we try to limit *our investigations* to one area, but in doing so, we may advance explanations that are faulty. The overlap among modules is admittedly great, but *our need* to substantiate modules as autonomous is also great. *Our fear* is that 'confusion will reign' if we attempt to approach the whole picture at once" [emphasis added].

14. M.A.K. Halliday 1978.

15. Ellis 1986:166.

16. What Casey (1976:9) once said about imagination could as well be said about memory: "It is just such detailed description that is patently lacking in many previous accounts of imagination. These accounts all too often rely on scattered descriptive remarks, and on this insecure foundation they attempt to erect an intricate theoretical edifice. . . . The consequences can be disastrous. One [such consequence] is that the reader may come to feel that what is being discussed is not at all akin to his own concrete experience."

17. Lutz quotes Orwell's 1946 essay "'Politics and the English Language'": "The great enemy of clear language in insincerity. When there is a gap between one's real and declared aims, one turns as it were instinctively to long words." V. C. Barnes (1990:517) notes that "Lutz also cites a study in which English teachers are found to prefer convoluted passages . . . to passages that say the same thing in simpler prose."

18. Felder & Henriques (1995:23) provide a list of "*the* five human senses" [emphis added]. Their list does not include "kinesthetic."

19. The list, devised by G. H. Betts, was reported in Sutherland et al. (1987:97).

20. Zurif & Caramazza 1974:170.

21. Zurif & Caramazza 1974:185.

22. Sacks 1985:76ff.

23. Bogoch 1968:25.

24. Pulvermüller & Schumann 1994:708.

25. Brierly 1966:34.

26. Schumann 1994:231.

27. Pulvermüller & Schumann 1994:686.

28. Whissell 1991.

29. Hamilton 1983:4f.

30. Klein 1956:175.

31. Richter 1966:96.

32. Schank 1982:92.

33. Pulvermüller & Schumann 1994:686.

34. Weinstein & Mayer 1986:321.

35. Snyder 1982:727.

36. Snyder 1982:732f.

37. I am here using the word "motivation" in the older and more general sense that includes reasons for studying the language. This contrasts with a more

recent and more specialized sense used by Gardner and others; see, for example, Gardner and Tremblay (1994:361).

38. Motivations will be explored more fully in Part II, on meaning. Dörnyei (1990:70) identifies four components of motivation in the study of foreign (not necessarily second) languages: an integrative subsystem, an instrumental subsystem, the need for achievement, and attributions about past failures.

39. Ahsen 1981:162.

40. Lennon 1989:384.

41. Sharwood Smith (1986:242) observes that "a foreign-language learner in a formal classroom setting may be said to be exposed to linguistic data in a comparatively pure form. But even here, there are other concerns which presumably force that learner to involve other knowledge systems as well: the expectations of the instructor, the expectations of fellow-learners, the desire to excel or not to lose face may all induce the learner to resort to various strategies that are not directly to do with the structure of the language, but which affect the comprehension and production of the target language."

42. Maslow 1970.

43. Ahsen 1981:161.

44. Maslow speaks of a fourth and highest need: for "self-actualization," for "becoming what one is potentially, [whether] painter, poet, ideal mother,]" or whatever. It seems to me, however, that in the very longest of perspectives at least, aiming at unique excellence for its own sake is an empty quest. To me the greatest good is not self-knowledge (Socrates), or self-actualization (Maslow), or self-realization, but self-giving. This idea is developed further in the last chapter of Stevick 1980, and in the last half of Chapter 5 of Stevick 1990.

45. Ahsen 1981:161.

46. Bruner 1967:11.

47. Sadow 1994:243.

48. Murphey 1995:35.

49. Freudenstein (1992:549) relates a very similar experience with a young North Korean man who claimed to have learned German largely by listening to short wave radio.

50. Taken from Coggins & Carpenter 1981.

51. Finocchiaro & Brumfit 1983:61–66; for definitions, see p. xiv of that book.

52. Coggins & Carpenter 1981. From within the linguistic profession, Flowerdew (1990:90) comments: "It is interesting to note in this respect that so-called functional language teaching materials tend to focus on the relatively well defined acts—requesting, offering, thanking, apologizing, etc. It might legitimately be asked, however . . . if this state of affairs might not in some way be per-

nicious. Are these acts selected and graded solely according to need, frequency, etc., or are they there because they happen to be the most easily characterized?"

53. Compare Flowerdew's remarks (1990:88) about speech acts: "There are in fact no limits to the size of the formal realization of a speech act. . . . On the other hand, one sentence can express more than one act."

54. Spolsky (1989:160) makes this point when he says that "a language may be learned for *any one or any collection of* practical reasons" [emphasis added].

55. Boxer & Pickering 1995:45.

56. Oxford & Shearin 1994:12.

57. Clément, Dörnyei & Noels 1994:441.

58. Simon 1974.

59. D. K. Dickinson 1984:360f.

60. Peters and Menn (1993:772) show that children may have partial knowledge of these as well as other facts about morphemes as they proceed in the learning of their first language.

61. Rabinowitz 1990:72; Fendrich, Healey & Bourne 1991:150.

62. Compare, for example, "Ed's" or "Frieda's" accounts with "Carla's," in Stevick 1989.

63. It takes three or more language teachers to change a light bulb: one to do the actual work, the others to offer unsolicited and mutually contradictory critiques of the methodology.

64. Based on ideas from Davis 1988:616f.

65. Eckman 1985:293; Bley-Vroman 1989:52f.

66. Krashen & Terrell 1983:42; Widdowson 1989:135.

67. The present list includes material from what in Chapter 2 will be seen as various "kinds" of memory. For example, the physical acts of spoken and written production depend on what in Chapter 2 I will call "procedural memory."

68. Dickinson 1984:360.

69. Cohen 1987:51f.

70. Fox & Routh 1975:339.

71. Gibson & Levin 1975:17ff.

72. Santee & Egeth 1980.

73. Baron & Kaiser 1975:303.

74. Molfese 1985:296.

75. Gardiner & Java 1990:29.

76. Spolsky 1988:392.

77. No doubt this claim could be supported by a citation from Aristotle, Thales, or Cleobulus, but never mind. See endnote 3, above.

78. Fischman 1985:462.

79. Gibson & Levin 1975:20.

80. Ard (1989:251) comments that "every phonological theory utilizes an abstract phonological representation, although of course the degree of abstraction varies."

81. The highest level of linguistic abstraction is implied in Bley-Vroman's (1989:52f.) assessment of the position of an adult language learner: "The learner *will expect* that the foreign language will have a syntax, a semantics, a lexicon which recognizes parts of speech, a morphology which provides systematic ways of modifying the shapes of words, a phonology which provides a finite set of phonemes, and syllables, feet, phonological phrases, etc. Universals of this sort are available to the foreign language learner merely by observing (not necessarily consciously) the most obvious large-scale characteristics of the native language . . . and by making the very conservative assumption that the foreign language is not an utterly different sort of thing from the native language" [emphasis added].

82. *Remembering.*

83. Nelson & Schmid 1989.

84. Clark & Clark 1977:168.

85. Rumelhart (1980:33) points out an OED quotation from Kant: "Any of certain forms of rules of the 'productive imagination' through which the understanding is able to apply its 'categories' to the manifold of sense-perception in the process of realizing knowledge or experience."

86. Bransford 1970.

87. Nelson & Schmid 1989.

88. Rumelhart 1980:34.

89. Bransford 1979:181ff.

90. Rumelhart 1980:34.

91. T. Wolf 1976:148.

92. All of the pianists in Wolf's study were men.

93. Neisser 1984:33.

94. Such as background knowledge about the structure of the type of oral or written text one is dealing with (Carrell, Pharis & Liberto 1989:647), or the structure of words or parts of words (Cohen 1987:51f.).

95. The little fleas have lesser fleas / Upon their backs to bite' em. / The lesser fleas, still lesser fleas, / and so ad infinitum (Anon).

96. Sadow 1994.

Chapter 2
"Kinds" of "Memory"

Questions I Asked Myself

☐ In what contrasting ways does the mind manifest its ability to be modified by experience?

☐ What are the most rudimentary tasks that human memory equipment performs?

☐ How do research-based categories of memory relate to what takes place as my students study a new language?

INTRODUCTION

The second metaphor commonly used in talking about memory is spatial, for example, by saying that one or another piece of information is "in" one or another "kind" of memory. This chapter is about some of the "kinds" that have been postulated, and about the observations behind them. As we consider them, we will do well to apply to "memory" what Casey[1] said about "imagination": "We must remain open to . . . the multiplicity of the mental. Within this multiplicity there is no strict hierarchical structure—only a proliferation of unforeclosable possibilities. An acute and continuing sensitivity to the multiplicity of the mental will allow us to acknowledge what is unique in each mental act and thus to [evaluate it] on its own terms." In plain English, "If we try to make things too simple too soon, we will miss a lot of what is in front of our noses."

SENSORY PERSISTENCE

In one series of experiments, subjects saw an array of 12 single numbers and letters—arranged as three horizontal rows of 4 characters—flashed on a screen for just a tenth of a second. The subjects generally reported not only that they had seen all 12 characters, but that their view of the array persisted after the screen had gone blank. When they were asked to report the characters, however, the subjects could come up with no more than 4 or 5 of them. What had happened to the rest?

23

Part of the answer to this question became apparent as the experiments continued. Now, immediately after the visual display ended subjects heard a tone signaling them which part of the display to report: high tone for the top line, mid for the middle line, and low for the bottom line. They could ignore the other two lines. It was discovered that under these conditions, the subjects' performance was nearly perfect. So they had indeed been correct in their impression that their mental picture of the array was persisting. The data they had earlier been unable to report had simply gotten lost because the display had faded during the time it took to report the first few characters.[2]

The terms applied to observations like these are "iconic memory" for visual data and "echoic memory" for auditory data. The other senses seem to behave in comparable ways. The cover term for all this is "sensory persistence," which stands for a phenomenon that lasts only very briefly—about a second. Apparently the data of sensory persistence as reported above (1) are undiminished and (2) are not yet interpreted. The latter point means that the capital letter T, for example, is preserved as raw visual data—as a horizontal and a vertical line segment in a certain configuration. At this stage, it is *not* any such concept as "the 20th letter of the alphabet," or "the last letter in *EAT*," or "a consonant made in such-and-such a way."

SHORT-TERM MEMORY AND LONG-TERM MEMORY

More frequently mentioned than sensory persistence is the contrast between "short-term memory" and "long-term memory." Let us look first at some non-human data. In one series of experiments, individual monkeys were placed in an apparatus that limited their freedom of movement. First, they learned that an item of food might appear in either of two windows, and that they could get the food by pressing a lever under the window. In one experiment,[3] a monkey was shown where the food was, and then a blind was lowered. Between the time when it saw the food (the "cue period") and the time when it was allowed to press the levers, the monkey had to remember where the food was.

Electrodes inserted into the brains of the animals showed that the greatest amount of electrical activity among the prefrontal neurons took place at the transition from the cue period to the delay. On the basis of other research, we also know that this is *the same period during which electrical shocks applied to the brain cortex are most likely to disrupt memory.*[4] Other investigators have also noted that the pattern of electrical activity of the brain changes significantly at the time when a new memory is being consolidated.[5] From this sort of evidence, scientists have inferred that at least one component of the physical side of memory is electrical. This is not surprising when we remember that the neurons that bring auditory, visual, and other sensory inputs to the brain communicate with one another by means of electrical discharges.

If we put a rat into a compartment with an open door leading into another compartment, we can be sure that before long the rat will explore the second compartment. But suppose that a second or two after the rat sets foot in the second compartment it receives a mild but unpleasant electrical shock to its feet. The next time it is placed in the same apparatus, it will avoid the second compartment. Wandering through the door this time would indicate that, in some sense, the rat had "forgotten" what had happened to it earlier. On such a stage, hundreds of rats have played out their parts in dozens of experimental scenarios.[6]

A basic finding of this research was that a second shock, strong enough to produce convulsions, might produce exactly this kind of apparently forgetful behavior, or it might not. The important factor was the timing. If the electroconvulsive shock (ECS) came within a very few seconds of the footshock, then the animal would, when next placed in the apparatus, go through the door without hesitation. If the ECS was delayed very long, however, the animal would "remember" to stay in the first compartment. The inference from this research is that the status of the electrical representation[7] of an experience changes very soon after it is formed, and that ECS somehow disrupts the changeover from the electrical to the nonelectrical form.

We also know that when rats are trained to use one paw in preference to another,[8] or when catfish are trained to respond differently to different odors,[9] their brains exhibit measurable biochemical changes. The biochemical entities involved are various proteins and ribonucleic acid. This and other evidence[10] leads to the further inference that another part of the physical side of memory must be nonelectrical, and presumably biochemical.

The busy language teacher will likely suggest a further conclusion: that the technical details of the chemical side of memory lie far outside our direct professional concern. This is of course a correct conclusion. But that same busy language teacher might still be interested to know that a widely varying list of influences may, under some circumstances, interfere with these chemical processes and so delay or prevent the consolidation of memories. Such influences include drugs, anesthetics, and lowered body temperature.[11]

The physical side of memory, then, may take either of two forms. According to a view that has been the basis for much of the research in this field, an original and fairly short-lived electrically disruptible storage is somehow converted into a longer lasting nonelectrical storage pattern, which is more durable.[12]

Now it is time to turn to human data.

Subjects in one frequently cited experiment[13] heard a set of three consonants (e.g., F, B, S), followed immediately by a number. They were then required to count aloud backward by 3's, beginning with that number, until they were asked to give the three letters that they had heard. When they were required to count backward for only 3 seconds, their recall of the letters was nearly perfect. Longer periods of counting produced more and more mistakes *up to a point*. At about 15 to 18 seconds, the subjects' average accuracy reached a low of about 18% (still better than they could have done by mere chance) *and leveled off there*.

We get a similar picture from experiments in which subjects tried to recall, in any order, a list of words that they had heard or seen. The words at the end of such a list are among the ones most likely to be recalled *if the subject is allowed to begin recall immediately.* If there is some interruption, however, this is not the case. The name that has been assigned to this phenomenon is "the recency effect."

The bend in the recall curve at about 15 to 18 seconds is one piece of evidence that has been used to support the idea of a distinction, especially for verbal material, between two discrete "kinds" of memory. Furthermore, experiments with human patients who were about to undergo ECS therapy showed a discontinuity of about the same magnitude,[14] and similar to the effects of ECS with animals. (p. 25) The noun phrases that are commonly used to refer to all such observations of this discontinuity are "short-term memory" and "long-term memory." They stand for the observable counterparts, or effects, of two media for storage: electrically disruptible storage and nonelectrical storage.

In 1976 I said that of all the findings that have come from research on memory, this distinction between short-term memory and long-term memory is the one that language teachers seem to have heard most about.[15] The same appears to be true today. Neisser, however, has complained that "[the topographical metaphor of talking about information as being in one or another kind of memory has] helped to reify[16] the concepts of short-term memory and long-term memory, to almost everyone's subsequent regret, and might better have been avoided."[17] More recently, Logie et al. say that "the notion of a single, flexible, short-term memory system has in recent years largely been replaced in the literature by the concept of working memory. It is now well established that there are likely to be a number of components of the cognitive architecture that are responsible for different forms of processing and temporary storage, and working memory often serves a a collective term for these various components."[18] So it appears that the term "short-term memory" may have been an example of the difficulties that can flow from the too facile naming of observations. We are reminded again of Casey's warning (noted above).

In any case, as I remarked earlier, we still need to notice when we are using these two terms for:

□ Memory as *place* (e.g., saying that a given piece of information is "in" short-term memory or long-term memory, or that it "moves between" them); and when we are using these terms for

□ Memory as *thing* (e.g., saying that converting short-term memories into long-term memories may be one of the problems of learning).[19,20]

WORKING MEMORY, HOLDING MEMORY AND PERMANENT MEMORY

For the purposes of language teaching, however, I think we will be better off with two departures from the familiar short-term memory/long-term memory dichotomy. The first is to go along with those contemporary scientists who talk more about "working memory" and less about short-term memory.[21,22] The second departure is to divide long-term memory into two parts, which in this book will be called "holding memory"[23] and "permanent memory."

Before going on to explain what I mean by working memory, holding memory, and permanent memory, I would like to go one step further, and replace these three terms with metaphors. My reason for selecting metaphors instead of more standard labels is not at all to brighten up my prose. I am aware of the dangers inherent in the use of any figure of speech.[24] But I am still more concerned about the dangers of such expressions as "short-term memory," "working memory," and the like. Such expressions, it seems to me, can be even more treacherous than metaphors are—mostly because they are less conspicuous. They can very easily become a means of obscuring complexity by simply giving it a name—the "reification" that I mentioned in Chapter 1. Readers who prefer the terms working memory, holding memory, and permanent memory are free to substitute them.

□   WORKING MEMORY

A critical aspect of the working memory concept is that "it involves the simultaneous storage and processing of information, and requires the maintenance of some information during the processing of that or other information."[25] Language teachers will be interested to know that one of the principal functions of working memory is as a vehicle for interpreting and producing spoken language.[26]

The metaphor that I used in 1976 for working memory was "the Worktable."[27,28] Several researchers have concluded that such a picture may be too simple.[29] More recent findings point toward viewing working memory not as one "work space" but as several. In fact, research measuring localized brain activity by means of positron emission tomography (PET) suggests rather strongly that "different cortical regions harbor verbal and purely visual short-term memory."[30] Clinical evidence from brain-damaged patients suggests that even vowels and consonants may be handled by different mechanisms, possibly in different locations within the brain[31,32]—a fragment of evidence for the neurological reality of these traditional categories. Experimental evidence with normal subjects also supports this idea.[33] It has been suggested that working memory may actually consist of a number of separate modules, and that various combinations of these modules may be activated according to the characteristics of the task at hand.[34] Each combination of modules could then be labeled as a different "strategy."[35]

One such model that has been successful in accounting for a wide range of data has been proposed by Baddeley and his colleagues.[36] Their model consists of three main components:

□   A central controlling executive involved in on-line cognitive processing such as problem solving and calculation, and in coordinating the activities of the other two.

□ An articulatory loop for temporary storage of verbal information, with

- an active subvocal rehearsal process, closely linked with the speech production system; and

- a passive phonologically based store, whose contents are subject to decay but can be refreshed by subvocal rehearsal.

□ A visuospatial scratch pad, similarly subject to decay and refreshment, with

- visual, and

- spatial components.[37]

Overall, then, perhaps a more accurate word picture for working memory would be of a number of small worktables connected by little ramps or bridges along which information can be slid.[38] For the sake of brevity, however, I will retain the singular "Worktable," with the understanding that it is almost certainly does not refer to an undivided entity.

The Worktable (or working memory) is often confused with our old friend short-term memory. They are alike in that each concept has been derived from observed limitations of mental functioning. It is by no means clear, however, that both are derived from the same limitations. "Short-term memory" comes mainly out of experiments with span memory, in which subjects try to retain strings of words, syllables, or digits. "Working memory," on the other hand, comes from the study of more complex processing. But span memory does not represent the limited span of consciousness. So I think we would be better off to resist the temptation to interchange the two terms.

In fact, however, we find a certain amount of overlap and inconsistency among the researchers in their use of these two terms.[39] What follows is therefore my own simplification, which is designed to reflect frequent usage among language teachers. According to this simplification, there are at least three important differences between short-term memory and working memory. One difference is that short-term memory is a stage through which information passes on its way to long-term memory. The Worktable, on the other hand, is really not a *stage*, but a *state*—a biologically describable state. A second difference is that with short-term memory, we are mainly interested in what *passes through* it. With the Worktable, we are mainly concerned with what *happens on* it.[40] Third, the very name "short-term memory" focuses on limited *duration*—on the 20 seconds or less that new material, freshly arrived from the eyes or the ears or elsewhere, can remain freely and directly available for processing. With the Worktable, we are more interested in its limited *capacity*, that is, in the fact that only a relatively small amount of information can be in the Worktable state at any one time.[41] In summary, then, long-term memory refers to one physical part of our memory equipment; short-term memory refers to what another part of the equipment allows us to do with new data coming in through the senses; working memory refers to a capability for consciously handling data from both external and internal sources.[42]

□ HOLDING MEMORY AND PERMANENT MEMORY

Now let us look at the observable counterpart or effect of nonelectrical storage, called long-term memory. By process of elimination, the expression "long-term memory" has been used for pretty much whatever remains available in memory after the expiration of the 20 seconds or so that short-term memory supposedly lasts. As we all know, however, some things that are available for longer than 20 seconds are in fact available years and even decades later.[43] This is what the term "permanent memory" refers to. Such material is metaphorically "in the Files."

But we also know all too well that other information—information that was still clearly available in memory after 20 seconds or even after 20 minutes—is gone a day or two later. This sort of everyday experience is what the concept I am calling "holding memory" is about.[44] Metaphorically, we can say that such material is "on top of the filing cabinet." It is there at hand; it is ready to be fitted into the Files; but it is also subject to being knocked off onto the floor and lost.

□ COMPARISON OF WORKING MEMORY AND LONG-TERM MEMORY

There are, then, four positive points about the "working memory" aspects of our mental equipment:

- □ The first and most conspicuous thing working memory gives us is access to whatever is currently in electrically disruptible storage—the question the teacher has just asked, for example. This means that in working memory we *hold onto* things without trying. In an everyday example, if someone tells us a phone number while we are busy addressing an envelope, we can often go ahead and finish writing the address, and then "play back" the spoken telephone number in our heads without difficulty. The same ability is being used whenever a language student repeats a word or a sentence that someone else has said a few seconds earlier.

- □ As we or our students play things back in working memory, we consciously *notice* things about them, things we perhaps didn't notice on first exposure: that the suffix on the Turkish word *festivali* appears to violate one of the rules we learned about vowel harmony, for example.

- □ Noticing two or more things that are in working memory at the same time allows us to *compare* them with each other: for example, the vowels of the possessive endings in Turkish *canım* "my life" and *evim* "my house."

- □ All this noticing and comparing allows us to do things with the contents of working memory *intentionally*: we can repeat them, we can arrange them in new combinations, check the Files to see what else we know about them, and the like. In Chapter 3, we will look more closely at the traffic between the Worktable and the Files. Conscious management of this two-way traffic is where we apply "strategies."

But there are also four negative points about working memory:

- □ It has no permanent content. Again, it is like a worktable, not a filing cabinet.
- □ Insofar as working memory gets its material from electrically disruptible storage, it must do so within about 20 seconds.
- □ The capacity of working memory—the number of things that can be in that state at any one time—is quite limited.
- □ Some of this limited capacity of working memory can be preempted by cognitive by-products of affective states such as anxiety. (This last is probably a lot of what the widely used term "affective filter" is about.)

The obvious positive points about long-term memory are that it can retain an amazing amount and variety of information, and that it can do so for long periods of time. It does, however, have two very important limitations. One is that we cannot explore it directly; we can only draw inferences from its products as they appear on the Worktable.[45] The other is that we cannot change it directly; at most, we can do things on the Worktable that we hope will have a desired effect in modifying the Files.[46]

Two-way traffic between the Worktable and the Files is both continuous and complex. Configurations of sensory data are constantly appearing on the Worktable and evoking the retrieval of various kinds of memories from the Files. These memories in turn work with the other material on the Worktable to trigger the formation of new configurations for storage in the Files, and so on. In this sense, the contents of consciousness constitute a stream of the perceptible products of cognitive processes. That much seems clear.

But can we indeed "do things on the Worktable that we hope will have a desired effect in modifying the Files," or is that idea merely an illusion? Who, or what, is the "we" that "does" all this "doing"? Who, or what, does the "holding on," the "noticing," the "arranging," and the "drawing of inferences" that I mentioned above? Certainly not "consciousness," for consciousness is at most a state, not an actor.

The question is whether or not the stream of consciousness merely flows on of itself, guided only by a combination of inputs from the senses and from the Files, or whether there is at least some possibility of occasional intervention by the person who is its host—its bed, to continue the fluvial metaphor. To take the latter position subjects one to charges of trafficking in homunculi—certainly not an accusation to be taken lightly. It seems to me, however, that to hold consistently to the position that there is no "we," except perhaps as a spectator, leads to the conclusion that that position must itself be only another product of some confluence of the same kinds of blind forces. As a nonphilosopher, I find this conclusion even more unacceptable. In this book I shall therefore continue to talk about "us" "hoping" and "desiring" and "doing things on the Worktable."

□ "CHUNKING"

Combinations of items and relationships among items make possible what have come to be called "chunks." As Miller explained it when he coined the term, a single "chunk" may contain a small or a large amount of information. Nevertheless, the Worktable seems able to hold a fairly constant number of chunks, regardless of how much or how little information each contains. For example, the number of unconnected words that we can hold on the Worktable is about the same as the number of unrelated digits, even though a word contains much more information than a digit.[47]

I think we need to make a distinction between "chunks" and what we might call "segments." The number 14052823886 can exemplify both. A reader might notice that the number consists of 11 digits, that the first digit is 1, and that the third digit is 0. On the basis of these observations, the same reader might decide to treat it as a phone number and break it up into four *segments:* 1-405-282-3886. This might in turn set up a familiar and comfortable rhythm for practice of the number, but anyone wishing to memorize it would still have to remember which of 10 possible digits belonged in 9 of the 11 positions. For me, however, the number consists of four familiar *chunks:* (1) "access to long distance" (=1); (2) "area code for Oklahoma" (= 405); (3) "prefix from my aunt's phone number" (= 282); and (4) "number of our own first private phone" (= 3886). So all I had to memorize was the sequence of four meanings, and the numbers came automatically. In everyday life, after all, familiarity and meaningfulness usually go hand in hand.

The same contrast between segments and chunks applies to foreign languages. The Turkish saying "*bilmeyenbilmez*" is written as a sequence of 14 letters. A learner could *segment* it in various ways: letter by letter, syllable by syllable, or as subsequences beginning with *bilme-*, for example. This would provide a smaller number of targets, and perhaps a phonologically comfortable rhythm, but it would not reduce the memory load. A more advanced learner could identify small familiar (and meaningful) chunks: *bil-* (= "know"); *-me-* (= "negative") *-en* (= "one who"), and so on, and memorize these. A still more advanced learner would be familiar with total words: *bilmeyen* (= "one who doesn't know"); *bilmez* (= "doesn't know").[48]

The precise number of chunks in any given piece of language is not of urgent interest to the language teacher. Nor are we particularly surprised at a relatively constant number of chunks that increase in size as the student gains in experience. Students who on the first day of class are hardly able to reproduce *hasta mañana* are soon able to handle activities that require 10-word sentences.[49] What we perhaps sometimes overlook, however, are three points: (1) this phenomenon lends itself not only to observation but to deliberate exploitation; (2) the upper limit is much higher than we usually suppose; (3) chunking is effective over long, though not extremely short, periods of time.[50] A teacher who has faith in this phenomenon, and who works with it deliberately, can get some amazing results.

One spectacular example of storage of large chunks of information is exhibited in the work of the simultaneous interpreter. In a classroom example, students learning by Gattegno's Silent Way are regularly given silent dictation by a teacher who points rapidly to a series of isolated syllables or words on a wall chart. They manage to come back with sentences of incredible length, after only a few hours of instruction. The two ingredients that make this performance possible are presumably the skillful way in which the teacher builds the chunks up, and the joint faith of teacher and students that the students can do it.[51]

Using a relatively conventional technique of the audiolingual variety, John Rassias succeeded in getting students to memorize prodigious amounts of material in dialog form.[52] Again, the elements of faith and energy were apparently the reasons for this achievement.

Both the potential size of chunks and the degree to which their size varies with experience were dramatically demonstrated in the studies of memory for configurations on the chess board, quoted in Chapter 1.

DECLARATIVE MEMORY AND PROCEDURAL MEMORY

Another pair of terms sometimes cited in writings on language teaching are "declarative" and "procedural" memory. In the literature of cognitive science, these terms have been used in a variety of senses. This distinction has been conspicuous in the ACT*[53] model of J. R. Anderson and his colleagues. In 1984 Anderson himself talked about declarative and procedural "memory."[54] Lesgold, quoting Anderson, mentioned declarative and procedural "stages" in the learning process.[55] Other writers speak of declarative and procedural "knowledge."[56] For our purposes, the central question is again, "What are the behavioral observations that these terms are supposed to remind us of?"[57]

Perhaps a good place to start is with the tying of shoes (a dying art in the age of Velcro). All the children I have known have acquired this ability by following instructions such as: "First, take one end of the lace in one hand, and the other end in the other hand. Now cross the laces. Now . . . ." After a few weeks of patience and practice, they no longer need anyone to *declare* to them what they are to do next. They have mastered the trick, the *procedure*. Meantime, the adult who provided the instructions has been going through the opposite experience. The adult was able to perform the tying *procedure* with no trouble at all. What cost the adult some time and difficulty was finding the right sentences to *declare* to the child.

And so the term "declarative knowledge" is sometimes used for whatever contents of memory is *"articulable,"*[58] for whatever facts or relationships between facts *can* be or *could* be transmitted through words.[59] Since declarative knowledge is usually described as consisting of a number of logical "propositions," it is sometimes called "propositional knowledge."[60] The declarative knowledge relevant to shoe tying includes the propositions:

- □ That is a shoelace.
- □ The shoelace has two ends.
- □ This is my hand.
- □ This is my other hand.
- □ The ends of the lace are in my hands.
- □ The laces are not crossed.
- □ And many, many others.

Three points need emphasis here:

- □ By no means all of the declarative knowledge that is relevant—and even necessary—for performing the task actually gets "declared" (put into words).
- □ Although declarative knowledge can be put *into* language, it does not necessarily come *from* language.[61] It is *"like* an internal sentence, but it is not a piece of any natural language".[62] In fact, much declarative knowledge is accessible to nonhuman species. For this reason, it would probably be an overstatement to say that declarative knowledge is represented in terms of language-based units, or that its storage is inextricably related to language structure and meaning.[63]
- □ We need not assume that all learning starts with declarative knowledge, at least on the scale indicated in this shoe-tying illustration. Examples are an infant learning to swim; a child who adopts the voice quality of its parents or peers; even some children learning to tie shoes; anyone learning to recognize an odor.[64]

The expression that contrasts with "declarative knowledge" is "procedural knowledge." In the ACT* model, procedural knowledge is made up of "productions." A production takes the form: "IF (this is true)—THEN (do that)."[65] Two examples are:

IF the purpose is to tie shoes,
    and two ends of a lace are visible and within reach;
THEN grasp one end in each hand.

IF one end of the lace is in each hand
    and the laces are not crossed;
THEN cross the laces.

Information active in working memory provides for the assembly of "procedures." A procedure in this sense typically requires multiple productions.[66]

Notice also:

- □ The conditions listed in the IF part of a procedure consist of declarative knowledge.

- □ What follows the THEN of a procedure is *doing*, not just knowing what *ought* to be done: playing a satisfactory game of chess versus reciting rules and principles.[67]

- □ So although it may be profitable to distinguish between declarative and procedural memory, the two are not separate, watertight compartments. In fact, the purpose of the ACT* model from which these terms are taken is to account for how skills are built up by transition from declarative to procedural knowledge.[68]

In the above example, the child begins with declarative knowledge of shoe tying and ends with procedural knowledge. The declarative knowledge, at first useful, is quickly lost, and will have to be painstakingly reconstituted 20 years later if it is to be used with the next generation of children.

We can apply this same *declarative-procedural* distinction to language. We sometimes try to guide learners by means of declared information that we hope will soon move into their store of THEN material. Some of the "propositions" involved in producing the first sound in English "tie," if expressed in words, might be:

- □ The tongue tip is this far forward but not that far. ("This" and "that" in this sentence are known to the speaker acoustically and proprioceptively, but cannot ordinarily be declared in words.)

- □ There is complete momentary stoppage of the speech tract.

- □ Voice onset is delayed by this much but not by that much. (Again, this information is acoustic and proprioceptive but not declarable.)

A related production might be:

IF   purpose is to produce the sound that has already been met at the beginning of "tie, two, tea," etc.

THEN   place tongue tip here, create a stoppage, and delay onset of voice by this much. (Yet again, "here" and "this" are known by feel but cannot be defined in words.)

Similarly, negation in English includes potentially declarable information about word order, the parts of speech of surrounding words, and choice between "no" and "not." The corresponding productions specify what to do, and under what circumstances. When all of this information has become firmly established, we can say that the ability to form negative sentences has been "added to the learner's procedural knowledge" of the language. To say that a piece of procedural knowledge is properly constructed is to say that it gives the needed performance. With time, the declarative knowledge may become less and less declarable (as in the case of the adult who is attempting to teach shoe tying).

As with the shoe-tying example, the propositions in declarative memory that relate to how language works *are not sentences* in any language. In one's native language, in fact, they are seldom if ever even derived *from* any verbal formulation. This is the difference between what Sharwood Smith and others have labeled "implicit" knowledge (the ability to conform to the *regularities* found in the speech or actions of others) and "explicit" knowledge (the ability to recite *rules about* those regularities).[69]

And so it is that a native speaker trying to give explicit directions for producing a sound or for using a word or for controlling a structure is in three ways at a disadvantage compared to an adult who is merely teaching someone to tie shoes. The instructor in shoe tying (1) knows what there is to observe, and (2) shares with the learner a basic but adequate vocabulary for reporting self-observations: "lace," "finger," "around," and the like. In addition, (3) the instructor has heard, at least in the dim and distant past, a series of directions similar to those that are needed now. The naive explainer of language has none of these. The linguistically trained explainer of language, on the other hand, may have the observational power, and probably has seen and heard quite a few explicit formulations. He or she also possesses a suitable vocabulary (e.g., "noun phrase," "indirect object," "possessive case"). The difficulty comes when the learner does not share that vocabulary, and so is kept from profiting from what the teacher thinks she or he has conveyed.

For us, the above discussion of the declarative/procedural distinction leaves one fundamental question unanswered: *To what extent does eventual control of some bit of a language profitably begin with declarative knowledge anyway?* One reader of this chapter reported that all the children he had known had learned shoe tying by observation, and not by following verbal instructions as in my example. As for language, we know that declarable rules are available for only a small fraction of what a speaker or listener actually does, and that a child learning its first language is exposed to few if any of those. Recent years have seen much exploration of the possibility that even adults may acquire extensive command of a language just by understanding comprehensible input, without significant use of declared generalizations about how it works. To be sure, some successful learners testify that their mastery of this or that point began with certain declarative knowledge they found in a rule, but how can we be sure they are not falling into the fallacy of *post hoc ergo propter hoc*? Perhaps insofar as declarative knowledge does help, its role is comparable to that of the wooden forms into which concrete is poured: it shapes a combination of auditory, visual, and meaningful ingredients which over time solidify so that the forms can be removed and discarded.

Research on the uninstructed picking-up of grammatical relationships—part of what in Chapter 1 were called "operating characteristics"—provides an interesting sidelight to the declarative-procedural terminology. The experimenter had subjects memorize "sentences" of from six to eight characters chosen from the set P, S, T, V, X. The control group in the experiment learned random combinations of these letters. The experimental group learned combinations that were put together according to a set of rules, but the subjects were unaware of this fact. It was found that subjects working with structured data not only memorized better, but after they were told that there was a system they were also able to pick out which new "sentences" fitted that system, and even to point out which parts of the "wrong" sequences did not fit. They were not, however, able to describe the system in words. In the terminology of this chapter, they were able to respond to and even to point out consciously some of the "regularities," but they could not come up with explicit "rules."

□ RECALL, RECOGNITION AND IDENTIFICATION

Before going on to consider the next "kinds" of "memory," we need to look briefly at three tasks that get accomplished both in experimental contexts and in everyday life. They are recall, recognition, and identification.

I noted earlier that one very general observation about remembering, both inside and outside the laboratory, is that people can more or less accurately report—they can "recall"—what they have seen or heard in the past. In a narrower sense used mainly by research psychologists, however, people may or may not be able to "recall" what they saw or heard *during a particular period of time.* In everyday life, this is Karen remembering that *as* I walked up the hillside I *was carrying a lawn chair.* In a language course, I tell my classmate that *yesterday at the end of class* our teacher *told us to review Unit 5.* In the laboratory, a subject hears three lists of 10 words each, and then tries to reproduce words from the second list only. Or, again in the lab, a subject hears a series of pairs of words (*fan-monkey, sliver-kite,* etc.). Later, the same subject is given one word from each pair, and is asked to supply the word that went with it *in that particular series of pairs.*

Another observation is that people can often say whether what they are seeing or hearing or tasting or smelling or feeling is something that they have experienced before. This is commonly called "recognition." But "to recognize" is another term that can be used in broader and narrower senses. Most generally, we recognize something when we repeatedly respond to it in the same way as we did on some unspecified previous occasion. It is in this sense that we recognize a face or a melody. In the narrower sense used by research psychologists, however, to recognize something is to be able to report that we encountered it *on some specific previous occasion.* In the laboratory, subjects are in this sense asked to "recognize" whether or not a particular picture was or was not included in the stack of pictures they viewed *on the preceding day.* In the classroom, students try to answer true/false statements about the trivial "story" *they have just read.*

Yet another observation is that even when people have been exposed to only a part of a word or a situation or a picture or a melody, or have been exposed to the whole only briefly, their minds can often fill in missing details, either of the thing itself or of its meaning or its name or its operating characteristics. On the other hand, they cannot do this if the exposure was *too* fragmentary or *too* brief. The name for this phenomenon is "identification."[70] The question to be answered is, "Of all the words/people/colors, etc. I have met in the past, which one is this?"—which is a sort of matching task.

This ability to identify things we have encountered before is attributed by some writers to what they call "perceptual memory." According to those writers, the "perceptibility" of a given word "is typically evidenced in terms of either the accuracy of identification of words that are exposed at near-threshold durations, or the speed of identification of words that come into view gradually."[71] The expression "perceptual fluency" *for an item*, in turn, refers to a particular subject's ability to identify *that item* quickly and accurately.[72] It may be improved by a process called "perceptual priming." Some writers have conjectured that such tasks as perceptual identification may depend on a special perceptual representation system that uses parts of the brain different from those used for other kinds of memory.[73]

□ EPISODIC MEMORY AND SEMANTIC MEMORY

Another distinction that is being cited with increasing frequency in publications for language teachers these days is between "episodic memory" and "semantic memory."[74] This distinction apparently originated with Tulving.[75] One of the defining characteristics of the episodic system is "recollective experience." Recollective experience means conscious awareness of other information that was present *at the time* a word or other selected stimulus was encountered—next to the ink smudge near the top of a left-hand page. This other information may have to do with the physical appearance of the stimulus, or with the way it was presented, or with something one was thinking of or did during its presentation, or with something one did, or with anything else one may have noticed in the surroundings at that time.[76] Bransford says that "episodic memory refers to the storage and retrieval of personally *dated,* autobiographical experiences": for example, making a great shot at tennis, or encountering *boy* as part of an experimenter's list of words.[77] Klatzky, a bit more cautiously, speaks not of episodic "memory," but only of episodic "knowledge," by which she means knowledge that "concerns events of one's life; not only what happened but where *and when, context as well as fact.*"[78,79]

A further observation about remembering is that we not only report whole forms, as with recall, or fill in gaps in them, as with identification, or report whether or not we encountered them during some particular time period, as with recognition. We also know something about what *usually* goes with them: what other words and what other objects or actions or feelings or other sensations. Bransford says that "semantic memory refers to general knowledge of concepts, principles, and meanings that are used in the process of encoding or comprehending particular inputs."[80] Klatzky, again more cautious, says simply that "semantic *knowledge* is not tied to individual [incidents]; it is factual information that transcends a particular context. 'Cats are chased by dogs' is a semantic fact; 'My cat was chased by a dog yesterday' is an episodic fact"[81] [emphasis added]. So there is a close relationship between the contents of semantic memory and the "schemas" discussed in Chapter 1.

For the present, I think it would be fair to say that "episodic" refers to the question "What *went* with what *then?*" and that "semantic" refers to "What *is likely to go* with what *in the future?*" As I noted with respect to declarative and procedural memory, however, episodic and semantic memory are not separate, watertight compartments,[82] for semantic knowledge must ultimately be derived from episodes.[83]

Both recall and recognition, *in the narrower senses* described earlier, deal with whole words or other whole forms. They are instances of episodic knowledge, or of the operation of episodic memory:

> "What were the words that I saw flashed on the screen a few minutes ago?"
> "Was this word among those presented to me by the experimenter at this time yesterday?"

Identification, on the other hand, requires the filling in of gaps in what has been only partially perceived. Thus it relies not on episodic memory, but on procedural or semantic memory.[84] The general "production" here is:

IF   faced with a set of fragments that have occurred together in the past but which do not make up a familiar whole;

and the aim is to make sense of whatever is coming in;

THEN   try filling in various combinations of other fragments that have occurred regularly with these fragments in the past.

Nonlinguistically, if one sees two eyes and a mouth in familiar locations relative to one another, then one tends to interpret whatever is found in the nose position as a manifestation of a nose, and to report that what one is seeing is a face. In Lewis Carroll's line "All mimsy were the borogoves" we know that borogoves is a plural noun even though it has no meaning for us.

An example from language study is evident in English speakers' frequent mispronunciation of the Swahili word *karíbu*, which means "near." The error is to place the stress on the first syllable instead of the second. Apparently what happens is that learners register only an incomplete set of fragments—most or all of the vowels and consonants, but not the location of the stress. The above general production therefore leads many North Americans to identify[85] the Swahili word with English *cáribou*, which has similar vowels and consonants, and in the same order, but with stress on the first syllable. That identification then becomes the apparent basis for the mispronunciation "káribu."

□ DECISION ON FAMILIARITY

Before going on to the last two "kinds" of "memory," we need to look at yet another experimental task. Here, subjects are shown a group of letters, and are asked to indicate whether or not it is a word in their native language. In their decisions, they are answering the question "Have I ever met this combination of items before in connection with any meaning?" (The experimental literature[86] calls this the "lexical decision task.")

□   EXPLICIT MEMORY AND IMPLICIT MEMORY

The last two "kinds" of "memory" to be contrasted in this chapter are "implicit memory" and "explicit memory." These are best understood in terms of the tasks used in assessing them.[87] In a test of explicit memory, subjects are directed to consciously recall prior events and experiences[88] that were present at the same time as some experimental stimulus. Because explicit memory for an item makes use of that item's ties to context, it is widely assumed to depend on the episodic system.[89] Three such tasks are free and cued recall and recognition, in the narrower senses explained earlier in this chapter.[90] In implicit tasks, subjects are not directed to consciously recall prior events.[91,92] Identification, decision on familiarity, and pattern completion are examples.

Readers should be aware that these same two terms "implicit" and "explicit" are used with nouns other than "memory," sometimes in ways that are not clearly consistent with the above. In the shoe-tying example I referred to implicit or explicit "knowledge," depending on whether or not people were able to put into words the rules to which their language conformed.[93] Frensch and Miner explore the mechanisms of explicit (intentional) and implicit (incidental) "learning."[94] The relationship between these two similarly named kinds of learning and memory is the subject of continuing discussion.

□   TASKS EXPERIMENTAL AND PEDAGOGICAL

In examining all these "kinds" of "memory," we have encountered a number of tasks that are often performed by experimental subjects. It may be worthwhile to consider how each of these tasks relates to what language students have to do. Two of them actually come fairly close.

Decision on Familiarity

Here is an experimental task that is very much shared by learners of a foreign language. Most obviously, a language learner is constantly having to consider *incoming* data so as to answer the question, "Have I met this word or sound or construction before, or is this something new to figure out?" The answers to this question will guide the learner in choosing where and when to focus in the midst of a welter of possible targets of attention. Just as important, however, the learner must also answer this same question concerning *internally generated* forms. So, for example, a speaker who puts together "sewed" from "sew" + "-ed" will get a Yes answer, and will go ahead and produce the form. The same speaker, mentally producing "goed" from "go" + "-ed", will get a No answer, and so will either suppress the form or correct it if it has already been uttered.[95] Lack of a well-developed bank of information about past experience may be part of the reason why small children, at one stage of acquiring their native language, produce many forms (such as *goed) which are regular but not standard.

Identification

Unlike superior recognition, and unlike free or cued recall (in the special senses noted in this chapter), the ability to give an accurate answer to the question "Which familiar item is this?" is indispensable to anyone who is trying to use a foreign language. As we know, efficient readers do not focus on one letter at a time, and then sound out each word on a page. Rather, they construct a whole word from whatever of its fragments they have registered, or the gist of a whole paragraph by glancing through it. Similar statements can of course be made about oral comprehension: for example, understanding a short-wave broadcast in spite of fading and static. And comprehension cannot be fluent unless the answers are not only accurate but quick (i.e. perceptually fluent). Comprehension needs these answers for too many purposes, in the midst of too many simultaneous and competing processes.

Free Recall of Words

Three other experimental tasks are farther from what our students do than they might first seem to be. Thus the phrase "free recall" sounds very relevant to the learning and using of foreign languages. But we saw that the experimental task differs in two ways from what our students are required to do:

□ The experimental subject, motivated by a desire to cooperate with (or to frustrate!) the experimenter, is asked to "recall" words that were met at some specific time in the not-too-distant past. The language student is asked to "recall" from any time in the past words that are needed at the moment for some communicative motivation.

□ The words to be recalled in the laboratory are virtually always from the subject's native language. This means that while the words are being presented, the subject gets the meaning imagery for each from a stimulus that has been heard of read within a very few milliseconds, and with no noticeable effort. At recall time, the subject comes up with the spoken or written forms in the same way. The task consists largely in answering the question: "Which of the word-meanings in my total vocabulary were included in the list?" The subject does *not* have to spend time or energy in order to answer the next question: "What vowels and consonants will I need in order to report this meaning in my native language?" In speaking or writing a foreign language, the situation is reversed. The student already has the meaning in mind; what must be recalled is the right combination of phonemes.

Cued Recall through Paired Associates

This task also sounds reassuringly familiar, something like "What's the Spanish word for 'carrot'?" But again, there are differences:

- □ As with free recall, the experimental objects to be stored and brought back are words for which the linkages are already well established between meaning and acoustic image, or between meaning and pronunciation, or both. By definition, this is much less true with foreign languages.

- □ The words to be associated in the laboratory have been paired arbitrarily by the experimenter, on almost any basis *except* that they mean the same thing. The words on the two sides of a flashcard for language study are supposed to be as close as possible to identical in their meanings.

- □ The pairings in the laboratory are temporary. The goal is to remember pairings until the next list is presented, in which some of the same words may show up again, but with different partners. The pairings of native and foreign words are permanent, and the goal is to retain them for the indefinite future.

Recognition

This is something else we would like all our students to do well. But:

- □ In the restricted sense in which experimental psychologists use the term, "recognition" means being given a picture, or a word from one's native language, and saying whether it had been met at some specific earlier time.

- □ To "recognize" a foreign word, on the other hand, is to come up with the correct meaning for a form that has been heard or read.

It appears, then, that the psychologists' versions of free and cued recall and recognition are not immediately applicable to what our students do. Nevertheless, these tasks will be of interest in Chapter 5 as indicators of how things get into "holding memory."

■ ■ ■ *Some Answers I Reached*

Memory makes use of three media: sensory retention, electrically disruptible storage (commonly called "short-term memory"), and nonelectrical storage (commonly called "long-term memory"). These concepts are based on quite different sets of observations, and differ among themselves with regard to their physical bases. In place of "short-term memory" many writers use the term "working memory," though the two are not exactly synonymous. Metaphorically, we can think of working memory as a Worktable, and long-term memory as a set of Files.

Within long-term memory, our classroom experience has shown us that some information continues to be available to our students for weeks, months, and years. We know all too well, however, that other information, though clearly available to them after a few minutes, can be lost within the hour. I have used the terms "permanent memory" and "holding memory" as labels for the ends of this quantitative continuum within long-term memory. Qualitatively, there appear to be certain discrete "kinds" of long-term memory: declarative memory and procedural memory; episodic memory and semantic memory; and explicit and implicit memory. All of these "kinds" show up in the everyday study of foreign languages.

Among the simplest tasks for memory are the recall, recognition, and identification of items, and judging whether something new has become available from long-term memory. All are parts of what any language student needs to do. But teachers reading experimental reports should be warned that these terms have special meanings in the laboratory.

■ ■ ■   *Further Questions*

□ How do learners differ in their natural abilities with various kinds of memory? For example, does one person regularly hold on to more details of a field trip to an ethnic restaurant than another person under similar circumstances?

□ How can a learner use his or her greater strength with one kind of memory in order to compensate for lesser strength with another?

Notes

1. Casey 1976:19.

2. Sperling, quoted in Bransford 1979:20–21.

3. Fuster & Alexander 1971.

4. Fuster & Alexander 1971:654; Gurowitz 1969:6.

5. Hydén & Lange 1968:1373.

6. Quartermain et al. 1970; Paolino & Levy 1971.

7. Throughout this book, I shall understand the "representation" of an event (or part of an event, or series of events) to mean the physical changes that it leaves after it in the brain. In that respect, I think I am echoing Hatch, Shirai, and Fantuzzi (1990:711) when they say, "If we believe that language is made up of connections that are multiply distributed, exceedingly overlapping in nature, then it is this messy, fuzzy, overlapping picture that is real rather than the descriptions that we use to bring better order to the picture." The same authors comment on the dangers and limited value of abstract "representations" (710).

8. Hydén & Lange 1968.

9. Rappoport & Daginawala 1968.

10. Gurowitz 1969:76.

11. Sheer 1970:181.

12. Richter 1966:84ff.

13. Peterson & Peterson 1959.

14. Metcalfe 1966.

15. Lado (1965, 1971) in a series of studies explored some aspects of the short-versus long-term memory distinction in the context of foreign language learning.

16. The undesirability of reification has been mentioned by a number of writers, among them Gregg (1989:21) and Johnson (1991:150).

17. Neisser 1984:33.

18. Logie et al. 1994:396.

19. Carroll 1966.

20. Similarly Casey (1976:9) gives examples of how everyday use of the word "imagination" can be subtly misleading.

21. "In [some] models, working memory serves as a mental workspace. Its general characteristics [are] limited capacity and rapid forgetting. [These] correspond to commonly accepted generalizations about short-term memory" (Carlson, Sullivan & Schneider 1989:518).

22. Similarly McLaughlin (1990:630) remarks that "many recent researchers use the term *working memory* as a construct replacing such older constructs as *focal attention* and *short-term memory*. The reason why new concepts are adopted is [that] old ones have too much baggage and do not fit the empirical facts." Needless to say, proponents of new terms should try to avoid replicating the Mad Hatter's Tea Party!

23. In earlier drafts, I used the term "temporary memory" here. But that term had already been used in Anderson 1984 in another sense. In any case, "holding" may be better for my purposes because of its use in expressions like "holding tank" and "holding cell."

24. Stevick 1990b, Chapter 3.

25. Salthouse et al. 1989:508.

26. Nairne 1990:255.

27. "In the case of procedural skills, WM must be used to hold current task information and to integrate that information with long-term knowledge" (Carlson, Sullivan, & Schneider 1989:518).

28. Cf. Straight's paper titled "Consciousness as a Workspace" (1977).

29. The view that WM consists of a single workspace contrasts with [recent models of WM] in which storage and processing are distributed over multiple systems or regions" (Carlson, Sullivan, & Schneider 1989:518).

30. Strobel 1993:367.

31. Cubelli 1991.

32. Brennen et al. (1990:339 and passim) provide support for the idea that modally similar bits of information may be more closely connected neurally than dissimilar bits of information are.

33. Molfese 1985:296.

34. Miles et al. 1991:582.

35. Miles et al. 1991:581. This use of "strategies" refers to something nonconscious and automatic, quite unlike how the word has been used recently in the field of language teaching.

36. Baddeley & Hitch 1974; Baddeley 1986.

37. Logie et al. 1994:396.

38. Dark (1990:119) uses the apt metaphor of "scratchpads."

39. Thus Kingston & Diehl (1994:20), quoting the Schiffrin and Schneider model, say that "automatic" processes are unhindered by the capacity limitations of "short-term" memory. I would argue that "working" is the preferable term here.

40. Compare Nairne's (1990:267) description of "primary memory" (approximately equivalent to what I have here been calling "working memory") as "a continuous stream of internally and externally generated activity, rather than . . . a box containing experimenter-defined items that sit in a kind of mental vacuum."

41. Klatzky 1984: Chapter 2.

42. As noted at the beginning of this paragraph, some writers (e.g., Frensch & Miner 1994) speak of short-term memory as handling both information recently arrived from outside and information that has already been stored for some time.

43. Bahrick 1984b.

44. Comparable three-way distinctions, though with different terminology, have been made by a number of writers, including Chafe (1973) and Curran (1972).

45. Dunlosky & Nelson 1992, 1994.

46. Traces of many of the above points are found in various recent theoretical models, including Frensch and Miner's (1994) treatment of implicit and explicit learning.

47. Miller 1956.

48. Schmidt's (1992) comments on "chunking" seem to omit this distinction between "chunks" and "segments."

49. Lado 1965:3.

50. Kleinberg & Kaufman 1971:333.

51. Based on numerous personal observations.

52. Personal observation of Peace Corps training programs conducted by Rassias and his staff.

53. pronounced "act-star."

54. Anderson 1984:82ff.

55. Lesgold 1984:44; Schmidt 1992.

56. Klatzky 1984; O'Malley & Chamot 1990; Celce-Murcia 1993; Schmidt 1992.

57. Tom Scovel (private communication) points out that there is neuropsychological support for this distinction between "declarative" and "procedural" knowledge: aphasia is a manifestation of disruption of declarative knowledge but not of procedural knowledge, whereas apraxia involves disruption of procedural knowledge but not declarative knowledge.

58. Klatzky 1984:57.

59. Readers should be warned that these same terms are also used in a different way, in which "declarative" means "with awareness" and "procedural" means "without awareness" (Frensch & Miner 1994:96).

60. Klatzky 1984:57.

61. Kosslyn (1984:105) notes that "a propositional representation [is not English; it] is equivalent to a *sentence* in logic; philosophers use the term 'proposition' to refer to the idea itself, not to the expression of the idea in some language."

62. Klatzky 1984:57.

63. O'Malley & Chamot 1990:215.

64. One can still assume that most or all kinds of learning begin with at least fleeting, covert declarative knowledge on a microscale. Caleb Gattegno's use of the adjective "conscious" often seemed to imply that assumption.

65. Anderson 1984.

66. Carlson et al. 1989:517.

67. Gregg 1989:20.

68. Lesgold 1984:45.

69. Sharwood Smith (1981); Tarone 1983:155.

70. Notice that "identification" in this sense is quite different from "recognition," even though in everyday language the two words are often interchangeable.

71. Johnston et al. 1991:210.

72. Johnston et al. (1991) say that "perceptual fluency" is a synonym for "enhanced perceptibility," and Gardiner and Java (1990:28) appear to equate it with "familiarity," but these must surely be superficial imprecisions.

73. Church and Schacter (1994:521) describe the perceptual representation system PRS as "a presemantic system composed of a number of subsystems that process and represent information about the physical form and structure, but not the meaning or associative properties, of words, objects, and other stimuli. The PRS is assumed to be a cortically based system that is distinct from a system based in limbic structures (e.g., the hippocampus) that is necessary for explicit, episodic retrieval."

74. Oxford 1990: footnote.

75. Tulving 1972.

76. Gardiner & Java 1990:25.

77. Bransford 1979:168. Schank (1982:19) gives a similar definition.

78. Klatzky 1984:30.

79. A contrasting view: Two functions of episodic memory: (1) to "acquire new information and keep it available for some time" (2) to be up to date on information that is "required only for a short span of time or that is highly variable" (Kliegl, Reinhold & Ulman Lindenberger 1993:617).

From within the field of language teaching Rohrer is quoted in an interview as saying that "our episodic memory is the memory for things that are detailed in the general setup of things which we do not need to know in order to survive. For example, our survival doesn't depend on whether we know that $(A + B)^2 = A^2 + 2AB + B^2$. Therefore our episodic memory tends to forget it. [Perhaps] all school learning is of this type. School learning is learning things that you don't need." Rohrer contrasts "episodic memory" with "schematic memory": "Our schematic memory is based on . . . scripts. A script is [something that] we learn with great ease" (Woytak 1992:9).

80. Bransford 1979:169.

81. Klatzky 1984:30.

82. Bryant 1990:355f.

83. Klatzky 1984:31.

84. Allen & Jacoby 1990:271.

85. In the everyday sense, not in the technical sense defined on page 37.

86. For example, Keatley et al. 1994.

87. Gardiner and Java (1990:23f) point out that some writers use the terms "explicit" and "implicit memory" to stand for "memory expressed with or without awareness of remembering."

88. This is called recollective experience ("autonoetic consciousness"): "ability to become consciously aware of some aspects of what happened and what was experienced at the time the word was presented—such as something to do with the physical appearance of the word, the way it was presented, something one

was thinking of or did during the word's presentation, or something else one noticed in the laboratory at that time" (Gardiner & Java 1990:25).

89. Gardiner & Parkin 1990:579; Parkin, Reid & Russo 1990:508.

90. Parkin, Reid & Russo 1990:507.

91. Gardiner & Java 1990:23.

92. We have already seen the need for care in the use of technical terminology. That need is nowhere more evident than in discussions of the contrast between "explicit memory" and "implicit memory." Thus, a phrase like "implicit memory test" is structurally ambiguous. The word "implicit" here could be intended to modify either "memory" or "test." Authors sometimes use "tests of explicit memory" versus "implicit memory tests" in contexts that indicate that the two phrases are parallel (Fendrich et al. 1991:137). This would indicate that "implicit" is supposed to go with "memory" and not with "tests." On the other hand, when "implicit memory tests" are defined as tasks in which subjects are *not* directed to "consciously recollect prior events or experiences," and "explicit memory tests" are defined as tasks in which subjects *are* so directed (Gardiner & Java 1990:23), then "implicit" clearly goes with "tests" and not with "memory." I find this inconsistency confusing. It probably doesn't bother the cognitive scientists the way it bothers me, since they know their field so much better than I do. I only hope it doesn't confuse them. Confusion that one is not bothered by is the most dangerous kind.

93. Similarly but not identically, Schmidt (1992:380) writes of implicit or explicit knowledge in terms of the difference between memory-based procedures and rule-based procedures, and also in terms of the difference between analyzed and unanalyzed knowledge.

94. Frensch & Miner 1994:110. These authors comment that use of the terms "implicit" and "explicit" has not always been consistent even with regard to so narrowly restricted a subject as serial learning.

95. This is related to the concept of "monitoring" advanced by Krashen and others in recent years.

Chapter 3

Memory at Work: Basic Processes

Questions I Asked Myself:

☐ What is the nature of the basic equipment that supports my students' long-term memory?

☐ How do their long-term memory and their working memory interact with each other?

INTRODUCTION

We saw in Chapter 1 that many kinds of information stay in people's heads from what has happened to them earlier. These "leftovers from living and learning" are open to observation on two levels:

☐ They leave behind subtle neurochemical changes in the brain. These neurochemical changes are not only records of the past; they will also go far toward shaping future actions.[1]

☐ They are reflected in measurable correlations between events and whatever behavioral changes follow after those events.

In between these two types of physical observation lies the realm of theory building. Here we create terminologies: we select or originate words and then try to fit those words into statements that will both account for what we have found in the past and predict what we will find in the future.

Next, in Chapter 2, we examined the principal "kinds" of memory "in" which the data of Chapter 1 may be stored. Now in Chapter 3 it is time to talk about memory not as information, and not as a set of places, but as processes.

TWO PRELIMINARY MODELS

☐ THE DUAL CODING MODEL

What can be said about how the various "leftovers from living and learning" fit in with each other? One widely cited answer to this question comes from the work of Paivio (1971). Paivio and others had measured the degree to which people seemed to be able to form mental pictures from certain words. In Bransford's summary:

> Paivio [proposed] a dual-code theory, which postulates two separate but interconnected memory systems. One system is verbal in nature, and the other system is visual. A word like *alligator* that evokes images can be stored both verbally and visually; a word like *agreement* that does not so readily suggest an image will be stored only [EWS: or mostly] verbally. If people have two codes for information (verbal plus visual) rather than one, retention should be enhanced.[2]

This theory was tested in experiments measuring both free recall and the learning of paired associates, always with NL words.[3] Results supported the idea that easily visualized words are somehow more memorable than other words. We have seen, however, that the questions to be answered by subjects in activities of these kinds are a little distant from the questions that our students most often face when learning and using new languages. The differences stem from the contrast between working on the one hand with form-meaning linkages that are clear, firmly established, and of long standing, and on the other hand working to correct and solidify form–meaning linkages that are new, partial, and unstable.

□ THE ISM MODEL

An alternative to Paivio's formulation has been put forward by Ahsen, a practicing psychotherapist as well as a leading student of mental imagery. In his view, the totality of one's "leftovers" (my term, instead of "idea" or "image") about a person or a thing or a sound or a color or a complex activity or whatever, consists not of two major kinds of information, but of three: Ahsen says that each such "idea"[4] [EWS: of a given person, event, skill, etc.] is actually [EWS: a combination of] a multisensory "Image" plus "Somatic response" plus a "Meaning"—what he calls an "ISM."[5] Just what we should understand by these three components needs some elaboration.

A "multisensory image" as the term is used in studies of mental imagery:

□ is primarily visual, but involves perceptions from a number of sense modalities[6]; and

□ involves an interplay between what is consciously experienced and what happens to the neurons and synapses in the brain; and

□ is not static like a snapshot, but undergoes constant dynamic change.[7]

In the ISM model, then, knowing and thinking consist of constant interaction among many modalities, and not merely of the shuffling of whole words plus their attached whole meanings.[8]

In 1984 Ahsen believed that "it [is] difficult to distinguish between images and percepts"—between pictures that our minds produce for us and pictures that have just now come in through our eyes.[9] This statement must be interpreted in the light of later research that found a definite difference between subjects' retention of enactments that they had actually perceived, and similar enactments that they had only imagined. In general, apparently, enacted visual stimuli— things we have actually seen—are more vivid and detailed than the correspond- ing well-developed mental images are—things we have imagined. Products of active imagination are in turn more vivid and detailed than whatever incidental imagery accompanies mere descriptions in words.[10] In comparing these findings with Ahsen's statement, we must remember that in Ahsen's practice, patients or subjects generally experience a kind of imagery called "eidetic." Eidetic images are as clear, sharp, fully developed, and stable as anything that comes in via ordi- nary vision. They are thus much more vivid and stable than the images that were probably present in the research I have just cited. We should also bear in mind that the noneidetic type of imagery is closer to the experience of most of our stu- dents than eidetic imagery would be.[11]

□   AN ASIDE ON VISUAL IMAGES

Sheikh[12] mentions four possible kinds of visual images:

- □ Afterimages from visual input: rather full but fleeting (about 0.2 sec.) records of what has just come in through the eyes or other senses.[13] These are products of "sensory persistence." Everyone has them.

- □ Eidetic images, which in vividness, completeness, and stability resemble the images produced by what is coming in through the eyes. Some people have these, but not everyone has.

- □ Memory images, which may approach eidetic images in clarity and vivid- ness, but usually do not. They tend to be "pallid, fragmented, indefinitely localized, and brief." Their quality seems to depend on attention and affect. The extent and quality of these probably vary from person to person and from occasion to occasion.

- □ "Imagination images," which may occur on the edge of sleep, or result from hallucinogenic drugs or loss of sleep. These have little direct relevance to FL instruction. I include them here only for the sake of completeness.

People vary widely in their ability to form and sustain various kinds of images. At one extreme are individuals like Casey,[14] who seems spontaneously to generate continuing eidetic images. I have had a graphic and detailed account of this type of imaging from at least one other adult male. Ahsen's patients appar- ently fell into this same category. I know a third adult male who had originally been unable to form eidetic images, but claimed to have been taught to do so by Ahsen. At the opposite pole, I know a few people who claim to be unable to form any variety of usable visual image of anything they have not actually seen with their eyes, even though they can answer questions about minor details of things they *have* seen.

Most of my own visual images fall into Sheikh's third category: fuzzy, dim, and fragmentary. For example, my image for "agreement" includes a "pallid, fragmented, indefinitely localized, and brief" picture of people shaking hands. The movie *Moby Dick* (except for Gregory Peck) was an amazingly accurate, clear, unfragmented, fully localized and continuing reproduction of the "pallid, fragmented, indefinitely localized, and brief" images my mind had formed while reading the book. My ability to profit from an audiolingual course in French depended on my mind's quick and consistent formation of appropriate "pallid, fragmented, indefinitely localized, and brief" images to accompany the sentences of the dialogs and drills. I cannot fathom how anyone could have images of the kind Casey describes, but I am just as unable to fathom how anyone could fail to generate at least the quality of visual imagery that is so familiar—even so indispensable—to me. I am sure the people in the two extreme categories find each other's accounts even more incredible. Yet here we all are.

The implications of this Aside for language teachers are probably:

□ That these three groups (eidetikers, memory imagers, and nonimagers) may be represented in any sizable FL class. I should therefore not expect all my students to have the same powers—or the same limitations—that I have.

□ That the largest group is probably the memory imagers.

□ We noneidetikers may take comfort in the findings of investigators like Dickel and Slak, who reported that at least for some memory functions, the vividness of an image is less important than whether the image had been generated by the subject.[15]

Somatic response: Returning now to Ahsen's ISM model, when we see an image—whether an image we have derived directly from our senses or one we have generated ourselves—our bodies may respond in a number of ways: skeletally, muscularly, viscerally, and with endocrine changes.[16] My understanding is that in the ISM model, this statement applies in principle to all images. Such physiological changes[17] may be very noticeable and long-lasting in response to some images, but fleeting and negligible in response to most others.[18]

Meaning: In the ISM model, the "meaning" of a multisensory image includes what we usually think of as lexical meaning[19]: whatever combination of semantic features may be required in order to differentiate a word or proposition or picture or other item from other such items. It goes beyond lexical or propositional meaning, however, to include all of the subject's expectations of, and involvements with, and purposes related to the image.[20] For example, my "pallid, fragmented, indefinitely localized, and brief" image for "pharmacist" includes not only visual material, but also the kinds of services I have come to expect from such people.

Most typically, at least in Ahsen's psychotherapy, the *I*mage element leads to the *S*omatic element, followed by the *M*eaning element, but the three elements may occur in other orders as well.[21] (More recently, the three elements of Ahsen's model—imagery, comprehensive meaning, and somatic response—find counterparts in Pulvermüller and Schumann's [1994:707] reference to "entire sensory-emotio-motor network[s]," where they are definitely talking about physical networks in the brain.)

The ISM model contributes to our overall understanding of memory in five ways:

□ Its broad interpretation of "meaning" recognizes that *purposes* always play a part in cognition and memory. I would add that the relevance of a purpose does not depend on how sharply or how weakly defined it is, or how close it is to the center of attention.

□ Similarly, the ISM model assigns an essential role to *emotion* as one component of the "somatic" element.

□ It recognizes that in practical experience, the three major elements occur in one or another *chronological order,* rather than appearing and disappearing hand in hand like three dancing fairies on the page of a textbook.

□ Recognition of chronological relationships among the three major elements allows the model to accommodate two findings having to do with *speed*. One of these findings is that affective reactions may make themselves felt extremely rapidly, even before the subject has had time to identify the object that he or she has reacted to.[22] The other is that merely slowing down and repeating material available in one modality may bring material from other modalities into awareness.[23] This is why we ask someone to "run that past me again," for example. Both of these facts are of direct relevance to the language classroom.

□ The model recognizes that what has been thoroughly and richly *imagined* is more memorable than what has only been understood from words.

NETWORKS

□ WHAT I MEAN BY "NETWORKS"

Commenting on the ISM model, Jordan states that the parts of the brain where the *I, S, M* elements are handled have pathways that interact to form a "network."[24] Because this metaphor of "network" is found in so many writings on memory,[25] let us pause here for a closer look at it.

Readers of this book or of other writings on memory will need to be aware of two distinctions in how the term "network" gets used. The first distinction has to do with the analogies represented by the metaphor:

□ Some writers use the analogy of a broadcast network: a number of individual stations can both receive programs from a central source, and send program material in to that central source for retransmission to other members of the network. This is really just a tree diagram, or at most a flow chart with internal branching.[26,27]

□   Most writers (and this book) use the analogy of a fishnet (or tennis net): a number of nodes are connected with one another in such a way that it is possible to go from any one node to any other node by more than one direct or indirect pathway. Compare the much-talked-about "web" of the Internet. The major elements of the ISM model provide an example of the simplest such network:

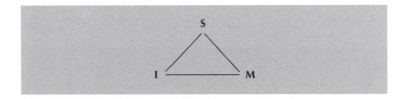

Here, we can go from M to I either directly or via S. The number of direct connections in such a network of n nodes is equal to $(n^2 - n)/2$, so that a network of 10 nodes would have 45 possible direct connections, and a network of just twice that many nodes would have 190.

The second distinction between uses of the term "network" pertains to whether it stands for something abstract or something concrete:

□   In the abstract sense, a network consists of hypothetical connections among nodes, which are something like concepts, or items of information.[28]

□   In the concrete sense, a network consists of neurons, which are connected with one another through synapses.[29]

I'm not sure anyone claims to have a clear idea about exactly *how* the physical networks of neurons in the brain are related to the conceptual networks of information in memory.[30] I am certain, however, that the relationship will turn out to be very, very complicated.

One component of this relationship may be found in an early speculation by Hebb, who predicted that any two neurons which tend to be active at the same time will automatically modify the connections (the synapses) between them.[31,32] After such modification, traffic along that connection will be easier (or faster? more probable?) than it had been before. In more recent years, Hebb's guess has been confirmed by laboratory research. Now, if there is indeed some kind of interdependence between the conceptual networks and the neural networks (and I think most investigators would agree that such an interdependence eventually has to be found), then when two concepts or fragments of experience are present at the same time in working memory, we should expect the connections (the associations) between those concepts or fragments of experience to be modified as well. In practical terms, this means that each of them becomes a more likely reminder of the other. This is after all consistent with common sense and everyday experience.

Let us make three additional assumptions about networks:

□ The individual nodes in a cognitive network can be at various levels of "activation."[33] Activation varies along a continuum from zero to some maximum.

□ When one node or item in a network receives additional activation, some of that activation can then spread along the paths of the network, and cause the activation level of one or more adjoining nodes to rise.[34]

□ When the activation of a particular item reaches a certain level, it shows up on the Worktable.

Perhaps surprisingly, the essence of the foregoing paragraphs lies not in the conspicuous "network" metaphor, but in the underlying assumptions: that the concepts and pictures and ideas accumulated from experience are discrete from one another in memory; that they are nevertheless somehow connected with one another; that at any given time each of them is at one or another level of activation; and that activation can spread among them. "Network" turns out to be only a cover term, one step farther from physical reality than are the concepts, their levels of activation, and their connections.[35]

If we view networks in this way, as cover terms and not as structures, then we are less likely to think of each large network as being made up of a number of smaller networks, which in turn include still smaller networks, and so on.[36] That picture would resemble a map collection that included a national highway map, state maps, street maps of cities showing major arteries, and neighborhood maps showing side streets. In going from 504 Highland Avenue in Joplin to 3412 N. 15th Street in Arlington, one may take any of numerous routes, but one necessarily goes from a side street to a major thoroughfare, to one or another important intersection, then perhaps along an interstate highway, then to a final series of intersections and major and minor streets to the final address. So in terms of cognition, one could respond to the question "Do canaries eat?" only by going first to the fact that a canary is one kind of bird, from there to the fact that a bird is one kind of animal, and then finding the answer somewhere down in one's file of general information about animals.

It would probably be more appropriate to think of direct pathways among *all* units of *all* sizes, with some pathways broader and smoother than others[37]: a person who feeds a canary every day will be quicker than most people in replying that canaries do in fact eat. So one's "image" of a canary will contain sound and color and motion, but the yellow color of a canary may remind one directly of the yellow in a certain dress or painting, and vice versa, without having to go through some total "canary unit." Similarly the canary's motion in picking up a piece of birdseed may remind one directly of a certain person's mannerism or of a melodic fragment in a sonata.

In general, we hold onto an item more reliably and have access to it more readily if it is involved in networks that are relatively rich and fully worked out—literally "e-laborated," as one psychological term puts it.[38] Each of these two words deserves a brief comment. A network (or subnetwork) can be called "rich" to the extent that it contains items of many kinds. For example, one's image accompanying the word "pencil" would include information about whatever information one's lay theory of pencils says are *necessary* in order for something to be called a pencil. But it would also include other, nonnecessary information that has been found in various past experiences with pencils: color, length, weight, state of the eraser, and so forth.[39] In this sense, the networks of one's first language are generally "richer" than those of any second language. This seems to be true even for proficient bilinguals.[40]

As for "work," it comes with "effort," and the amount of effort may in turn be influenced not only by the task, or by the available time, but even by the learner's perception of the power and reliability of the source.[41]

□ LANGUAGE DATA AND THE NETWORK CONCEPT

In the discussion of the ISM model, language teachers will have noticed that in one respect it is inadequate for our concerns: it says nothing about the system of verbal symbols called language. This is quite understandable, since the model was developed by researchers whose subjects or patients were working, by and large, in their native languages. We on the other hand must place linguistic data[42] on a par with Ahsen's sensory *Images*, *Somatic* responses, and *Meaningful* involvements, for words both shape and are shaped by all three of those.

One special point needs to be made about the subnetworks that store linguistic data. We ordinarily think of memory for a word as consisting of an association between some meaning and its corresponding "form," with this "form" in turn being connected both to a set of muscular movements and to some sort of auditory image:

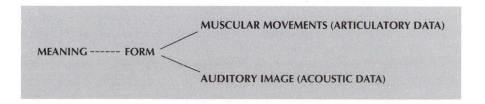

MUSCULAR MOVEMENTS (ARTICULATORY DATA)

MEANING ------ FORM <

AUDITORY IMAGE (ACOUSTIC DATA)

Straight has pointed out, however, that it would be more accurate to see these subnetworks as triangular rather than Y-shaped:

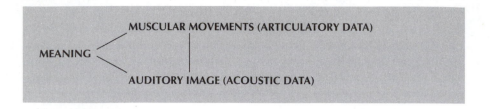

That is, the relationship between the articulatory and the acoustic data is independent of their separate relationships to the meaning, and no "processually neutral" "form" exists. In everyday speech, the triangular subnetwork is so well established, and works so quickly, that we are unaware of that independence. It becomes apparent, however, in special situations. In the laboratory, if a person tries to recite a familiar nursery rhyme onto tape while listening to his or her voice through a headset, he or she has no difficulty when the feedback is immediate. But if the voice is artificially delayed by perhaps a quarter of a second, speech is disrupted. The triangle is not working as expected. Similarly, clinical work with persons who have certain reading difficulties indicates that the path between form and meaning is not a single line. Straight has cited considerable psycholinguistic evidence that people, especially children and other language learners, may be very good at construing the meanings of words they hear or read, even though they are poor at using the same words fluently and appropriately, or may even use a word for a meaning which they would not have understood from it had they heard someone else use it.

So a baby in its prespeech months constantly experiments with its own speech apparatus, thus discovering certain parallels between what it does with its articulators and the sounds that reach its ears. This is the first side of the triangle to begin its development. Later, the child begins to notice meanings, and to realize that certain acoustic inputs regularly go with certain meanings. This is the second side of the triangle. Presumably the young child's initial attempts at speaking are pieced together by following these already established paths, first from meaning to auditory image, and from there to instructions for the speech muscles. With time the third side of the triangle, between meaning and muscles, begins to develop. Still later, the triangle becomes a quadrangle as visual data about the shapes of written words are added.

If the connections between pairs of the points on this triangle or quadrangle are strengthened sufficiently by co-occurring under conditions of successful use, the whole subnetwork comes to operate with great swiftness and dependability. This is why some people, on hearing a word in a language they know well, automatically get a visual image of its printed form, or on seeing a written word also "hear" it in their minds. Such experiences may produce the illusion that we are dealing with a single connection between meaning on the one hand, and some unitary "form" on the other. For certain everyday purposes this illusion is harmless enough, but it is not strictly accurate.

□   ACTIVITY WITHIN NETWORKS

What we commonly call long-term memory (cf. nonelectrical storage, or holding memory + permanent memory, or "the Files") then consists of nonverbal and verbal organized leftovers from living and learning, in a multidimensional network-type relationship with one another. Activation from the Worktable or directly from the senses hits matching items in long-term memory, and from there spreads through networks in which those items participate. This spreading is automatic, parallel, very fast, and not accessible to direct conscious inspection.[43] The result is that the levels of activation of other items in the Files are changed. Those whose activation exceeds some threshold are then registered on the Worktable, generally in the form of images or concepts.[44] So images and concepts do not reach the Worktable directly from the senses; they come from the networks of the Files. This is one respect in which the "Worktable" concept differs from "short-term memory."[45]

This "activation hypothesis" has received a wide range of support from the laboratory.[46] In one series of experiments, researchers asked subjects to try to recall groups of three capital letters they had seen; each letter was printed in a different color. They found that if they diverted or overloaded the subjects' focal attention, the letters and colors were mismatched in the subjects' reports. As they interpreted the results, incoming sensory material is first analyzed into its features, and these features are registered in memory. After that, activation from the features is used in the construction of integrated representations of the objects from which the features had originally been derived. The process of integration can be guided by focal attention, but it can also be guided by past experience.[47,48]

In other research, subjects were shown words that consisted of four letters, chosen so that they differed only in their second and third letters, such as COPE, CAPE, CONE, CANE. The performance of the subjects suggested that the presentation of COPE not only activated a representation of itself in the networks of the Files, but also partially activated other words that were similar to it *either visually, orthographically, or phonetically,* such as CAPE, CONE, CODE, or DOPE. So, for example, both COPE and CANE would partially activate both CAPE and CONE. Suppose that the two words that have been presented together are COPE and CANE. If COPE is used as the word to be responded to, and if the net activation of either CAPE or CONE surpasses the activation level of COPE, then it will be that word (CAPE or CONE) and not COPE that will be perceived.[49]

□ TWO-WAY TRAFFIC BETWEEN THE WORKTABLE AND THE FILES

The basic interaction between the Worktable and the Files involves a lot of query and response. Something that is presently on the Worktable somehow contributes to the activation of one or more items in the Files. As we saw previously, increased activation of these items in the Files contributes to the activation of still other items in the Files, and so on automatically, until a reply is created. This reply now becomes part of the contents of working memory, and this new item in working memory—an item that has just come from the Files—can in turn affect the activation of further items back in the Files. In this way, the incoming information is integrated into the networks that represent long-term knowledge.[50] My experience with *des Abendlandes* (discussed later in this chapter) will provide a good example. So there is a continual two-way interplay, producing "that ever-changing constellation of memories, sense data, anticipations, fantasies, rational thoughts and meanings" that we call the "stream of consciousness."[51,52] Straight's "cycles of reflection and creation"[53] go on and on.

But the new item can itself also be acted on within working memory—acted on by nonautomatic, conscious, deliberate, intentional processes, including what many people these days call "strategies."[54] The fact that material from inside the person and material from outside can and do compete with each other for the limited capacity of working memory[55] fits much more readily with the concept of working memory as a state, than it does with short-term memory as a stage between the sensory input and long-term memory.[56] One result is that, to paraphrase Halliday,[57] the structure of memory is always in transition, because every act of recall, and even every act of recognition, transforms it, however microscopically, from what it was into something else.[58]

Two-way traffic is a separate process. Evidence for repeated back-and-forth activity between the Worktable and the Files is found in work by Goodglass, Theurkauf, and Wingfield.[59] They showed subjects a series of pictures, and measured how long it took for a subject to provide the name of each picture. Some of their subjects were normal, but others suffered from various moderately severe types of speech loss. The researchers discovered that, at least for high-frequency words, the subjects with speech loss performed about as well as the normals. What is more interesting is that the subjects with speech loss seemed to fall into two groups. Those in Group A either got the word quickly, or they didn't get it at all. Group B subjects sometimes got the word quickly, but if they did not get it at first, they continued until it finally came to them. What may this observation mean?

One guess is that the members of Group B had available to them *not just one retrieval process, but two.* In the first process, the picture was transmitted directly to the Files, which with characteristic speed provided the corresponding word. The second process seemed to consist of a slower, often[60] conscious search involving the mobilization of associations, "with *repeated decisions* as to whether to continue" [emphasis added]. With pictures for which the first process worked, the second process was discontinued, but when the first process did not work, the second continued on to completion (or, as we will see in Chapter 4), to a "tip-of-the-tongue" [TOT] state. For some reason, this second process was not available to members of Group A. What interests us is that the normal subjects—the ones with no loss of speech, who include most of our students—are presumably like Group B in this respect. The importance of this distinction between two processes of recognition is affirmed in a recent article by Rugg.[61]

□   PRIMING

In the everyday world, to "prime" a pump is to bring the pump to the point where it is ready to put out water, even though no water has yet emerged from it. To "prime" a firearm is to supply it with powder for communicating fire to a charge, even though it has not yet been discharged. The staff of a politician may "prime" their boss for an anticipated question by preparing her or him to answer it fully, effectively, and without hesitation.

In the world of experimental psychology, a researcher may expose subjects to stimuli of various kinds. Later, the ability of those same subjects to produce or respond to some target word may be tested by means of a number of tasks. As noted in Chapter 2, some experimental tasks are more closely related to the needs of a language learner than others are. These tasks include identifying a word form on the basis of brief or fragmentary presentation, and making a decision about whether a particular string of letters or sounds has ever been met as a word. Such abilities are indispensable for fluent comprehension. Researchers have found that certain types of learning activity improve subjects' performance on tasks of these kinds, even when the subjects are unaware that their memory is being tested. The name for this effect is "priming."[62] Although priming is not easy to document outside the lab, it is probably a ubiquitous part of daily life and language study.[63]

Priming in the psychological sense may be either conceptual or perceptual. An example of conceptual priming is found in research reported by Meyer and colleagues.[64] In their experiments, subjects were shown pairs of letter groups on a screen, one group at a time. They were asked to press one or the other of two buttons as quickly as possible in order to indicate whether the letter group did or did not make a word in English (their native language). As soon as they indicated their decision, a second word appeared in place of the first, and the same decision was required. The experimenters measured the number of milliseconds needed for each decision. Possible pairs would be:

1. KEBED   (No)   GWAF (No)
2. BLEG   (No)   ZONE (Yes)
3. SHELF   (Yes)   TUVE (No)
4. TIGER   (Yes)   RAKE (Yes)
5. GARDEN (Yes)   RAKE (Yes)

The most interesting result from these experiments was found in comparisons of pairs like (4) and (5). The time required for a Yes decision about RAKE was significantly less if the word had been preceded by a meaningfully related word such as GARDEN than if it had been preceded by an unrelated word such as TIGER. To state this finding more generally, reaction to a given item will be easier (faster or more likely or both) if that item *or an item closely related to it* has been met within some limited period of time in the past.[65]

Conceptual priming is apparently the observable product of spreading activation.[66] Activation from the priming experience spreads through existing networks and raises the level of activation of the target word. This enables the subject to identify or accept that word more readily once it is presented.[67] The central link in this chain of spreading activation involves not the mere physical forms of the words, but their meanings, which is why this kind of priming is called "conceptual."[68] The process of conceptual priming involves one or more round trips between the Worktable and the Files.

Outside the laboratory, conceptual priming is an important element in comprehension. In language study, it helps to account for the advantage that coherent and interesting texts have not only over uncontexted sentences, but also over the perfunctory pablum that has sometimes been offered to students as "connected discourse."

Perceptual priming[69] is an entirely different phenomenon. In the study phase of a typical experiment, subjects meet stimuli of one kind or another: words, line drawings, and the like. Later, in the test phase of the experiment, subjects are given the same stimuli in some perceptually reduced form, and are asked to name them or categorize them.[70] If the stimuli in the study phase consisted of words, the test stimuli may consist of the same words presented very briefly, or of words with distorted or fragmented letters, or of words with blanks in place of some letters, or of just the first few letters. Or they may consist of strings of letters that may or may not form words.[71] The time that elapses between the study phase and the test phase may be anything from seconds to months.[72] Overall, these tasks are very much like what faces a language learner who is trying to deal rapidly and simultaneously with a flood of details about pronunciation or typography, plus the meanings of individual words, plus grammar, plus the intent of the speaker or writer.

Language teachers will be interested to know that perceptual priming is stronger when the experimental subjects (and presumably language learners) have simply read a word, than it is when they have been required to generate the word for themselves.[73] Apparently this exposure strengthens the connections among items in the networks that correspond to the words,[74] and thus makes the word more readily available later on. So perceptual priming, unlike conceptual priming, does not involve traffic between the Worktable and the Files. Perhaps for this reason, perceptual priming works even with deeply amnesic patients, with very young children, and with adults who show some degree of mental deterioration.[75] We can reasonably expect that it will work for our students too!

Of course, comprehension may benefit from both kinds of priming at the same time: research has shown that it takes less phonological information to identify words heard or seen in context than to identify words heard out of context.[76]

□ OUTPUT FROM THE NETWORKS

What, then, can we infer about the source of a language learner's observed behavior in speaking and writing? What is behind it? The distinctive emphases of this book so far have been:

- □ That we are working primarily with two kinds of physical reality:
  - observable behavior; and
  - neurochemical networks, which support cognitive, conceptual networks.
- □ That these networks are essential to memory.
  - The networks contain data of many more kinds than we usually think of.
  - The countless connections that make up the networks are in constant change, each along a continuous range of values.

Tarone once summarized three views on the nature of what underlies the output of people who are learning a new language. Is it a single unified system of knowledge? Or is it actually a continuum of styles? Or does it consist of two completely independent systems?[77] The assumptions I have just outlined clearly fit better with the idea of the continuum, for every impact of a new configuration of stimuli upon the networks is in principle unique. This is true either because the configuration itself is new, or because the networks have changed since the last impact, or for some combination of both reasons.

A PAIR OF DIAGRAMS

□ FIGURE A

Two-way traffic between the Worktable and the Files (i.e., between working memory and long-term memory) is inconsistent with the unidirectional picture commonly associated with the short-term memory/long-term memory terminology. We see this picture in Figure A.

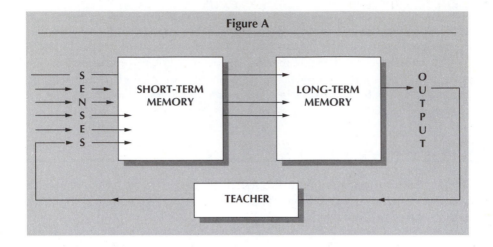

Figure A

Three features stand out in this diagram:

☐ In Figure A, short-term memory and long-term memory are really treated as two stages—almost as two places—to which and through which information passes.

☐ Information passes to and through these stages in a kind of unidirectional flow: from the senses to short-term memory; through short-term memory to long-term memory; from long-term memory to output.[78]

☐ In this view, information is just a commodity, something like a cargo to be moved. It is not a creation. There is no place in Figure A for imagination.

The view of memory implied in much that is written and said about language teaching these days is something like what we see in Figure A. In the context of language study, what Figure A says is that a student is exposed to a large amount of variegated input; that some but only some of this input gets into short-term memory; that some but only some of what finds its way into short-term memory is then stored in long-term memory; and that when output is needed, it is drawn from whatever finally wound up in long-term memory. In ordinary, nonimaginative teaching, as I read the diagram, the teacher hears the student's output and realizes that something is amiss in the student's long-term memory. She (the teacher) therefore provides new input, which eventually reaches the student's long-term memory and modifies it. There is some evidence that adult learners can and do profit from feedback of many kinds.[79] This process continues in one way or another until the student's output shows that the modification was indeed the one the teacher had hoped for. So Figure A fits conventional teaching very neatly.

□ FIGURE B: AN INCIDENTAL GUESS

Since cognitive science is a field in which I am only an amateur in both senses, I am reluctant to venture into abstract reasoning about it. Figure A does, however, imply two crucial assumptions:

- □ At least at the beginning of any new experience, whatever is in short-term memory has come from the senses. *Comments:* These sensory data are raw and undiminished. But we must assume that they are also uninterpreted in the light of past experience. (Figure A has not yet provided a point at which interpretation could have taken place.)
- □ The material that passes from short-term memory into long-term memory consists of word forms ("the," "say," "from"), people (my first-grade teacher), actions (writing, bouncing), and so forth. *Comments:* Each of these is a concept, and exists only in relation to a host of other concepts. These concepts have been derived from past experience.

That is to say, we have here a theoretical construct (short-term memory) some-how taking in *data* and putting out *concepts*. Yet the most frequently cited qualities of short-term memory are that it is limited, temporary, and devoid of any permanent content of its own. How could it then be able to transmute data into concepts? We can only conclude, then, that Figure A needs to be fundamentally revised or even replaced.

These terms *data* and *concepts* figure in a number of contemporary writings on memory. Performance on certain memory tasks can be improved just by exposure to appropriate input, without a lot of thinking and processing of that material. These are tasks that we carry out "automatically,"[80] almost "mindlessly."[81] They involve relatively little two-way traffic between the Files and the Worktable. Such tasks include deciding whether or not a word (or a face, or a color, or a flavor) has been met before, and filling in the missing parts of a word or a sentence or a schema. (p. 16) Here is where "semantic" memory—"what generally goes with what." (p. 38) Here too is where the best-known effects of "priming" show up. A number of theorists have used the term "data-driven" to describe the processes by which such tasks are carried out.[82] The principle seems to be that units that occur together tend to become better connected to one another.

Performance on certain other memory tasks is helped very little by mere exposure, but profits greatly by various kinds of conscious processing such as generation. We will see that this is true of the learning of lists, or of reporting whether or not a particular word was in the story that was heard yesterday, or learning which NL word is close in meaning to which FL word. Cognitive experiments with these tasks have most often depended on "episodic" memory—on knowing "what went with what on a particular occasion." The same theorists call the processes behind these tasks "concept-driven."

I would therefore suggest, though with considerable diffidence, the following eight points:

1. Various combinations of sensory data may trigger various concepts through spreading activation of networks in the Files. (Compare punching a required combination of buttons on an electronic lock in order to get a door to open.)

2. What reaches the Worktable consists largely of conceptual material from the Files.

3. What is currently on the Worktable can itself trigger further activity back in the networks of the Files, resulting in further input to the Worktable.

4. What is on the Worktable can be consciously inspected and manipulated or edited by the user. The results of this manipulating or editing can in turn be transmitted to the Files.

5. Whatever comes to the Files, whether from the senses or from the Worktable, can alter slightly the weightings of the connections that make up the networks of the Files.

6. What has entered the electrically disruptible Worktable will be lost from the Worktable within about 20 seconds unless it is reintroduced or deliberately repeated (what the psychologists call "rehearsal").

7. Output is the THEN-half of an IF-THEN "production" (p. 33) triggered either by activity entirely within the Files, or by something that has come from the Worktable.

8. It may be that some material that passes through the senses never makes a significant impact on the Files.

Figure B is an attempt to represent some of these eight fairly complex points as a simple two-dimensional map.

Figure B fits more easily with the concept of two-way traffic between working memory and a long-term memory that consists of dynamic networks within which activation spreads rapidly and automatically, so that at any given time the contents of working memory is likely to include both material derived from what has just come in through the senses *and* material derived from one or more round trips between the Worktable and the Files.

Quantitatively, the length of time it takes to send a stimulus from working memory to the Files and to get back some sort of reply or response is a very, very tiny fraction of the time that things can stay in working memory—perhaps 1% or 2% by some estimates. This means that once an item has reached working memory, a lot of work can be done on it, with it, and from it while it is still in working memory. This large ratio between how long we have something available in working memory and how long it takes us to get the reactions of the Files to that something has been called "an important element in complex cognitive operations."[83]

But as rapid as two-way traffic between Worktable and Files may be, it does take time, and this time can affect the performance of language-using tasks. An example is found in a report by Leow.[84] In his experiments, learners' intake of linguistic items from written material did not appear to depend heavily on the comprehensibility of that material. This contrasted with an earlier study by VanPatten, which showed that for auditory material input needs to be easily understood if it is to become intake.[85] Leow reasoned that the difference may stem from the fact

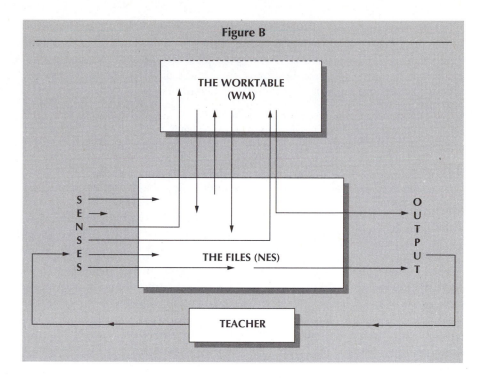

Figure B

that in reading, unlike in listening, learners have more time in which to do things they already know how to do[86]—for example, rereading, or consulting what they have in holding memory—that will help them to process the text.

Even recognition can become a complex operation, depending on the circumstances. A learner of Turkish, for example, who hears the word *heyecan*, may have to go through three round trips from working memory to the Files and back: (1) Have I heard this word before? Yes. (2) When, and in what context? Last week, in a discussion of popular music. This may lead to identification: (3) What did it mean in that context? It meant something like "excitement." Such queries and replies can be time-consuming and, as the cognitive scientists would say, they can also be capacity-depleting. From the learner's point of view, this identification process distracts attention from whatever further input is being presented while it is going on. Again, the concept of working memory as a state reflects this fact more clearly than the concept of short-term memory as a stage in a unidirectional flow does.

COTERMINOUS PATHWAYS

Diagram B, then, begins to reflect some of the amazing flexibility of memory processing.[87] A further point, fairly well documented in research but seldom mentioned among language teachers, is that one and the same query from work-ing memory may produce two or more responses from the Files.[88] For example, Bradley and Thomson[89] observed a number of patients who suffered from one or another form of dyslexia, and they found three quite different routes by which a person can perform the task of pronouncing a word off a page:

□ By one of these routes, which Bradley and Thomson called the lexical-semantic route, the Files generate a *meaning* that goes with the overall graphemic representation of the word, and then they generate a *pronunci-ation* that goes with that meaning.

□ By a second route, the Files respond to the overall graphemic shape of the word and generate a *pronunciation* for it without any dependence on meaning.

□ By the third route, the Files respond to *one grapheme at a time*, generating a *pronunciation* for each and in this way piecing together a pronunciation for the whole word.

And all three of these outputs can show up in working memory, either simulta-neously or one after another, but still well within the time span that will allow working memory to deal with them together. In normal readers, the three replies almost always agree, so there is no problem, and thus the existence of more than one reply is concealed. But in those cases where the replies don't agree, working memory compares them and notes any discrepancies. Then some of its limited resources are briefly devoted to choosing which of the replies to accept. This, of course, will entail further inquiries to and responses from the Files.[90] We can refer to such routes as "coterminous pathways" (CPs). In plain English, CPs are two or more different ways of getting from the same input to the same or differ-ent outputs, more or less at the same time.[91,92]

A more general concept is "alternative pathways." One might say that there are two kinds of alternative pathways from any point in an associative network: divergent and coterminous. As an example of the former, exposure to the word "elevator" might lead to more than one series of associated responses:

□ elevator → grain elevator → Thomas, Oklahoma.

□ elevator → an elevator ride to the top floor of the old Connor Hotel in Joplin, Missouri, a dizzying nine stories above street level.

But when each of these divergent pathways leads further to a shared item—a pic-ture of my father—then the two pathways become "coterminous."[93]

The concept of CPs is found in the foreign language field. One theory of vocabulary proposes that the representations of (for example) Portuguese *alface* and English *lettuce* are stored in separate, language-specific modules. As transla-tion equivalents, they are connected to each other. But each is also connected to an image representation in a separate image store, and the combination of these connections (*alface*—image and image—*lettuce*) provides a second pathway between the two verbal systems.[94] (This indirect pathway is in fact the one that

I most often find myself using when I have to hesitate for a word in a foreign language.)

Some investigators have concluded that even so simple and routine an act as the semantic categorizing of nouns normally draws on two distinct processes, often operating side by side. A person may draw on the features of meaning necessary for membership in a given category. This kind of categorization is deliberate, analytical, and capable of providing explicit justification for the decision: "I call this thing a lamb because it is a young animal whose parents were sheep." The other kind of categorization is more automatic and holistic, and cannot be used to supply convincing justification: "I call this thing a lamb because it's about the size of the lambs I've seen in the past, is frisky, and has tightly coiled hairs." In language as in reasoning, both processes commonly operate together.[95]

The output of any pathway, or of any combination of CPs, gets compared with whatever purposes are in effect at the moment. So production by the Files is not a process that just runs on unchecked.[96]

The CP phenomenon may be fairly common in day-to-day work with a new language. Here are two recent examples from my own adventures in reactivating the German I learned some decades ago.

□ AURAL COMPREHENSION

A news broadcast contained the phrase "*des Abendlandes.*" What I was aware of on my Worktable, in chronological order, included:

- □ I don't get a meaning for this word. Initiate search!
- □ *Abendlandes* appears to be made up of *Abend* plus *Land* plus the inflectional ending -*es.*
- □ *Abend* means "evening" and *Land* means "land."
- □ Therefore *Abendland* means literally "evening land."
- □ In the evening, the sun goes down in the west.
- □ Maybe *Abendland* means "west."
- □ Now I remember that I once met it in the phrase *Niedergang des Abendlandes* "decline of the West."
- □ Therefore *Abendland* must indeed mean "west."
- □ Terminate search!

If what came into consciousness on my Worktable is any indicator, this bit of comprehension must have followed a tortuous series of pathways, with several shuttlings back and forth between the Worktable and the Files. It certainly had the effect of blotting out what the newscaster said for the next few seconds.

Another, simpler way of recovering the meaning of *Abendland* would have been:

- ☐ Have I ever met this word before? (Yes.)
- ☐ Where? (In a government course in college.)
- ☐ What did it mean there? ("West.")

This would have been parallel to the Turkish example of *heyecan* (discussed previously), which is a manifestation of episodic memory. Unfortunately, the necessary linkages in the networks of my Files were not strong enough to do it this simpler, faster way.

A still quicker and simpler recovery would have occurred if my circuitry had been more like that of a native speaker, with numerous direct or very short linkages to appropriate material in the *I*magery, *S*omatic response, and *M*eaning categories of Ahsen's model. This would have been straight semantic memory. (p. 37) I would probably have responded in this way to *Augenblick* "moment" (literally, "eye-blink").

☐ PRODUCTION

Comparable alternatives would have been available if I had been using the word *Erde,* "earth," in the genitive singular, and had needed the appropriate ending for the definite article. Some of the information of which I might have become conscious, though not necessarily in this order, are listed below. Explicit rulelike information has been so labeled:

- ☐ The German word for "earth" is *Erde*.
- ☐ RULE: Most nouns that end in *-e* are feminine.
- ☐ RULE: But not all are.
- ☐ The one exception familiar to me is *Ende*, "end."
- ☐ The title of a chapter in a book we read in class was *Das Ende* "The End" (neuter gender).
- ☐ Therefore *Erde* is not the exception, and so must be feminine.
- ☐ RULE: The nominative, genitive, dative, and accusative forms of the definite article for the feminine gender are respectively *die, der, der, die*. (This information I get from a pallid but legible visual-type image.)
- ☐ Therefore the needed form should be *der Erde,* "of the earth."
- ☐ This is confirmed from the Files by dative form in the title of Mahler's *Das Lied von der Erde*.[97]

Here we see an intimate and subtle interplay among word, larger utterance (the chapter title), and rule. In the actual use of any language, whether native or foreign, we can produce our utterances from scratch, starting with rules plus a list of the smallest sized meaningful units. But we can also produce them by starting with whole utterances and modifying them to suit the context, employing for the purpose whatever kit of rules or regularities (p. 35) we may have under our control in the language. In the latter case, the rules are "not so much generative

[as] regulative and subservient [to memory]."[98] I would suggest that both methods may be in operation at the same time, as "coterminous pathways," and their results are then compared.

In the preceding example, if my networks had been more like those of fluent speakers of German, I could have come up with the form much more directly and therefore more quickly.

What I am saying here is *not* that progress in mastery of a word or a point of grammar consists in a more efficient or more accurate "process" or "strategy" *replacing* (eliminating) a more primitive, slower process or strategy.[99] That may very well prove to be true. For the time being, however, I think it is more cautious to assume only that all these alternative pathways in the Files are followed automatically until the search is terminated, and that they may even interact and blend with one another. In this more general view, progress will consist in modifying the relevant networks so that the search will be terminated more rapidly, and so that any discrepancies between the replies from various CPs will be resolved accurately. The nature of network modification will figure in the next section.

□ CONNECTIONISM

Recent years have seen a large amount of experimentation in a type of research called "connectionism." Connectionist researchers use computer hardware and software in order to try to approximate some of the learning behavior observed among humans.[100]

In a connectionist view of language, the rules and words and tenses and all of the other elements that we normally think and talk about are just a broad-brush, approximate way of thinking about the *outcomes of processes*. These processes themselves involve very large numbers of *very-small-scale units*. In fact, these very-small-scale units are so small that individually, no one of them corresponds to anything that we can normally even think about.

A connectionist learning device consists of a layer of input cells, a layer of output cells, and often an intervening layer. Some of these units accept input from the outside world. Other units emit output to the outside world. Many of them, however, are connected only to one another. Each of the connections between the cells has its own *numerical weighting*, and each of these weightings varies along a continuum.

These processes involving smoothly varying quantities are what mathematicians call "stochastic." That is to say, the processes occur randomly under the control of functions that specify the *probability but not the certainty* that under a given set of conditions a certain thing will happen. And these stochastic processes, involving continuously varying values of units too small to think about, occur in large *networks* of interconnected units.

In brief, some set of the input units of the network are turned on by a stimulus—for example, the infinitive form of a verb—that is provided from outside.

On the basis of the existing weightings of the connections among its cells, the network responds by turning on some set of its output units—in the same example, indicating the network's guess as to the past tense form of the same verb. Then comes the learning part. The computer takes this guess and compares it with the correct form, which has also been provided. It then goes on to increase the weightings of whichever connections were behind what was correct in the network's guess, and to decrease the weightings of whichever connections were behind the wrong parts. This means that a learned pattern of behavior does not correspond to a fixed pattern of the connections themselves. Rather, a learned pattern of behavior corresponds to *a pattern of weightings* on the connections.

As a matter of fact, one connectionist program was designed to learn to produce past tense forms for 506 English verbs when it was given the present tenses. After 200 cycles of training, the computer was 91% correct in its guesses about the past tenses for a group of verbs it had never met before. What was even more interesting, the program reportedly approximated the same three stages commonly observed in children learning English as a native language: (1) irregular past tenses came out right; (2) wrong past tenses were produced for irregular verbs, by analogy with regular verbs; (3) correct past tenses were produced both for regular and for irregular verbs.

This line of research has been somewhat controversial among linguists.[101] The chief issue at stake seems to be whether the connectionists have succeeded in producing languagelike performance with equipment that neither recognizes nor stores what we ordinarily call "rules." To the extent that they have indeed done so, it is sometimes asked, "Do not their results deny the very concept of language as rule-governed behavior?"

I wonder whether this issue is largely a matter of how we have used words. Perhaps the crux of the matter lies once more in using a noun *(rule)* as if it stood for a thing (or even an actor), and then making that thing (or actor) the subject of a transitive verb *(govern)*. This comes about in approximately the following way:

□ We notice that in any one language, or in language in general, there are certain things that happen over and over, and certain other things that do not happen at all.

□ We try our hand at making statements that will pull together what we have noticed.

□ To some extent, we disagree about which rule statements, and even which *kinds* of rule statements, work best—even about which kinds of rule statements are permissible. For example, must such statements be confined to the patternings that could be discovered by cutting sentences into pieces and then reassembling those pieces *(She cut some wood. / She cut several flowers.)*? Or may they (must they?) take into account the relationships among sentences that are related in content but different in form *(She cut some wood yesterday. / The wood cut yesterday . . . .)*? Is learning a language merely a matter of becoming able to duplicate statistical properties of a body of existing sentences, or is it more a matter of producing and rejecting sentences as a native speaker would?

□ By and large, however, we find that the making of such rule statements is a workable way to keep track of what has or has not already happened, and to predict what will or will not happen later on.

Then we take a crucial next step:

□ We conclude (or at least we let our figures of speech give the impression) that these statements, the work of our minds and our hands, must be the cause (or must stand for the cause) of what we have observed, and we express this conclusion by saying, "Rules *govern* behavior."

I find it confusing to see the same word *rule* standing now for the statements themselves, and now for what they describe. Perhaps we would be better off if for the former we continued to use "rule," and spoke of the latter as "regularities." This word "regularities" works best not as a subject, but as an object: "What regularities have we observed?" and "What causes these regularities?" A possible answer to the second question is:

□ The *kinds* of regularities reflect inborn characteristics of the physiological equipment we use for networking. Some of these characteristics are very subtle, as yet undiscovered, and absent from the mechanical and electronic equipment used in connectionist investigations.

□ The *specifics* of regularities come from what has previously happened to our networks.

Hatch, Shirai and Fantuzzi[102] quote an early-20th-century statement that "[the learner] is neither a pure associative machine nor a sovereign constructor of concepts. Rather his speech is based on the continuing interaction of external impressions with internal systems which usually function unconsciously. It is thus the result of a constant 'convergence.'"

For me, then, the great wonder is (1) that the regularities/predictabilities of human speech are such that at least some of them can be described by explicit statements called "rules"; (2) that some of the rules are as complex and as subtle as they are; and (3) that we have been given minds that are able to construct and appreciate and test explicit rules. This is—and I think always will be—beyond our knowing. Just how the brain does all this—whether by connectionist-like mechanisms or in some other way—is not a wonder, but only an as-yet-unsolved puzzle.

The shaping of the networks of long-term memory will be the subject of the first parts of the next chapter.

■ ■ ■   *Some Answers I Reached*

Items of stored information can be compared to a set of points that are connected to one another in networks. At any given time, each item is at some level of activation. If a set of items is stimulated by something coming from the senses or from working memory, the stimulation raises the level of activation of those items. That activation then spreads to other items that are connected with them, and from them to still other items. In this way, the activation of certain other items is eventually raised to a level that allows them to reach consciousness, and to appear in working memory. The classroom implication is that our students do not have direct access to the networks of long-term memory, so what is done on the Worktable is of great practical importance.

Exchange of information between our students' working memory and their long-term memory does not take the form of a unidirectional flow. Rather, it is constant complex two-way traffic, sometimes almost instantaneous, but sometimes lasting a noticeable period of time. Teachers need to respect the complexity, and to allow the time.

A single incoming stimulation may bring back two or more replies from long-term memory. These replies may agree with each other, or they may conflict. This fact is probably part of the explanation for self-monitoring and self-correction. It also helps to account for the well-known advantages in presenting the same material in more than one medium.

■ ■ ■ *Further Questions*

□ How are the cognitive networks studied by psychologists related to the complex interconnections of the brain?

□ How can we in practice tell when we have not allowed enough time for a student's long-term memory to do what it can? How can we tell when we have allowed too much time?

Notes

1. Physical changes in the nervous system related to learning and forgetting have been clearly demonstrated in the nervous systems of sea snails and some other animals (Johnson 1991:59). Comparable studies would of course not be feasible with humans.

2. Bransford 1979:90.

3. Much of the evidence I will cite in this chapter and in Chapters 4–6 is taken from experiments with the learning of individual words or other uncontexted items. Such subject matter is relatively easy to design and vary for investigative purposes, and so is understandably a favorite of scientists, who are concerned with making and testing hypotheses, and in building theories from the ground up. At the same time, however, Scovel (private communication) points out that foreign language learners retain contextualized words much better than they retain lists. This observation is consistent with common experience, as well as

with the contrast between "concentrated" and "diffused" learning (see Chapter 5), and with emphasis on the importance of "rich and complex images."

4. Other writers, quoting or referring to the ISM model, use language such as "the structural eidetic *image* . . . involves visual *images* [plus the S and M components]" [emphasis added] (Jordan 1984:54); "a model of *imagery* that includes a somatic component as well as *image* and meaning components" [emphasis added] (Hanley & Chinn, 1989:110). I prefer to avoid juxtaposing uses of this same stem *image(ry)* on two levels.

5. Ahsen 1984:34.

6. Jordan (1984:54) believes that "the inferior parietal lobule serves as an association area in human beings where input from the occipital, somatosensory, and auditory areas of the brain converge."

7. Jordan 1984:64.

8. Jordan 1984:64.

9. Ahsen 1984:34.

10. Gehring & Toglia 1989:95.

11. Most people apparently do not experience eidetic images at all. I never have.

12. In Singer & Pope 1978:200f.

13. For a summary, see Brown & Herrnstein, in Block 1981:19–26.

14. Casey 1976.

15. Dickel & Slak 1983.

16. Ahsen 1984:34.

17. Hanley & Chinn 1989:111.

18. If the ISM model, with its intimate interrelationships among imagery and physiology (including what are commonly called "feelings") and meaning, is to be credible, it needs at least some support from neuroanatomy. Both Ahsen (1984:23) and Jordan (1984: 52, 63)quote findings that the neural connections between the limbic areas (responsible for affective processing) and the inferior parietal cortex (where intermodal connections are made) are, though sparse, sufficient for this purpose. Schumann (1994) has provided a readable description of the role of one brain structure, the amygdala, in maintaining the relationship between what we see and what we can expect from it.

19. Jordan 1984:52.

20. Ahsen 1984:34f.

21. Ahsen 1984:35ff.

22. Jordan 1984:52.

23. Jordan 1984:55.

24. Jordan 1984:52.

25. "Network" (Bower 1988; Carrier & Pashler 1992; Hamilton 1983; Kail et al. 1984; Johnson 1991; Keatley et al. 1994; Luria 1974; McLaughlin 1990; Perrig & Perrig 1988; Schmidt 1992; Seliger 1984; Smith & Sloman 1994; Thompson 1986; Werbos 1988) is one of the most widely used terms in this field (though it runs a distant second to "strategy").

26. For a simple example, see Hamilton (1983: 71).

27. This hierarchical meaning for "network" appears, for example, in Schmidt (1992:362).

28. Anderson 1984:61.

29. Anderson 1984:64.

30. I for one have never found the further metaphor of "mapping onto" very helpful.

31. Hebb 1949.

32. For a summary of this and related research, see Johnson (1991). Hebb's principle is also a fundamental part of the neurobiological model proposed by Pulvermüller and Schumann (1994).

33. Anderson 1984:61; O'Brien & Albrecht 1991.

34. Anderson 1984:61.

35. Straight (1993:199) argues that "language is best viewed not as a specifiable set of interpretable and expressible events, but rather as a mechanism for the interpretation and construction of such events." I would want to add that networks in the sense used in this paragraph are at the center of that mechanism.

36. See Chapter 1, endnote 95.

37. See the discussion in Bransford (1979:172f).

38. Similarly, H. D. Brown (1987:68) observes concerning forgetting that meaningful learning is not only a more efficient process than rote learning, but its products are also more resistant to interference with the passage of time.

39. Smith & Sloman 1994:385.

40. Keatley et al. 1994:77.

41. Salomon 1983:42. On "effort," see endnote on Salthouse et al. in Chapter 1, endnote 11.

42. See Chapter 1, p. 12.

43. Bryant 1990.

44. Over the years, the threshold concept has appeared in a number of writings on memory, for example, in Warren (1972:91) and in Wayland, Wingfield, and Goodglass (1989).

45. "A person perceiving a familiar object is not aware that what is perceived is as much an expression of memory as it is of perception" (Tulving & Schacter 1990:302).

46. An everyday example is the "Flaggenheisch Incident," discussed in Chapter 4, p. 96.

47. Treisman & Schmidt 1982.

48. Mozer 1983:532; Church & Schacter 1994.

49. Mozer 1983:544.

50. Weinstein & Mayer 1986:320.

51. Singer & Pope 1978:3.

52. This and the next few paragraphs are modified from material in a plenary address delivered at JALT 1992, and from Stevick (1993).

53. Straight 1977:4.

54. For a brief survey of how this word has been used in our field, see Stevick (1990a).

55. The Worktable is what Brown and Herrnstein (1981:48) describe as "a level of experience where stimulus input and imagined output meet and have common characteristics."

56. Laboratory examples of material in competition with overt or covert language include tapping with the right index finger (Soares 1984) and white noise in the 0–4000 Hz range used by speech (G. J. Smith 1985).

57. Georgetown Round Table 1992.

58. The idea of two-way traffic appears in Nairne's (1990:252f.) statement that "[like] many other memory models . . . , [this model assumes] that primary memory traces can be formed through the encoding of *externally* presented information . . . , *or* through the action of internally generated retrieval processes. Primary memory traces . . . do not exist in a vacuum, but rather are part of a stream of representations containing many *internally* generated traces. . . . For example, subjects formulate strategies for retrieval, rehearse previous items, and so on, and *all* of these activities may produce representations in primary memory" [emphasis added]. (For "primary memory" read "the Worktable" or "working memory," and for "secondary memory" read "the Files" or "LTM.")

59. Goodglass, Theurkauf & Wingfield 1984.

60. This search need not always be conscious or deliberate. One afternoon as I was mowing the grass, I noticed a German-speaking neighbor passing by on the street. I wanted to remark to her that the afternoon was humid, but a quick search of my vocabulary resources convinced me that I did not know, and had never known, any appropriate German word. So I went on mowing. A minute or so later, however, the word *schwül* came to consciousness, apparently from nowhere. I "sent the word to my Files," got back a meaning picture that was consistent with humidity, and decided that *schwül* could indeed be have been used for that purpose. It was only several days later that I remembered the

"episodic" information about where and when I had learned *schwül*: in the weather section of a borrowed newspaper, only 2 or 3 years earlier.

61. Rugg 1995.

62. Weldon 1991:526; Tulving & Schacter 1990:301b, par. 2. This definition of "priming" as a phenomenon or effect seems at odds with Tulving and Schacter's statements on the same page, that priming is a "*form* of human memory," or a "*kind* of implicit memory," or a "*category* of learning and memory."

63. Tulving & Schacter 1990:302.

64. Meyer, Schvaneveldt & Ruddy 1974.

65. McClain 1983:644.

66. McNamara (1994:519) reports that attempts to explain the priming phenomenon without assuming spreading activation as its mechanism have not been very successful.

67. An earlier statement of this idea is found in Warren (1972:91).

68. It is also called "semantic" or "associative" priming; see Tulving and Schacter (1990:305, note 2).

69. Also called "repetition" priming; see Tulving and Schacter (1990:305, note 2).

70. Tulving & Schacter 1990:301.

71. Weldon 1991:527.

72. Tulving & Schacter 1990:301.

73. Jacoby 1983.

74. Tulving & Schacter 1990:305.

75. Tulving & Schacter 1990:302.

76. Wayland, Wingfield & Goodglass 1989:477.

77. Tarone 1983:156f.

78. A more recent and more sophisticated unidirectional model appears in VanPatten and Cadierno (1993:226f).

79. Carroll & Swain 1993.

80. Shiffrin & Schneider 1977.

81. Ellen Langer, quoted in Salomon 1983:43f.

82. E.g., Fendrich, Healy & Bourne 1991; Gardiner & Java 1990; Rappold & Hashtroudi 1991.

83. Klatzky 1984:29.

84. Leow 1993.

85. VanPatten 1990.

86. More learned: "to activate existing strategies."

87. Miles et al. 1991:583.

88. As Straight (1978:3) put it, "[A] conscious experience is an interpretively neutral representation of the results of internal or external information processing. By interpretively neutral I mean that a single conscious representation is subject to multiple chains of successive or even simultaneous interpretive processing."

89. Bradley & Thomson 1984.

90. For other clinical evidence for CPs, see Bub and Kertesz (1982).

91. Perecman (1984:61) suggests that the difference between "compound" and "coordinate" as applied to the performance of bilinguals may refer not to how the languages are wired into the brain, but to alternative strategies for getting at the necessary information, and that a polyglot may resort to one strategy at one moment, and to the other at the next moment.

92. For other instances of "coterminous pathways," see Logan and Stadler (1991:495) and O'Brien and Albrecht (1991:94).

93. If one wished to sound learned here, one could perhaps hellenize this description:

- □ alternative pathways = "polydromes"
- □ divergent pathways = "allodromes"
- □ coterminous pathways = "isodromes"

with the corresponding adjectives in -ic.

94. Summarized in Keatley, Spinks and de Gelder (1994:70). This theory is derived from Paivio's dual coding model.

95. Smith & Sloman 1994.

96. Schmidt 1992:366f.

97. Here, der is dative and not genitive, but one of our rules has already told us that the feminine forms for these two cases are identical.

98. Widdowson 1989:135.

99. "Strategy" refers here more to internal processing by one or another combination of pathways than to consciously adopted techniques for going at a memory task.

100. Unless otherwise noted, this account of connectionism is derived from Sampson 1987.

101. S. Carroll 1989:537.

102. Hatch, Shirai & Fantuzzi 1990:709.

Chapter 4

Processes of Memory: What Happens within the Files

Questions I Asked Myself:

☐ What do the networks of long-term memory do?

☐ What are some everyday examples of "two-way traffic" between working memory and long-term memory?

☐ How do affective factors such as stress or anxiety fit into the operation of my students' networks?

☐ Are there perhaps any general differences between the networks of one student and those of another? How might such differences show themselves in practical performance?

INTRODUCTION

In Chapter 3, I introduced several key terms that will be basic to further discussion of how memory works, and tried to clarify the frequently contradictory ways in which they are used in the literature. I also sketched some of the basic processes of memory. Now in Chapter 4, we will look in greater detail at these processes, and at how they may shape the contents of the metaphorical Files of long-term memory. Finally, we will explore further the pivotal roles of comparisons in shaping memories, and of construction in using them.

HOW LONG-TERM MEMORY CHANGES

Figure B in Chapter 3 says, among other things, that the effect of feedback is ultimately not to "shape *behavior*"—to "reinforce" a desired *response* from the learner or to "correct" an undesired *response*. It is rather to shape the *source* from which the behavior came. To give an encouraging reaction to a student's production of a vowel or a word or a tag question or any other behavior is therefore not simply to increase the likelihood that that behavior will recur in the future. It is to increase the likelihood that the behavior will recur *from the same source*—the same combination of "pathways," whether shallow (e.g., mimicking) or deep (e.g., expressing personal meaning)—*that produced it this time.* The same can be said for reinforcement of mental processes that have led to correct interpretation of the words, structures, and visual or auditory contrasts of incoming signals.

Let us begin with three research reports that cast light on how the resources in the Files get shaped through experience. This will at least appear to parallel what the computer does as it modifies the networks in connectionist research. By coincidence, each of these three reports makes some kind of reference to the use of flashcards, a primitive and perhaps regretable, but still-flourishing, technique for the learning of vocabulary. Many writers these days consider word lists and flashcards obsolete. I certainly agree that such devices have often been misused as substitutes for more meaningful activities, and my purpose in this chapter is not to recommend them. As I have explained elsewhere, however, I myself would still use them in certain ways[1] in my own study for purposes of what in 1989 I called "stockpiling,"[2] or what in Chapter 10 of this book I call "spanning." In a recent statement, Nation also seems to find a place for cards and lists.[3]

□   EVIDENCE FROM THE REPETITION EFFECT

The first report was about a study of something called the "repetition effect,"[4] which psychologists have found to be very robust.[5] In this series of experiments, subjects were given several lists of numbers, and were asked to enter them on a keypad. Each number consisted of three digits (e.g., 398, 710), and each list consisted of 10 such numbers. Carrying out this task certainly involves the subjects' muscles, which must receive signals from the brain, *and* respond to each signal, *and* press appropriate keys, *and* return to rest position. But the task also requires much from the brain: to decode the visual cue, *to prepare a muscular response,* and to send the necessary signals to the muscles.

The experimenters discovered that if one of the lists in an experiment is identical with a list that the same subject had typed earlier, the subject will type it faster the second time. (This is what is meant by the "repetition effect."[6]) For each entry of each three-digit number, the researchers measured two intervals. One was the delay between the appearance of the visual stimulus and the first keystroke. They called this the "encoding time." The second interval was the time required for entering the second and third keystrokes. This was the "execution time." The researchers discovered that with the first presentation of a list, encoding time was much longer than execution time. They interpreted this finding to mean that during encoding time the mind and muscles not only must do everything they will have to do for the later keystrokes, but will also have to register and encode the visual stimulus and prepare the entire response. With later presentations of the same list, encoding time was again greater than execution time was, *but it was much smaller than it had been the first time.*

This piece of research has an incidental payoff for language teachers because one of the experiments in the series used pseudowords (e.g., *nef, ibu*) instead of numbers. This obviously resembles work with flashcards, since the combinations of letters have no preexisting well-established representations in memory, and no meanings firmly attached to them. And of course it is common experience that a new word or phrase comes more easily off the tongue the tenth time than it did the first time. On the other hand, we must not forget that work with pseudowords is unlike FL vocabulary study in at least three ways:

☐ Subjects readily recognize that the pseudowords are artificial, arbitrary, and of only temporary interest.

☐ Pseudowords require no new skills of articulation or of recognition of printed characters.

☐ Pseudowords are not, and never will be, supported in memory by occurrences in meaningful contexts.

Principally, however, this research contributes toward our understanding of memory in general by showing that *between stimulus and outward response something time-consuming and improvable is going on in the head of the subject.*

☐ EVIDENCE FROM JUDGMENTS OF LEARNING

In a second body of research, the subjects simulated a student who has just 1 hour in which to prepare for tomorrow's vocabulary quiz in Kigeni 101. Facing the student is a stack of 100 flashcards, each with a Kigeni word on one side and a NL equivalent on the other. Obviously the student will want to spend at least a little time even with those cards that already seem to be under control. (This is what these authors call "doing preventive maintenance."), but proportionately more time with the cards that are still causing trouble ("corrective maintenance," or reestablishing access to nonrecalled items). In order to distribute the available time among the cards as efficiently as possible, the student must try to make "judgments of learning." Research has shown that students who are accurate at this kind of "metacognitive monitoring" do best on tests, *and* that this skill can be picked up over time.[7]

Under these circumstances, the student needs to make two kinds of decisions:[8]

☐ *What* to look at: The NL stimulus alone? The NL stimulus and the Kigeni response in immediate succession?

☐ *When* to attempt the judgment: While still looking at the card? After looking at one or two other cards? After looking at several other cards?

In these experiments, *judgments of learning* were much more accurate when subjects made them after looking only at the NL stimulus, and when they were not made until at least 30 seconds after the subject had last seen the NL stimulus and the Kigeni response together. The authors report that typically, *accuracy of actual performance* is also greater when preventive maintenance is done by looking only at the NL stimulus.

If we wanted to give a flashcard user some advice consistent with these findings, we might suggest:

- If you found you were able to give the response side of a card correctly before you looked at it, put that card at or near the *bottom* of the pack.

- If on the other hand you had trouble giving the response, put the card about 10 cards below the *top* of the deck.[9]

For the moment, however, our concern is not with techniques for language learners. We are interested in what points this report implies about the working of memory in general. One such point is that *a judgment of learning depends on a making a comparison* between the correct Kigeni response and whatever Kigeni response the learner has been able to supply.

- If the comparison is made at least 30 seconds after the most recent exposure to the correct Kigeni form, then the *supplied* Kigeni form has presumably come from the nonelectrical storage of long-term memory and indicates what long-term memory is likely to produce on the quiz.

- If the comparison is made earlier, a supplied Kigeni form may still have come from long-term memory, but the same form or some different form may also have been supplied from the electrically disruptible storage of working memory, or forms may have been supplied by both working memory and long-term memory simultaneously. Under these circumstances, the usefulness of the comparison is reduced because the relevance of one of its terms is uncertain. As the authors put it, when an immediate judgment of learning is attempted, the response from working memory may "add noise to" or "dominate" or "distort" or "blot out" the response from long-term memory, so that long-term memory's contribution cannot be reliably assessed.[10]

The other member of the comparison is the *correct* Kigeni form. It may of course have come from outside—from peeking at the Kigeni side of the card. Two other possible sources are internal: (1) if not too much time or distraction have intervened, it may have come from something that is still in working memory (short-term memory); or (2) it may have come from long-term memory, which is also internal. No matter which internal source the Kigeni reply came from, *once it is on the Worktable it in turn triggers the networks of the Files (long-term memory). The* NL *reply that comes from the Files is then compared with the original NL stimulus, which is still on the Worktable.* If the two are alike, then an affirmative judgment of learning is reached.

□ EVIDENCE FROM THE VALUE OF RETRIEVAL

In the last of these three reports,[11] each subject was seated at a personal computer. The experiment went as follows:

- □ Subjects were exposed to 30 pairs of items on the screen, one pair at a time. One member of each pair was a number (e.g., *8, 43*), and the other was a nonsense syllable (e.g., *flev, zo*). The subjects' task was to learn these pairs so that if they were given the first member (the stimulus) they would be able to come up with the second (the response).

- □ The first time through the list, subjects saw each pair for 15 seconds. On the second presentation the same pairs appeared, but this time in a different order, and each pair stayed for only 10 seconds. During this 10-second period, subjects were free do anything they liked mentally with what they saw.

- □ Next, subjects were presented with a series of 5 pairs taken at random from the original 30-pair list. Each pair was on the screen for 10 seconds. (The "10-see" treatment.)

- □ Following their viewing of this sublist, subjects were given a distractor task consisting of pairs of words. For each pair, subjects were required to speak aloud an original sentence that contained both words. This distractor activity lasted for a little over 2 minutes. Its purpose was to override/wash away any direct access to the material studied, particularly the material studied toward the end of the activity. The reason for this particular duration of the sentence-production activity was to get beyond the length of working memory, which as we have seen is usually estimated as around 20 seconds.

- □ Then subjects were shown the first members of these pairs, and were asked to supply the second member of each pair. If they could not actually produce an answer from memory, they were invited to guess. They could take as much time as they needed.

- □ Following this work with the first 5-pair sublist, subjects saw 5 more pairs from the original 30-pair list. Now, however, the first member of a pair came on for the first 5 seconds, and then both members of the same pair for another 5 seconds. (The "5-try-5-see" treatment.) A third and a fifth 5-pair sublist were presented like the first sublist, and a fourth and a sixth like the second. By the end of the sixth 5-item sublist, subjects had met all 30 of the pairs in the original list. Each sublist was followed by the same 2-minute distraction-plus-test that was described for the first sublist.

But what exactly was going on in all this study-plus-testing activity? Let's look at two views. According to View X:

- □ The units in memory are connected to one another in networks.

- □ Whenever a configuration of two or more units (e.g., including Units A and B) are active at the same time, the connection strengths among them are increased.

□ If later on some part (e.g., A) of that same configuration is met, this new
pattern of connection strengths will tend to supply the missing parts
(including B).

Of the two treatments used in this research, the 10-see treatment was more
consistent with View X than was the 5-try-5-see treatment. The reason is that in
the study phase, the full configuration (i.e., both members of the pair) was present for a longer period of time. View X also harmonizes with the account of the
repetition effect, which implies that the oftener or the longer a particular configuration is met, the stronger will be the connections among the units involved;
and the stronger the connections, the quicker the response.

View Y is somewhat different:

□ As in View X, units in memory (e.g., including A and B) are joined into
networks.

□ Again as in View X, the strength of the connection between any two units
in long-term memory (in this example, A and B) can be changed.

□ When later on Unit A is presented to the network in long-term memory,
the network will produce its *guess* as to the missing part of the configuration (B_g). In real life, no network has a simple history, and no network is
free of overlap with many other networks. For this reason, B_g may be
entirely like the original B, or it may be partly like it, or it may be entirely
different from B.

□ If within the span of working memory the correct form B is present
together with B_g, the two are compared. This is the same sort of comparison mentioned at the end of the preceding section.

□ Modification of the connections within the network is then carried out in
accordance with the information that has come from this comparison of
B_g with B. This kind of modification figured in the discussion of connectionism in Chapter 3.

The 5-try-5-see treatment is more consistent with View Y than the 10-see
treatment because it allows time for a clean guess during the first 5 seconds, followed by a 5-second opportunity for comparison. The evidence reported by
these researchers showed that under these conditions, most subjects performed
better under the 5-try-5-see treatment.[12] Notice that in the 5-try-5-see treatment,
the items that jointly occupied the Worktable during the first 5 seconds included
Unit A, plus a guess B_g supplied from long-term memory (probably holding
memory). During the last 5 seconds, the Worktable contained Unit A, plus a
record of B_g from working memory, plus the correct form of Unit B. In the 10-
see treatment, the items on the Worktable during the 10 seconds were at least
Unit A (from working memory) plus Unit B (also from working memory), and
possibly some kind of B_g (from long-term memory).

According to View Y, the main disadvantage of the 10-see treatment is
that the very presence of a full, examinable Unit B from working memory may

interfere with the retrieval of a reliable B$_g$ from long-term memory. Even if that is not the case, the presence of B may contaminate what is retrieved. In this way, it may prevent accurate assessment of what long-term memory is likely to produce in the future. As a result, reliable information for modifying the strengths of the connections in the networks of long-term memory is not available. *If "learning" means "changing what is in memory so as to produce better performance in the future," then learning takes place* after *retrieval has generated B$_g$ and after the suitability of B$_g$ has been estimated by comparison with B or in some other way.*

Pedagogically, View Y and the results of this third set of experiments lend support to the flashcard procedure outlined in Chapter 3, which allows plenty of opportunities for the learner to try out whatever guess long-term memory is likely to produce, followed immediately by a way to estimate the suitability of that guess.

Like the experimental design used in the study of the repetition effect (discussed previously), this research is partially unlike what our students would do with flashcards:

□   Words were not taken from any connected context.

□   Subjects sense the connections between the items in a pair to be arbitrary and artificial.

□   Motivation is temporary and superficial.

□   Timing is not under the control of the subjects.

□   RAPID COMPLEX SIMULATION

The practical teacher is interested only in those mental processes that take place in normal students under ordinary circumstances. Yet it is often the exception that casts light on the ordinary—that "proves the rule," as the saying goes. Let us therefore turn and look briefly at some findings of scholars who have studied three special states of consciousness: out-of-body experiences, apparitions, and dreams.

In an "out-of-body experience," a person seems to perceive the world, often including his or her own body, from a location outside the physical body, most often from above. These experiences may take place during a close brush with death, but also in meditation, relaxation, life-threatening stress, or other situations.[13] Out-of-body experiences are by no means rare; in fact, surveys have reported that somewhere between 8% and 25% of the general population have had out-of-body experiences.[14] During an out-of-body experience, the subject is perceiving a dynamic image in the visual modality, the same modality that is normally fed by impacts of photons on the optic nerve. But now the image is not being so fed. It must therefore be coming from—be generated by—the mind. Yet the visual aspect of an out-of-body experience is as clear, stable, and apparently complete as ordinary visual images that seem to have come directly from the usual external source. It is a mental *simulation* of the world.

In a second type of altered consciousness, an apparition is perceived in the context of actual physical surroundings. The apparition obscures real objects that are behind it, and is itself obscured by real objects in front of it. According to one interpretation of this phenomenon, *"[T]he entire environment* seen during an apparitional experience may be hallucinatory, not just the apparitional part"* [emphasis added].[15] This sort of imagery has been "reported as being capable of providing a precisely imitated reproduction of the physical environment, and . . . it is apparently possible for a subject to enter [this] state without noticing any discontinuity."[16]

If this interpretation is correct, then we have further evidence of the power of the mind to generate clear and apparently complete images, and to do it so quickly that the product simulates what comes in from external sources. This product can then enter into comparisons. Perhaps this same power, not in connection with any apparitions, is what allows us to detect spelling errors, regional accents, or (both by sight and by hearing) the fact that the carpet has been removed from a familiar room, as in the example I will present on page 91.

The third special state of consciousness at which we shall look is dreaming. Tart uses the expression "state of consciousness" to stand for "a[ny] dynamically interacting and *stabilized* system."[17] He proposes that "the neural patterns that awareness perceives or cognizes as its world—the simulated world the mind perceives—involve essentially the same brain areas and neural patterns that are involved in waking state perception of the external physical world." He therefore believes that "what the mind perceives is . . . of equal [EWS: apparent] reality/intensity/substance in both states. . . . In both dreaming and waking, an active, complex world simulation process is going on, basically identical in kind."[18]

According to Tart, the difference between the waking state and the dreaming state lies in what he calls "stabilization": "In waking, the world simulation process must constantly [EWS: be compared and kept] consistent with a steady inflow of sensory information originating in the external world and the physical body." That is to say, "ordinary waking consciousness is especially stabilized by two major feedback routes: via the external world and the exteroceptors, and via the internal world, the body, through the interoceptors."[19] This requirement does not apply to dreaming.[20]

In each of these three special states of consciousness, we have met something that could be described as a "complex world simulation process." The speed of this process is so great and its product is so much like what comes from external reality that it is often hard to detect.

The question that concerns language teachers is of course whether this process has anything to do with what goes on inside the learners in our classrooms. If somewhere between 75% and 92% of the general population do not have out-of-body experiences even rarely, and if even fewer people ever see apparitions, then reports on those states by themselves are of no direct interest to us. But the mental simulation process that we found in those states shows up also in Tart's description of dreaming, and dreaming is something that everyone does. I would suggest that rapid complex simulation by the Files in fact goes on all the time. It must be the kind of thing Straight had in mind when he remarked that "the skilled listener or reader unconsciously employs expressive processes to anticipate the speaker's or writer's output."[21] If this is so, than rapid complex simulation is an integral part of the perception and memory processes that shape and constantly reshape the networks of the Files.

□ THE "DIN IN THE HEAD"

During rapid complex simulation the Files are throwing onto the Worktable images which are largely visual, and which are both vivid and complete. There is a second phenomenon in which the Files again throw vivid material onto the Worktable, but this time the material is largely auditory, and is typically incomplete. In a brief note published in 1980, Elizabeth Barber reported on something that happened to her while she was trying to use Russian in Leningrad. Although she had studied a little Russian some years earlier, her mastery of the language was nowhere near sufficient to allow her to speak correctly, at least not at a rate that would have enabled her to interact with Russian monolinguals. So she just went ahead and did her best. She tells us:

> By the third day . . . , I [began to notice] a rising Din of Russian in my head: words, sounds, intonations, phrases, all swimming about. . . . The sounds in my head became so intense that I found myself chewing on them like so much linguistic cud, to the rhythm of my own footsteps as I walked the streets and museums.[22]

I have had firsthand experience of this sort of involuntary verbal playback. I once spent 2 weeks in a training program for a group of Scandinavian (mostly Swedish) English teachers near a small town in Sweden. During the first week, all the sessions were conducted in English for my benefit, since I knew no Swedish at all. I did, however, spend much of my spare time learning to read Swedish newspapers. In this enterprise I was helped by my previous knowledge of German, and by courses that I had taken 25 years earlier in Anglo-Saxon and Old Norse. In the second week, however, the sessions were mostly conducted in Swedish. At first I understood nothing, but gradually as I sat at the back of the room listening and sketching, I found I was understanding longer and longer chunks of what was being said. On Thursday morning (compare Barber's "on the third day"), I woke up with Swedish words and phrases tumbling through my head like laundry past the window of a clothes dryer, and at breakfast I enjoyed trying these expressions out on two of the Swedish-speaking participants, somewhat to their amusement. Whatever speaking ability I may have had on that morning quickly evaporated after I left Sweden at the end of the week, but I did have the clear impression that given a few more weeks in Sweden I would have been able to speak Swedish reasonably well.

Krashen[23] reports a similar experience with German, though his preexisting background in that language (he had spent 10 months in Vienna 18 years earlier) far exceeded either mine in Swedish or Barber's in Russian.

Since Barber's note appeared, other writers have studied this "din phenomenon" both to find out how widespread it is, and to determine the conditions under which it occurs. Some have also ventured interpretations of what causes it, and of what it indicates.

The first such interpreter was Krashen.[24] He hypothesized that the occurrence of this kind of din was an indication that the so-called language acquisition device (LAD) had somehow been stimulated. As I have noted earlier, however, such noun expressions are temptations to reification, and reification leads too easily to blurring of details. I would therefore prefer to expand and paraphrase Krashen's suggestion as follows:

1. Exposure to a new language leads to two kinds of *product*, each of which is a special kind of *knowledge*. *Acquired* knowledge is by definition available quickly and without conscious thought. Access to *learned* knowledge, by contrast, requires time and attention to form and knowledge of rules.

2. Certain *processes* or combinations of processes in the brain lead to one of these *products* or to the other. The processes that lead to "acquisition," plus the inborn neurological equipment they depend on, are collectively called "the language acquisition device."[25]

3. Certain overt *activities* are likely to set off some or all of the internal *processes* that lead to acquisition, while others tend to set off some or all of the processes that contribute to what is in this special narrowed sense called "learning."

Krashen offered the hypothesis that Barber's "din" indicates that processes of the former kind are under way. This is what he means by saying that the activities which regularly precede dinning have "stimulated the LAD."

Krashen also predicted that:

4. If input is to set off this kind of dinning, it will have to be comprehensible to the student.

5. It must also be "interesting."[26]

6. It must contain significant quantities of structures that are just beyond whatever structures the learner has already acquired. (Krashen's shorthand for this is "$i + 1$.")

These three conditions are the same as those found in other activities that Krashen had already identified as leading to "acquisition"—as "triggering the LAD." The best-documented among those activities are responsive listening, real conversing, and interested reading.

Accordingly, Krashen went on to predict that:

7. If dinning is indeed a by-product of the activity of the LAD, then listening, conversing, and reading will lead to noticeable dinning.[27]
8. On the other hand, activities like discussing grammar, memorizing rules, and doing drills, which lead to learned knowledge but not to acquired knowledge, will be followed by little or no dinning.[28]
9. Advanced performers will not experience dinning, since they have already acquired most of the structures, thus removing one of the three conditions (6, above) required for setting the acquisition processes in motion.[29]

To summarize and augment (but not, I hope, to distort) Krashen's LAD hypothesis about the verbal "din": *Involuntary verbal rehearsal ("verbal dinning") brings to consciousness specific linguistic material*[30] *that has been met within the past day or two.*[31] *It occurs when and only when all or at least some of the psychophysical processes that integrate new experiences into "acquired" knowledge are under way.*

The evidence cited by Krashen in favor of this interpretation of the verbal din requires careful examination. Krashen quotes data from studies by Bedford[32] and de Guerrero[33] showing that many students experience dinning after listening and reading, as well as after conversation. This agrees with his prediction (7, above) and thus is consistent with his hypothesis.

But the Bedford and de Guerrero studies also show that dinning is common after "grammar in class," "grammar at home," and "drills in class." In fact, the highest rating in the Bedford study was shared by "listening to comprehensible input" (an "acquisition" activity) and "drills in class" (a "learning" activity). This is hard to reconcile with Krashen's prediction (8, above), and so challenges his LAD hypothesis.

Furthermore, neither the Bedford nor the de Guerrero study found that their most advanced learners experienced significantly less dinning than did learners at the beginning and intermediate levels. At this point, therefore, these two studies fail to support Krashen's prediction (9, above).[34] However, a brief paper by Parr and Krashen[35] does support it.

Another bit of data that casts doubt on (9) is Krashen's own experience of the dinning phenomenon in German 18 years after he had spent nearly a year living in Vienna. It is surprising that one who appropriately describes himself as "a professional linguist who came into linguistics partly because [I] enjoy language acquisition"[36] could have been exposed to that much comprehensible input without absorbing most of the important structures of German.

Krashen's overall explanation of verbal dinning is that it "occurs when we are experiencing something new and attempting to integrate it"[37] into what I have metaphorically been calling "the networks of the Files." If this is true, one might ask whether perhaps the din is generated by some kind of temporary special activity taking place at synapses that represent connections whose strengths have been altered by recent experience. But this is only the speculation of a rank outsider, and is not to be taken seriously.

There is at least one other explanation for verbal dinning. Perhaps it results not from the LAD'S efforts at integration of new structures, but simply from the fact that the person experiencing the din has recently been paying close attention to a particular type of data. Dinning is produced by residual activity in whatever parts of the brain had been handling those data: *Involuntary rehearsal brings to consciousness material of the same general kind (though not necessarily the same items) that a person has repeatedly and sharply focused on within the past day or two.*

This alternative hypothesis would accommodate the findings of Bedford and de Guerrero that dinning is also found after "learning" activities. And if further investigation supports Parr and Krashen's preliminary findings that extremely advanced learners notice very little dinning, then that fact could be explained by those learners' reduced need to focus on linguistic details.

My own experience of dinning in Swedish was consistent with both hypotheses. That is to say, what I was hearing in the din was material that was new and not yet integrated into my Files, and the material was also something on which I had recently been focusing my attention.

I experienced a very similar din a few years ago when I began to listen to German on the radio, nearly 50 years after my two college courses in the language. I had not previously heard Germans speaking to other Germans. Although my academic exposure to the language was relatively brief, I did internalize virtually all the usual structures, and have retained an enjoyable amount of ability to use the language with some fluency, though within a noticeably limited vocabulary. According to Krashen's prediction (9), this degree of mastery should have disqualified me from dinning.

The content of my German din was in some respects consistent with Krashen's LAD hypothesis, but in other respects it was not. (In the following examples, read the symbol > as "produced" or "was followed by.")

> After recent reading of Luke 10:29, DIN > *Er wollte sich verteidigen,* "He wanted to ——— himself" > uncertainty as to precise meaning of the verb *verteidigen.* In subsequent days, the word kept coming up out of the din, along with the question "defend"? "justify"? This was resolved by the eventual occurrence of *Verteidigungsministerium,* obviously meaning "Defense Ministry," in a radio broadcast. This sounds very much like Barber's comparison with chewing of cud. The incident also fits Krashen's LAD hypothesis in that it involved integration of new material. It did not, however, involve integration of any "$i + 1$" *structures.*

> DIN > *Versitzung* > *versitzen* > a set of principal parts for a verb: *versitzen, versaß, versessen.* All of this was accompanied by a feeling of certainty that this verb didn't exist in German, which in fact it doesn't. This is hard to reconcile with my understanding of Krashen's LAD hypothesis, since I had obviously not been exposed to the nonexistent word *versitzen* either recently or at any time in the past.

> DIN > the isolated three-word phrase *mit einer solchen,* "with such a" > "English has different word order." > "Should it be *mit solch' einer*"? > Remembered quote from a story in college German *Solch' eine Dummheit kann bloss ein Esel machen,* "Only a jackass can do such a stupid thing!" >

"Or was it *So eine Dummheit . . . ?*" Saying the phrases aloud gave me the clear impression that *So eine Dummheit . . .* had been the form in the story. Cud-chewing again, possibly triggered by recent exposure to this *kind* of material, but certainly not by recent exposure to this particular sentence.

Some writers cited by Krashen[38] have noted that involuntary playback occurs with other aspects of experience as well, and they have speculated that it may be related to the verbal din of foreign languages. One of these other kinds of playback is visual. Earlier I mentioned that my own visual images are almost invariably "fuzzy, dim, and fragmentary." In at least three settings, however, this has not been the case. In the first of these settings, I was given a hoe and put to digging out a certain type of weed in a vacant area behind the planing mill where I was working. Whenever I closed my eyes during the next 24 hours, I got very sharp and vivid flash images of the same kind of weed. In another setting I had the job of cutting plexiglass with a jigsaw, following red lines that had been inscribed into the material. Again, closing my eyes brought a series of vivid, though not identical, images. Most recently, I have had a similar though less vivid experience on nights after picking raspberries. What all three settings have in common is that I was focusing very sharply on material that was defined by a relatively small and clear set of criteria, and that I was doing so for a simple purpose. A violin maker and his apprentice who read this account of my experiences assure me that the same thing regularly happens to them. A clergyman of my acquaintance had quasi-retinal pictures of Hebrew letters after his first week of study, even with his eyes open. (One may wonder whether these experiences are actually very mild examples of a mechanism similar to the one that produces the vivid flashbacks of a soldier's post traumatic stress disorder.)

This kind of experience obviously does not depend either on the presence of "$i + 1$" structures, or on the integration of new material. On the other hand, it seems to fit easily with the attention hypothesis. But as others have already pointed out, the relationships among this kind of involuntary visual replay, the verbal din reported by Barber, and songs that get stuck in our heads are far from clear.[39]

In the earlier parts of this section, we looked at some of the phenomena that have given rise to the term "din." We then considered two hypotheses about where dinning comes from. A final question is, "How, if at all, can dinning be useful to those of us who learn or teach languages?" By either hypothesis, the "din" places material on the Worktable. Such material at the very least modifies the content of the Files by providing fresh instances of words, phrases, and intonations for possible storage in the Files, and some of this material may then be subjected to further conscious, deliberate cognitive processing on the Worktable as in Barber's "cud-chewing." We can assure students that hearing the din (or not hearing it) doesn't mean they are weird. Having done that, we can go on to teach them the "strategy"[40] of deliberately exploiting it for the purpose of strengthening or clarifying what is in their Files. If the LAD hypothesis is correct, then presence of the din carries an additional benefit: it can tell us that the processes of "acquisition" have been set into play by a particular activity.

As Murphey remarks in summarizing his article on the din, "[T]o a certain extent one could say we are recordings of everything we come into contact with and everything we experience, as we tend to mirror, echo or rehearse these things throughout our lives. But thank God we have the power of choosing at least some, if not a good portion of our thoughts to think, and experiences to experience."[41] This conclusion applies equally to both the LAD hypothesis and the attention hypothesis.

EXAMPLES OF COMPARISON

Comparisons lie at the hub of the use and management of memory. Some of the most important will be sketched below.

□ "WHAT'S DIFFERENT?"

Suppose:

1. It's dark as P (a person) enters a familiar room. On all previous visits, the room had been carpeted and had contained upholstered furniture. This time, both the carpet and the furniture have been removed. P closes the door, thus making a slight noise.
2. The noise enters P's ears, triggers the Files, producing and sending back to the Worktable an anticipated echo E_p, even though P had never before consciously noticed any echo in that room.
3. The noise also produces an actual echo E_a, which enters P's ears.
4. On the Worktable, E_p and E_a are compared.
5. P wonders what has been changed in the room.

We are dealing here with an ordinary nonlinguistic experience. Points to remember from this scenario: (1) *without comparison there could be no surprise;* (2) *without information from the Files, there could be no comparison;* (3) *the entities being compared need not be sharply defined, intended, or the objects of past conscious attention, or even definable in words.*

□ "WHO DO I SOUND LIKE?"

P is trying to learn the first consonant sound in the Shona word for "now" (one of the so-called whistling fricatives of that language).

1. P plays a tape recording of the word. The first consonant S_t triggers the Files and sends to the Worktable:
2. the English consonant sound in the middle of "pleasure." This sound in turn triggers:
3. A visual image of the spelling *zh*, which also goes to the Worktable.

4. One or both of these items on the Worktable trigger from the Files a set of muscular adjustments.

5. *P* pronounces the word from that setting of the speech apparatus, producing a sound S_p (in my experience, usually the consonant from *pleasure*).

6. S_p enters *P*'s ears, and is compared on the Worktable to S_r.

7. Any discrepancy may become the occasion for modification of the networks that control the muscular adjustments, followed by hearing the result of the modification and comparing it with the model. These steps may be repeated many times, possibly until even the ear of a Shona speaker would be unable to distinguish *P*'s output from the model.

In (1), a mental composite of what has been heard many times in ordinary discourse could replace the tape recording.

About this scenario, we know that learners are quite diverse in a number of respects:

□ Their ability to retain accurately, over short or long periods of time, the sounds that will be needed as models for comparison.

□ The relative extent to which what is triggered (S_p) in (4) is influenced by (2) or by (3).

□ Whether their own judgments in (6) will be sufficiently accurate, or whether their judgments will need help from an outside expert.

□ The extent to which in making the modifications in (7) they need or can profit from explicit hints from teacher or textbook (e.g., "Round your lips more.").

Points to remember from this scenario:

1. Learners vary in their abilities to retain and to use certain types of data.

2. The articulatory and auditory facts about this sound are not directly connected to each other: they are not simply two different uses of a single underlying phonetic representation.[42]

Originally, each is connected to particular words that contain this consonant, or to certain spellings, or to both. With practice, and with the passage of time, the two may indeed develop a direct linkage, but this linkage will be constantly open to verification and renegotiation. As Straight has put it:

[T]his mutual adaptation between processes of understanding and processes of speaking is never perfect. Even within a single listener-speaker, whatever congruence exists between the objects acted upon and constructed by the processes of reception and expression probably derives from and is maintained by the continual interaction of these objects in actual language activity.[43]

Straight was writing with primary reference to NL use, where the articulatory and acoustic facts are relatively familiar and stable. How much more true this must be in establishing and fine-tuning relationships involving the brand-new facts of a foreign language!

□   **"DID I SAY WHAT I MEANT?"**

1. *P* has something we can loosely call a communicative intention.
2. This intention triggers appropriate items in the networks of the Files.
3. The reply from the Files sets off appropriate muscular activities in the speech apparatus, which in turn produce sounds.
4. The sounds enter *P*'s ears. From there, they trigger in the Files and send to the Worktable:
5. Certain speaker-specific auditory targets, complete with the effects of skull-bone resonance and other factors unique to that speaker. The sound that has just come in is compared with that target.
6. The sounds in (5) also trigger the same kinds of images and meanings that would have been triggered by the same sounds coming in from another person. This nonverbal reply from the Files is then compared with the intended effect, which is still on the Worktable.
7. If either comparison turns up a discrepancy, *P* may undertake a correction.

This happens constantly and continuously, drawing on *P*'s ability for rapid complex simulation.[44]

Sometimes in (6) two separate nonverbal counterparts come back from the Files: what was intended, and something quite different.[45] Puns are an obvious example: "I've told you a million times, don't exaggerate!"[46] may have been intended as simple hyperbole, but is subject to ridicule as self-contradictory. Social nuances provide more subtle examples: "What time is it?" is likely to elicit desired information about the time, but it could also be taken as a hint to leave.

A point to remember from this scenario: *some kinds of comparison are large scale, continuous, and nondeliberate.*

□   **"AM I MAKING MYSELF CLEAR?"**

1. As in the preceding example, *P* is producing an utterance *U* addressed to A.
2. *U* triggers in the Files a range of reactions R_p that *P*'s previous experience with the addressee *A* might suggest.
3. *A*'s actual reaction R_a is compared with R_p.
4. Any discrepancy may become the occasion for amendment of *P*'s communicative intention, and probably of *P*'s future expectations of A as well.

This is another ongoing process that relies on *P*'s capacity for rapid complex simulation.[47] A point to remember from this scenario: *without frequent comparison and verification of this kind, communication would rapidly deteriorate.*

□ "AM I SAYING IT CORRECTLY?"

1. P has a communicative intention.
2. This intention triggers appropriate items in the networks of the Files.
3. The Files produce and send to the Worktable an as yet unspoken utterance U_u.
4. This utterance on the Worktable triggers in the Files a list of word classes, sounds, structures, and grammatical categories exemplified in U_u. These linguistic items are sent to the Worktable.
5. Some of these linguistic items combine to trigger in the Files, and send to the Worktable, an explicit rule X.
6. Together with U_u, which is still on the Worktable, X triggers a reply U_m from the Files.
7. U_u and U_m are compared on the Worktable. A discrepancy may become the occasion for corrective action.
8. P speaks the utterance, possibly incorporating corrections.

This is pretty much the scenario to which Krashen[48] has applied the term "monitor use." As I said earlier, people differ in the details of their neural circuitry. A person whose relevant circuits in Steps (4), (5), and (6) are clearly defined, well established, and accurate will go through this scenario fast enough, and with enough success, so that it is not prohibitively bulky and frustrating. Individuals with the very best circuitry may even qualify for Krashen's ranking as "Optimal Monitor Users."[49]

Points to remember from this scenario:

□ Access to the rules can be very time-consuming if it requires several round trips between Worktable and Files, and intervening conscious attempts to deal with fragmentary rules on the Worktable.

□ The conscious parts of this activity compete for limited Worktable capacity with all kinds of distractors, including cognitive by-products of emotions.[50]

□ Instead of relying on explicit "rules," P may refer to remembered fragments of the usage of trusted speakers of the language.

Notice that the scenario accounts for Krashen's "three conditions for monitor use," which are time, attention, and knowledge of the relevant rule or rules.

MEMORY AS CONSTRUCTION FROM FRAGMENTS

Here are four multiple-choice questions:

□ Do all of the available bits of data from an external stimulus enter working memory?
  a. Yes. Isn't that what "available" means?
  b. No.

□ How much of what enters working memory eventually reaches long-term memory?

a. All or most of it.

b. That depends.

□ When the Files send back a face or a word to the Worktable, does this reply contain all of the information that would have been available from the original face or word?

a. Always, or almost always.

b. Never, or almost never.

□ What happens if only part of the information needed for a serviceable rendition of the face or the word is available from the Files?

a. Nothing; the person simply "draws a blank."

b. Plenty!

Most of what we have said up to this point is consistent with the (a) answers. The (a) answers are also consistent with the folk view of memory. In fact, however, the correct answers are probably all (b). Three types of evidence can help us to see why this is so.

□ THE "WORSE THAN AVERAGE" ILLUSION

Over the years, I have posed the following question to audiences totaling hundreds of people:

> At a party, you are introduced to someone you have never heard of before. The conversation continues. A minute later, an occasion arises where you need to introduce that person to a third person. For this purpose, you must recall the name. *Compared with the population in general, how good do you consider yourself to be at this task? Better than average? About average? Worse than average?*

Respondents report that they would find it easy enough to recall the gist of what had been said during the intervening minute, but by a show of hands (often accompanied by audible groans) at least 90% have always rated themselves "worse than average" when it comes to recovering the actual name. What can be the source of this illusion?

The answer, I think, is not that they heard the words of the name any less well than they heard the words of the conversation. In fact, only certain fragments of each ever reached the networks of the Files. The difference is that the fragments from the conversation, once they reached the networks of the Files, were able to activate meanings in the Files. When recall was needed, the meaning elements plus the retained fragments of sound combined to fill in the blanks, and so returned to the Worktable an image complete enough to be usable for production. The fragments from the name, by contrast, did not benefit from this constructive redundancy. For this reason, what came back to the Worktable was too full of gaps to serve as a basis for production. (Of course, the description of the typical process assumes that the name did not bring with it some unusual meaningful feature, such as being the name of a beloved friend.)

This implies that memory does not begin with the storage of whole neurological analogues to—"mappings of"—the total range of sensory data that are available. Nor does it end by reconversion of such analogues into quasi-sensory images back on the Worktable. Rather, it begins with sampling of the available sensory data, and with these resulting fragments initiating spreading activation within the networks of the Files. (p. 57) What later comes back to the Worktable for use in recall or recognition or whatever, has been constructed by activity in those same networks.

The preceding paragraph was a little abstract. What it says, however, is quite consistent with the experience of learners and teachers of languages. It offers an explanation for the fact that at first, students often are unable to repeat new words, whether in isolation or in context, no matter how distinctly those words may have been spoken. It also reminds me of my occasional impression, while listening to a FL broadcast, that an otherwise very careful speaker has mumbled certain words while continuing to speak clearly otherwise.

□ THE FLAGGENHEISCH INCIDENT

Many years ago, I came back from lunch and found a message slip on my desk. It said I was to call a "Mr. Flaggenheisch" at the Center for Applied Linguistics. Unfortunately, I didn't know any Mr. Flaggenheisch, either at the Center for Applied Linguistics or anywhere else. So I thought for a minute, then phoned Irwin Feigenbaum at the Center for Applied Linguistics, and he thanked me for returning his call. Later I asked the secretary how much time had elapsed between Irwin's phone call and the time when she wrote out the message slip. She assured me she had filled out the slip immediately, and she seemed quite confident that she had it right.

As I interpret this incident, the secretary did not register all parts of the name "Feigenbaum." She did however retain several of its features: the initial consonants for the first and second syllables; the number of syllables; the stress pattern; the whole second syllable; the fact that the name was somehow German-sounding. These fragments triggered the networks in her Files. The networks then filled in the gaps and sent their finished product back to the Worktable. They did their work so well and so rapidly that the secretary had no reason to suspect anything was amiss. This interpretation of the Flaggenheisch anecdote is supported by the experimental findings of Mozer and of Treisman and Schmidt discussed in the notes to Chapter 3.

The difference between the "worse than average illusion" and the Flaggenheisch incident lies only in their outcomes, and not in the process behind them. What came back to the Worktable in the former was insufficient to serve as the source for any production, while what came back in the latter was sufficient but wrong. This of course again reminds us of something about FL learners: that they frequently come up with nonexistent "words."

But this process is not limited to producing nonexistent forms. One time I said something to a colleague about a friend whose last name was Ash. A few days later, my colleague referred to what I had told him about "Mr. Bush." This sort of outcome is even more instructive than the Flaggenheisch example, for it allows us to make inferences about what may have gone on within the networks of my colleague's Files. We can notice phonetically that both names were monosyllables ending with -*sh*; semantically that both can be used to stand for a large kind of vegetation; statistically that the surname my colleague retrieved is more frequently heard than Ash is. The same sort of outcome is common in FL study: saying *hombre* instead of *hambre* in Spanish, for example.

Most often, this same process promptly produces the correct, intended form. When it does, we don't notice it.

The same process operates on all levels of size and abstractness. Some years ago, in an investigation on the genesis of rumors, Gordon Allport would show an individual subject a picture of a group of people on a subway train.[51] He then removed the picture. One by one additional subjects were brought in, and each described to her successor what she knew about the picture. Allport found that, as the story passed from person to person, there was an inexorable tendency for it to change so as to conform to ethnic and other stereotypes that were common to the culture of the subjects.

Allport's demonstration makes clear a fundamental fact about how memory operates. In everyday thinking, we assume that to "remember" something is like playing back a tape, even though the tape may be marred by gaps or static. The references to memory in the popular book *I'm OK—You're OK*[52] also used this terminology. But the Allport experiment shows that this view is not wholly adequate.

□   "THE NAME'S RIGHT HERE ON THE TIP OF MY TONGUE!"

Sometimes the outcome of this same process is neither a blank nor a quick wrong reply, but something called a "tip-of-the-tongue" (TOT) state. The boundaries between failed recall, a TOT state, and successful recall are quite delicate and indistinct.[53] In a TOT state, most of the needed word or expression is supplied to the Worktable by the Files—enough so that the person is sure the expression is there, but not enough to enable its production. The TOT state may last for a few seconds or for weeks. Because of its duration, psychologists are able to glean from it hints about what goes on in the networks of the Files. This is not the place to summarize their findings,[54] but a few points are of interest to us:

- □   Definite sequences of steps can be inferred from the study of large numbers of TOT states and of how (if at all) they were resolved.[55]
- □   During some TOT states a spurious solution presents itself, but it is usually recognized as wrong and rejected.[56,57]
- □   The resemblances between the sought-for word and the spurious solutions may be in some aspect of sound, in some aspect of meaning,[58] or in

both. This implies that what has been going on in the networks of the Files is complex.

☐ On the way toward solution of a TOT state, certain indicators often show up. Among the most frequent are similar sounds, the first or last letter, the number of syllables, or the primary stress.[59,60] These may be of interest when a teacher wants to assist a student who can't quite remember a word, but does not want to short-circuit the student's retrieval process entirely.

☐ People get into similar "almost-but-not-quite" states over matters other than words. A few weeks ago I confidently called the teenaged daughter of a friend "Grace," only to be reminded that her name was Ruth. I have a strong certainty that my error was due to the existence, somewhere in my past, of an in-some-way-similar friend with a teenaged daughter named Grace. I can almost see the people, but not quite. The names are both at hand. All that is missing is one of the referents. Compare this with the language student who sees (or even supplies from memory) a word, can give certain parts of its meaning ("It's from sports, a favorable term"), but doesn't have enough of the meaning to be able to use the word.

☐ The same thing can happen with grammatical information. That is the present state of my control of the Swahili word *kamwe*, about which after many years of not speaking the language I seem to remember only two facts: "It's sort of negative," and "The places where it can occur in a sentence are sort of unique to it."

EMOTIONS

The process that figures in the formation of memories is at best fragmentary: not all of the available sense data get registered on any one occasion. The process is also complex, since it may involve multiple round trips between the consciously inspectable Worktable and the covert intricacy of the Files. Certain factors tend to fragment and complicate it still further. Most conspicuous among these factors is emotion, and the emotions most frequently cited are negative: anxiety and stress.

A number of attempts have been made to observe the effects of anxiety and stress by means of small-scale experiments. One study, in which subjects viewed a violent incident, led to the conclusion that this sort of experience does something that could cause a narrowing of attention to a limited range of information, especially while the information is on its way in.[61] In a later study, subjects viewed a nonviolent incident, but the time when one of the characters was onstage was accompanied either by a pure tone or by white noise, which was assumed to be more stressful than the tone. The subjects who were exposed to the white noise were able to recall significantly less information about that character than were the subjects who heard the pure tone.[62]

Some years earlier, Easterbrook had proposed that emotional arousal narrows the range of information that we use. He said that this may be either an advantage or a disadvantage, depending on what we are trying to do,[63] but that in general "cerebral competence is reduced in emotion."[64] More recently, Reason has concluded that there is a strong connection between stress on the one hand, and various kinds of slips and lapses on the other.[65] So the experimental psychologists have provided considerable small-scale evidence that emotion can interfere with the workings of memory.

Just where and how that interference takes place is another question, one that has been addressed on a larger scale and within the context of FL learning by MacIntyre and Gardner. In one article, they suggest that interference may occur at one or more of three separate stages[66]:

□ As new information is *on its way in,* anxiety may interfere with full attention. This may prevent full initial processing of data, so that less information gets registered. In terms of the general process outlined above, perhaps fewer data are getting through from the senses to the networks of the Files. Or perhaps as many data are getting through, but there is some biochemical reason why they do not trigger as much spreading activation within the neural networks.[67]

□ While new information is *being processed*—during the period in which there is lots of two-way traffic between the Files and the Worktable—emotion causes relatively little interference if the task is simple, but more trouble with more difficult tasks. This would be consistent with the idea that the Worktable is limited in its capacity,[68] and that emotional aspects of experience carry with them their own cognitive by-products.[69]

□ At times when the subject is *trying to retrieve* information from memory, anxiety can again get in the way. This is another place where we must not rule out some sort of biochemical basis. Or perhaps negative emotional by-products that had been stored along with the cognitive data may impede retrieval.

In studying the effects of anxiety, MacIntyre and Gardner administered questionnaires to a large number of English-speaking students of French. Through statistical analysis of the responses, they were able to isolate two different kinds of anxiety. One, called "general anxiety," was based largely on a combination of "trait anxiety" (Typical questionnaire item: "I sometimes feel jittery.") and "state anxiety" (Typical questionnaire item: "I feel calm right now [in the midst of filling out the questionnaire]."). The authors found that general anxiety was not reliably related to language behavior.

The second broad category was "communicative anxiety." It included French class anxiety (Typical questionnaire item: "I was generally tense when participating in French class."); English class anxiety (Typical questionnaire item: "I was generally tense when participating in English class."); French use anxiety (typical questionnaire item: "It would bother me if I had to speak French on the telephone."); and audience sensitivity: (Typical questionnaire item: "If I came late to a meeting, I'd rather stand than take a front seat."). Communicative anxiety did turn out to have a negative effect on performance,[70] and a later study by the same authors suggested that almost all of the experiences contributing to FL class anxiety resulted from attempts to speak the language.[71]

In another phase of their research, MacIntyre and Gardner further found that state anxiety is more closely associated with performance on the test that *preceded* its measurement than it was with performance on the text that *followed* it. They pointed out that this can lead into a circular effect:

1. Communicative anxiety interferes with performance.
2. Poor performance increases state anxiety.
3. Repeated episodes of state anxiety within the context of FL study may solidify into FL class anxiety, a major component of communicative anxiety, which in turn interferes with later performance, and so on round and round.

In summary, then, we have found effects of stress and anxiety at all stages of storage and retrieval, and we have seen that one kind of anxiety may work differently from another. Moreover, emotions or their by-products are stored in association with all other kinds of data. This picture of the influence of emotional material is much more complex and subtle than the picture of an "affective filter" was.[72] There, the result of anxiety was only to "raise" a "filter," whose sole function was to screen out some of the data that might otherwise have reached the "language acquisition device." The Filter metaphor was however heuristically useful in that it served as a placeholder, reminding us that we needed—and still need—to learn much more about this aspect of the language-learning process.[73]

REASONING

The following text was taken from an elementary logic textbook of many years ago:

IF   all pigs have wings; and
         that animal is a pig;
THEN   that animal has wings.

This was given to us as an example of "reasoning," which apparently meant the disciplined marshaling and manipulating, through words, of largely visual images plus abstractions associated with them. Ability to succeed at that kind of enterprise is of undoubted value, and has long been at a premium in formal education. This kind of reasoning is not just a manipulation of words. What has to be manipulated consciously on the Worktable consists of those largely visual images, plus some abstractions associated with them. These images and abstractions have been derived from words, but they do not consist of words. In order to succeed at this kind of reasoning, a person:

- Must already have stored certain kinds of data in long-term memory (information about pigs, wings, etc.).
- Must be able to take in certain types of data (words) through the senses.
- Must retain those types of incoming data ("All pigs have wings") in working memory pending the arrival of other such data ("That animal is a pig").
- Must obtain from long-term memory replies that are relevant to those types of data (the largely visual images).
- Must be able to compare and manipulate the data on the Worktable.

To those of us who are reasonably good at holding these kinds of data in working memory or long-term memory, and at bringing up the appropriate replies, the above listing of steps in syllogistic reasoning will seem tediously detailed and pedantic. But consider the same steps in the work of a professional tea taster:

IF   this tea tastes like a particular reference variety;
        and not like a particular other reference variety;

THEN   give it such-and-such a rating.

In order to carry out this line of "reasoning," the taster:

- Must already have stored certain kinds of data in long-term memory (smells and tastes of various types of tea, along with their names and relative desirabilities).
- Must be able to take in certain types of data (smells and tastes) through the senses.
- In order to judge a series of teas, must retain those types of incoming data (smells and tastes) in working memory, keeping the data from earlier samples in storage while going on to later ones.
- Must obtain from long-term memory replies that are relevant to those types of data (the names of the varieties, and the relative desirabilities).
- Must be able to compare and manipulate the data on the Worktable.

Now the list of steps seems much less trivial and obvious, at least to me.

Language learning requires its own kinds of reasoning: IF this word has a certain ending, and IF it is in a certain grammatical context, THEN it can be expected to have a certain other ending in certain other contexts. The kinds of data to be retained in working memory or reproduced from long-term memory consist of word fragments and subtle grammatical relationships. Or as I noted earlier, improving one's pronunciation depends on retaining and manipulating data from how one's speech muscles once felt, plus the noises made by oneself and one's models. We language teachers need to remember that our students, who may greatly surpass us at the "reasonings" necessary for tea tasting or for tennis, are unlikely to be as at home with the linguistic types of data as we are.

Howard Gardner has proposed that there may be as many as seven distinct "intelligences," each consisting of "the ability to solve [certain types of] problems or to fashion [certain types of] products that are valued in one or more cultural settings."[74] One cannot solve a problem or fashion a product without trying out competing solutions mentally, *and* this "trying out" requires control of the relevant smallest fragments, *and* this control in turn requires ability to retain and manipulate. Perhaps differences between "intelligences" come at least partially from quantitative differences in qualities of memory.[75]

An approach that seems to fit well with this speculation is "Neurolinguistic Programming" (NLP). According to NLP, all people make use of the same visual, auditory, and kinetic modalities, but they differ in which of these modalities is central or most fundamental to their cognitive functioning. One can communicate with an individual more effectively if one can correctly assess which modality is central for him or her, and then emphasize one's own use of that modality. NLP provides ways of making such assessments and of adjusting one's communication accordingly. So the system sounds attractive not only to psychotherapists and sales personnel, but also to teachers. On the other hand, a number of studies have failed to confirm some of NLP's basic predictions.[76] My own tentative conclusion, therefore, is that until the research findings are clearer, we would do well to approach NLP's theory, and to use its techniques, with some caution.

■ ■ ■ *Some Answers I Reached*

New information, whether from the senses or from working memory, triggers spreading activation within the networks of long-term memory. This may send back to working memory a complete and usable new image (e.g., remembering someone's name, or the meaning of a word), which may be either correct or incorrect. Or it may result in a partial image (e.g., remembering part of the person's name, or some aspect of the meaning of the word). Or it may not even produce that much. But the output of the networks is compared with what is present in working memory or in the senses. On the basis of these comparisons, the networks may undergo modification.

One time-honored way of improving a particular part of the networks of long-term memory is through the use of repetition. But the value of repeating an item is affected by what happens when the item reappears. Timing is relevant in two ways. First, reappearance of an item (word, sound, structure, or whatever) seems to be more helpful when it gives the learner a bit of time for making some kind of guess, followed by verification of the accuracy of the guess. Second, depending on the interval between appearances, the guesses may come from what is still in working memory, or from one or another part of long-term memory. For the long run, teachers are concerned with guesses that have come from students' permanent memory rather than with those that come from holding memory.

We should not underestimate either the speed with which guesses can be created, or the pervasiveness of the process. Comparison between what the mind has generated and what is coming in through the senses is found in a wide variety of simple everyday tasks. This ongoing process is necessary for detecting errors, inconsistencies, and even foreign accents.

Affective information has an effect on all stages of storage and retrieval. It is itself also one kind of information that is stored and retrieved along with other kinds. Teachers should not allow preoccupation with language or teaching procedures to crowd affect out of their planning or monitoring of student activities.

Perhaps people differ with regard to the types of data they store best and retrieve most dependably. If this is true, it may cast light on interpersonal differences in success at different tasks, as well as on differences in how two or more individuals go at the same task.

■ ■ ■ *Further Questions*

- □ Which familiar language study activities contain opportunities for verified guessing?
- □ What are the possible positive and negative affective concomitants of verified guessing?

Notes

1. Stevick 1982:77.
2. Stevick 1989: "Frieda" chapter.
3. Schmitt 1995:5.
4. Fendrich, Healy & Bourne 1991.
5. Ferrand et al. 1994:431.
6. I was interested to learn that the repetition effect held true even when the numbers were kept the same but the keyboard layout was switched from telephone-style to computer-style, or when the key positions were kept the same but the numbers were changed. (E.g., the keys for 123 on the telephone are in the same positions as the keys for 789 on the computer.)
7. Dunlosky & Nelson 1992:374; 1994:564.
8. For the sake of concreteness and clarity, I will develop this example on the assumption that the upcoming quiz is going to require the student to give Kigeni words in response to NL cues. The principles would be unchanged if the roles of the two languages were reversed.
9. This advice is hardly astonishing. I have been following it myself and offering it to others for at least 40 years, and I have no reason to think I am either the first or the last language learner to hit on it independently.

10. Dunlosky & Nelson 1992:379; 1994:564.

11. Carrier & Pashler 1992.

12. Other evidence that sheer time in exposure to an intact stimulus is not as important as accompanying mental activity is provided by Hirshman and Mulligan (1991).

13. Blackmore 1987:53.

14. Blackmore 1987:54.

15. Green & Leslie 1987:69.

16. Green & Leslie 1987:71.

17. Tart 1987:154.

18. Tart 1987:155.

19. This idea is hardly new. Hatch, Shirai, and Fantuzzi (1990:709) quote Stern and Stern's *Die Kindersprache* (1907): "[The learner] is neither a pure associative machine nor a sovereign constructor of concepts. Rather his speech is based on the continuing interaction of external impressions with internal systems which usually function unconsciously. It is thus the result of a constant 'convergence.'"

20. Tart 1987:154.

21. Straight 1994:43.

22. Barber 1980.

23. Krashen 1983:42.

24. Krashen 1983.

25. Pulvermüller and Schumann (1994:684) equate the "language acquisition device" with the brain as a whole, but I prefer the narrower definition.

26. This point is from Krashen (1993:7, 8). The other points are from Krashen (1983). In his 1993 paper, Krashen seems to equivocate regarding the importance of "interest." At one point he explains the lack of dinning as due to the absence of input that is "truly comprehensible *and interesting*" (8), and states more generally that dinning occurs "only after *interesting,* comprehensible input, *not after grammar drills*" (7) [emphasis added]. Yet in explaining Bedford's finding of relatively high incidence of dinning after drills, he accepts Bedford's suggestion that the drills "may have provided *comprehensible* input" [emphasis added].

27. Krashen 1983:43; 1993:7.

28. Krashen 1983:44; 1993:7.

29. Krashen 1983:43; Parr & Krashen 1986; Krashen 1993:8.

30. Barber 1980.

31. Krashen 1983:44.

32. Bedford 1985.

33. de Guerrero 1987.

34. In response to this evidence from de Guerrero, Krashen (1993:8) expresses doubt that any of her subjects were really "very advanced acquirers." Yet de Guerrero (1987:540), in describing her participants, tells us that her "advanced" group consisted of students who were in the same class as a number of English-dominant students.

35. Parr & Krashen 1986.

36. Krashen 1983:44.

37. Krashen 1993:9.

38. Krashen 1993:9.

39. Murphey, 1990; Krashen 1993.

40. In the sense commonly used in language teaching these days.

41. Murphey 1994:61.

42. Straight 1979:58f.

43. Straight 1979:58. Straight (1980:64) suggests that the connections between auditory input and articulatory output begin to be established sometime within the first half-year of life.

44. Straight (1980:315) calls this "self-comprehension" or "monitoring."

45. Straight 1977:5.

46. Straight (1975:5) points out that "puns are not created, they are discovered."

47. Straight (1980:315) calls this "other-production" or "anticipation."

48. Passim.

49. Krashen & Terrell 1983:143.

50. Hamilton 1983.

51. I once watched a public demonstration of Allport's procedure.

52. Harris 1967.

53. L. T. Kozlowski, 1977f:481.

54. A particularly full and interesting treatment of this topic may be found in Reason and Lucas (1984).

55. Reason & Lucas 1984:62ff.; Brennen et al. 1990:339.

56. Reason and Lucas call these spurious solutions "Cinderella's ugly sisters," who live at a similar address but don't quite fit. See also A. R. Luria (1974:9).

57. Reason and Lucas's (1984:66) tentative conclusions about the mechanism of rejecting wrong solutions fits well with Straight's (1977:1; 1980:314) insistence on "two sets of processes, one for the reception and one for the production of linguistic data."

58. A. R. Luria 1974:9.

59. L. T. Kozlowski 1977a:477.

60. These are among the factors that were traceable in the Flaggenheisch Incident. The Flaggenheisch Incident, of course, did not involve a TOT state. This is a minor shred of evidence that the same basic process may be at work.

61. Clifford & Hollin 1981:368.

62. Hollin 1984:266.

63. Easterbrook 1959:183.

64. Easterbrook 1959:198.

65. Reason 1984:116.

66. MacIntyre & Gardner 1989.

67. "The notion of spread of activation describes a cognitive process that must be fundamental not only in memory search but in the act of perception" (Hamilton 1983:77). Hamilton elsewhere points out that there is a two-way relationship between memory and perception (52).

68. McLaughlin (1987: Chapter 6) develops this idea fully.

69. Hamilton 1983:5.

70. MacIntyre & Gardner 1989:269.

71. MacIntyre & Gardner 1991:297.

72. Krashen 1982; Dulay, Burt & Krashen 1982.

73. For further comments on the Filter metaphor, see Stevick (1990:48–50).

74. Gardner & Hatch 1989:5.

75. A helpful summary of this work from the point of view of language teaching is provided by H. D. Brown (1987:73).

76. See Salas et al. 1989; Poffel & Cross 1985.

Chapter 5

Managing Memory: The Mechanical Side

Questions I Asked Myself:

☐ What factors under my control can affect the shaping of my students' long-term memory?

☐ How does activity within the student's mind affect retention?

INTRODUCTION

Suppose, then, that these kinds of memories (see Chapter 1), in these kinds of memory (see Chapter 2), act in approximately these ways (see Chapters 3 and 4). How can our students get their resources to working for them as fully and as efficiently as possible? That question will occupy us in the present chapter and in Chapter 6. First, however, let us consider a further distinction.

CONCENTRATED LEARNING VERSUS DIFFUSED LEARNING

In Chapter 4 I noted that "learning" involves a process of adjusting "networks" in ways that will lead to quicker and more certain production of appropriate responses in the future, whether those responses be in producing what is needed, or in correctly interpreting what one has heard or read. This process may be either *concentrated* or *diffused*.

☐ CONCENTRATED LEARNING

Such adjustments may be concentrated as relatively large changes in the connections among a relatively small number of items in the Files. Thus I learned my serial number the night after I was inducted into the Army by saying it over and over to myself 40 or 50 times. This was a military prototype of one approach to FL skills. For example, one can do rote repetition of "'to dance' = *plinsjan, plinsjan* = 'to dance.'" (The language of this illustration is Gothic, chosen with a tip of my cap to William G. Moulton, who in 1953 guided me cheerfully and competently through Wright's introduction to it.) Or one can memorize the statement that "In choosing between the Russian words *nye,* "not," and *nyet,* "no," remember that they are the opposite of their English counterparts with regard to presence or absence of final *-t.*" These sorts of modifications can be accomplished in fairly short order. On the other hand, if for any reason some of the individual changes in weightings get weakened or lost or influenced by related concepts, the desired behavior becomes unavailable. There is little or no redundancy. This is approximately what Krashen (passim) and others have labeled "learning." Material met in this way tends to be "in holding memory," readily lost unless while it is in holding memory it gets used in diffused learning.

□   DIFFUSED LEARNING

Such adjustments may also involve relatively small changes diffused among a relatively large number of items. Another linguistic item that I needed immediately on my entry into military service was "sergeant." Simply to have memorized "three stripes = *sergeant, sergeant* = three stripes" would not have been adequate for very long. The full, rich imagery I still have for that piece of vocabulary came from several exemplars, over many separate occasions. This imagery, and the word that stands for it, are not likely to be lost. Similarly in FL study, one can come to control the *nye/nyet* distinction by understanding texts (as in the Natural Approach) or by memorizing (as in Audiolingualism) a large number of sentences that contain one or the other of these two words. If individual connections are lost or weakened or subjected to other influences, the remaining connections are likely to do whatever filling in or correcting may be needed in order to produce a quick and reliable reply from the Files (*Feigenbaum,* not *Flaggenheisch*). In Krashen's terminology, this is "acquisition," comparable to what a child does with its first language. In the terminology of this book, the products of "diffuse" learning are likely to be "in permanent memory." (Needless to say, I intend "concentration" and "diffusion" to represent opposite directions on a continuum; they are not mutually exclusive qualities.)[1]

□   THREE APPROACHES TO MANAGING MEMORY

New information gets into holding memory in any of a number of ways. The best-known way is by "rehearsal," repetition of the material while it is still on the Worktable. This was the mainstay of the dialog memorization and the massive structure drills in Audiolingualism. But it was also assumed in the paradigm recital of even more traditional methods.

In the light of the above distinction between concentrated and diffused learning, three possible approaches present themselves:

1. Rely almost entirely on concentrated learning, do lots of donkey work, and have patience. (That was how I got through 9th-grade Latin.)

2. Rely almost entirely on diffused learning, do lots of interesting work, and have patience. (That was how I picked up what Spanish and Portuguese I know.)

3. Rely on diffused learning for the final product. Rely on interesting activities (including the understanding of interesting texts) to get things into permanent memory and produce diffused learning. Use concentrated learning as one means of getting material into holding memory and so making it available for the interesting activities. Do lots of work. Be patient.

Approach 1 has been with us for centuries. Approach 2 has been thoroughly expounded and described during recent years.[2] I hope one of the effects of this book will be to cast a bit of new light on Approach 3, which treats holding memory as a kind of bridge[3] from where a student is right now to where that same student may be by this time tomorrow. The remainder of this chapter will examine research findings on how to get various kinds of material from outside the learner's head, and at least into holding memory.

EFFECTS OF TIME

In Chapter 1 we saw that some of the kinds of information that make up the *contents* of memory have to do with time. But the *passage of time* is relevant to the *process* of memory too.

□   HOW LONG THINGS STAY IN WORKING MEMORY

We have already met experimental evidence of both electrical and nonelectrical kinds indicating how long new material can remain in working memory without being reintroduced. We can find corroborating evidence for these results outside the laboratory, in the experience of simultaneous interpreters, skilled typists, telegraphers, and court reporters. All these people normally produce their output—typed or spoken words, or dots and dashes—several seconds behind the input that they receive, and they do so while new input continues to pour in. The length of this delay may amaze the rest of us, but it still does not exceed 20 or 30 seconds.[4]

This information has a number of potential uses in the design of teaching methods. It means that after any verbal input to the student's eyes or ears, there is a period of time that is neither too short nor too long for us to work with in the classroom. So we and our students need not panic when a new item is presented. The item will remain at hand for several seconds. We might, for example, safely allow a few seconds to pass between the time when students first hear a new word and the time when they first repeat it. In free conversation too, or in question-and-answer sessions, teacher and students often seem to operate by the convention that if the student does not immediately understand what has just been said, the teacher should immediately repeat it. But if there really is a short-term memory—or if material really can stay on the Worktable for a while without having to be reintroduced over and over—then it is also possible for student and teacher to operate by a different convention, under which the student would have a few seconds in which to replay and listen to his or her own short-term recording.

The nature and duration of this interval should also be of considerable interest to designers of materials to be used with computer-assisted language learning.

□ THE PRIMACY EFFECT

In Chapter 2 I discussed the recency effect: the fact that the last few seconds of what has just been heard remains for a short time more recallable than what went before it. But the recall of words in a list is not simply a flat curve that rises at the end. As Figure 5.1 shows, the first few words in such a list are also more likely to be recalled than the words that follow them. Furthermore, this phenomenon, called "the primacy effect," is present whether recall is immediate or whether it is delayed. If the list of words is presented at a slower rate, the number of words at the beginning of the list that benefit from the primacy effect increases, while the number that benefit from the recency effect decreases.

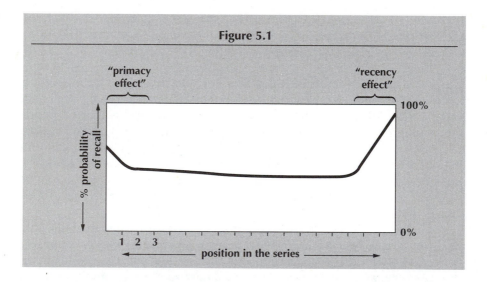

Figure 5.1

What do these contrasting outcomes mean? The decrease in the number of words covered by the recency effect is presumably due to the relatively fixed duration of short-term memory/electrically disruptible storage. The primacy effect, on the other hand, is evidence that the longer an item is held in short-term memory without being disturbed by new input, the more it can trigger material in the Files and form associations there. (This traffic from short-term memory to the Files may or may not involve the Worktable.) Later, when the subject is asked to recall words from the list, any of the word shapes *or anything else they triggered during the presentation phase of the experiment* can become a basis for the subject's report. As I noted in Chapter 2, we are dealing here with the "explicit" and "episodic" aspects of memory.

For our purposes, the practical point to remember here is the one about undisturbed time in short-term memory (or on the Worktable) allowing for more interaction with the Files. This point is further substantiated by an experiment in free recall of lists in which it was discovered that words that immediately followed high-priority or attention-holding words were themselves relatively *un*likely to be recalled. Apparently the processing resources of the Worktable had continued to work with the attention-holding items in the list.[5] Here we find a second reason for using pauses as a teaching tool: they allow the student not only to rehear a word or sentence, but also to process it and to begin integrating it with other contents of memory. The process of integration helps to establish the item further in holding memory.

□   TIMING

No matter how "memory" is divided up by one theoretical model or another, memorization remains a dynamic process that continues long after the original event.[6,7] Further, not all kinds of input are consolidated at the same rate. In one study, an experimenter presented familiar and unfamiliar material to psychiatric patients just before shock therapy, and then tested their retention of this material 5 hours later. The results of the study suggested that memory traces for familiar types of material got consolidated rapidly enough so that they were not disrupted by electroconvulsive shock that was applied a minute later; unfamiliar material was still vulnerable to disruption.[8]

Other scholars believe that what is important and emotionally charged tends to be more rapidly embedded than material that is emotionally neutral or unimportant.[9] This is of interest in the present chapter, but will take on even greater importance in the context of Chapter 6.

Probably related to this point is an observation that Miller[10] reported concerning a relationship between memory and sleep: "Where meaningful stories are recalled . . . the details essential to the story are remembered as well after waking activity as after sleep; the irrelevant details are recalled better after sleeping than after the same amount of time spent in wakeful activity." Also, forgetting of nonsense syllables is dependably slower during sleep. The memory traces for what is unfamiliar and only partially understood need a longer time without disruption from new inputs.[11] The language teacher will have no difficulty in seeing the relevance of this principle to getting unfamiliar or undigested words or structures into holding memory.

☐ SPACING

One of the "laws of learning" that was once proposed by some psychologists stated that "the amount learned is a function of study time regardless of how that time is distributed."[12] A large amount of evidence runs against this law, however. In studies that contrasted "massed practice" (numerous consecutive exposures to an item) with "distributed practice" (the same number of exposures interspersed among other items), distributed practice consistently proved to give superior results. This was true both for free recall of individual items and for the learning of paired associates, which as we saw in Chapter 2 is partially comparable to the learning of vocabulary in the study of foreign languages. It was also true when subjects tried to learn discrimination between pairs of words one of which was arbitrarily designated as "correct."[13,14] In addition to better recall, subjects also perceived the distributed items to have occurred more frequently than the massed items.[15] Furthermore, the distributed practice effect appeared to persist over much longer time lags than the benefits from massed practice do.[16] This spacing effect is still recognized as an extremely robust phenomenon.[17] Some possible applications of these findings in the foreign language classroom are again obvious.

Much remains to be learned about the precise mechanics of distributed practice. As the interval between two repetitions of an item is increased, performance improves up to a point *and then declines.*[18] Some writers suggest that the superiority of distributed practice lies in the fact that it allows the mind to store a greater variety of cues instead of storing multiple copies of essentially the same image.[19] Under these circumstances, having two or more nonadjacent images may help to nullify the effects of "crowding," as I will use that term later in this chapter.

My experiences in freshman German, described more fully in Chapter 11, may cast some light on how distributed practice works. Our course followed the Reading Method.[20] We began with a series of 10 specially prepared softbound booklets, mostly stories. A central principle in the preparation of these readers was that once a new word was introduced, it had to come up again five or more times, at increasingly long intervals, within the next so many pages. I recall that each encounter with an as yet unmastered word was in effect a test, calling on whatever relevant resources might be in my permanent memory—what in Chapter 4 was called a "guess." If those resources were inadequate, and if some information from the previous encounter was still in holding memory, then I could use that information for the purpose of either filling out, correcting, or verifying the guess from permanent memory. Possibly we have here another, larger scale example of what we saw in the "5-try-5-see" treatment, (p. 82) where permanent memory's "guess" is checked against something that is still in holding memory, and adjustments are made accordingly.

The trick for the writers of our 10 booklets was to place each occurrence of a new word far enough after its last preceding occurrence so that the needed information was no longer available from short-term memory, but close enough so that it would still be available from holding memory, and at the same time to keep the narrative both plausible and fun!

□ PACING

Even if we eventually learn the answers to some of the questions about spacing of distributed practice, we probably should not use such knowledge to design precisely timed presentation devices for use with all students. Two separate studies point away from any such applications.

In the first study, subjects were presented with sequences of 12 letters, one letter at a time. Memory was considerably better when the subjects were allowed to move from one letter to the next at their own pace, compared to seeing the same material presented in the same total amount of time but at a constant rhythm.[21] Perhaps the lesson to be drawn from this experiment is that because our students' minds all work a little differently, consolidation times cannot be predicted exactly. And because students are able to recognize and to some extent control their own mental processes, they can profit from freedom to do so.

The second study involved a quite different task, the learning of paired associates, for which an unannounced retention test was given a week or two later. One reason advanced by the investigator[22] to explain unusually high retention in the experiment was that the subjects were allowed to move through the test at their own pace. Maybe another reason was that the subjects didn't have to use any of the capacity of their working memory for monitoring the time—and the experimenter!

□ CROWDING

One slightly surprising fact about remembering and forgetting was discovered in the 19th century by Ebbinghaus: if a subject requires 10 trials in order to learn to a given standard a list of 10 items in his or her native language, then in order to learn equally well a list of 20 comparable items, the same subject will require 20 trials. Since each trial of a 20-word list takes twice as long as a trial of a similar 10-word list, the total time is four times as long to learn twice as many items. To put the same idea in another way, it takes twice as much time to learn a 20-word list as it takes to learn two 10-word lists. There is a catch, however. Although tests administered shortly after learning (when holding memory is still available?) will show that the lists have been learned equally well, a test administered a week later (and depending on permanent memory only?) will give quite different results. At that time, the subjects who learned the 20-word list will be much better able to recall the material than those who learned the two 10-word lists. The reason, of course, is that they had to learn the individual items better in the first place.[23]

Suppose, now, that a subject learns two 10-word lists with a given degree of thoroughness, and that none of the individual items are the same. To help in recalling the lists a short time later, the subject will have at hand whatever coding or processing he or she did for the items, plus the very important temporal clue of knowing *when* each was learned.[24] With the passage of time, however, this latter difference between the lists, or among individual items, becomes a smaller and smaller percentage of the total period that has elapsed since the time of learning. By the end of even one day, the temporal clue will have become almost useless. This phenomenon is found when the subject is asked to recall items, but not when he or she is asked to recognize them or to remember which items were associated with which other items.[25]

EFFECTS OF ACTIVITY

Overt and covert activities can also help or hinder the passage of information into holding memory.

□ AN EFFECT OF FREE RECALL

We have been looking at how certain factors can influence a person's likelihood of recalling items from a list. An interesting variation on the word-list experiments was reported by Darley and Murdock.[26] Subjects studied a series of ten 20-word lists. After studying each of five of the lists, the subjects were allowed to recall as many words as they could. After studying each of the other five lists, subjects were required to count forward by 3's—a simple but distracting activity. After the final list, half of the subjects received a final free recall test over all the lists, while the other half were tested for their ability to recognize which of the words had been on the lists.

The main conclusion was that the prior free recall increased quite dramatically the subjects' ability to recall words later on. As language teachers, we may be able to derive from this experiment some helpful suggestions about working with word lists, beyond what we saw in Chapter 4. But it is suggestive for textual material as well: "What do you remember from this videotape?" is perhaps not only a comprehension check, but an aid to future availability as well—the kind of availability from holding memory that will support the interesting activities that are to lead toward permanent memory.

□ THE WORKTABLE AND SUBJECTIVE ORGANIZING

In these or in other ways, human learners are constantly examining the material that for the moment occupies their Worktables, selecting appropriate material from the Files, and combining the two sets of information.

Experimental Evidence

There is evidence that a certain amount of conscious, nonautomatic subjective organizing goes on in any memorization task, whether the learner has been instructed to do so or not.[27] If for some reason the mind is unable to function in these ways while new material is available for processing on the Worktable, future ability to retrieve the material or to recognize it is seriously affected. This has been demonstrated in studies with marijuana[28] and with thiopental.[29] The drugs had much less effect on the same subjects' ability to retrieve or recognize material that they had learned *before* the drugs were administered. In the absence of drugs also, there is evidence that for long-term memory tasks but not for short-term ones, people who normally do a large amount of subjective organizing perform better than low subjective organizers.[30] The organizing that they do presumably takes place while the material is on the Worktable.[31] As we saw with the primacy effect (discussed earlier in this chapter), when a subject is given a list of new items, the first few items undergo more thorough processing of this kind, while processing of the later items encounters interference from the earlier ones.

In one series of experiments, subjects were given three nouns and required to remember them after 3, 6, or 24 seconds of distracting activity. Some subjects were instructed to read the nouns aloud, while others either counted the letters or labeled each word according to a simple semantic criterion. After 3 or 6 seconds (still within "short-term memory"), those who had read the words aloud performed better, but after 24 seconds of the intervening activity they performed as poorly as the others. Later experiments in the same series required that some of the subjects put the nouns into sentences; there were not any very decisive results. But when subjects were told to form one sentence that would contain all three words, retention was 2 or 3 times better than in the preceding experiments.[32]

Bower and Winzenz had subjects study pairs of unrelated concrete nouns, at the rate of 5 seconds per item. One group of subjects rehearsed each pair silently. A second group read aloud a sentence that contained the nouns. A third group made up their own sentences and said them aloud. A fourth group visualized a mental picture in which the referents of the two nouns were in some kind of vivid interaction with each other, but said nothing aloud. The second group performed better than the first, the third better than the second, and the fourth best of all. These investigators concluded that "the student's memory benefits from actively searching out, discovering and depicting," as contrasted with rote repetition, sentence reading, or even generation of their own relatively unimaginative sentences.[33]

Another study[34] reached a similar conclusion. In it, subjects were given a series of words at intervals of 3.2 seconds. One group used the time after each new word to repeat it aloud six times. The other group had the time free to think about the word and process it mentally. The recall performance of the second group was superior.

In any event, and by whatever devices, subjects are able, through exposure to the learning of previously meaningless linguistic responses to familiar stimulus items, to develop skills that are specifically useful in just this kind of task.[35] One of these skills certainly involves the use of mediators, but Postman et al. suggest that skills may also include "the adoption of a suitable rate of overt responding" and "efficient distribution of rehearsal time between hard and easy items."

Depth of Processing

A final set of experimental data center around the work of Fergus Craik and his associates. Two key concepts that appear in their investigations are "cognitive depth" and "Type 1 and Type 2 processing."

In one experiment, subjects were given a list of letter sequences. About each word they were asked one question, but not all the questions were alike. There were, in fact, five different questions: (1) "Is this a word?" (2) "Is it printed in capitals, or in lower-case letters?" (3) "Does it rhyme with ———?" (4) "Is it a member of the ——— category?" (5) "Does it fit into the following sentence?" Each question was assumed to require subjects to process the word to a greater "cognitive depth" than the question that precedes it in the list. Craik defined "cognitive depth" in terms of the meaningfulness extracted from the stimulus.[36] In this experiment, deeper decisions required some additional time, but they also led to dramatically better performance both on a recognition task[37] and on a recall task.[38] Craik believed that when attention is diverted from an item that is in what he called "primary memory" (approximately what others have called "short-term memory" or "working memory"), "it will be lost from primary memory and will be forgotten . . . at a rate appropriate to its level of analysis."[39]

Building on this concept of "depth," Craik went on to distinguish two types of processing that may take place while the subject has an item in "primary memory." In "Type 1 processing," the subject merely repeats whatever analyses he or she has already carried out. In "Type 2 processing," the subject continues the processing of the stimulus on to a deeper level. This is reminiscent of the "complexity" and "richness" of cognitive networks discussed in Chapter 3. Craik cites experimental evidence to support the idea that Type 2 processing increases long-term retention, but that Type 1 processing does not.[40] In a language-learning situation, Oller[41] has demonstrated that sentences are easier to learn if the student meets them in a meaningful context. One reason for Oller's finding may be that the meaningful context permits (and requires!) complex processing.

We should not be too quick to draw sweeping generalizations from this appealing conclusion, however. In 1977, another group of researchers replicated Craik's work.[42] Bransford (1979:66) has summarized their results:

> [Subjects were presented with] two different types of incidental orienting tasks. Task A involved deciding whether a target word fitted meaningfully into a sentence frame (e.g., A ——— has ears: frog). Task B involved judgments about rhyme information (e.g., " ——— rhymes with log: frog"). After acquisition, participants received target items (in the preceding example, frog) plus

foils in a single-item recognition test. Results indicated that semantic processing (Task A) resulted in better performance than did more superficial processing (Task B). These results replicated those of Craik and others.

The important aspect of the study . . . was the performance of a second group of participants. These people experienced identical acquisition situations but received a different type of test. They were presented with a completely new set of words and required to decide which of these words *rhymed* with target words heard during acquisition and which did not. Under these conditions, people were better at recognizing rhymes of acquisition target words that had initially been processed in a rhyming rather than a semantic mode. Subsequent experiments showed that the superiority of rhyme over semantic processing (given a rhyme test) persisted even when there was a twenty-four-hour delay between acquisition and test.[43]

It appears, then, that deep processing is actually just a special case of what is sometimes called "transfer-appropriate processing."[44] It is of value as preparation for many types of "interesting work," but not for some of the more mechanical types of tasks.

Of course, the design and selection of tasks is home territory for any language teacher. A recent research study strikingly demonstrates how the differences between, for example, (1) merely hearing or seeing a word, (2) visualizing what the word stands for, and (3) making inferences or judgments related to the word can influence performance on identification.[45] In Chapter 3 I noted that identification is a task rather close to the everyday needs of language students.[46]

Clinical Evidence

Luria[47] once wrote a whole book about a man who illustrated this sort of memory functioning to an incredible degree. The man earned a living by giving performances in which he recalled large amounts of data that were presented to him by an audience. These data included word lists, tables of arbitrary numbers, mathematical formulae that he did not understand, and sentences in foreign languages. It is probably significant that even this man required that there be a few seconds pause between items on a list, and on the other tasks he was of course free to set his own pace in processing the information. He was able to imprint a table of 20 numbers in about 40 seconds, and a table of 50 numbers in 2½ to 3 minutes. If he was required to remember such a table after several months, he needed some time to revive in his mind the entire situation in which he had learned it, but once he had recovered it, he could read from it as fast as he had been able to originally.

This man had another unusual characteristic that was not obviously connected to his phenomenal memory, but that interacted with his memory in an interesting way. He was subject to "synesthesia," in which an input from one sense might register in one or more other senses. Thus, if someone in the audience happened to cough while he was reading mentally from a table of numbers that he had recalled (i.e., while the image from his long-term storage was laid out on the Worktable), the cough came out not only as a sound, but also as a blob or blur of color over that part of the image that he was looking at, and obscured that number in future attempts to recall it.

His handling of the number tables illustrates one of the two basic mechanisms he used. The other mechanism converted words into visual images of the things they stood for. When he used this mechanism, any failure to recall an item was more a defect of perception than of memory as such. Thus, he once "forgot" from a list the word "pencil." He explained that in his mind he had placed the pencil near a picket fence, where it was hard to see. At another time, the same thing happened to "egg," which he had inadvertently placed in front of a white wall. The next time he had to deal with the word "egg," he made it into a larger image, and saw to it that the place was well lit by putting a street lamp nearby.

It would be a mistake to suppose that this man was just another clever but genetically ordinary person who had become adept at a few parlor tricks. He was apparently born with this ability, which in the long run actually proved to be at least as much a curse as a blessing. Nevertheless, all of us use both of his basic mechanisms every day: we register on the Worktable configurations of data (whether visual, auditory, or other) that are tied to the same moment of time; we bring from the Files something that has in the past been associated with the whole configuration or some part of it, and which we think will make our present memory task easier; then on the Worktable we put together a new combination, and it in turn is stored in the Files. The man Luria described had such a good memory that he was seriously troubled by not being able to forget things, but even this may perhaps be regarded as a tremendous quantitative difference in the number of items per image, rather than as an absolute qualitative difference from other human beings. It is also true that he seemed immune to the effects of "crowding."

As we saw in Chapter 4, the act of remembering is to a large extent an act of construction. We do get back some features of the original experience as though from a tape. But another large part of the process consists of generating a new image that contains elements from that "tape," and then recognizing whether that new image is like the original.[48,49,50] Judgment about whether the generated image is like the original depends on criteria that already existed within the individual. Here again we meet the competition between two or more replies from the Files in response to the same stimulus.

Classroom Evidence

This principle helps to illuminate many things that we see in the process of language acquisition. Outside of formal instruction, FL learners and also adult learners of second languages, when corrected on a matter of grammar, sometimes seem not to have heard the correction. Instead, they respond to the content of what was said.

The same phenomenon appears in organized language instruction. A preliminary example appeared in the discussion of *karibu* in Chapter 2. I have frequently noticed that students have little or no trouble in producing an acceptable mimicry of the "whistling" /zv/ of Shona if they do it immediately, without sufficient time to form associations with familiar sound–spelling correlations. But these same students, asked a few minutes later to produce the same sound from memory or from a written symbol, find it very difficult. In fact, knowledge of the written symbol used in written Shona even seems to interfere with their ability to mimic the sound.

Students of Swahili provide another dependable example of the same principle. As all language teachers know, *th* in English has two common pronunciations, unvoiced as in *thigh* and voiced as in *thy*. Most English speakers have no difficulty with differentiating this pair of words, either for comprehension or for production. But it is also true in English that the voiced sound as in *thy* occurs almost exclusively in a fixed list of Anglo-Saxon words, some of them very frequent, while *th* spellings in Greek-derived and other unfamiliar words are always pronounced with the unvoiced sound in *thigh*. Swahili has both these sounds, the unvoiced one spelled "th" and the voiced one spelled "dh." If we looked only at the phonetic contrasts of English, we would have to predict that the Swahili sounds would cause no confusion for speakers of English. In fact, however, many students have an almost ineradicable compulsion to say *nathani* for *nadhani* ("I think"), and so forth. The recalled part of the pronunciation is "something that in English we would spell th." Since both Swahili and English have two sounds for *th,* this criterion is inadequate. The student who is trying to pronounce such a word must therefore supply the missing information from his or her own inner criteria, one of which is "in unfamiliar words, use the unvoiced sound."

The first hour of work with one early version of the Silent Way often provides a striking example of the same phenomenon. The student hears a new word such as "rod" at most once from the teacher, but produces it many times in response to various nonverbal cues. A student may produce such a word successfully 20 or more times at intervals during the first 10 or 15 minutes, and then suddenly appear unable to say it. It is as though, up to that point, the student had been copying the word from some sort of short-term resource, even though the most recent occurrence of the word may have been as much as half a minute earlier, and so must have had it at least in some minimal networks of holding memory. Suddenly, for some reason, the same student tries to produce the same word on the basis of whatever facts have been noticed about it, but these "inner criteria" are not yet adequate for the job. (p. 80) Holding memory can deteriorate all too quickly!

THE GENERATION EFFECT

In 1978 Norman J. Slamecka and Peter Graf of the University of Toronto reported a series of five paired-associate experiments. Subjects in these experiments worked with a deck of 100 cards, each of which had printed on it a pair of words. For some of the subjects, the second word on each card was printed in full just like the first one, so that subjects had only to read it *(rapid-fast)*. For other subjects, however, the second item was represented only by its first letter *(rapid-f————)*. The subjects were also given various kinds of hints as to the relationship between the words in the pairs: that the second was an antonym of the first, or a synonym of it, or a rhyme, or whatever.

As soon as the subjects completed the deck, they were given a sheet with groups of three words, and were asked to select from each group which one of the three had actually occurred in the deck. They were also asked to indicate how sure they were about their selections. Slamecka and Graf discovered that there was a highly significant difference between the performance of the two groups of subjects. Those who had had to generate the second word on each card not only recognized words much more accurately, but also had much more confidence in their selections from the recognition list. This turned out to be true no matter which kind of hint the subjects had had as they were studying the lists in the first place, and it held good for recall tasks as well as for recognition tasks.

Numerous other researchers have performed experiments related to those of Slamecka and Graf, and have reached similar but not identical results. Dickel and Slak[51] used 45 pairs of nouns that had been selected for their imagery potential. In this research, one group of subjects created and described a visual image that included the objects that the two words in each pair stood for. They had 10 seconds in which to do this. The experimenter recorded these descriptions and later transcribed them. The other group of subjects did not make up their own images; instead, they heard the descriptions that had been produced by other subjects for the same pairs of words.

Following the 45th pair there was a brief rest, after which the subjects in both groups were given recall sheets on which one noun from each pair was printed in capital letters. Subjects were asked to recall the image that each noun had participated in, and then to write the noun that had appeared with it. Those who had *made up their own images* were able to recall significantly more of the target nouns than subjects who had used someone else's images. Moreover, Dickel and Slak were able to determine that *a vivid image was no more helpful for this purpose than an image that was not so vivid.* All that mattered was whether or not the subjects were working with the images that they themselves had put together, or with something else. This is comforting to those of us for whom whole visual images are "pallid, fragmentary, indefinitely localized, and brief."

Just what makes self-generated information so effective, at least for recall, is not entirely clear. It appears not to be merely a matter of added effort.[52] Jamieson and Schimpf suggest that self-generated imagery is superior because it is formed in a different way from externally supplied imagery.[53] Dickel and Slak venture that "when someone generates his own image of all the images that could possibly be developed, that particular image is the most likely or the easiest for that person to develop. Because each person will have a particular image that is most likely to be generated, when recall is required it will be easier to generate that same image. If the image generated at recall is the same as the one generated during original stimulus presentation, the required response will also be recalled easily."[54]

Another investigator of "the generation effect" is Rabinowitz,[55] whom I mentioned in Chapter 1. Rabinowitz reports on work done by herself and Glisky,[56] and also on some more recent experiments of her own. In the Glisky and Rabinowitz study, whenever subjects generated words, they did their generating from word fragments (AL_OHO_). By now we will not be surprised to learn that the subjects did better at recognizing those words that they had generated from fragments than those they had simply read. But Glisky and Rabinowitz also found what they called a "specific generation enhancement effect": for those items that were initially generated, recognition performance was improved if at the time of testing the subjects generated the items again, rather than merely reading them. Glisky and Rabinowitz therefore argued that a complete account of the generation effect must include a specific processing component, and that some kind of record of cognitive operations gets stored as part of the memory trace of the stimulus event. They failed to find this effect when the letters that were omitted on the test were different from the letters that had been omitted originally (AL_OH_L), so that the process of generation was slightly different. They also failed to find the effect when the same letters were missing, but the retrieval process was guided by some different type of information (booze— AL_OHO_). Just how the information about cognitive operations gets stored is another matter, of some interest to those who are concerned with the use and teaching of "learning strategies." This question became the focus of Rabinowitz's later experiments.

Also on the topic of generation, Gathercole and Conway[57] found that "although acoustic information may generally enhance memory (especially when compared to reading silently), this enhancement is greatest when the acoustic information is self-generated." Of course, it is also true that the act of reading aloud provided an additional set of articulatory/kinesthetic data for storage along with the visual and auditory data.

As is the case with "depth of processing," however, we need to look for the limitations as well as the exciting prospects. In particular, there seems to be a rather clear dissociation between the effects of generating a word as opposed to simply reading it, depending on what the subject is asked to do later on. As we have just seen, the episode-based tasks that draw on explicit memory (discussed in Chapter 2) benefit dramatically from the generation effect. On the other hand, the pedagogically important task of identifying a word quickly and accurately is helped more by reading than by generating.[58] We have here a second example of "transfer-appropriate processing."

A further caution about generation is raised by Schooler and colleagues.[59] They present evidence that memory is affected not only by exposure, but also by what they call "the act of commitment." If this is so, then a subject who for whatever reason has committed to a wrong response may suffer memory for it later on. The writers suggest that "generated inaccurate responses may impair memory more than does passively acquired inaccurate information." A language teacher who wants to take advantage of the generation effect in order to establish material in holding memory should make sure that students receive a quick exposure to a correct version of what they have just generated. Such exposure need not be in a pedantic "teacher voice"; it can just as easily be the reply of an interested partner in a conversation.

"MNEMONICS"

The chain of associations noted in Chapter 3 regarding the German word *Abendlandes* may run on freely. One most essential and, at the same time, distinctive feature of human thinking, however, is that we can to some extent assume control of the chain and use it for our own purposes.[60] This is the basis for some useful mnemonic devices. In language-learning circles, probably the best-known mnemonic device is the so-called keyword method[61]—actually not so much a "method" as a simple technique. Kasper[62] summarizes literature showing that the technique works with learners of all ages, from 1st grade to adult. Unfortunately, in the studies she cites, comparison seems to have been with control groups who studied the same lists by rote rehearsal alone. It is not clear how the keyword technique would have fared alongside learning vocabulary through understanding interesting messages, memorizing interesting dialogs, or even playing "Concentration," for example.

Thompson gives the example of an English speaker who wants to remember the German word for "egg," which is *Ei* (pronounced something like English "eye"). By the keyword method, the learner uses some kind of visual or quasi-visual mental image, an image that already has a strong tie with the *pronunciation* of the word in one language, and also a strong tie with the *meaning* of the word in the other language: a fried egg with eyelashes, or the like. ("Key-*picture*" might be a more apt description than "key*word*".)

Without the image, learning the connection between the meaning <egg> and the word *Ei* could be diagrammed something like this:

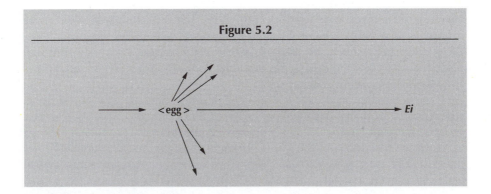

Figure 5.2

In words, Figure 5.2 stands for the fact that when the meaning <egg> is for any reason activated in the speaker's mind, that activation spreads to a number of items with which that meaning has been associated in the speaker's past experience. We hope (often in vain) that enough of that activation will spread to *Ei* so that the activation of the German word form will increase sufficiently to make it available for conscious use. But here, the only source of activation for *Ei* is the meaning <egg>.

The keyword mnemonic device actually involves constructing on the Worktable a very simple network, in the sense in which I used that metaphor in Chapter 3. Three points in that network are obvious:

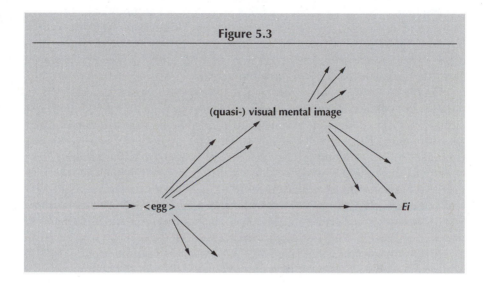

Figure 5.3

(quasi-) visual mental image

<egg >   Ei

This diagram means that some of the activation that spreads from <egg> reaches *Ei* directly, as in Figure 5.3. Some of the rest of the activation reaches the mental image. As the activation of the image is raised, there is a further spread of activation from the image to other items, including *Ei*. So *Ei* now receives activation both directly and indirectly.

But there is at least a fourth point in this simple network: the time (TI_r) at which the network was constructed. There is after all no compelling reason why this particular triangle of associations should have any particular status. In order for the keyword method to work, therefore, the learner must remember *what happened to go with what at a particular time*. This is of course a major characteristic of episodic memory as described in Chapter 2.

There may be still other reasons why the keyword method works. For one thing, as Dickel and Slak have stated, self-generated cues are superior to others' cues for the explicit and episodic purpose of aiding recall, and for this reason it is worthwhile for users of mnemonics to go to the trouble of creating their own cues.[63] Another point is that any elements of vividness, bizarreness, or humor will tie in with some of the learner's deeper and more general needs, even if some of those needs are peripheral to the task as viewed by the teacher. Under these circumstances, the resulting networks may be richer as well as more complex, and may therefore remain effective longer. And as Curran pointed out,[64] the very knowledge that the keyword is there may contribute to the learner's sense of security, thereby reducing any distracting and deleterious effects of anxiety.

Language students for centuries have stumbled onto and used the keyword principle.[65] There is also evidence from laboratory learning of paired associates that if one or both members of each pair in a list consist of an unfamiliar form, subjects commonly make spontaneous use of some kind of mediator.[66] At least one brief introductory language textbook was designed around the technique,[67] and a group of language teachers reported an experiment contrasting the results obtained through use of such "interactive imagery" with results obtained in other ways.[68] Overall, this classic trick is for many learners[69] a tried and true way of making new words available in holding memory.

In the last analysis, a keyword is like a bumpy but passable road that gets the motorist to the destination while a smoother, faster highway is under construction. Or in another travel simile, it is like a detour that the learner takes while waiting for the direct highway to be built.[70] The technique works fast enough so that the FL and NL equivalents are brought together on the Worktable. Each time this happens, the direct connection between the two increases in strength. Finally this direct connection becomes strong enough so that a second "coterminous pathway" is created. The keyword gradually becomes superfluous, recedes from consciousness, and is finally dropped. The remaining pathway is more direct, faster, and makes less of a demand on processing resources. A keyword (better called a "key picture," as I said previously), which is mostly nonverbal, thus plays the same role in the mastery of vocabulary that a "rule," which is primarily verbal, can play in the mastery of grammar.[71]

■ ■ ■ *Some Answers I Reached*

In working with any new language, our students need to retain information not only about discrete items such as words, word classes, and sounds, but also about the relationships among those items. For long-term mastery, all this information must eventually come to be available from permanent memory. One way to add to permanent memory is to get information first into holding memory and then use it in some interesting way. Success in moving information into holding memory depends not only on what is done with the information, but also on how the doing is timed.

Externally controllable factors that affect the shaping of the networks of long-term memory include the choice between studying discrete points and working with the meanings of texts; where an item is placed; how much time is available for absorption of one set of material before new material is met; and the interval between successive occurrences of the same material.

A student is more likely to recall material if she or he has previously recalled it; or has noticed relationships between it and other items or categories; or has at least partially generated it using her or his own existing networks.

Further Questions

□ How are these factors reflected in existing types of activity?

□ Do they suggest any new types or activity, or the modification of any old ones, or the placing of greater emphasis on certain activities than on others?

Notes

1. Compare the summary by H.D. Brown (1987:65) of Ausubel's distinction between "meaningful" and "rote" learning. There, meaningful learning is described as "a process of relating and anchoring new material to established entities in cognitive structure," and rote learning is described as "the mental storage of items having little or no association with existing cognitive structure." My terminology is intended to highlight the small-scale mechanics of these processes, rather than their characteristic products. Perhaps it can also help us to treat the difference as continuous rather than as dichotomous.

2. References to Krashen et al. 1982; Dulay, Burt & Krashen 1982; Krashen & Terrell 1983.

3. As this word is used in Chapter 11.

4. This paragraph is based on informal interviews with such people.

5. Tulving 1969.

6. Russell & Newcombe 1966:21.

7. Benson & Geschwind 1967:542.

8. Metcalfe 1966:10.

9. Brierly 1966; cf. the role of "salience" in Chafe 1973.

10. Miller 1951:218.

11. For another discussion of the effects of sleep on memory, see Fowler et al. (1973).

12. Underwood 1970:573.

13. Underwood 1969, 1970; Melton 1970; Ciccone 1973.

14. As foreign language teachers, we may be reminded here of the use of minimal pairs of words in the study of pronunciation. Minimal pairs are now out of fashion

as a means of establishing pronunciation, though they are still seen by some as "consciousness-raising" (Sharwood Smith 1981).

15. Underwood 1969.

16. Melton 1970:604.

17. Parkin, Reid & Russo 1990:511.

18. Bjork 1970.

19. Melton 1970; Gartman & Johnson 1972:808.

20. This method is described in Bond (1953). The readers we used (some years before Bond's book came out) were written by Peter Hagboldt.

21. Pinkus & Laughery 1970.

22. Nelson 1971.

23. Ceraso 1967.

24. Shiffrin 1970:387.

25. Ceraso 1967.

26. Darley & Murdock 1971.

27. Tulving 1962.

28. Abel 1971.

29. Osborn et al. 1967.

30. For a dramatic example of this, see the interview with Derek in Stevick (1989), summarized in Chapter 12 of this book.

31. Earhard 1970.

32. Kintsch et al. 1971.

33. Bower & Winzenz 1970; cf. also Modigliani & Seamon 1974.

34. Glanzer & Meinzer 1967 in Bjork 1970.

35. Postman et al. 1968:783.

36. Craik 1973:49.

37. Craik 1973:58.

38. Craik 1973:60.

39. Craik 1973:51.

40. Craik 1973:51–54; see also Craik & Lockhart 1972.

41. Oller 1971.

42. Morris, Bransford & Franks 1977.

43. Bransford 1979:65–68.

44. Rappold & Hashtroudi 1991.

45. M.C. Smith 1991.

46. One closely related example from the field of language teaching is the treatment of line drawings in Stevick (1986:74).

47. Luria 1968.

48. Deese 1958:274.

49. Martin et al. 1968:566.

50. Hogan & Kintsch 1971:565.

51. Dickel & Slak 1983.

52. Zacks et al. 1983:754f.

53. Jamieson & Schmipf 1980.

54. Dickel & Slak 1983:124.

55. Rabinowitz 1990.

56. Glisky & Rabinowitz 1985.

57. Gathercole & Conway 1988.

58. Allen & Jacoby 1990:270; Rappold & Hashtroudi 1991:109; Roediger & Blaxton 1987; Allen & Jacoby 1990:276.

59. Schooler et al. 1988:250.

60. Atkinson & Shiffrin 1968:90 et passim.

61. Thompson, in Wenden & Rubin 1987.

62. Kasper 1993:2.

63. Wall & Routowicz 1987:121f.

64. Curran 1968:341.

65. One example is provided by "Fred" in Stevick (1989:114f.).

66. Bugelski 1962.

67. Groberg 1972.

68. Ott et al. 1973.

69. Though not for me!

70. In still another related figure of speech, Sharwood Smith (1986:253) recommends willingness to use "short-cuts" which will facilitate and even bypass natural developmental sequences.

71. For an excellent statement of a related view, see Sharwood Smith (1981).

Chapter 6

Memory and the Whole Person

Questions I Asked Myself:

☐ What does it mean to "communicate"?

☐ How does depth of communication figure in language use outside the experimental laboratory?

We don't really follow the news that closely. I'll be doing my work, changing Paul Junior's diapers or washing the dishes and I'll hear the news, but when the music comes back, I'll suddenly realize that I've been listening to five minutes, *five minutes* of the news and I haven't heard a single word the man spoke, not a word. If you ask me what he said, I'd have to say nothing, nothing I can remember.

—Robert Coles, *The Middle Americans*

INTRODUCTION

In the preceding chapters, I have from time to time emphasized the place of *purposes* and *emotions* in the memory process, and in Chapter 3 I said that the most important aspect of images is their *richness* and *complexity*. Now, in closing the *Memory* section of this book and looking ahead to the section of personal meanings, I would like to bring these ideas to center stage in relation to a concept called "depth." This concept will be illustrated both by experimental evidence and by application to certain specific language teaching methods.

COMMUNICATION AND "COMMUNICATION"

Though a student may repeat over and over the forms of the language, in doing so he or she may not be using the language. This point has been made by a number of writers, especially during the past 25 years. Language use, these writers say, requires communication, and communication means the resolution of uncertainties. A person who says "I think they close at 6:00" in response to the question "What time do the stores close?" is communicating—resolving the questioner's uncertainty—unless the two of them are in a language course recit-ing a dialog containing these lines.

This position is useful insofar as it forces us to notice what we are and are not doing in a class, and also insofar as it suggests ways in which we can do bet-ter. That is, it has both a corrective and a heuristic value. Even outside of the classroom, it helps us to understand Paul Junior's mother (see the chapter epi-graph). What was coming over the radio was not just linguistic forms: for some listeners, the announcer's words were resolving uncertainties about what was going on in the world that day. But Paul Junior's mother, immersed (as one might say) in the diapers and the dishes, had no unanswered questions beyond her own neighborhood. This was why there was no communication, and because there was no communication there was no retention.

This view of communication and language use, as I have said, has certain values. There is, however, one rather limited way of interpreting this view that is seriously inadequate, and that may therefore blind us to a—or *the*—central fact about memory and about learning in general. This interpretation assumes (usu-ally tacitly) that information—that which is "communicated"—consists of facts (including fictional pseudofacts). Examples are the answerer's name, if the ques-tioner doesn't know it and would actually like to know it; questions and answers in a game of "Twenty Questions," or a statement about the edibility of a persim-mon made to someone who is trying to learn to judge such matters. According to this view, a student who is reciting a memorized dialog in class is not convey-ing information, and hence is not communicating and not really using language. This is the sense in which one can say that the (subphonemic) "distinctions which cumulatively lead to foreign accent are nonfunctional in language use situ-ations."[1] In restricting attention to the "fact–fict" band of information, this view represents an unfortunately narrow brand of cognitivism, which would allow us to assume a dichotomy between body and mind, or between intellect and emo-tion. Beyond "Just the facts, Ma'am," full communication conveys tone and atti-tude and readinesses and loyalties, and much, much more.

THE DIMENSION OF "DEPTH"

What this limited brand of cognitivism misses is a whole dimension that runs at right angles to the "fact-fict" continuum. In Chapter 5 we saw that mental activ-ity on the part of the subject, whether intentional or unintentional, has a power-ful effect on memory. Most of the mental activity in those studies was primarily "fact–fict." The missing dimension, the subject of this chapter, is what Craik called "depth." We saw in Chapter 5 that depth of processing is not relevant to all *experimental* tasks. I believe, however, that it *is* very important in a large num-ber of the *day-to-day* tasks faced by language learners.

Some examples may clarify what I mean by "depth." Many years ago, I still thought that because we ordinarily perceive language through acoustic and muscular media, language learning was therefore primarily an acoustic and muscular process. At that time, I hit on an idea for improving my fluency in Swahili, a language that I could already speak and understand to some extent. On my cassette tape recorder, I would simply listen to half-hour Swahili news broadcasts, repeating what I heard aloud as I listened. That is to say, I would operate as a simultaneous interpreter does, except that I would not change languages. When I put this plan into practice, however, I was disappointed. I was indeed able to repeat along with the tape fairly well, but the experience produced only fatigue, with no perceptible improvement in my Swahili. The words were going into my ear and out my mouth all right, but they were not disturbing anything in between. In the metaphor of "depth," the words were flowing over my mind so fast that they had no time to sink in to "modify my Files." Instead, they remained on the surface, and evaporated almost immediately.

The research findings of Craik, Tell, and Ferguson and of Kappel et al. (discussed in Chapter 5) give one set of reasons why I should not have been surprised at the results of my bright idea. The narrow-band cognitivists to whom I referred previously would of course point out in addition that my repetition of the announcer's words involved no communication, and only an outward appearance of language use. They would be right. My reason for recounting the story here is only to illustrate one extreme in the depth dimension: the shallow end of it.

Even the simplest old-fashioned grammar drill, one that includes no fact–fict communication, such as

book   The book is on the table.

pen   The pen is on the table.

money   The money is on the table, etc.

can be carried out at more or less depth. Shallowest is purely mechanical substitution of one word for another in the same slot. A bit less shallow is substitution accompanied by brief visualization—even the most pallid, fragmented visualization of what the sentence means. Choice of substitution items can help here: in the above example, "money" would probably produce a fuller, more complex response than "pen" would. Letting students draw up the list of cues would guarantee a certain amount of imagery for at least three reasons:

☐ No one can suggest a word without having first thought of its meaning.

☐ Sharing in preparation of the list adds a social component to the upcoming drill.

☐ Time available for visualizing is more leisurely than with a prefabricated list reeled off by the teacher, and is also self-paced.

I recognize that in my early years as a language teacher, such drills were assigned too central a role—and too a large share of my students' time—in our attempts to produce language mastery. Even so, I am not as ready as some to discard them entirely. The purpose of the previous example, however, is not to recommend this type of drill. I have used it only as a vehicle for illustrating variation along the "depth dimension."

We could think of a series of usual classroom activities that lie at successively "deeper" levels: retelling a story, verbatim or in one's own words; improvising variations on a memorized dialog; writing an autobiographical statement based on a model. These allow varying amounts of fact–fict communication.

A crucial point on this continuum is found in the work of the simultaneous interpreters mentioned in Chapter 2. Unlike the student who is doing even the most complex drill, these remarkable people must react to the full range of structure and to the full range of lexical meaning, and come out with an equivalent in another language. But any simultaneous interpreter works under one limitation that is essential for understanding this meaning of "depth": she or he must not allow the content of what is coming in to make any personal difference to her or him.[2] For example, suppose an interpreter who interprets a statement that the weather is going to be unusually cold in Winnipeg this week, expects to be in Winnipeg the following day. If she makes a mental note to take along an extra sweater, she will for a moment partially or entirely lose the ability to listen and speak at the same time. I have interviewed a large number of simultaneous interpreters on this point, and all have readily acknowledged the existence of this boundary, which is apparently rather well defined. Yet although this line lies far "deeper" than the level at which I was "speaking" Swahili along with the tape, it is still true that all normal use of language takes place at levels that lie even deeper. Below this line lie the connections with our plans, with our most important memories, and with our needs. These are not mere fact–fict information. As we saw in Chapter 1, and will further explore in Chapters 7 and 8, needs are arranged in a complex hierarchy, and include strong emotional or affective elements. The lowest reaches of this dimension lie beyond our conscious awareness.

This meaning for "depth" is then not entirely unlike the use of the same word in the phrase "depth psychology." At the same time, it extends Craik's meaning of the word (discussed in Chapter 5). It also suggests a more adequate interpretation of the oft-repeated statement that foreign language students should "use the language for communication." If "communication" means "making a difference," then a single speech act may communicate on a number of different levels at once. Or the same utterance that on its "fact–fict" surface is totally noncommunicative (e.g., a sentence in a substitution drill) may carry important meanings (i.e., make important differences to speaker and hearers) on deeper levels. The fact that both speaker and hearers may be unaware of these meanings does not alter the truth of this statement. Chapters 7 and 8 will be concerned with some of the deeper meanings for students, while Chapter 9 will deal with possible meanings for the teacher. In this chapter, we shall confine our attention to relationships that have been demonstrated experimentally between depth and memory.[3]

TOTAL PHYSICAL RESPONSE

One kind of unmistakable communication takes place when the speaker gets hearers to commit the long muscles of their arms and legs in the way the speaker intended. This commitment guarantees a certain minimum depth of processing, which probably accounts for its powerful effects on memory. Asher and his collaborators have demonstrated these effects in their use of "Total Physical Response" (TPR) instruction.

Early experiments with TPR involved the teaching of a relatively small number of phrases in Japanese[4] or Russian.[5] The subjects were either children or college students who learned only to comprehend the language, not to speak it. A total of about 30 minutes of training was divided among three training periods. The experimental group carried out commands in the language, beginning with single words and going on to strings of three or four multiword commands. The control groups listened, and then either (1) watched someone else execute the commands, or (2) heard an English translation of the commands, or (3) read the translations silently. As the years have passed, TPR principles have been extended and developed much further, as is evident in the title of Seely and Romijn 1995.[6]

Not surprisingly, the experimental group had better comprehension immediately after training. More striking, this group's comprehension deteriorated hardly at all after weeks and even months, while the control groups forgot the material rapidly. Here is a clear example of the difference between what in Chapter 2 I called "permanent memory" and "holding memory."

A 1974 report[7] suggested that "most linguistic features can be nested into the imperative form, and if the approach is used creatively . . . , high student interest can be maintained for a long-term training program." During the years since that time, TPR has enjoyed wide reception throughout the language teaching profession. I interpret its success as vindicating two of its most conspicuous characteristics:

☐ It encourages—indeed, practically forces—multisensory involvement and resulting multisensory images.

☐ It meets in an integrated way needs that are physical and social as well as cognitive.

Perhaps TPR is a special case of what Klein and others (quoted in Chapter 1) had to say about response in general: new material is more quickly and firmly embedded in memory if it is tied to experience, to emotion, and to existing motivations.

THE EFFECTS OF PERSONAL SIGNIFICANCE

In 1970, a group of researchers[8] varied the usual paired-associates experiment to include a factor of emotional involvement on the part of the subjects. The subjects, given a list of names of public figures, were asked to say whether they liked, disliked, or felt neutral about each one. They then learned meaningless trigrams (groups of three consonants, such as RTG), which were paired with the names of these people. The trigrams that they learned best were those paired with the names of people they liked. Next were the ones associated with disliked persons. Least well learned were those that were tied to neutrally regarded figures. This was the case both when the subjects tried to give one member of a pair in reply to the other member, and also in later trials of free recall.

Another experiment, with a quite different format, produced comparable results. The subjects were undergraduate students of psychology. Before the start of the experiment, subjects had filled out a personality inventory form and had been warned that they would be tested immediately on the ideas contained in a passage to be read to them. In the experiment itself, individual members of the control group were read a short passage describing an unnamed person. Their recall for the same passage was tested again 2 days later, but without prior warning. The experimental group was treated in exactly the same way, except that each was told that the passage was derived from that individual's own personality inventory and applied to her alone. The passage itself was carefully constructed to contain 12 items that were favorable, 12 that were unfavorable, and 4 that were ambiguous.

The statistically significant results of this experiment showed that the ego-involved group recalled the unfavorable items better than the other group did, both immediately and after 48 hours. After 48 hours they were also superior in recall of the favorable details of the passage. Over the 2-day period, the involved group did less forgetting than the control group.[9]

A particularly interesting series of studies have been devoted to a concept called "arousal." In one key experiment, subjects tried to learn paired associates in which one member of each pair was a word, and the other was a number. Some of the words (e.g., money, rape, slut) were emotionally loaded, while others (e.g., white, pond, berry) were emotionally more neutral. Using a device that measures the electrical resistance of the skin, the investigators discovered that the emotionally loaded words produced a large change in skin resistance—certainly one kind of "physical response," even though it is neither "total" nor conscious. The neutral words produced little or no change in skin resistance. This physical change was therefore used as a conveniently quantifiable manifestation of arousal.

At some time after the learning trial, subjects were asked to look at the words and give the numbers that belonged with them. Those who attempted the recall immediately after the learning trial did rather well on the pairs that had produced a *small* change in skin resistance (the low-arousal words), and very poorly on the pairs that contained high-arousal words.

Other subjects tried to perform the same task not immediately, but 20 minutes after learning. These subjects remembered both types of pairs equally well: less well than the immediate recall group for the low-arousal pairs, but better on the high-arousal pairs. For a third group of subjects, whose recall was delayed until 45 minutes after learning, the results were the reverse of what happened with the immediate recall group: recall of the *high*-arousal pairs was about three times as good as recall of the *low*-arousal pairs! Subjects tested after a week showed the same excellent recall for the high-arousal pairs, but no recall for the low-arousal pairs.[10] Similar results were obtained when nonsense syllables were used in place of numbers as responses—a task very close to one way of learning foreign language vocabulary. The absence of forgetting over the period of a week is strongly reminiscent of the results obtained in the TPR experiments. The common factor is presence or absence of physical response—muscular and visible in one series, galvanic and invisible in the other. This is similar to what Curran[11] called the presence or absence of "self-investment."

Another experiment showed similar results when arousal was produced in a different way. Subjects studying an ordinary list were told either that their intelligence was being evaluated, or that the word list itself was. Those in the first group showed poorer retention when tested on the paired associates 2 minutes after studying them. After 45 minutes, however, their retention was better than that of the other group.[12] The same investigator had previously reported the same effect for the difference between being observed or unobserved while studying the list, and found that the effect was particularly striking when the two factors were combined.

We might be tempted to conclude that if we want our language students to have good long-term retention, we should make them as nervous as possible while we are presenting new material. This is not necessarily the case, however. Taft,[13] commenting on the effect of this sort of thing on memory, warned that "in some instances, ego involvement tends to raise the defensive process and results in lower recall values, while in others it tends to raise the sensitization process and lead to increased recall." This distinction foreshadowed those drawn by Bruner between "defending" and "coping,"[14] and by Curran between "defensive" and "receptive" learning.[15] More recently, Ehrman and Oxford have replaced Taft's quantitative distinction with a qualitative one between "facilitating" and "debilitating" anxiety.[16]

"DEPTH" AND MEMORY

It has been demonstrated that stimuli carrying high priority or a strong emotional charge can disrupt memory for stimuli that are presented immediately before or after them.[17] These are relatively mechanical effects, in which the stronger stimuli somehow prevent their neighbors from getting their proportionate share of time on the Worktable. The arousal phenomena discussed above operate in a different and more general way to facilitate or to interfere with retention. Bruner has suggested that emotions may operate on memory, and on learning in general, on a still larger scale and in a way that is different from either of those I have just mentioned:

> When early learning is hemmed about with conflict . . . , it becomes highly charged or libidinized. . . . These cognitive structures remain in being into adult life. . . . [When learning becomes overly defensive], it finally implicates so much of the patient's world . . . that he is truly crippled.[18]

Rapaport made an even bolder assertion about the relationship between emotions and memory. Emotions do not merely expedite or inhibit memory, he said. They actually provide the principle on which memories are organized.[19] Just as gestalt psychology had shown earlier generalizations about memory to be special cases of its own laws that were stated in terms of meaningfulness and logical organization, so Rapaport hoped for a second revolution, in which "the memory laws based on logical 'meaning' and 'organization' of the memory material refer only to special cases of memory organization; the more general theory of memory is a theory based on 'emotional organization' of memories, i.e., the organization of memories by strivings."[20] The fact that Rapaport's revolution was never realized in the profession as a whole[21] does not destroy its interest in the light of the other ideas presented in this chapter.

Two views of the relationship between depth and memory are found in the work of Curran, a clinical psychologist, and of Lozanov, a psychiatrist. Their conclusions are of particular interest to language teachers because both men developed and tested their theories in actual language classes, and not just in controlled experiments of limited scope.

Curran, whose method will be discussed more fully in Chapter 11, believed that people learn best from utterances in which they have a strong personal stake, or "investment." Partly for this reason, each class session in his method includes a certain amount of group conversation. During this time students, with the help of a "knower," say whatever they wish to in the foreign language. These sentences, in the students' own voices, are recorded on tape as the session proceeds. Later, these sentences become the basis for grammatical analysis, manipulative practice, and so forth. These relatively conventional activities gain in effectiveness because the students have felt in their own shared experience the meanings of the sentences, and heard their own voices speaking the sentences from the tape.[22]

Lozanov's work is particularly relevant to a discussion of memory because his method is supposed to produce what his translators have called "hypermnesia": students were reported to learn hundreds of words at a session, with little or no forgetting over long periods of time.[23] Because Lozanov's work is still more widely mentioned than understood in many parts of the world, and because it has value for understanding methods other than his own, I shall sketch my own understanding of some of the main outlines of his thought.[24]

Lozanov's view of learning is derived from three observations. (Lozanov would emphasize that they are in fact observations based on controlled experiments, and not mere speculations.) The first is that people are able to learn at rates many times greater than what we commonly assume to be the limits of human performance. The second observation is that learning is a "global" event, in the sense that it involves the entire person. The third and most characteristic of Lozanov's observations is that a person is constantly responding to innumerable influences, a few of which are conscious and rational, but most of which are either nonconscious or nonrational or both. The science that Lozanov calls "Suggestology" is concerned with the systematic study of these nonrational and/or nonconscious influences.

But the number and strength of these outside influences requires us to develop antisuggestive barriers of at least three kinds. These barriers are necessary if a human being is to preserve personal identity in the face of a constant stream of outside influences. They must therefore not be removed. Nevertheless, they may also act to interfere with learning. They do this not only by rejecting new material, but also by preserving the results of previous suggestions, extending back for many years, concerning the limitations on our ability to learn. Lozanov's answer to this impasse is "Suggestopedia." Suggestopedia is the application of suggestological principles, summarized above, to the art of teaching. Lozanov attacks the problem in two directions, and on two planes. The two directions are, first, to "desuggest" the limitations that have resulted from earlier suggestive influences and, second, to suggest various positive ideas. Of the two, Lozanov seems to regard the former as the more important.

The two planes are the conscious and rational plane and the plane of the nonconscious and nonrational. Lozanov emphasizes that inputs on these two planes should support each other, rather than partially canceling each other. This in itself is not a new idea, but perhaps Lozanov has made a qualitative leap in the extent of his attention to the details of the relationship between the two planes.

The antisuggestive barriers, then, are to be circumvented and not destroyed. When this has been achieved, the learner reaches a state of that Lozanov's translators call "infantilisation." (I suspect that the existing English expression "regression in the service of the ego"[25] would mean about the same thing.) In this state, the learner retains all previously acquired knowledge, but becomes more open, plastic, spontaneous, and creative. It is in this state that "hypermnesia" supposedly becomes possible.

"DEPTH" AND COMMUNICATION

Within the language teaching profession in recent years, we have said and written much about the desirability of "communication" in the classroom. We may evaluate this emphasis in terms of "depth." It is easy enough to devise some kind of communication scale whereon the rote repetition of meaningless material is at the zero point; the giving of meaningful but prescribed responses to stimuli from teacher, tape, or textbook is slightly more "communicative"; the selection of a situationally appropriate response from among a set of previously practiced responses is still more "communicative"; and conversing freely about matters of real and urgent interest is most "communicative" of all. This is reminiscent of the fact-fict dimension discussed earlier in this chapter.

Such a scale would, however, coincide only partially with the dimension of "depth." Much of the difference between the two would be found in the degree of attention given to the same nonconscious and/or nonrational needs that Lozanov has explored. These needs (for teacher as well as for students) may be subtle and submerged, but they are, for all that, no less potent. The surrealistic story that on paper looks asinine may, in the hands of a teacher who understands its use and who obviously believes in what he or she is doing, become an instrument for producing astonishing degrees of retention both lexical and structural.[26] On the other hand, talking about real objects or events that have nothing to do with long-term needs, either intellectual or practical, aesthetic or social, is notoriously unproductive. My guess is that an increase in "communicativeness" enhances retention and improves pedagogical effectiveness to the extent that it increases the average "depth" of the experience, but only to that extent. This subject will be developed more fully as we examine Meaning in Part II.

■ ■ ■ *Some Answers I Reached*

As I understand the term, "to communicate" is to make a difference in some other person, whether in that person's immediate actions or in his or her long-term memory, or in both. Communication takes place at various degrees of depth, which is to say that the comprehension or production of language "makes differences" on many levels. These levels are reflected in memory performance.

In addition to cognitive processing (discussed in Chapter 5), some of the factors affecting depth are arousal, personal significance, and the types of response that one makes or receives in the course of language use.

A wide variety of procedures can be profitably examined for the depth of communication they are likely to produce—or to inhibit. The same is true of whole methods, including those of Asher, Curran, and Lozanov.

■ ■ ■ *Further Questions*

□ Does the concept of "cognitive depth" apply to the processing of form as well as meaning?

□ How can a learner control the depth at which he or she is working from moment to moment?

Notes

1. Seliger et al. 1975:20.

2. This is presumably why these people commonly have poor recollection of the content of what they had been interpreting only a short time earlier.

3. My *Teaching Languages: A Way and Ways* (1980) was intended primarily not as an exposition of certain unconventional approaches, but as an exploration of the deeper meanings of learning and using a new language.

4. Kunihara & Asher 1965.

5. Asher 1965.

6. Seely & Romijn 1995.

7. Asher et al. 1974:30.

8. Lott, Lott & Walsh 1970.

9. Kamano & Drew 1961.

10. Kleinsmith & Kaplan 1963.

11. Curran 1968: passim.

12. Geen 1974.

13. Taft 1954.

14. Bruner 1967:129 and passim.

15. Curran 1968:337.

16. Ehrman & Oxford 1995: 69, 84.

17. Tulving 1969; Ellis 1971.

18. Bruner 1967:132–133, 147.

19. Rapaport 1971:270.

20. Rapaport 1971:268.

21. Luborsky 1971.

22. Curran 1968: Chapter 14.

23. In the current psychological literature, "hypermnesia" has a quite different meaning. There, it refers to "incremental recall": the fact that under some conditions, recall actually increases with the passage of time, rather than decreasing (see Thomas & Allen 1991:193).

24. My account of "Suggestopedia" in Stevick (1980: Chapters 18 and 19) is fuller than what is given here. It is also more authoritative, having been revised on the basis of Lozanov's own reactions to an earlier draft.

25. Schafer 1958.

26. Lipson 1971.

Part II
Meaning

Chapter 7
The Meaning of Speaking

Questions I Asked Myself:

☐ What may be the relationship between personal meanings and pronunciation?

☐ How may data about personal meanings interact with other data in shaping—and limiting—pronunciation?

☐ How may personal meanings influence ease of speaking?

INTRODUCTION

In Part I of this book, I referred frequently to the roles that "purpose" and "emotion" play in the working of "memory," and in Chapter 6 I talked about how language use makes various kinds of differences to those who are engaged in it. Now in Part II, I propose to develop this point of view further by looking at the "meaning" of some aspects of language study. This term "meaning" will, however, be used in a very special and restricted way. It will not refer to dictionary definitions or translation equivalents, or even to the relation of referent to symbol. Rather, continuing from Chapter 6, it will refer to whatever differences participation in a given activity—information-gap exercise, listening comprehension, or Spanish club picnic—makes to an individual relative to his or her entire range of drives and needs. In this chapter and in Chapter 8 we shall take a brief look inside the student, to see what some of these forces are, and how they may affect language learning. In Chapter 9 we shall take an even briefer look inside the teacher, and then examine some of the forces that are at work among the human beings who gather within the walls of a language classroom.

MacIntyre and Gardner[1] have reported a study in which they asked students to write brief essays about language-learning experiences that they had found either positive and relaxing, or stressful and anxiety-producing. One finding of this study was that almost all of the anxiety-producing experiences had had to do with trying to speak. Let us look first, therefore, at some meanings of "speaking." In exploring this one side of speaking, I do not mean to minimize the importance of the cognitive and biological sides that have been investigated by others.

This topic can be divided into "*How* we speak" (pronunciation) and "*How readily* we speak" (ease in speaking).

THE MEANING OF HOW WE SPEAK

It is common knowledge that people who have learned a language after puberty seldom sound exactly like natives[2] (though I have known two or three who did). We also know, however, that some speakers of a foreign language, even those who learned it as adults, have much better accents in it than others have. Certain ones are difficult to understand at all, others at first impression sound like natives, and the rest fall somewhere in between. Let us consider these differences first in a general psychodynamic framework, and then in terms of the processes of memory.

□ SOME PSYCHODYNAMIC MEANINGS OF PRONUNCIATION

What does accuracy of pronunciation "mean" to nonnative speakers—including students—of a language?

The Social Significance of Subtleties

We may look at pronunciation in two ways. First, and especially within the tradition that has viewed language teaching as one kind of applied linguistics, we may see it as consisting of control of a number of discrete features that have been called "phonemic distinctions." Thus we have often been counseled to try to bring our students to a pronunciation that is at least "phonemically accurate."[3] That is to say, they will make some kind of distinction between *sheep* and *ship*, or between *light* and *right*, even though the exact sounds they use for these distinctions may be noticeably foreign. This is pronunciation with attention to the things that critics might put their fingers on. We may call this the "analytical" (or "digital") view of pronunciation.

The second point of view takes pronunciation as a continuum. Although no two human voices are identical, nonnatives may produce their utterances, their intonations and rhythms, their vowels and consonants, in ways that are or are not closely parallel to the patterns that are shared by native speakers. This is a matter of degree, with no sharp dividing lines between correct and incorrect. We may call this the "holistic" view of pronunciation. I would like to suggest that with respect to the needs and anxieties of students, the "analytical" and the "holistic" points of view lead to different results.

Our attitudes toward these two kinds of pronunciation accuracy sometimes find explicit statement. One of my daughters, doing rather well in 8th-grade

French, explained to me that she could have spoken French so it would sound like the voices on the tape, but she didn't want to sound unacceptable to her classmates. This is an oft-related story in junior high school, but adults sometimes react in the same way. As we reach maturity, we become part of groups of all sizes, some very small and others numbering millions of people.[4] We depend on these groups as we establish and maintain our images of ourselves, and as we establish routines that protect us from the ravages of "overchoice,"[5] and as we provide for our physical and economic security. One natural way of showing which of these groups we are loyal to is through our speech,[6] and particularly through those aspects of speech that are least accessible to conscious choice. The analytical aspects of pronunciation (e.g., the distinction between *u* and *ou* in French) are much more accessible than the "subphonemic," nondigital aspects (rhythm, voice quality, precise vowel quality, etc.). When listeners (including ourselves) who are members of our own in-groups hear us go beyond the gross and digital kind of accuracy in an outsider language, they may feel a threat at Maslow's level of "belonging"—that we are somehow showing ourselves disloyal to the group of which they and we are both members.

This is why, at least during one period of English history, no gentleman who was learning French would "stoop to adopt the effeminate and obviously degenerate way of speaking that is used by the French people."[7] To do so would be "integrative" toward a dangerous out-group and for that very reason "*dis*integrative*" toward the in-group. This feeling on the part of listeners is not entirely mistaken: in my own study of foreign languages, even dead ones, I have regularly developed an "integrative" attitude toward the peoples who speak or spoke them. Seliger et al.[8] report that among a group of people who had learned a foreign language after puberty, those who learned it without an accent had relatively few close friends who spoke the same first language as they did, compared with those who learned the same new language with an accent.

The Guiora Studies

One widely cited body of research on the relationship between pronunciation ability and other aspects of personality made use of a distinction similar to the one between the analytical and the holistic points of view. In a crucial part of this research, subjects were taught a few brief dialogues in Japanese. Then they were tested in two ways: first by engaging in a simple conversation with the teacher, and later by repeating after the teacher five simple sentences based on patterns that they had met during the training phase. Competent judges then rated what they had said according to (1) "general authenticity" (comparable to the holistic point of view) and (2) "specific criteria" (comparable to the analytical point of view).

Each student in the Japanese experiment thus received four scores: general authenticity on (1) spontaneous production and (2) repetition, and specific criteria on (3) spontaneous production and (4) repetition. The aim of the researchers was to find statistically reliable correlations among these scores and other measurable characteristics of the subjects. Not very surprisingly, the strongest relationship turned out to be between these scores on the one hand, and the Scholastic Aptitude Test-Verbal Ability scores on the other.

Of considerably greater interest was the strong positive correlation between the "spontaneous specific criteria" scores and the subjects' scores on a test devised especially for this research. In that test, a subject watched a motion picture of a patient during a psychiatric interview. The subject was to watch for fleeting changes of facial expression. In one of the experiments, the film was played at successively slower speeds. Subjects differed markedly from one another in their ability to detect these "micro-momentary expressions" (MMEs). The researchers discovered a strong correlation between relative authenticity of pronunciation and relative ability to pick out MMEs.[9] This was particularly true for the specific criteria under the condition of spontaneous production. Note that although the judges were listening "analytically" as they evaluated the specific criteria, the subjects had not been drilled on these points as such. They had thus picked up these isolable features of pronunciation in the course of a largely nonanalytical reaction to the language.

The meaning of this relationship requires some interpretation. The experimenters' purpose in recording the subjects' sensitivity to MME's was to measure their ability to achieve "empathy" with other people. This quality they described as a process of comprehending, in which boundaries between the self and an object outside the self were temporarily weakened. In this way, the subject is able to achieve an "immediate emotional apprehension of another's emotional experience, and then to use this experience cognitively to gain some understanding of the other person."[10] They assumed that the more sensitive a person is to the feelings and behavior of others, the more likely that person will be to perceive and recognize the subtleties of a second language and incorporate them into his or her own speaking.[11] They pointed out that language development and the ability to empathize came along at about the same time in the life of a child, and that both depend on a warm and close relationship between the child and a nurturing person.[12]

The same authors developed an even more comprehensive picture of the relationship between pronunciation and personality. In their view, the language ego, like the body ego, has definite outlines and firm boundaries.[13] Ehrman, trained both in language education and in psychotherapy, tells us that the "thickness" (in Guiora's metaphor, the "permeability") of ego boundaries is a relatively stable aspect of personality.[14] As studies by Guiora and others have shown, however, what is stable here must be only the range *within which* "thickness" or "permeability" may vary for a particular individual, and not the absolute value of this quality.

In the view of Guiora and his colleagues, pronunciation is perhaps the most critical and the most valuable of the contributions that the language ego makes to total self-representation.[15,16] They believe the empathic process may act on the boundaries of the language ego. Guiora defined "empathy" as "a process of comprehending in which a temporary [melting] of self-object boundaries, as in the earliest pattern of object relations, permits an immediate emotional apprehension of the affective experience of others, this sensing being used by the cognitive functions to gain understanding of the other."[17] This means, among other things, that the empathic process depends on the ability to suspend, if only temporarily and partially, the functions that maintain one's separateness from others.[18] Because this suspension moves in the direction of an earlier mode of psychic functioning, it is in the psychiatric sense "regressive," but because it is temporary and partial, this regression remains under cognitive control and in the service of the ego.[19]

Some of the evidence presented by Guiora and his colleagues shows that "empathy," at least as they measured it, is in fact one predictor of pronunciation accuracy.[20] One factor in the empathy dimension is "tolerance to anxiety caused by awareness of affective stimuli."[21] I would suggest that alien pronunciations may be perceived as "affective stimuli."

What We Can Expect

This negative reaction to alien "affective stimuli" is particularly likely for a person who is psychologically very dependent on a monolingual (or even monodialectal!) peer group. Hill[22] pointed out that in some cultures, details of pronunciation become the focus of much attention as a mark of ethnic, regional, or sexual identity, while in others it is much less so. She therefore challenged the assumption that a person who learns a language as an adult never completely gets rid of a foreign accent. I myself have known at least three speakers of other languages who have learned accent-free American English well after puberty, and one other, a native speaker of British English, who did the same thing. Krashen[23] has cited evidence that the acquisition or nonacquisition of accent-free pronunciation has less to do with brain maturation than with the socialization that takes place at about the time of puberty.

People vary, then, both individually and culturally, with respect to the significance that pronunciation has as a medium for expressing their self-concept. They also vary with respect to their tolerance for the affective impact of hearing themselves or someone else sound foreign. At least a part of this tolerance seems to depend on events that took place in the earliest parts of their lives.[24] The reasoning of Guiora and his colleagues seems to suggest that a combination of these two types of difference may go far toward explaining individual variations in pronunciation ability.

But the boundaries of the factors are set for each individual only in the sense that each individual has a limited range within which he or she can fluctuate.[25] One study experimentally altered that flexibility by "lowering of inhibitions" through the use of alcohol.[26] One finding of this study was that there did, indeed, seem to be an optimal amount of alcohol that could significantly improve pronunciation of a foreign language. Presumably, this was an amount that lowered inhibitions (i.e., increased tolerance for anxiety about self-image and about alien noises from other people), while not yet interfering with cognitive control. But the same effects that the alcohol seems to have achieved here can also be reached by social means. This is where "receptivity" (discussed in Chapter 10) and "controlled regression" (discussed in this chapter) become urgently important to the teacher and the learner of pronunciation.

If the reasoning of Guiora et al. is correct, then certain kinds of life history may actually predispose one to pronounce foreign languages extraordinarily well. For example, a child who in infancy had "a warm and close relationship with a mothering person"[27] but who never achieved full integration into an adolescent peer group, and whose family was oriented toward groups outside the dialect area to which his or her peers belonged, might have not only the emotional basis for the necessary empathy, but also a definite positive affect attached to the experience of sounding foreign.[28] Such a person might even try, unconsciously, to use her or his good foreign pronunciation as a means for getting from outsiders the acceptance that adolescent peer groups had withheld.

This small venture into psychoanalytic interpretation is an extrapolation from the Guiora studies, and in the first edition of this book I did not intend it to be taken too seriously. In the intervening years, however, I have heard from at least eight individuals, excellent mimics with highly accurate pronunciation of various foreign languages, who have said, in effect, "That's me!" Though their reports obviously do not validate my guess, they may at least suggest that it is a conjecture worth testing. Yet even if this sketch is wrong in detail (or fully applicable only in certain instances), it is still an example of an additional angle on the meaning of pronunciation. Deep emotional attitudes have the power to facilitate or inhibit pronunciations. I do believe that intelligent awareness of factors such as these will do more to improve the teaching of pronunciation than all the charts, diagrams, and mechanical devices that we sometimes depended on in the past.[29]

□ MEANING AND MEMORY

I have already listed a number of kinds of data that can be stored in memory. Four categories are sensory input (5S), emotion (EM), purpose (PR), and time (TI). These four have to do with information that language can convey. I also listed language itself as a category, with all its forms and structures. Some of its subcategories are:

□ *Audible sound*(s), whether coming in from outside, or generated internally (AU). Since the topic is pronunciation, a few special observations about this category are in order:

- The phonological representations found here have been constructed from experience by each individual.[30]

- Native speakers are able to hear many phonetic differences that linguists would say are redundant or nondistinctive in their languages.

This is the speaker's principal source of information about dialect, mood, and the like.[31] So AU covers not only the recognized "distinctive features" of one or more languages. It also includes subtle subphonemic distinctions.

- The physical differences that contribute toward identification of a given vowel or consonant may extend before or after the duration of that segment. For example, word-final /-t/ and word-final /-b/ have different influences on the vowel that precedes them, as in *wrote* and *robe*.[32] This principle is also at work in the well-known umlaut process.

☐ *Articulation* (AR): the physical acts of tongue, jaw, and so on necessary to produce a spoken form.[33]

☐ *The physical motions* (WR) needed for the act of writing.

☐ *Spelling* (SP): a sequence of individual letters, whether coming in from outside, or generated internally.

☐ *The overall appearance* (OA) of a written form.

Figure 7.1 shows six of these kinds of data that are particularly relevant to pronunciation. The dots stand for individual representations of the types indicated by the two-letter symbols.

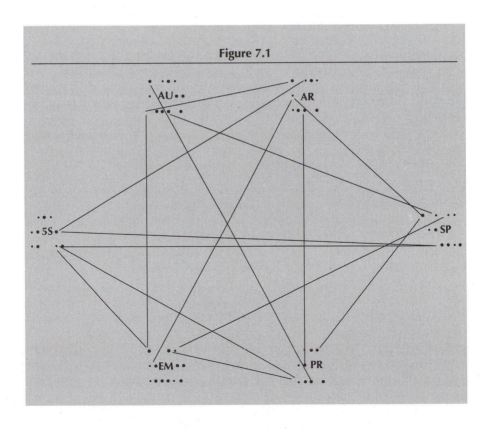

Figure 7.1

Chapters 1–6 suggest some basic reasoning about any memory that is composed of various kinds of data:

1. As a result of any particular experience many, or even all, of these kinds of data may be stored. *This is true for all neurologically normal people.*

2. But not all kinds of data are stored with equal clarity, permanence, or level of activation. *People differ as to which types of data they store best, or as to which types are most readily accessible to them, or both. Some but probably not all of these differences in performance are due to genetically determined differences in wiring.*

3. Connections are probably formable between data at any of the pairs of dots in Figure 7.1.[34] Just which of these potential connections actually get formed or strengthened on any given occasion, though influenced by context, is still partially a matter of chance. *Again, this is true for all neurologically normal people.*

4. It follows that not all of the connections are equally strong, or equally fast. *People differ also with regard to the relative strengths of the various kinds of connections. At least some of these differences in performance are due to differences in past experience, including but not limited to deliberate practice.*

We can apply this reasoning to three sets of examples.

EXAMPLE 1: Pronunciations of "Stevick"

Every bearer of the surname "Stevick" I have encountered over the years has pronounced the first syllable with the vowel of "leave." People who have only heard the name, and who later try to pronounce it aloud, fall into four main groups. How can we account for the differences among these groups in terms of the above reasoning?

The overall process, common to all four groups, must be something like the following:

1. Personal identification data (face, age, gender, social background, etc.) come in and are stored. Most of these are sensory, and so will appear in Figure 7.1 at 5S.

2. At the same time, audible phonetic data come in from whatever has just been heard and activate representations (of vowels, consonants, etc.) at AU in Figure 7.1 .

3. Activation spreads from AU to all other categories, *along paths that have been established by previous experience.*[35] (In Western culture, the strongest/best-established paths from auditory data are likely to lead to old data about spellings and personal identification.)

4. Part of this secondary activation in turn spreads further to data at 5S.

5. When on a later occasion the same personal identification data in 5S are activated by new sensory input (e.g., when people see me again and want to introduce me), activation spreads from the data at 5S to the data in other categories with which the 5S data were connected earlier.

6. Activation from various categories, and especially from SP and 5S, spreads to AU.
7. The result of what happens at AU is transmitted to the Worktable and becomes the basis for oral production of some version of the name.

The four groups of pronouncers are:

Those who can't come up with the name at all. This is a relatively large group, for "Stevick" or for any other surname. (In fact, as we saw in Chapter 4, most people think they are worse than average when it comes to reproducing surnames they have heard for the first time just a minute or so earlier.)

For these people, the data stored at AU, plus any activation reaching AU from other categories, are insufficient to produce any name at all.

□ If the data activated at AU are very few, the person typically reports "drawing a blank."

□ If almost but not quite enough data are activated to produce a name, the person may say "It's on the tip of my tongue," and may even report partial data: "It begins with an S" or the like.

Those who pronounce the first syllable with the vowel of "let." Of those who come up with any name at all, nearly everyone uses this pronunciation.

Here, the pronunciation that comes to the Worktable from AU is heavily influenced by data that had earlier been stored in the SP category, analogous with "seven." These data override whatever may have been stored in the AU category itself, or in any of the other categories. I've found that even pointing out the difference between this and the original pronunciation seldom has any effect on how these people pronounce the name the next time they need it, either. It is not clear whether this version of the name is due to superior storage *at* SP, or to better established connections *between* certain SP data and certain AU data, or to some combination of these.

Those who use the vowel of "fit." Few people do this, but I can't remember hearing it at all before the advent of the TV series "All in the Family."

Here, the original AU material apparently had activated 5S data having to do with Archie's Polish-American son-in-law Mike Stivic. When a name needed to be produced later, activation from those data overrode competing activations at AU, and the result went to the Worktable. (Many years ago, some people used the vowels of Sea-Tac, apparently due to a similar process involving the bandleader Charlie Spevack. I haven't heard that pronunciation of "Stevick" for at least 25 years.)

Those who pronounce the first syllable with the vowel of "leave." This is a relatively small group. Possibly:

□ People in this group have stored the original phonetic data well at AU. These data are strong enough to override any secondary activations coming to AU from other categories.

- Or they reach their AU outcome in the same way as those in the second group, except that their previous experience leads them to follow the analogy of "even" rather than the analogy of "seven."
- Or a combination of the above.

EXAMPLE 2: Degrees of Foreign Accent among Adult Language Learners

I have already noted that after the age of puberty, most individual learners of new languages continue to sound like obvious foreigners. Others, with equal or even less exposure to the same language, seem not only to control the gross phonemic distinctions of a new language, but also to achieve a high degree of mastery of the nuances of vowels, consonants, intonation, rhythm, and voice quality that together add up to a "good accent."

Those who "have tin ears." Within the above reasoning, and with reference to the basic process outlined earlier, the possibilities are:

- The FL phonetic data that arrive at AU activate NL spellings in SP. Later, when production is needed, these spellings from SP activate their NL associates at AU strongly enough to override any phonetic data that may have been stored there from the target language itself.
- The most important data activated by incoming AU are not in SP, but in the area of meaning: 5S, PR, and especially EM. That is, they respond relatively more to the meaning of what has come in through their ears and to its meaning-bearing features, and ignore the nuances of the sounds that brought it to them.
- They may be sensitive to the nuances, but just prefer not to sound too foreign.
- More than one of the above may operate simultaneously.

Those who "pick up the accent naturally." There are again three obvious possibilities:

- These people store raw phonetic data from the new language better than their fellow learners with the tin ears, and better than they store the corresponding data in SP.
- The 5S, PR, and EM associations with the foreign language and culture are positive for such individuals, so that these associations tend to strengthen the influence of the target language phonetic data on the outcome from AU to the Worktable.
- Both of the above may operate simultaneously.

Hints as to what is going on here may be found in reports from adult learners with "good ears." Much of the evidence I am about to present here will be taken from my own experiences. I recognize that this evidence is anecdotal and largely introspective. Nevertheless, it has the merit of providing contrasting pictures from within a single personality.

□ In the languages that I have learned to use since age 18, my "accent" has commonly been good enough so that nonnatives thought I sounded native, and natives had to listen at least a moment or two to be sure that I wasn't. This is as true of German, which I learned in the absence of any phonetic knowledge, as it is of other languages that came along later. Even when I have had phonetic information available, I have made little or no conscious reference to it as I learned to speak.

□ I can also speak these same languages with a strong American English accent. This however requires conscious effort. I do it only to amuse others, and I cannot continue it for communicative purposes. This indicates important effects of data in PR, EM, and 5S.

□ My accent in Swahili was always "very good." After a number of years, I had a chance to hear the language spoken by a woman (Annie Håkonsdatter) who had acquired it during her adult years by attaching herself to a Swahili-speaking family and having them teach it to her as they would to a child. I recognized immediately that her accent was incomparably better than mine. Subsequently, if I picture her in the back of my mind, my Swahili accent is much more African. She seems to be a living assurance that a person from the culture she and I share can after all sound that way.[36] I can do this even in continuing communication. Again, the relationships between 5S, EM, and PR data on the one hand, and AU data on the other, seem to be central here.

EXAMPLE 3: Use of Varying Styles or Accents within the Native Language

People vary greatly with regard to their occasional use of more than one regional or social accent within their native language. Some (including my father and my wife) seem to shift accents relatively seldom, and within a narrow range. Perhaps they have no wider range of alternative accents available to them. If they were computers, we would say that their printers had only a single typeface available, though with corresponding italic and bold variants. Others (including my mother and me) do have more than one accent available—more than one typeface—and shift among them easily.

With regard to speakers who control more than one accent within their NL, we must distinguish between shifts that can be chosen or avoided deliberately, and those that are outside conscious control.

Consciously controllable shifts:

□ Certain individuals are thought of as "excellent mimics." Two such are Tracey Ullman and Whoopi Goldberg. In a television interview some years ago, these two actresses agreed that "We don't do accents, we do people." The colleague who reported this interview to me, himself an amazingly accurate mimic with a wide repertoire, said that the same was true for him. This is reminiscent of how the picture of Annie Håkonsdatter influences my accent in Swahili, and further emphasizes the connections between 5S-EM-PR and AU.

□ I can do reasonably accurate and (to some people) amusing imitations of English as spoken by speakers of some of the more common European languages with which our culture has a joking relationship. I cannot usually do so for Portuguese, Turkish, or Swahili. To do so would seem to me to be making fun of the individuals from whom I learned the language. This points to the 5S-EM-PR and AU relationship again.

A unique exception confirms this suggestion. One day, a Swahili teacher and I were looking over the transcripts of the proceedings of an East African legislative body. The language of the proceedings was Swahili, but the speakers had made frequent use of English words and short phrases. Both the teacher and I were surprised—and therefore sometimes amused—at the speakers' choices of which meanings to put into English. As we went through the transcript, I occasionally read one of the quotations aloud. After a few minutes, we both noticed that in my reading of the English portions I had used an East African accent. Evidently the teacher's participation had allowed me to feel free to have a little fun at the speakers' expense. Since that time, the East African accent in English has again become completely unavailable to me, presumably because of the (to me) disrespectful implication of my use of it.

Shifts that are beyond conscious control:

□ Many people volunteer the information that they speak with different accents at different times. I am one of those people. Probably none of my ways of speaking is totally without the influence of the southwest corner of Missouri, which is where I grew up.[37] Even so, several people besides myself have noted accent shifting in my spoken English. Most obvious are what in the first edition of this book I called my "down-home" accent and my "educated" accent. Which of these I use seems to depend on who I am being at the moment. I typically use the "down-home" variety to exert force with unfriendly strangers, and to convey solidarity with friendly strangers who themselves speak with similar accents. At a time when the "educated" variety seems needed, the "down-home" variety is completely closed to me, and vice versa.

Shifting from one accent to the other is for me therefore not at all a matter of beginning from some one "basic" way of speaking and then using a set of "rules" in order to convert the "basic" way into some other accent. Unless circumstances change, such a shift is an impossibility. It is thus quite different from "doing accents" for fun.

THE MEANING OF EASE IN SPEAKING

To close this chapter, let us look briefly at something that for want of a better term I shall call "ease in speaking." Ease in speaking is not quite the same as "fluency." Schmidt[38] cites several definitions for the latter term: ability to fill time with talk; ability to speak in a way that is "coherent, complex and dense"; ability to say the right thing at the right time; ability to control aesthetic and other nuances of the language; and overall ability to use the language well. Under "ease in speaking" I would like to include a number of observable characteristics that will be familiar to anyone who has ever taught or used a foreign language:

□ One characteristic is similar to Schmidt's first definition of "fluency": the ability to fill time with speech. By this I understand not only syllables per second once someone has begun to speak, but also a minimum of pauses, or of hesitancy before beginning. But there are three additional characteristics not found in Schmidt's list.

□ Willingness to speak or try to understand the language rather than avoiding it.

□ Willingness to use words or constructions rather than avoiding them, even when it appears likely that listeners may disapprove of them.

□ Overall, an ability to concentrate on communication without spending time and Worktable resources in planning, rehearsing, and correcting utterances before producing them—what Krashen might call "monitoring."

In using this cover term "ease in speaking" for all four characteristics, I have not constructed it from statistical analysis of any body of scientifically collected data. I am only offering an experimentally supportable or falsifiable conjecture that these characteristics may generally go together in people's everyday use of foreign languages.

□ WILLINGNESS TO USE THE LANGUAGE

Nida[39] gives a striking example of how concerns about identity may influence readiness to interact through the use of language. An Aztec woman who lived in a Spanish-speaking village in Mexico seemed to be able to speak Spanish only when she was drunk, but then she spoke it fluently and with great accuracy. Nida speculates that her failure to speak Spanish while sober was not simply stubbornness; rather, it was at the same time a part of playing her social role of "dumb Indian," and one way of expressing her resentment and her refusal to identify with the dominant culture.

Insistence on using one language with certain people and another language with others is a phenomenon that is commonly observed in bilingual children. It is most acute at the same age (roughly 2 to 3 years) when a child is in the process of forming an image of itself as a person separate from other people. As we grow older, we no longer refuse absolutely to speak "the wrong language" with others, but fluency may be strongly affected by these same considerations—my daughter-in-law speaking Portuguese with me, for example.

The fluency requirement may threaten a self-image at other points besides this one. Obviously, other things being equal, a person who sees herself or himself as the "strong silent type" will resist verbal interaction more than someone with an "outgoing, gregarious" self-concept. More important, though less obvious, is the fact that many other threats to a student's ego may result in a withdrawing type of defense mechanism. "I usually succeed at what I try" is threatened by failures small or large; theoretically at least, "I'm no good at languages" might feel temporarily threatened by success. "I'm a professional preparing for an important job" is threatened by materials that seem irrelevant, and "I'm eye-minded" by the withholding of written materials; "I'm a student, and students are supposed to be taught" reacts badly either to a poor teacher, or to a good one who is less directive than expected. Varying difficulties arise in a language classroom for those who have no patience with details, for those who must have something to conform to, and also for those who bridle at the demands of any authority.

Any of these threats to a student's ego will produce some kind of adaptive reaction, many of which are of a defensive nature. Some defensive reactions are aggressive, while others consist of one or another form of withdrawal, and the latter generally bring partial (or occasionally complete) loss of fluency. It would be interesting to notice which students habitually direct inward their annoyance at having made a mistake (apologizing, slapping forehead, muttering "Stupid!," etc.) and which ones customarily direct it outward ("Dammit," manipulation of objects, etc.), and to see how these two patterns correlate with overall fluency.

Unfortunately, there is no way to dissolve all of the frustrations and potential ego threats; there is not even a single, magical formula to minimize them. Nevertheless, there is one fundamental change in our approach that might improve our chances of dealing successfully with problems of this kind. During most of my years in language teaching, I have focused my attention on the linguistic material—the sounds, the words, and the structures—that my students were learning. Their emotional reactions, the relationship between what they were experiencing and how it made them feel, were at the periphery of my thinking. I was conscious of those matters only when a student showed gross and overt signs of being upset. As my career progressed, however, I tried to reverse my priorities. Student attitudes now began to take chronological priority. This means that I no longer care how much of the language they learn during the first week. Although I would not tell them so, the linguistic material presented during that time is only a vehicle for getting acquainted and for finding and reducing anxieties. Even during the remainder of the course, the first question is "How are they learning?" and the second is "What have they learned?" It is now content, and not morale, that I tend to place in the background unless it threatens to cause trouble. Needless to say, I still give much attention to content and to accuracy; what has changed is the focus.

□   RESTRICTION IN RANGE OF SPEAKING

But threats exist at the level of interaction as well as at the level of identity. One experimenter measured the fluency, rate, and total verbal output of a series of subjects who thought they were addressing an ordinary audience. Actually the audience was primed by the experimenter to react in one of two ways. In the first mode, various members of the audience manifested positive kinds of behavior, including smiling, maintaining eye contact, sitting in a comfortable but erect posture, note taking, and absence of fidgeting. With other speakers, the same audience fidgeted, withheld eye contact, looked around the room, and doodled. The difference between these two modes of audience response produced the expected differences in fluency, rate, and total output, although these effects were not always statistically significant.[40] If these variations in hearer response can produce this sort of effect in subjects who are speaking their native language, we should not be surprised to find stronger effects on people who are trying to speak a foreign one.

A different pair of experiments in the same general area produced statistically significant results. In both, the dependent variable was not total output or general fluency; rather, it was a number called the "type-token ratio." This is the ratio between the total number of words used and the total number of *different* words used.

In the first experiment of this series, the control subjects were simply asked to tell two familiar folk stories selected by the experimenter. The experimental subjects told the same two stories. After the first story, however, they were required to count backward from 15 to 1, alternately subtracting 3 and 4. As they attempted this fairly difficult task, the experimenter interrupted them frequently, showed contempt or irritation when they made errors, and was generally unpleasant. After this aggressive behavior on the part of the experimenter, the subjects went on to tell the second story. Not surprisingly, their type-token ratios were down. Apparently, in response to a threat, they had "reduced their perimeter" by sticking to a leaner vocabulary than they would otherwise have used.

In a related experiment, the subjects were invited to the experimenter's home and, in the course of the visit, they were asked why they had chosen psychology as their major field of study. The control subjects were allowed to answer freely, while the experimental subjects were criticized, interrupted, and made to feel misunderstood. As in the previous experiment, the second group showed a drop in type-token ratio. In this informal setting, the difference between groups was even greater.[41]

□ THE IMPORTANCE OF EASE IN SPEAKING

I think all language teachers would agree with Peirce's assumption that practice in a new language is a necessary condition for learning it.[42] But real, high-quality practice depends on willingness to speak, and that in turn depends on ease in speaking. What I have said in this and the preceding chapters indicates at least three ways in which "ease in speaking" can be valuable:

- Most obvious is its *social* value in making conversation more comfortable for all concerned.
- When the people the learner is talking with are comfortable, they are likely to provide richer *input* to the learner, and to do so for a longer period of time.
- From the point of view of *memory organization* (Part I of this book), a new item of vocabulary or structure is more likely to get used. When used, it will be processed at greater depth, be integrated into richer and more

complex networks, and be more likely to get beyond holding memory and into permanent memory if in times of real and intense communication it is used and not avoided.

In summary, ease of speaking is not just "nice"; it is also useful.

Yet as Peirce cogently points out, "willingness" and "ease" with a language depend on motivation and on social identity, and these are undergoing constant modification and reconstruction in the very process of using the language.[43] She also argues that a key factor in this process is the unequal and often inequitable distribution of social and personal power. I will have more to say on this subject in Chapters 8 and 9.

■ ■ ■ *Some Answers I Reached*

A group of people who are loyal to one another over a long period of time generally develop a shared kind of pronunciation that differs in small details from the pronunciation of groups around them. Loyal participation in a group is by far the most frequent way—though not the only way—of attaining conformity with respect to those details.

Therefore conformity to a group's pronunciation is widely—and usually correctly—taken to signify membership in it or at least loyalty to it. This sort of conclusion is all the more powerful because both the conclusion and the pronunciation details themselves are often outside of conscious notice.

Group loyalties are an important component of anyone's self-image. For this reason, details of pronunciation are intimately involved with self-image.

Protection and management of self-image are high-priority concerns of almost everyone. Therefore the adoption or rejection of details of pronunciation carries important personal meanings.

Personal meanings interact with other data in the networks of long-term memory, whether in the choice of phonemes or in nuances of pronunciation, both in one's native language and in foreign languages.

Personal meanings may also influence one's rate and smoothness of speaking, how long one speaks, and the richness of the vocabulary one uses, as well as one's willingness to speak a language at all.

■ ■ ■ *Further Questions*

□ On average, would a class exposed to sustained sympathetic portrayals of another culture in fact come out with better accents in the language of that culture than would a comparable class that had not had such exposure?

□ What is the relationship between getting an accent *perfectly* (which is what Scovel's 1988 book is about), and getting *relatively close* to it (which is the subject of much of this chapter)?

Notes

1. MacIntyre & Gardner 1991.

2. Scovel 1988.

3. MacCarthy (1978:31) offers a more subtle treatment, with five levels of priority for various phonetic discrepancies between the learner and the community of established speakers. Highest priority is assigned to phonemic features: those distinctions that "[give] rise to actual minimal pairs of words differing in meaning."

4. Tiger 1969.

5. Toffler 1970:234.

6. Labov 1966:487ff.

7. Rivers 1968:132.

8. Seliger et al. 1975:20.

9. Guiora et al. 1967.

10. Guiora et al. 1967.

11. Taylor et al. 1971:147.

12. Taylor et al. 1971:147.

13. Guiora 1972a:144.

14. Ehrman 1993:332. Ehrman's treatment of ego boundaries as they affect the language learning process deserves careful study, both in this paper and in Ehrman and Oxford 1995.

15. Guiora 1972a:145.

16. A summary of this series of studies is Guiora et al. (1975).

17. Guiora 1965:779.

18. Guiora 1972a:148.

19. Guiora et al. 1967; cf. Schafer 1958.

20. Guiora 1970:536, and earlier citations.

21. Guiora 1970:536, and earlier citations.

22. Hill 1970.

23. Krashen 1973.

24. Taylor et al. 1971:147; Guiora 1972a:144.

25. Guiora 1972a:144.

26. Guiora 1972a.

27. Taylor et al. 1971:147.

28. "Frieda" (Stevick 1989:119f.) is an example of this.

29. Straight (private communication) reminds me of another neglected avenue of pronunciation improvement: being willing to focus on the development of the receptive abilities that will enable learners to develop their expressive abilities in their own time but with a broad experience of and deep sensitivity to variations in sound.

30. Ard 1989:243.

31. Ard (1989:248f.) cites evidence from Russian, but the same must certainly be true in other languages.

32. Ard 1989:249.

33. The ways in which learners perceive new sounds and the ways in which they produce them are not always neatly parallel. Evidence for this dissociation is summarized in Leather and James (1992:314f).

34. For a neurobiologically explicit development of ideas comparable to those in this and the following paragraph, see Pulvermüller and Schumann (1994), especially pp. 691–697.

35. Leather and James (1991) summarize evidence that learners tend at first to perceive the sounds of the new language in terms of the categories of their native language (311–314), and that connections between the sounds one hears oneself making and the feelings one gets from one's own speech muscles gradually becomes stronger with experience (316).

36. Compare Murphey's conclusion (1995:35) that "[students] need role models, people who they can identify with more closely than [they can identify with their] foreign teachers. When they see, *or even hear of,* someone with whom they can identify easily (someone who resembles them in some way), and this person has learned [the same FL fluently], then . . . changes in behaviors come easier . . ."

37. V. Shoemaker, private communication.

38. Schmidt 1992:357f. This entire article is exemplary in its handling of cognitive issues as they relate to language learning.

39. Nida 1972.

40. Blubaugh 1969.

41. Höweler 1972.

42. Peirce 1995:14.

43. Peirce 1995:15.

Chapter 8

Interpersonal Meanings

Questions I Asked Myself:

☐ What personal meanings are my students likely to pick up in the process of their academic study of a language?

☐ How are these meanings exemplified in well-known procedures?

INTRODUCTION

There is interpersonal meaning not only in what we say, but in how we say it; not only in what we teach, but in how we teach it. In particular, the acts and the events of the classroom, are always bound up in relationships of power. I would further suggest that the oft-repeated goal of (to use a currently stylish term) empowering students, however far upward or however far outward it may hope to reach, needs to find solid footing in how we treat those same students day by day.

TWO SETS OF CONCLUSIONS

Having made this generalization, let me be more specific: first a little more specific, and then very specific. To begin with, here are two rather distinct sets of conclusions that a student might draw from his or her experience in a foreign language class. I have put them together largely out of some of the things Leo Loveday said in his book on *The Sociolinguistics of Learning and Using a Non-native Language.*[1]

☐ ARCADIAN[2] CONCLUSIONS

One set of conclusions is the set that Loveday seems to think we should enable our students to reach. (Page numbers refer to Loveday 1982.) Working for this set of conclusions is thought of by some as enlightened, by others as starry-eyed. Probably more teachers subscribe to this goal than manage to pursue it consistently.

☐ Language is a medium (134) for creating (130) one's own meanings (141), and for exchanging meanings with other people.

159

- In this process of creating and exchanging meanings, one discovers one-self (130) more fully.
- The process of creating and exchanging meanings also provides opportunities for expressing one's freedom (127) and autonomy (137), and for developing them further.
- At the same time, one also recognizes and affirms the freedom, autonomy and uniqueness of others. (Contrast with "intolerance" [129], "judgmental" [125, 134].)
- In the process of learning a language, one should be freed from unnecessary social pressures (145).
- In order to exchange meanings with other people, one needs to know how they will react to various possible ways of using words (125f.), as well as how to respond appropriately to the words of others. That is to say, one must be able to use the "conventions" of the language and of the culture in question.
- In the production of language, conformity to norms of correctness is less important than comprehensibility is.
- The teacher is primarily a resource and a facilitator.

These are conclusions that are likely to be drawn by students in a learner-centered curriculum, as described by Nunan[3] and others.

□ UTOPIAN CONCLUSIONS

In dramatic contrast to this set of conclusions is the set that Loveday believes are too often reached by people who have sat or worked their way through a language course. Working for these conclusions is seen by some as realistic and responsible, by others as hidebound, and as inconsistent with the learner's needs as a person:

- Language must be treated as an object for a long time before it can be treated as a medium.
- Spoken language should not depart too far from written language. (Say "pro-ba-bly" and not "probbly.")
- The most important thing about language as an object is its form. This means that what I say is less important than how correctly I say it, and that guessing the meaning of a paragraph is less important (less honorable?!) than being able to account for all the grammatical signals it contains.
- Some conventions that affect the form of language are acceptable (e.g., "It doesn't"). (These conventions are what Loveday calls "norms.") All other conventions are entirely unacceptable ("It don't").
- Decisions as to which linguistic and which social conventions become norms are made by a small group of socially powerful people. By enforcing conformity to these norms, this oligarchy—actually, the upper middle class (174)—both expresses and perpetuates its own power at the expense of larger groups of subjugated and despised speakers (175).

□ The language of monolinguals is—or at least may be—acceptable by those norms; language that is not consistent with acceptable monolingual usage is not acceptable at all.

□ If I follow unacceptable conventions, I will be unacceptable as a speaker of the L2, and my utterances may be rejected, ridiculed, or ignored by competent (i.e., conforming) speakers.

□ In production, conformity to norms is more important than comprehensibility is.

□ Therefore learning a language is first of all a process of learning to conform to norms (social as well as linguistic); success in a language course first of all requires the learner to demonstrate his or her willingness and ability to conform.

□ The teacher is primarily a judge and corrector (134).

□ I will be judged every time I open my mouth.

Here is the same contrast in a nutshell: two quotations from people to whom I had put the question, "What besides language did you learn from your language class?"

□ "I learned that it is important for a learner to explore, and not just follow what's given by the teacher."

□ "I learned the importance of what the teacher's voice conveys. I also learned anxiety and anger."

Richards and Rodgers analyze methods in terms of three levels: approach, design, and procedure.[4] Either of the sets of conclusions described above can make itself felt on all of these levels. If, for example, we recognize the effect of such conclusions on the purposes and emotions of learners, and if we further recognize that a learner's purposes and emotions are intimately involved in memory even for cognitive material, then that recognition becomes part of any theory about the nature of language learning (the "approach" level). On the level of "design," that knowledge will in turn affect choices of activity types, and of the roles to be assigned to learners and to teachers. Finally, those choices will encourage certain "moment-to-moment techniques, practices and behaviors," and will also discourage other teaching behaviors (the "procedure" level).

□ CONTRASTING TECHNIQUES FOR DOING THE SAME THING

Let me illustrate these two sets of social meanings by describing a minimal pair of techniques—two quite different ways of implementing a single format, which is the pairing of a picture with a dialog. This format has been with us for centuries, but it is still the object of comment in the literature. Hammadou,[5] for example, cites research that seems to indicate that cuing readers about an upcoming topic with a picture aids comprehension more than teaching vocabulary does, and that this is a particularly useful technique for low-proficiency students.

A Utopian Technique

First let us look at a fairly standard audiolingual procedure with seven very familiar steps, which I personally encountered as a student in an audiolingual French course:

1. The students look briefly at the picture. The purpose is to establish at least a bit of meaning in their heads before bringing in the linguistic forms.
2. The students close their books and listen to the dialog. This allows and requires them to focus on the linguistic forms.
3. The students repeat the dialog bit by bit after the teacher, and the teacher corrects their pronunciation. Focus is still very much on form.
4. The students listen again, this time with their books open. Now they are matching audible forms with visible forms. At the same time they may be picking up a little of the meaning.
5. The students read the translations that have been provided in a parallel column. The focus here is on meaning.
6. The students repeat the dialog numerous times, both for further polishing of their pronunciation and in order to commit it to memory. Emphasis is once again on form.
7. The students become able to recite the dialog correctly and unhesitatingly. The product is linguistic form, although we of course hope that as they practice, students will also have in their heads the meanings they picked up in Steps 1 and 5. (I suspect that students for whom audiolingual instruction worked may have played mental videotapes as they drilled the forms. I know I did.)

An Arcadian Technique

Now here is an alternative technique,[6] also using a picture-dialog combination, and also in seven steps:

1. Before the students come into contact with the dialog in any form, they look at the picture and describe it in whatever words or phrases they can supply in either language. They also guess what the people in the picture might be saying to each other. The teacher reflects what the students say, using an interested, appreciative tone and correct target language. The students do not repeat after the teacher. Focus is on meaning, which is expressed through linguistic forms that the students themselves already to some extent control.

2. The students listen together to the full text of the dialog, and report what they think they have heard. The teacher writes their contributions on the board, without filling in gaps and without correcting. Focus is on form, but students are unlikely to suggest forms for which they have no meanings.

3. The students listen again, this time with their books open. They now check the forms that they have suggested against the forms on the page. At the same time, they pick up at least a little meaning. Here, they are comparing the incoming material with some of the contents of holding memory.

4. The students indicate what they have not understood. The teacher explains or demonstrates meanings.

5. The students work on pronunciation either by conventional imitation-correction, or by using some learner-initiated technique such as The Human Computer.™ Focus is on form.

6. The students practice together in dyads, working for greater familiarity and fluency, though not necessarily for absolute memorization.

7. The students take turns acting out the dialog or some variant of it. Their purpose is to interest or amuse. Focus is on combination of forms and meanings.

Comparison of These Two Techniques

In the second technique, as Allwright[7] put it, classroom interaction is being managed by all present, not just by the teacher. It is not hard to guess some of the conclusions that a learner might draw from these two ways of handling the dialog-plus-picture format. From the first way, he or she might decide (1) that both the meanings and the words necessarily originate with the management, not with me; (2) that both the meanings and the words through which I am to express them are the property of management; (3) that whatever meanings I might contribute would at worst be inaccurate (be semantically wrong), at best would divert class time from the task at hand (be socially wrong), and would in any event eventually be rejected, so why bother? (4) that whatever forms I might contribute from experiences outside of class or from other sources would at worst be linguistically wrong, and at best would again be a distraction from the task at hand (be socially wrong)[8]; (5) that I'm expected to use the part of my brain that copies, but not the part that creates; (6) that power—both the power to decide what is to be done and the power to decide whether it has been done acceptably—is in the hands of the teacher; (7) that any initiative is to come from the side with the power; (8) that my conformity should be not only complete, but also quick and unhesitating; (9) that my fellow students are at worst sources of undependable models, and at best are sources of competition for the teacher's time and approval.

The second way of handling dialog-plus-picture obviously leads toward very different conclusions. Some of those conclusions would likely be (1) that my perceptions, my meanings, and the past experiences on which I base them are of interest here; (2) that whatever language I already know is going to be valued even if it isn't exactly what is in the book; (3) that initiative from me is welcomed, even needed; (4) that the person with the linguistic and administrative power—the teacher—will respond to my initiatives in ways that help me; (5) that it's all right for me to use the part of my brain that creates; (6) that guessing and approximation are acceptable; (7) that guesses and approximations do not lead me to wrong learning if I am careful to verify and correct them; (8) that I can safely assume some of the responsibility for evaluating my own accuracy; (9) that there is value in working together with other learners at almost every step in this technique.

None of this second set of conclusions can be drawn from the first technique. On the other hand, if the second technique is well executed, the first set of conclusions are unlikely to flow from it. There are of course numerous other ways to combine pictures and sample dialogs. It would be worthwhile to examine each of them to see which of these two sets of conclusions they would lead toward.

And that would be an interesting, perhaps even a profitable intellectual exercise. In the real world, however, the question is what we should do, which technique we should use, and there is no one clear answer to this question. Our answers will depend on which of a number of possible aims we are trying to reach. Let me list just a dozen such aims:

□ Provide a *linguistic sample* that the students can rely on.
□ Provide clear *overall structure* for the activity.

These two desiderata are well served by both of the two techniques I have sketched. The rest however are not:

□ Provide clear *moment-to-moment structure* for the activity.
□ Provide a few *clear models* for learning.
□ Work for maximum accuracy in *copying* of models.
□ Work within *familiar* power/status relationships.
□ Achieve *closely specified* outcomes.

These five make for very clear cognitive focus. They are consistent with the larger aims of having the class go smoothly and efficiently, and of preparing students for standardized—or for standardizable—tests. They are well served by the first of my two techniques, but poorly served by the second.

On the other hand, we may have a quite different list of desiderata:

□ *Enrich the meanings* of the forms being practiced.
□ Reduce the *status/power* differential between teacher and students.
□ Encourage the students to take *initiative.*[9]
□ Encourage *cooperation* among the students.
□ Provide *clear and reliable checks* against uncontrolled inventions of students in the early steps of this technique.

These five are much better served by the second technique than by the first. They are consistent with the larger aim of producing independent, resourceful, and responsible language users outside of the class.

TRANSACTIONAL ANALYSIS AND THE LANGUAGE CLASSROOM

We can explore a quite different side of interpersonal meaning by looking at the three "ego states" of Transactional Analysis, a brand of popular psychology still represented today, after over a quarter of a century, on book counters in drug stores and airline terminals. This interpretation of human functioning was originated by Eric Berne, but its most widely circulated exponent has been T. A. Harris.

□ EGO STATES DESCRIBED

Ego states are contrasting systems of reacting and operating that coexist within each individual. At any given moment, according to Transactional Analysis, one or another ego state is dominant over the others and largely controls how the individual is functioning. The names given them in Transactional Analysis are Child, Parent and Adult.

The Child: The ego state that Transactional Analysis calls the Child is based on memories of how one thought and felt in the early years of life. There are numerous signs that indicate when the Child has been activated. Display of emotion, either pleasant or unpleasant, is one of them.[10] Specific nonverbal signs, in some cultures at least, include rolling or downcast eyes, shrugging shoulders, and raising the hand for permission to speak. Verbally, where the Parent makes sweeping and judgmental statements, the Child is likely to emphasize lack of responsibility by using such words as "I wish" and "I dunno." The Child is interested in comparisons, and particularly in establishing that "Mine is Better" than anybody else's. When the Child ego state wants something, it has no patience with delay, but wants it now![11] People of any age can act from this ego state.

Berne differentiates between the Natural and the Adapted Child.[12] The *Natural Child* is self-expressive; the *Adapted Child* seeks to avoid trouble with the outside power structure, and to get what it wants,[13] whether by compliance, by whining, or by dissimulation. The Natural Child is the one that learns languages; the compliant variety of the Adapted Child works for good marks.

The Child is useful because it is the source of spontaneity and creativity.

The Parent: This ego state draws on memories of how things have been in the past, and acts on whatever conclusions the individual has reached about how things ought to be. Of course, one does not need to be physically a parent, or even a grown-up, in order to operate in this state. A 4-year-old who admonishes another 4-year-old that "You're not *supposed* to do it that way!" is providing an example of the Parent ego state.

When used for the benefit of a person in a less powerful position, this state is called the *Nurturing Parent.* We see this in the teacher who is very conscientious in providing the best of materials, and in encouraging students, and in generally looking out for their interests. When used in order to protect one's own interests and perpetuate one's own power, Berne speaks of the *Controlling Parent.* Here is the teacher who keeps a tight rein from moment to moment, with little trust for students' initiatives. Numerous clues indicate the moments when a person is probably under the control of the Parent ego state. Nonverbal clues may include a furrowed brow, a pointing index finger, a "horrified" or disapproving look, sighing, and patting another person on the head. Some verbal cues are "always" and "never," which are consistent with a long-standing system of conclusions that are not open to new data; evaluative words, both favorable and unfavorable; "If I were you . . ." "should," and "ought."[14] In addition, a person in this ego state is likely to use a tone of voice, gestures and specific facial expressions learned many years ago from her or his own parents.

The Parent is useful as a source of stability and continuity, and of the amount of conformity necessary to keep a society or a class from flying apart. It thus helps to control the unpredictabilities of the Child.

The Adult: Transactional Analysis applies the term Adult to the ego state in which a person "appraises her or his environment objectively, and calculates its possibilities and probabilities on the basis of past experience".[15] This is the self as it reaches out and tries to make sense of the outside world. This ego state comes into play at least as soon as an infant is able to move itself around, so that it must begin to choose among alternatives; Gattegno[16] thought it begins at the moment of conception. The incessant asking of questions, so typical of young children, is a striking manifestation of the Adult and not of the Child, just as Gattegno's emphasis on "the subjection of teaching to learning" is a call for the teacher to operate in the Adult instead of in the customary Parent state.

The Adult is sometimes compared to a computer. It reconciles what the Child wants with what the Parent will allow; it then figures out whether the result is advisable under present circumstances and, if so, how to achieve it. Some indications that the Adult is in charge are alert movement of eyes, face, and body; questions like Who?, What?, Why?; and tentative expressions like "probably" and "in my opinion," instead of dogmatic statements.[17]

Some readers will be reminded of the id, superego, and ego of classical Freudianism. The principal value of either set of terms is as a metaphor for the power relationships, emotional states, cognitive processes, and interpersonal behaviors found in the organized study of language. They should not be given the kind of reification or personification I warned about in Chapter 1.

By whatever name, all three ego states are necessary to a healthy personality. What is difficult is to keep them in proper balance with one another, and this task too is grist for the Adult's computer. The Adult, unfortunately, is also the ego state most likely to be swept aside by the others under the pressure of external events.

As Berne and Harris saw life, the ideal condition of any human being is that of being and feeling "OK." For various reasons, however, people usually see themselves as more or less "NOT-OK." Much of what they do in the three ego states is then motivated by their reactions to feeling "NOT-OK"—trying either to escape that feeling, or to live with it, or to show that others are even more "NOT-OK." This gives rise to a wide variety of what Berne and Harris call "games."

□ EGO STATES IN LANGUAGE STUDY

The old standby technique for dialog-plus-picture is a natural habitat in which the teacher's Controlling Parent and the learner's Adapted Child can coexist and reinforce each other. Indeed, some of the audiolingual courses I have observed or participated in as a learner seem to presuppose and demand this combination of ego states from start to finish. Too many students have gone through their entire language training in this relationship. I suppose we should not be surprised that after the training is over, such people often tend to put the language out of their minds entirely, or to become noticeably uncomfortable when confronted with a need to use it. The most successful audiolingual teachers I have personally observed were Marilyn Barrueta, who taught one of my daughters Spanish, and John Rassias, both of whom provided frequent and rich opportunities for the Adult and the Natural Child to take over, and both of whom turned out students willing and able to use their new language.

The second technique I outlined above, in requiring and welcoming the learners' interpretations of the picture, draws on the creativity of the Natural Child. It also allows the teacher to show Adult-type interest in what students have come up with, instead of having to judge each of their utterances Parentally as to whether it is the one expected. Repeating correctly what a student has said in faulty language is likely to be a sign of the Nurturing Parent, in contrast to the Controlling Parent's "Not quite right. Now repeat after me." This depends partly on tone of voice. When this same technique has learners compare their guesses with what they have actually found on the tape or on the printed page, it is providing an environment that calls for the learners' Adult. The closing step, in which learners perform the dialog instead of merely reciting it, again allows room for the creativity, even the whimsy, that comes from the Natural Child.

Yet we cannot bring forth the spontaneous, creative, fun-loving Natural Child just by calling for it. The primary requirement here is security. If, for example, the learner is linguistically insecure due to lack of resources, then any technique that depends on the Natural Child is likely to founder. One page in Abbs and Sexton's *Challenges* provides a positive example.[18] It features eye-catching, photographically professional photos of six attractive young adults. This in itself is almost certain to produce pleasant reactions in the students' Child. The same page ends with an invitation to compare and discuss those reactions. In between, however, the authors provide language samples in the form of tapes about the people in the pictures, and exercises that require students to extract and write down information about them. This augments the students' existing resources and so reduces whatever linguistic insecurity may be present.

The Natural Child is also likely to remain unavailable if the learner suspects there is a judgmental Controlling Parent lurking behind the invitation to create. Some of this will depend on the teacher's demeanor at the moment, but it will also depend on the students' previous experiences with him or her. Using formats that are already familiar to the learner also helps to establish a safe environment.

Then there is the learner who personally disapproves of any teacher who is *not* a Controlling Parent. This learner really wants to be allowed to be an Adapted Child, and may be very slow to participate fully in activities designed for the Natural Child. Such a situation is an occasion for the teacher's Adult to patiently observe, experiment, observe again, and experiment again.

Various configurations of these three ego states appear also in the various ways of pursuing the control of grammar. Soaking the point up gradually through the understanding of interesting and diverting samples of language the way a child does sounds, in fact, like the Child. The old-fashioned way of studying a rule, memorizing it, and then applying it in the translation of sentences for correction by the teacher exemplified the familiar Controlling Parent–Adapted Child nexus in action again.

□   A SIMPLE EXAMPLE: CLASSICAL DRILLS

The same Controlling Parent–Adapted Child nexus is found with the standard audiolingual drill format as it is usually administered:

Cues by teacher	Responses expected from students
B	ABCDEF
S	ASCDEF
T	ATCDEF
U	AUCDEF
V	AVCDEF

A fairly ordinary procedure for using such a substitution drill is very simple. It consists of two steps:

1. Teacher reads aloud each line of the drill, and students repeat it. Comprehension is checked. (This step is sometimes unnecessary, and is often omitted.)

2. Teacher reads aloud the first line of the drill, plus the cue word for the next line. A student then tries to give the entire next line in response to the cue. The teacher continues through the drill giving successive cues, to which the students reply with the corresponding whole lines.

Although students may repeat Step 2 several times, either in class or in the lab, this is ordinarily the last step. When it has been completed up to a certain performance criterion, students go on to the next drill.

It will be worthwhile to look at this common procedure from two points of view; first, in the light of what we know about human memory, and second in the light of the Transactional concepts just discussed.

With respect to the formation and storage of memories, students in the first of these two steps reproduce the utterances from what has just come in and is still in short-term memory. Research has indicated that oral production of the material carries certain advantages, at least for short-term recall. If, at the same time, students are conscious of the meaning of what they are saying, then in the networks of long-term memory the connections between the form and the meaning are strengthened. Also included in this process are the physical surroundings of classroom or lab, the fact that the connection was formed in the context of a manipulative drill, and feelings of empathy, apathy, or antipathy toward the teacher. On the other hand, there is unlikely to be found in this newly formed image much that comes from or leads to the student's own purposes, needs, or interests.

In the second step, the student is doing cued recall. Since the material that is being recalled was stored only recently, it is likely to come from the less-well-consolidated part of long-term memory (what in this book I have been calling "holding memory"). They are easier to recall now than they would be 5 minutes or 5 hours from now because they have not yet been subjected to much "crowding." Recall is achieved through a combination of rote memory, visual and acoustic images, and ad hoc mnemonic devices. As the student recalls the total utterance and finds it to be correct, new relationships among all of these memoranda are perceived, examined, and (in the Skinnerian sense) reinforced. This whole experience is then stored in its turn. It is separated by perhaps a minute or two from the corresponding image that was formed during the first step. The two images are distinct, but because they were formed so close together and under virtually identical circumstances, they soon merge as a result of "crowding." The chief value of having in Steps 1 and 2 a large number of instances containing a given utterance lies less in the number itself than in the opportunity for additional perception, examination, and reinforcement of relationships among the parts of the total configuration. One reason for the superiority of distributed practice over massed practice may be that in the latter, where the same item is repeated several times in succession, the "perceptions" do not have time to change. If this is true, then a student who is required to repeat the same thing many times at increasing speed as a means of "burning the pattern into his brain"[19] may profit from deliberately shifting the focus of attention from one part of the utterance to another as the repetitions go on.

So much for the basic drill procedure as seen from the vantage point of research on memory. Let us now look at the same activity from the perspective of Transactional Analysis.

In a conventional drill, control of what is to be said is entirely in the hands of the teacher. The student's performance is therefore necessarily limited to working with what has just been given, and involves no origination. She has available to her neither the joys nor the risks of revealing her preferences, her extracurricular activities, or her life history. With regard to communication, she is in the sheltered position of a child, or even of an unborn fetus. It is therefore only natural that her ego state during these two steps of a drill should be that of the Child: the noncreative and therefore the Adapted Child. If that Child happens to be "compliant"[20] and possessed of a fair amount of language aptitude, it will use the occasion to seek approval from the teacher's Parent by conveying the message "Look-Ma-How-I-Straightened-Up-My-Room" (i.e., by performing very well on the drill). If the teacher's ego state is that of Controlling Parent, she will accept this message as not only natural but desirable; she then will respond with a message of her own, saying in effect "That's-my-Kid." If this exchange is interrupted, such a teacher may feel seriously threatened and become noticeably upset.

The perspectives of memory theory and Transactional Analysis are not completely separate from each other. (The first chapter of Harris's book, in fact, draws heavily on the work of one pioneer in memory studies.) The storage of feelings alongside, and inextricably bound together with, linguistic material may cast light on the etiology of a disorder that sometimes appears among graduates of even the most advanced language programs. This is lathophobic aphasia (unwillingness to speak for fear of making a mistake).[21] Symptoms I have observed include avoidance of foreign language situations; addiction to continuous classroom training while resident in a country where the language is spoken; and the conviction that foreigners, some of whom want to practice the student's native language with her, would not also welcome her use of theirs.

A possible contributing cause of this condition, which can produce atrophy of language competence even in the midst of thousands of native speakers, may be that ego states are stored along with basic sentences and structural automaticities. If most or all of these ego states are Adapted Child, then subsequent attempts to speak or understand the language will inexorably revive this ego state along with the words and phrases. Even in so-called free interaction sessions, some teachers feel compelled to keep track of and eventually comment on every error. But Rivers [22] has told us that by maintaining an unbending attitude toward mistakes, we may be impeding ourselves from a "great leap forward."[23]

I would suggest, then, that we add three steps to follow the two that almost everybody uses:

3. Students give sentences from the drill, in any order, without cues. Teacher serves as referee.

From a mnemonic point of view, the students are now doing "immediate and uncued free recall." Some experimental evidence suggests that this activity enhances the ease of future, delayed free recall of the same material.[24] During this step, the student is doing something that only she can do; she is searching through her mind to see which images are available readily, which ones are less clear, and which ones seem to be unusable. This may lead to further perception and examination of relationships—an Adult function. It will at least provide an opportunity for the student to become aware of which elements and relationships she needs to listen for the next time she hears a particular sentence.

With this information about her own inventory of images, a student who is doing free recall may decide to play it safe by selecting only those that are strongest and clearest. Or she may decide to be adventurous, and select an image that she is not sure of, with the hope of filling in the missing parts and so producing a more satisfactory image for use next time. Or, finally, she may choose one that is clear because it is recent, but which she wants to reinforce quickly before it fades. This is from the mnemonic point of view.

From the Transactional point of view, the student has a range of choices opened to her, among the decisions outlined in the preceding paragraph as well as among the sentences themselves. The availability of choices is the condition that most naturally brings the Adult into play. Moreover, each of the choices is right and acceptable (though the student may still make a linguistic mistake); thus the occasion for reproach and contrition is absent.

4. Students take turns suggesting sentences that are grammatically similar to those in the drill, but that contain other vocabulary. Teacher again serves as referee.

In this step, as in the preceding one, the student has two kinds of choice open to her; the decision to be bold, cautious, or whatever, and the selection of the lexical items themselves. For the latter, however, she is no longer drawing on material that she has reheard within the past few minutes as a part of the drill. The words that she inserts into the pattern may come from very recent learning (holding memory), or from the very first day of the course (perhaps permanent memory). I believe this is a useful difference between Steps 3 an 4.

On the Transactional level, there is a parallel difference between Steps 3 and 4; the choices that lie open to the student's Adult now make it possible to express at least some of the things that she (her Parent, her Adult, or best of all her Child) would actually like to say. This leads to the final step.

5. Students use sentences derived from the preceding steps in ways that they hope will draw reactions from teacher or classmates.

One such reaction can be laughter, but others are verbal or nonverbal expressions of interest, sympathy, agreement, disagreement, and so on. The giving of genuine information is yet another possible reaction. At this stage, the whole personality may become engaged with other whole personalities, still within the framework of the drill.[25]

Although the three extra steps have been discussed separately, in practice they may be merged, and sometimes one or another of them may be omitted entirely. I have discussed them at length, but all these steps taken together should probably consume only 1 to 5 minutes of class time at the end of a drill. I would also like to state explicitly that I am *not* recommending drills as either the only or the best starter of free communication. It is essential, however, that the teacher have a clear view of the options available, and be aware of what is going on, both mnemonically and in the personality of the student.

Steps 3, 4, and 5 are more than a mere appendage to Steps 1 and 2. They can go far beyond just a superficial mitigation of a mechanical and mindless charade (which is how many teachers view drills). The activation of the Adult, which goes along with Steps 3 to 5, can extend backward and begin in Steps 1 and 2. When this happens, the purpose and also the effects of Steps 1 and 2 are transformed. No longer are they simply a relatively sterile means for mechanically "practicing and forming habits." Instead, they become a way for the learner to explore a structure, and to verify or modify his or her more or less explicit hypotheses about it. Depending on how they are used, Steps 1 and 2 may become an arena for "conscious reasoning."[26] They may even serve as an additional, very special, medium for meaningful interaction among the people in the classroom.

CHOOSING OUR MEANINGS

At the beginning of this chapter, we looked at two sets of interpersonal meanings that our students may carry away from their hours with us. Later we met a similar contrast, this time stated as the difference between configurations of ego states: Parent–Child or Adult–Adult. Some might find that a difference between "humanistic" and "nonhumanistic" crops up in each of these sets, but for reasons I have explained elsewhere,[27] I prefer to avoid that terminology.

The illustrations were taken from two widely known formats:dialog-plus-picture and simple drill. But the same points could have been made about other types of activity: reading, aural comprehension, pronunciation, and others. The examples I have given should, however, be sufficient to raise a question that would only be intensified after further illustration. That question is, Which of the larger aims do we actually choose most of the time? (Or which *should* we choose?) And I'm afraid that even after we have exercised our greatest ingenuity, we do have to choose. Those choices will be the subject of Chapter 12.

■ ■ ■   *Some Answers I Reached*

One set of personal meanings lies in the conclusions that our students reach about the nature of language, about the nature of learning, and about themselves. I have illustrated these meanings in contrasting procedures for using a picture with a matching dialog.

Another set of meanings is found in the sides of themselves and of us that our students see in action. The terminology I have used in looking at this has been borrowed from Transactional Analysis. Here the illustration consists of three suggested steps for supplementing a well-known drill procedure.

All these distinctions are perhaps just different ways of looking at a choice which the teacher constantly makes, deliberately or not, between two general aims.

■ ■ ■ *Further Questions*

□ How do these meanings figure in other types of class activity?

□ How might it be possible to combine the desirable features of the Arcadian and Utopian styles, or of the Adult and the Parent?

Notes

1. Loveday 1982.

2. As I did in 1980 and again in 1990, I am borrowing the Arcadian/Utopian distinction from W.H. Auden's *Horae Canonicae*.

3. Nunan 1988.

4. Richards & Rodgers 1986: Chapter 2.

5. Hammadou 1991.

6. From Frankel & Meyers 1991.

7. Allwright 1984.

8. This may have been one of the most destructive aspects of "Carla's" experience in her German course (Stevick 1989: Chapter 3).

9. I have discussed more fully the contrast between "control" and "initiative" in Chapter 3 of *Teaching Languages: A Way and Ways* (1980).

10. Harris 1967:118.

11. Harris 1967:91

12. Berne 1972:13.

13. Berne 1972:104.

14. Harris 1968:90.

15. Berne 1972:11.

16. Gattegno 1973.

17. Harris 1967:92.

18. Abbs & Sexton 1978.

19. Brown 1968:4.

20. Berne 1964:26.

21. Straight (private communication) points out that there is also lathophobic apraxia, an unwillingness to trust one's own comprehension sufficiently to act on it.

22. Rivers 1972:81.

23. Berne 1964:26; 1972:104.

24. Darley & Murdock 1971.

25. Goldstein 1963, quoted in Curran 1968:348.

26. Diller 1971:73.

27. Stevick 1990.

Chapter 9

The Language Class as a Small Group

Questions I Asked Myself:

☐ What are some of the personal meanings that the events of the classroom may hold for the teacher?

☐ What kinds of power structure may be found in formal education?

INTRODUCTION

Chapters 7 and 8 discussed some of the things that go on inside students as they encounter various aspects of the process of language study: that is, what the activity of study can "mean" to them. This chapter will begin with a hasty glance at what a language course may "mean" to the teacher, and will then go on to summarize a bit of literature on the interpersonal "meanings" of power structures, trust, and "community."[1]

THE TEACHER

The concentration in Chapters 7 and 8 on the anxieties, frustrations, and defensive actions of the student may have left the impression that the teacher is relatively free from such feelings, or has no need to engage in such maneuvers. This, of course, is not the case. Teachers are human too!

☐ INSIDE THE TEACHER

For reasons one may darkly suspect, the literature about what goes on inside the teacher is much slimmer than the literature about students. The language teaching profession seems to have been particularly neglected: Silberman's well-known *Crisis in the Classroom*[2] contained no significant reference to our field; Miles[3] mentions FL learning as one area in which we need to use "an analysis of here-and-now events," but he does not elaborate; Lyon's[4] book on humanistic

175

education contains specific examples from mathematics, science, and NL teaching, but none from foreign languages. Yet the fears and anxieties of teachers are probably no less than those of their students: they differ only in form. Teachers, too, are human!

As the terms are used in this chapter, "fear" differs from "anxiety" partly in that fear is occasioned by external, relatively objective threats: an onrushing car, a sinister-looking group in the shadows near the bus stop, seeing one's child pick and swallow what may have been a poisonous mushroom. In contrast, a large component of anxiety comes from inner or subjective conditions.[5]

The inner, subjective conditions that contribute to anxiety are, to a large extent, the same "NOT-OK" feelings mentioned in Chapter 8. A person in the occupational status "teacher" may seek protection or relief from those feelings by operating in the Parent state. The teacher patterns her Parent stage after one or more of those powerful figures who in her own early childhood were the very embodiment of OK-ness, goodness, and adequacy. From raw materials such as these, she may construct an image of herself which she shows to the public, and in which she also comes to believe.

Rogers[6] described the self-concept as "an organized configuration of perceptions of the self which are admissible to awareness." If, as Darwin said, self-preservation is the first law of life, then preservation of the symbolic self may be the fundamental principle of human motivation.[7] Threats to this image therefore constitute a rich and inexhaustible source of anxieties. Disparities between those motives that are admissible to awareness and those that are not are the basis for a wide variety of what Transactional Analysis calls "games."

This is not to say that everything teachers do is merely an expression of one or more anxieties, or that all their actions are moves in unwholesome "games." Mutually respectful, nonexploitative relationships can exist in a language class, and sometimes do. Some "games" even make social contributions that outweigh the complexity of their motivations.[8] The results of unacknowledged motives may still be benign.

Thus Curran[9] spoke of the creative thinker as being "sick to teach," as suffering from a powerful and partly irrational craving to have people understand him or her on the intellectual level. This craving exists in addition to the basic human need for acceptance on the emotional plane. Any teacher who plans a lesson with care and imagination is, in that respect, a creative thinker with a "sickness" to receive appreciation. A native-speaking teacher (or even a nonnative one who has made a heavy personal investment in the target culture) may see learning of the language as acceptance of him and of his culture, and failure to learn as rejection. This is another normal and generally benign kind of "sickness," to which language teachers are more susceptible than most of their colleagues. The passion to help one's students grow in their own individuality, becoming emotionally more whole, and intellectually more self-sufficient,[10] is perhaps the most benign of teacher attitudes. It requires great personal strength. (What are its sources?)

□   A HYPOTHETICAL QUESTIONNAIRE

"A teacher cannot make much headway in understanding others or in helping others to understand themselves unless he is endeavoring to understand himself. If he is not engaged in this endeavor, he will continue to see those whom he teaches through the bias and distortions of his own unrecognized needs, fears, desires, anxieties, and hostile impulses."[11] In the pages that follow, we shall therefore look at some of the ways in which a single act may be compatible with one purpose on the public, acknowledgeable, social level, and with a quite unrelated, not-so-acknowledgeable motive on the psychological level. In other words, we shall explore a few of the "games" that language teachers sometimes play. This material is set out in the shape of seven replies to a questionnaire. The responses are imaginary, but they are drawn from my observation of a number of very real teachers, including myself. Although they make rather speculative use of Transactional terminology, they are not intended as a poor folks' guide to individual psychoanalysis. They are only an attempt to suggest some of the complexities of teacher motivation (Items b and c), and to show how challenges (Item d) to the self-concept (Item a) may contribute to anxiety.

The four items of the questionnaire are the following. (Note that while Items c and d in each reply are potentially consistent with Item b in the same reply, they do not necessarily go along with it.)

QUESTIONNAIRE

I am a teacher, and as a teacher _____(a)_____.
This is true or necessary because _____(b)_____.
   (Social level: real reason, or publicly acceptable excuse?)
I also *feel* this way because _____(c)_____.
   (Psychological level: additional bonus, or actual motive?)
What bothers me most is _____(d)_____.

The following sets of replies are imaginary, but are based on people (including myself) whom I have met over the years:

1. a. I am a teacher, and as a teacher I know my subject matter.
    b. This is true or necessary because I am the students' link with the realities of the foreign language.
    c. I also *feel* this way because whatever I do must be accepted as right. (A Parent posture, but related to a NOT-OK Child who is trying to escape being "wrong.")
    d. What bothers me most is someone claiming that I have made a mistake.
2. a. I am a teacher, and as a teacher, I know more than my students know.
    b. This is true or necessary because I am a native speaker of the language, or have studied it for many years.

   c. I also *feel* this way because I can always win the basic Child–Child game of "Mine is Better."

   d. What bothers me most is a student who has made his way into my class in spite of coming from a home where the language is used, or having lived where it is spoken.

3. a. I am a teacher, and as a teacher I must correct my students when they make mistakes.

   b. This is true or necessary because I am their link with the realities of the foreign language.

   c. I also *feel* this way because in correcting them (or in praising them when they are right), I identify with my own OK-Parent sources, who were always evaluating my conduct for me, who was a NOT-OK Child.

   d. What bothers me most is the suggestion that I could teach as well or better if I would limit my interventions so as to require and allow more independent mental activity from the students.

4. a. I am a teacher, and as a teacher I must decide what is to happen in the class, and when.

   b. This is true or necessary because I have had more experience in language classes than the students have had, as well as professional training in linguistics and pedagogy.

   c. I also *feel* this way because in controlling my students, I identify with my own OK-Parent sources (perhaps my actual parents, or my own teachers, or some combination of these), who were always controlling me, a NOT-OK Child. Besides, it's a matter of finally getting a little respect, which I as a NOT-OK Child never got.

   d. What bothers me most is petitions, suggestions, or complaints from students regarding my procedures.

5. a. I am a teacher, and as a teacher I should do my best to meet the expressed needs of my students.

   b. This is true or necessary because their expressions of desire or preference can provide me with valuable hints about what they are ready to respond to.

   c. I also *feel* this way because by complying with their requests, I may be able to win from them the kind of OK strokes that my Child has always lacked. Or perhaps by doing so I may identify with my own Parent sources as a provider of necessities and a granter of boons.

   d. What bothers me most is close, authoritarian supervision, or a heavy workload, or whatever prevents me from complying with my students' requests.

6. a. I am a teacher, and as a teacher I respond to opportunities as they arise; I therefore have no need to prepare for classes.

   b. This is true or necessary because fresh material is generally more stimulating than material that is cut and dried.

   c. I also *feel* this way because my Child doesn't like to carry responsibility and, anyhow, it would rather spend the time in other ways.

    d. What bothers me most is suggestions that I would teach better if I made detailed, written lesson plans. To do so would restrict my creativity, cramp my style.

7. a. I am a teacher, and as a teacher I should tend to business.

    b. This is true or necessary because if too much time is spent in ways that are unrelated to the task at hand, the task will not get completed.

    c. I also *feel* this way because by limiting the scope of my contacts with the students, I can avoid expressing or perceiving emotion, thus keeping from view the Child that I either distrust or am ashamed of.

    d. What bothers me most is suggestions that I should encourage the expression of honest feelings as a part of the learning experience.

Notice that if we paste together the b items from the seven replies shown in the questionnaire we come out with the qualifications of a rather fine teacher:

> Someone who knows the language either natively or very well, with thorough knowledge of the subject matter. Has been trained in linguistics and pedagogy, and has also had classroom experience. Tends to business, but uses fresh material and is open to suggestions from students.

If in the same way we combine all the c items, we arrive at a picture of a miserable wretch who is compulsively passing on to her students the same unpleasantness that she experienced at the hands of her own elders. This is a person who will resist bitterly any attempt to deprive her of "the gratifications that reside in the central, highly differentiated teacher role" and who has strong "fears of fallibility and loss of status."[12] This is also the person about whom Lyon wrote the words that were quoted earlier in this chapter, and who leads Williams to assert that professors are more likely than most people to ridicule ignorance, to beat down imagination and creativeness, and to be unsympathetic toward universal human weakness.[13]

It should be emphasized that the picture that has just been painted on the social level (Items b) and the picture on the psychological level (Items c) are not necessarily found together; they may be found in the same person, but either can, of course, exist separate from the other. Most of us probably embody some kind of mixture, for a conscious wish (e.g., Items a) usually has more than one motivation[14] and drives are interrelated, not mutually exclusive.[15]

To say that our laudable aims (Items a) sometimes rest on motivations that we would rather not talk about is not a condemnation either of the aims themselves or of the motivations. It is merely analogous to the observation that a person may produce a linguistic analysis (or write a book like this one) as part of a game of "Mine is Better" or "Look-Ma-No-Hands." The analysis may be valid or invalid, and the thesis of this book worthy or unworthy of attention, independent of the psychological state of the people who wrote them. But there is one respect in which the analogy between teacher and writer fails. Insofar as a teacher is working from c-type motives, he is susceptible to threats of the kinds represented by Items d. These threats produce anxieties, which in turn become the occasion for defensive reactions on the part of the teacher. These reactions become an involuntary, partially subliminal, but for all that more compelling, component of the teacher's input to the continuing interchange between him and his students. Jersild, a veteran observer of the educational scene, believes that "many teachers and students have lived with anxiety day after day, scarcely knowing that the burden might be lightened. . . . Schools and colleges have usually offered them little in the way of help except academic activities that sidestep anxiety, or perhaps even increase it."[16] He further points out that "there are few unforbidden, frank and direct channels for expressing hostility in education but ["and therefore"?! EWS] much of what is done in the name of education or scholarship is, indirectly, a means of venting hostility" (9). (I wonder to what extent this statement is also true for "love" or "affection," as well as for "hostility.")

What, then, is the teacher to do in the face of her internal inconsistencies and the complexities of her own personality? Clearly, she must get herself sorted out, and that is a job for the Adult. But how is the adult to take control? Jakobovits and Gordon[17] did not use the terminology of Eric Berne, but one of the recurring themes of their book was exactly that. Their chief suggestion was that the teacher participate in "Encounter Transaction Workshops." On a more immediate and mechanical level, I suspect that one of the most important effects of Interactional Analysis[18] was to put the teacher into her Adult mode.

This ends our very brief look "inside the teacher." In Chapters 7 and 8, we examined in greater detail some of the things that go on inside the learner. We turn now to the interactions that go on *between* teachers and learners.

AUTHORITY STRUCTURES

The most fundamental fact about any social system, including a language class, is the way the power issues have been settled.[19] On the chessboard of academic-style education, the most powerful single piece is the teacher. Society invests him or her with authority, which is the right to exercise power. The personal style with which she or he wields that authority is a principal determinant of the power structure of the class. It is at these issues that we shall look first.

Zaleznik and Moment described four prototypical patterns of authority. The first of these they called paternal-assertive. This pattern is characterized by aggressiveness, dominance and initiation of interaction on the part of the authority figure. This figure avoids tender feelings, but may be deeply concerned with the advancement and reward of subordinates, particularly the ones who accept his or her form of authority.[20] One of the problems common under this type of authority structure is that the subordinates—in our case, the language learners—may develop anxiety about their own capacity to act assertively. Much of what is called "traditional" language teaching—Grammar-Translation and

Audiolingualism—usually fitted this pattern, but the same can be said of the simplest forms of computer-assisted instruction.

Zaleznik and Moment's second authority pattern is maternal-expressive. Here, the leader avoids initiation and aggressiveness, but concentrates instead on creating affective ties with subordinates, exercising control over them by withdrawing affection and thereby threatening them with rejection. If the subordinates fail to get enough attention from this kind of authority figure, they may react with anger or with depression. This absence of initiation and aggressiveness by the "knower" is found in the first three stages of Community Language Learning (Chapter 11), but at no stage in that method does the knower attempt to control the learners by threatening to reject them.

In the fraternal-permissive prototype, the leader consciously minimizes any status differentiation, aiming instead at equality. Authority resides in something outside the group, such as a task (e.g., learning a language, or preparing for work in a foreign country) or a set of ideals (such as various Arcadian motivations). The needs of the subordinates appear to dominate in this relationship. The leader shares with his subordinates as much responsibility as possible, and tries to encourage them. An example in our field is the learner-centered curriculum. In this style of teaching, not everything is planned before the class meets. Rather, the learners participate in ongoing decisions about what is to be taught and how it is to be taught.[21]

In many ways, this third pattern might seem to be the one at which a personally secure language teacher ought to aim. Considerable evidence indicates that when subordinates exercise significant amounts of control over what is going on, their performance and productivity improve.[22] Perhaps this is another aspect of what in Chapter 5 was called the "generation effect." Much has been written in our field about individualization of foreign language instruction, and "learner-centered" education is stylish in many circles. Zaleznik and Moment, however, warn that the fraternal style may not be ideal for a task-oriented group, and a language class is, by definition, task-oriented to a large extent. If the emphasis is too much on the group itself, with corresponding deemphasis of evaluation and status differentiation, this may keep the needed work from getting done; if this happens, it, in turn, may produce anxieties related to the professional or academic reasons that caused the students to take the course in the first place. In the terminology of Lambert, if the "integrative" side of the enterprise crowds out the "instrumental" side, there is likely to be trouble. But even without this kind of concern, there are some students—and some teachers too—who simply need a given style of authority of one parental variety or the other.[23,24]

One may speculate that the supreme affront to a "paternal" leader is refusal to obey; that the most upsetting experience for a "maternal" leader is to feel that he or she has not been properly appreciated; and that the ultimate disappointment for a leader who has aimed at a "fraternal" style is to realize that others will not give up their demand that he or she be parental.[25]

The fourth and last authority pattern that Zaleznik and Moment list is the rational-procedural. It avoids some of the pitfalls of the other three by minimizing emotional and interpersonal relationships. The person in charge seeks to invoke the constraints of impersonal authority, in the form of objectives, laws, and regulations—or an externally imposed syllabus or a very detailed set of teaching materials. Unfortunately, however, this prototype also has its disadvantage: by failing to reach individuals at sufficiently deep levels in their emotional experience, it may produce very little involvement or creativity.

If authority systems in language teaching were arranged along a continuum from authoritarian to permissive, the first extreme would surely find its embodiment in the work of Borden and Busse,[26] two "speech correctionists" of the 1920s. The people with whom they worked were not called "students," but "patients," many of whom suffered from "defects of foreign dialect." These "defects" were apparently regarded as being comparable to catarrh or cleft palate. The style of "treatment" employed by these authors to remove one common symptom was the following:

> If the patient stubbornly [!] persists in substituting T as in TOWN for TH as in THIN . . . hold the blade of his tongue forcibly down in its proper position by means of a wire form [called] a "fricator." If he persists in substituting TH for S, push his tongue back into its proper position with a forked metal brace . . . known technically as a "fraenum fork."

The therapist is warned that once the patient can make the sound in isolation, he must practice it in larger units. He must also "ruthlessly eliminate the old defective sound from his speech—even from colloquial speech with intimate friends." The fraenum fork and the fricator make Borden and Busse's method seem bizarre to us, but how many of our more recent methods have been more sophisticated in their approach to personality, or less authoritarian in their assumptions about the distribution of power?

Zaleznik and Moment find that there is much evidence that, under certain conditions, a participative and relatively permissive style of leadership has been accompanied by marked improvement in group productivity, morale, and emotional involvement. The reasons why this is so are not entirely clear, but these authors suggest that a major factor is that in this pattern there is more attention to what they call "reality-testing." But if reality-testing is, in fact, the essential element, they point out, it is compatible with a great range of leadership styles, from permissive to stern.[27]

Curran apparently was thinking along the same lines when he wrote about "the maturity and therapy of limits."[28] In a language classroom, we tend to think first about the limits imposed by the subject matter, beginning with the structure and vocabulary of the language itself. The student certainly needs to learn to deal with these. But in a class, as in any group process, the very presence of others imposes limits on each student.[29] There are also, of course, the limits that any human being carries from his physical nature and his past history. The struggle, at once collective and individual, to live with these limits is an essential element of the process of maturing.[30] It is also a principal source of forces that are latent or active in every classroom, potentially supportive of learning, but seldom harnessed to the constructive purposes of the teacher.[31]

As students set out to test reality in its many aspects, they meet the teacher at every turn. There are at least four ways in which this is true. Most obviously, perhaps, the teacher's culturally conferred status makes her or him a link with the reality of those rewards and punishments (e.g., grades, promotions, recommendations) that society attaches to performance in the course. From another point of view, her or his superior knowledge of the language and its related subject matter make her or him an indispensable link with the realities of whatever content the students hope to learn. Third, the teacher's training and accumulated experience mean that she or he is a potentially useful medium through whom to deal with the realities of organizing the work to be done. Finally, because of her or his pivotal position in the classroom, the teacher is, for each individual, one important link with the realities that are represented by the other students.

In each of these respects, the teacher is a door that is either open or closed. Or, to change the figure of speech again, the teacher is a bridge. Before a student is willing to venture out on a reality-testing expedition in one or another of these directions, she checks to see whether the bridge that leads in that direction looks safe. If it appears shaky or slippery she will, according to her temperament, be cautious or aggressive, obsequious or resentful, but in any case learning will be affected.[32] This brings us to the crucially important question of building mutual trust in a small group such as a language class.

INTERPERSONAL TRUST

There is a fairly large body of literature on this subject. Perhaps its most fundamental and, at the same time, most controversial concept is that trust is produced by behavior that can be changed, and that, in turn, it is functionally related to desirable changes in the behavior of groups.[33] In contrast to this idea is the view, held by many teachers, that "people are the way they are": a teacher who presumes to try to do anything with adolescent or adult students except impart information to them is aiming at a goal that is as inappropriate as it is unattainable. If students are assumed to be "plastic learners in a fixed cultural environment,"[34] these teachers seem to regard them as plastic only in the most narrowly cognitive sense, and as being in other respects quite rigid.

The primal importance of trust is implied in Gibb's summary of the deepest and earliest concerns in the life of a group. They occur, he says, in the following order: first "acceptance," then "data flow," then "goal formation," and finally "control."[35] In everyday English, this means that people must feel relatively secure with those around them before they will say what is really on their minds; that only after a group knows what its members have on their minds can it figure out what it wants to do; and that there is no point in trying to decide how to use the time, energy, and other resources of a group until its goals have become clear.

Gibb was writing primarily about the "T-Groups" so popular at that time— therapy groups with no preestablished goals or control mechanisms. In a language class, of course, the intellectual parts of the goals are already well defined and the administrative aspects of the control mechanisms are fairly clear. I believe, however, that if we take into account the nonintellectual and nonadministrative aspects, Gibb's scenario is valid in our world as well as in his. Koch, in fact, found a very similar sequence in intercultural workshops in Germany; the workshop atmosphere reduced inhibitions and established an initial level of trust; within this atmosphere, participants felt a strong need to communicate with one another ("data flow"); and in this context, superior language learning took place.[36] Levertov, teaching creative writing to native speakers, observed that her students seldom made really sincere suggestions as long as they felt that they were among strangers whom they could not trust.[37]

A brief article by Giffin summarized much of what had been written up to that time concerning the variables that tend to build trust or destroy it. Some of the factors listed by Giffin are the following:

1. B is more likely to trust A if B feels that A has acted in a way that has shown conditional trust in B; and if A seems to expect that B will in turn act in a trustworthy way; and if A indicates that she herself is ready to reciprocate whatever trust B shows for her.

2. B is more likely to trust A if A makes an enforceable promise to him.

3. Certain kinds of communication from A tend to increase B's trust in her:

   a. Communication in which B feels that A is describing what she sees, rather than passing judgment on it.

   b. Communication in which B feels that A is interested in solving a problem, rather than in controlling him or someone else.

   c. Communication in which A seems to be stating tentative rather than final conclusions.

   d. Communication that B sees as spontaneous and sincere, not motivated by some concealed purpose.

   e. Communication that means to B that A is personally involved in the exchange, and not just an aloof observer.

To anyone who has read Chapter 8, these five criteria for communication will have a familiar ring. Points 3a–c mean, in Transactional terminology, that a trustworthy communicator is a person who is operating in her Adult ego state; points 3d–e say that the communicator who wants to be trusted must avoid the appearance of engaging in ulterior transactions.

These same five criteria are also reminiscent of some of the characteristics of what Curran called a "counseling response"; warmth, understanding, and acceptance, with the communicator involved but at the same time able to deal objectively with emotional data.[38] As students explore the realities of the limits listed above, they often become anxious. They may then react against the person or persons who are the voice or the occasion of these limits. Here I have described in three different ways the kind of response by teacher or parent that can aid such a student to begin to distinguish the limits from the people who represent them, and so to deal with his own negative reactions and conflicts.[39] This is a major step in building an atmosphere of mutual trust.

In this light, we may take a fresh look at what is essential in the role of "teacher." As Chastain[40] has rightly pointed out, the teacher should first of all appear to the students as a strong person, a source of stability. Otherwise their deepest need, at the level of security, will remain unfulfilled. Attempts to motivate them at less fundamental levels will then prove largely futile. This does not mean, however, that strength can be manifested only by ubiquity, omnipotence, omniscience, or inflexibility. Frank,[41] writing not about teachers but about trainers in T-Groups, said that dependency on the trainer should be limited to looking to her for general guidance on how to proceed, and for clarification of what is happening.

A language class is not a T-Group, of course. The most inevitable difference is that the former is committed to the task of learning a language, while the latter has no outside commitments at all. We must therefore assign to the teacher at least the additional role of an information source. But some of the activities at which teachers spend great amounts of time do not fall clearly under any of these three rubrics. None of these functions, for example, requires the teacher to emit a steady stream of praise and blame, or of confirmation and correction. None requires him to be one of the participants in every exchange, or to do 50% or more of the talking, or to give the students detailed guidance at every step. None requires him to display either wittiness or erudition, or to be "buddies" with his students. While any of these styles may be compatible with good teaching, none is essential. Each of them, furthermore, is sometimes used by teachers for their own personal reasons; when this happens, these kinds of behavior may begin to interfere with learning.

A GOAL: "VOICE IN COMMUNITY"

The preceding parts of this chapter have perhaps concentrated too much on the seamy side of teacher–student relationships. Let us turn now to the more positive side, and to description of a desirable style of dynamics for the language classroom. I shall label it "Voice in Community."

Rivers[42] says that a class "consists of individuals who have gradually been welded into a group with some knowledge of each other's activities, and some interest in each other's affairs." This description implies that a certain amount of "data flow" is taking place within such a class, and this in turn means that some level of interpersonal trust exists. It does not, however, tell us how pervasive the trust is, or the "depth" from which the "data" are flowing.

A sustained examination of the role of group forces in language learning was found in the Northeast Conference report on "motivation."[43] Libit and Kent, in their contribution to that report, mention the obvious fact that "accomplishment is a source of motivation." This observation relates principally to the level of "esteem" in the student's Maslovian "hierarchy of needs." The writers precede that statement, however, with the more profound observation that "fear is one of the first obstacles to be eliminated." This, of course, is the deeper "security" need in the same hierarchy. They go on to urge teachers to remember that "it is a 'soul'—a self—that the student wants to express in the foreign language." Curran goes even further when he says that a student learning a language under conditions of minimum anxiety may actually develop a "new language self."[44] He would concur with Libit and Kent in emphasizing the importance of the group as a source of motivation in foreign language learning,[45] and in their belief that "a classroom can be an intimate place where each student knows his place in the group, and knows that others recognize him." Libit and Kent, Curran,[46] Wilson and Wattenmaker,[47] Moskowitz,[48] and Rivers[49] are unusually rich sources of concrete ideas for expediting "data flow" in language class.

Lambert, too, agreed that "the challenge for the teacher is to go beyond the mere achievement motives of students, and to link language teaching with more appropriate and more productive motives."[50] Some of these motives, surely, must be found in the many "informal and quasi-formal communities" that may come into being either in the classroom or outside it.[51] In such a community all members—"teacher" as well as "students"—see that if any one of them is to get ahead, he or she must depend on the others. People who perceive themselves to be in such a relationship tend to act in ways that are consistent with that perception.[52] Then, as realities come to be not only experienced individually but also shared, learning becomes more profound for students and teacher alike.[53]

Some beautifully perceptive remarks about classroom communities appear in a brief essay by the late George Elliott,[54] a teacher of creative writing at Syracuse University. They are worth quoting at some length:

> A good class pulls together into a kind of community. It is only an occasional community [and] there is no way to prescribe how to bring such a community into being. . . . Freedom to make or not to make a community of a class is essential if you are to make it at all.
>
> An alternative to squatting sequestered in the fastness of pedantry is to strive in the classroom to let come into being a fragile community. The extraordinary ingredient in making communities is not possessing the power to make them, but exercising that power, wanting them enough to risk failure. Our life is so far from nature now . . . that many no longer know they have the power of communion, of making even fragile communities, and many have too little hope of exercising that power successfully even to try, even to want to try. The faith must be restored. What can we who are believers but not great prophets do to restore this faith except exercise that power as best we can?

It is in a community such as this that the student can, in several senses, find her "voice." Most literally, she is more likely to use her larynx for purposes other than mimicry. In addition, and more important, her unique presence will be felt by those around her, and her personality will express itself in what she says.[55] If the teacher's own ideas about how he ought to act are not too rigid, he too may come to have a voice in this kind of community.[56] If he is fortunate, he will even find himself sharing with other human beings his knowledge, experience, and enthusiasm on subjects of mutual interest!

■ ■ ■   Some Answers I Reached

Teachers' pictures of what they should be for their students vary. Each such picture rests partially on objective fact, but partially also on inner needs. Different kinds of inner need may make teachers susceptible to different kinds of frustration and threat.

In dealing with a class, a teacher may rely mostly on exerting authority, or on giving or withholding affection, or on eliciting initiative and cooperation from the students, or on appealing to their concern for the subject matter. Each of these styles can work, but each has its drawbacks. For language classes especially, a suitable goal is often to help students develop their own "voices in community."

■ ■ ■   Further Questions

□ How feasible is it, or even how wise, for a teacher to try to teach in a basic power distribution that does not come naturally to him or her?

□ What might make such a redistribution of power easier for the teacher, and more likely to succeed?

Notes

1. Although the references on which this chapter is based are much the same as those for the corresponding chapter of the first edition of this book, I was interested to find that its basic conclusions are at least consistent with an outstanding review of the subject found in an unpublished paper by Zoltan Dörnyei, which I was privileged to read.

2. Silberman 1970.

3. Miles 1964:473.

4. Lyon 1971.

5. Jersild 1955:27.

6. Hayakawa 1962:229.

7. Hayakawa 1962:226.

8. Benne 1964:163.

9. Curran 1972:114.

10. Lyon 1971:197.

11. Jersild 1955:14.

12. Miles 1964:470.

13. Lyon 1971:32.

14. Maslow 1970:22.

15. Maslow 1970:25.

16. Jersild 1955:8.

17. Jakobovits & Gordon 1974.

18. Moskowitz 1968, 1971, 1974; Krumm 1973.

19. Ilfeld & Lindeman 1971:588; Gibb 1964:283; Bennis 1964:251.

20. Zaleznik & Moment 1964:273.

21. Nunan 1988:2.

22. Bachman 1964:272.

23. I myself am personally drawn to the fraternal-permissive style of teaching, and of relationships in general. It is not a panacea, however. I remember an otherwise cordial colleague who once wrote me a very angry note because of my espousal of such principles. And in a class that I was attempting to conduct on this basis, one of the military students felt strong outrage at being asked to participate in decisions about content and procedures, but his personal interpretation of military discipline did not allow him to express this feeling to me. Apparently for this reason, he developed an acute psychosomatic reaction which resulted in a week's hospitalization. And I once heard a respected colleague publicly and contemptuously refer to the first edition of this book as "Memory, Meaning and Madness."

24. Carl Rogers in LaForge 1971:58.

25. LaForge 1971:48.

26. Borden & Busse 1925:183.

27. Borden & Busse 1925.

28. Curran 1968: Chapter 10.

29. Curran 1968:211.

30. Curran 1968:213.

31. Bradford 1960, quoted in LaForge 1971:47; Miles 1964:469.

32. Jersild 1955:62; Curran 1968:231.

33. Giffin 1967:233.

34. Benne 1964:24; Miller 1964.

35. Gibb 1964:283.
36. Koch 1972.
37. Levertov 1970:159.
38. Curran 1961:81.
39. Curran 1968:215.
40. Chastain 1971:370.
41. Frank 1964:449.
42. Rivers 1968:167.
43. Nelson et. al. 1970.
44. Curran 1961:92.
45. Nelson et. al. 1970:79.
46. Curran 1972.
47. Wilson & Wattenmaker 1973.
48. Moskowitz 1978.
49. Rivers 1972.
50. Nelson et. al. 1970:87.
51. Nelson et. al. 1970:61.
52. Loomis 1959:305.
53. Levertov 1970:188.
54. Elliott 1970:50.
55. Hawkes 1970:96.
56. Gibb 1964:302.

Part III
Method

Chapter 10

Three Views of Method

A Question I Asked Myself:

☐ How might what has been said in the chapters on memory and meaning be applied to methods in the actual teaching of languages?

INTRODUCTION: THE RIDDLE OF THE RIGHT METHOD

In 1950 I received a master of arts degree in what was then called "Teaching English as a Foreign Language." At that time, I knew all that anyone could ever need to know about our field—all about how learning of languages proceeds and about how teaching should be carried out. My native land, pedagogically speaking, was a lovely little country called "the Oral Approach."

I am no longer so wise as I was then. After a few busy but uncomplicated years, my omniscience was first shaken as a result of experiences preparing language study materials in Africa during the years 1956 to 1958, then finally demolished between 1964 and 1970 by frequent consultation and travel for the Peace Corps. During these years, I visited new methods and unfamiliar approaches—foreign "countries" with such names as "Cognitive Code Learning," "Programmed Instruction," and "the Silent Way." In some of those countries, I even became a resident alien and took out working papers. To which of these, I wondered, will I give my final allegiance?

The answer has turned out to be "None of them." Instead of becoming a citizen of any one country, I have for better or for worse become an explorer of Terra Incognita, an unknown land that does not lie anywhere on the terrain whose boundaries are made up of differences in linguistic analyses or textbook formats or overt classroom techniques.

One of the circumstances that turned my eyes toward Terra Incognita may be stated in the form of a riddle:

> In the field of language teaching, Method A is the logical contradiction of Method B: if the assumptions from which A claims to be derived are correct, then B cannot work, and vice versa. Yet one colleague is getting excellent results with A and another is getting comparable results with B. How is this possible?

Sometimes the same riddle (and I believe that it *is* ultimately the same riddle) takes a different form:

> Why does Method A (or B) sometimes work so beautifully and at other times so poorly?

My guess, briefly stated, is that if we leave the methodological space whose dimensions are linguistics and technique and overt behavior, we may find that each method, when used well, fulfills in its own way a set of requirements lying beneath and beyond any one of them. The answer to just what these requirements are lies largely in Terra Incognita. That is how the first edition of this book came to be written, and why after 20 years I have ventured this update.

Earlier parts of this book have included occasional comments on specific techniques, but always with the main focus on other matters. Now it is time to look more directly at some existing methods in the light of what I have been saying about "memory" and "meaning." What, then, do these thoughts on *Memory* and *Meaning* tell us about our final topic, which is *Method*? In this chapter we will look at method from three different but mutually complementary points of view: a general psychodynamic sketch, the communicative approach, and a format I will call "bridges." Then in Chapter 11 we will examine close-up a half dozen specific methods. Finally in Chapter 12 we will probe the tension that often exists between diversity and tradition in our field.

A VIEW FROM INSIDE THE LEARNER

A Turkish class in its 30th hour was drilling itself on a pattern that usually is reserved for about the 150th hour. With very few interventions by the teacher, the students were making up the drill as they went along, proceeding with deliberation, but smoothly. There was noticeable lack of tension. As their supervisor, I complimented them and their teacher, at which one of them replied in Turkish "we-thank-you" (*teşekkür ederiz*), a form that he had never heard. This happened to be the very form that had been the subject of discussion among the staff only a few days earlier. We had noted that even our advanced students failed to come up with this form when they needed it, using instead *teşekkür ederim* ("I-thank-you") as an all-purpose translation of English "thank you." So this particular class session was doubly delightful to me. How did it happen? I'm not sure, of course. But the following are my best guesses.

☐ PERFORMANCE: SELF-STARTED OR REFLECTIVE?

We may begin by distinguishing between two kinds of performance: that which is *self-started* and that which is *reflective* or echoic.[1]

Insofar as a student is bouncing back what the teacher is throwing at him, his performance is reflective. The extreme case is mimicry of pronunciation, where the meaning of a word, even if the student knows it, is unimportant. But substitution drills, transformation drills, and other conventional kinds of grammatical calisthenics are commonly about as reflective as phonetic mimicry is. Even retelling of stories, answering questions about a dialog, or discussing a reading selection, though they contain some elements of productivity, are still largely reflective.

Insofar as performance is self-started, on the other hand, the student does not start from the assigned task of following a language model that the teacher or the textbook has provided. Instead, he starts with something that he wants to say and with a person to whom he wants to say it. He then draws on the models that are available within himself, in order to fulfill his purpose. The Turkish class that I described above had been working in a self-starting manner, rather than reflectively, for most of its 30 hours. The students had been both allowed and required to notice what they were doing, and to piece together their own individual pictures of how Turkish works. This is, I suspect, the reason why one of them arrived quite naturally and spontaneously at the form "we-thank-you." It also may account for the performance on which I had complimented them in the first place.

Language teachers have produced a constant flow of articles about how to get back from students the responses that we want them to give; we like to worry about the best way to design materials for this purpose, and the most appropriate kinds of teacher behavior; we construct fascinating and sometimes useful models of what must go on in the student's head as he acquires the ability to repeat a dialog or go nimbly through a drill. Whenever we do these things, we are concentrating on reflectivity; indeed, it is this variety of performance that has received almost all our attention. From this point of view we ask ourselves "how?": "How" do learners use their brains in learning.[2] Or "how" does the learner become able to encode or decode grammatical sequences?[3] Next we analyze the various levels of the linguistic side of "what" they say.[4] But we rarely ask "where" the content of the sequences comes from, or "when," or "why." We forget that social decisions are made prior to linguistic constructions.[5] Rivers[6] has remarked that "unless [the students'] adventurous spirit is given time to establish itself as a constant attitude, most of what is learned will be stored unused, and we will produce individuals who are inhibited and fearful in situations requiring language use."

□ LEARNING: DEFENSIVE OR RECEPTIVE?

Chapter 6 introduced the idea of a "dimension of depth," using evidence from studies of human memory. Chapters 7 and 8 tried to show what may be found along that dimension, borrowing theoretical equipment first from Maslow and then from Berne and Harris. Using this same metaphor, self-started performance comes from somewhere deeper within the student than reflective performance does. The chapters on memory generally support the belief that, other things being equal, the "deeper" the source of a sentence within the student's personality, the more lasting value it has for learning the language. This carefully qualified conclusion is not likely to cause much argument. What is likely to be more controversial is a further assertion that I believe to be justified by experience if not by experiment: that this same "depth" factor, far from being an additional, minor consideration to be taken into account only when weightier factors are equal, is in fact more to be reckoned with than technique, or format, or underlying linguistic analysis.

"The deeper the source of a sentence, the more lasting value it has for learning a language." But an utterance can only come from as deep within the student as the student herself has allowed the language to penetrate. Performance, whether it is to be self-started or reflective, depends on the quality of previous learning. There is, I think, a terribly important difference between learning that is defensive and learning that is receptive.

"Defensive" learning sees the foreign language as a vast set of sounds and words and rules and patterns that are to be transferred from the teacher or the textbook into (or onto!) the mind of the student. In this view, the teacher—and, later on, the speakers of the language in the host country—are seen as hurling darts at the student. If a dart strikes an unprotected area (i.e., if the learner is unable to come up with the correct response in speaking or understanding), the experience is painful. Prabhu suggests that fellow students, among whom exist "likes and dislikes, loyalties and rivalries, ambitions and desires to dominate, injured pride and harboured grudge, fellow feeling and jealousy", can be an ever "fiercer" source of threat.[7] Similarly Clément, Dörnyei, and Noels tell us that classroom activities which expose students to negative evaluations *by the teacher or by peers* may promote anxiety, and that anxiety and self-perceptions may in turn affect achievement.[8] What the learner tries to do, therefore, is to see to it that there are as few chinks as possible in her armor, or in Prabhu's metaphor, she tries to build a shell around herself.[9] Learning thus becomes a means of adapting to academic requirements, or to life in a foreign country; but like a suit of armor it is a burden, to be worn as little as possible and cast off entirely (i.e., forgotten) at the first safe opportunity. Meantime, the teacher is viewed as an adversary (at best a congenial sparring partner), against whom the learner may defend herself in a number of ways: by learning some of what she is told to learn, of course, but also by daydreaming, by ridiculing the teacher behind his back, or by damaging books and equipment associated with the course.[10]

"Receptive" learning is quite different. It is more like what happens to seed that has been sown in good soil. In this metaphor, we may compare language teaching to truck farming. The goal is a high yield, except that we language teachers measure our success in amounts of vocabulary, fluency, comprehension, or structural control per learner-year instead of in bushels per acre. Several factors will affect the yield.

One factor is the seed. Its counterpart in language teaching is the content of the materials, including the linguistic analysis on which they are based. We have for many years been aware of the importance of the seed, and we have spent considerable time and money in trying to improve it. We still have far to go, of course.

A second factor is the machinery used for cultivating the plants once they have sprouted and begun to take root. Again, we have long been conscious of the importance of methods and teaching aids. We produce a steady stream (eddy?) of innovation in method, and occasionally some careful research. (This is in many respects either healthy or necessary, and sometimes both.)

A third obvious factor is the richness of the soil, that is, the native endowments students bring with them to our training programs. A fourth is the weather, all the ephemeral variations that are physically beyond our control. Meteorological weather, with its changes in barometric pressure, is one example. Sprained ankles, chicken pox, family strife, and worry about international events are others.

There are, however, at least two factors I have not yet mentioned. The language teaching profession has tended to lump these two factors together with the weather, outside its area of responsibility. These are the boulders and the weeds—ego-defense reactions of withdrawal and aggression—that either prevent the seed from taking root in the first place, or very quickly choke it out. Those few writers who have looked steadily at this side of language learning are unanimous in emphasizing the importance of going back to an open, plastic, more spontaneous state that was characteristic of childhood: the soil needs to be soft and open and free. Boulders and weeds interfere with this.

No metaphor should be pushed too far, and this agricultural one has probably reached the point of diminishing returns. What I am saying is that, if we wish to promote "receptive" learning, we need to bring to our work an understanding of the ego defenses used by both student and instructor, and of the reasons why they use them. Defense mechanisms are triggered whenever either (1) a person is not sure what are the realities of the situation in which he finds himself, or (2) he does not know how to deal with those realities in a way that satisfies him. We teachers are quite accustomed to introducing students to realities and telling them how they ought to deal with them at the levels of attendance requirements and linguistic structure, but realities exist at all levels of personality. Full "cognition" requires more than five senses and an intellect.

For the intellect never comes forth by itself, any more than blood flows independent of heart, liver, kidneys, or lungs. The linguistic skills that a student gets out of some one element of a course are only the most superficial part of what that element has meant to him. (This point was made at some length in Chapters 7 and 8.) The same element that provides a learner with practice on the present subjunctive also has significance for him at deeper levels. It is these more profound meanings that will either bind the student's personality or release it, and only insofar as the whole person is free can the part that we call "mind" turn itself to "receptive" learning of the present subjunctive or the names of the animals in a barnyard. Clément, Dörnyei, and Noels remark that "given Horwitz et al.'s results on the genesis of language anxiety, the social processes and dynamics of the classroom probably play an important motivational role."[11]

What has been said about "receptive" learning up to this point has been metaphorical and very general, a discussion of the conditions under which that kind of learning can take place. Before going further, we should consider the relative desirability of "defensive" and "receptive" learning.

I have already asserted that the "deeper" the source of whatever the student produces, the greater its value for retention and assimilation. This assertion was based largely on experimental studies of human memory. If this is true, then one advantage of doing away with the boulders and the weeds is that we thereby open up greater "depths" within the student's personality. In addition, by reducing threats to the student's ego, we remove some of the occasions for playing what Transactional Analysis called defensive "games." Ausubel has said, "A central task of pedagogy . . . is to develop an active variety of reception learning characterized by an independent and critical approach to the understanding of subject matter." Rivers[12] states that fatigue often has an emotional rather than a physical basis.

What has come to be called "integrative" motivation, then, consists largely though not entirely of one kind of receptivity: the absence of certain types of boulders and weeds. Gardner and Lambert[13] tell us that an integrative motivation implies "a willingness or desire to be like representative members of the 'other' community, and to become associated, at least vicariously, with that other community." This in turn implies that the learner feels little or no threat from the "other" group. Lambert and a number of others have carried out a series of studies in a variety of cultural settings, all of which have supported the hypothesis that "an integrative motive, independent of intelligence and language aptitude, is important for second-language achievement."

This feeling of comfort with and openness to an "other" of course applies to individual teachers, and not only in their role as representatives of alien cultures. Elliott, who taught composition to his fellow Americans, told his colleagues that "your job as an English teacher is to get the students to use language your way in large part as a result of wanting to, not having to, be together with you."[14] Newmark long ago began to place heavy weight on the personal qualities of foreign language instructors, with an eye to promoting the kind of learning that I am calling "receptive," based on motivations that are analogous to what Lambert et al. have called "integrative."[15] This was contrasted with an "instrumental" motivation based on a desire to use the language for practical ends. I have already noted that this simple dichotomy is no longer seriously defended, but I will quote it in the paragraphs that follow.

The studies of contrasting "integrative" and "instrumental" motivations were based largely on nonadult students who are studying a foreign language while resident in their native culture. Larson and Smalley, whose experience has been primarily with adults living abroad in relatively small batches, have examined a process they call "dealienation." To some extent going through dealienation in a foreign culture means actually doing what the "integratively" motivated student back home was willing to do but didn't need to. When a person leaves her home culture, she becomes an alien. She is then faced with a decision that is often unconscious, but nonetheless important: "Will I coexist indefinitely without ever becoming a member of this new community, or will I submit to and seek to acquire the perspective of its members? Will I retire into an alien ghetto protected by imported surroundings, and choose my friends only from those who will move into my world, or will I learn to understand and participate in a new way of life?"[16] In other words, will she both seek and accept dealienation? One possible advantage of "receptive" learning, and of fostering "integrative" motivations, may be that to do so will ease any future process of dealienation.

□ THE ROLE OF THE LEARNER

In the preceding parts of this chapter, we looked at what kind of performance is asked of the learner, and at how the learner reacts to what is going on. Both are tacitly consistent with the traditional teacher–student axis, with initiative and moment-to-moment control and monitoring principally in the hands of the teacher. This relationship, if well handled, is capable of producing graduates who are able to use and respond to the language, but who are left with the conviction that the way to ability in a new language lies through good teaching.

A topic much discussed in recent years is how to create a new role for the learner as a member of the team, and how to build in the learner, alongside language *pro*ficiency, a new kind of self-*suf*ficiency in the learning process. That is the whole purpose of the recent movement to identify successful "strategies" and to teach them to students on a large scale. There are strategies for managing memory, strategies for managing time, strategies for managing one's own feelings and for evaluating one's own performance, even metacognitive strategies for standing back and managing strategies. At this writing, the best-known exponents of strategy training include O'Malley and Chamot,[17] Oxford and her colleagues,[18] and Wenden and Rubin.[19]

Among the precursors of the strategy movement are Gattegno (at whose work we will look briefly in Chapter 11), who began in the 1950s to urge the subordination of teaching to learning, and to insist on the importance of the learner's independence, autonomy and responsibility; and Holec, who in 1981 published an important book on learner autonomy.[20]

MITCHELL'S PRINCIPLES FOR THE COMMUNICATIVE APPROACH

In 1994, Rosamond Mitchell published a brief paper summarizing the communicative approach to language teaching, by then some 20 years old.[21] She listed six principles, the first three of them grounded in specific debates about language learning theory:

1. "Classroom activities should maximise opportunities for learners to use the target language for meaningful purposes, with attention on the messages they are creating [EWS: and receiving] and the task they are completing, rather than on correctness of . . . form and structure." This principle is of course reminiscent of the central position given to elements of purpose in my discussion of the overall workings of memory.

2. "Learners trying their best to use the target language creatively and unpredictably are bound to make errors; this is a normal part of language learning, and constant correction is unnecessary, even counterproductive." This principle is consistent with what I have said about learning as the gradual reshaping of networks within long-term memory, through a process of comparison between what one has done (either in a self-started manner or receptively) and other relevant data.

3. "Language analysis and grammar explanation may help some learners, but extensive experience of target language use helps everyone." Here is an example of the fact that the same data—auditory, visual, concrete, abstract, and so forth—presented to and even stored in two different brains, still may form in those brains networks that function quite differently from each other, depending primarily on different parts of what has been stored.

The other three principles have to do with more general educational debates about learning and teaching:

4. "Effective language teaching is responsive to the needs and interests of the individual learner." We know that present interests that are general and academic, or interests that are general and anticipated, are less powerful in forming and modifying the networks of memory than are interests that are specific and immediate; and that needs exist on many levels.

5. "Effective language learning is an active process, in which the learner takes increasing responsibility for his or her progress." This principle may be applied in one or more of several areas. We may say that the learner is responsible only for how he or she responds to and processes whatever the teacher has presented (his or her own "learning strategies"). But in some programs the learner shares responsibility for the timing and even for the selection of input. (We have seen on a smaller scale that memory generally profits from learner timing of exposure to what is being learned.) Another area, long assumed to be closed to students, is the evaluation of performance.[22]

6. "The effective teacher aims to facilitate, not control, the learning process." That is to say, learners may not only control timing and selection of input from the teacher or textbook, but also originate either content or procedures or both. Here is the generation effect writ large. Here also is exploitation of a new level of immediate needs and interests (Principle 4, above).

Overall, then, it appears that the communicative approach as described here harmonizes in several ways with what I have said about *Memory* and *Meaning*. It should also lead to learning that is relatively "self-started" and "nondefensive," as those terms were used in the first part of this chapter.

BRIDGES

As a third general view of method, I would like to describe a specific format, and then to derive from that format a set of three concepts. I will illustrate those concepts at the end of this chapter in terms of specific procedures, and then in Chapter 11 apply them to six existing methods.

The format will build on distinctions developed in earlier sections of this book. From the *Memory* chapters, the most conspicuous ideas are (1) the distinction among sensory persistence, working memory, holding memory, and permanent memory; (2) the role of richness and complexity of networks in getting material into permanent memory; and (3) the central role of purposes and emotions in the quality of networks.

Based on the *Meaning* chapters, the format notes a distinction between two directions in which an activity may be oriented:

- □ A *form-oriented* activity lets the student SAY (or HEAR or READ or WRITE) something that could be said (or heard or read or written), and that might turn out to be useful some day. But the situations are chosen to illustrate selected grammar points, competencies, etc.

- □ A *communication-oriented* activity lets the student DO something that he or she considers to be immediately relevant, or recognizes as essential to effectiveness in a foreseeable situation that he or she regards as in some way important. Language is chosen because it contributes to getting that something done.[23]

Another inference from the earlier sections has to do with the place of imagination in an activity:

- □ Some activities *require* the student to use imagination, for example, to imagine wanting to get to "Room 104" although he or she knows nothing about what is in Room 104 and therefore really needs also to imagine a reason for *wanting* to go there. Few if any students are likely to get around to all this imagining.

- □ Some activities *trigger* imagination by tying in with preexisting configurations of motivations, visual images, and the like. For example, in a role play a future security guard may have to decide whether or not to admit a person to a building.

□ THE BRIDGE FORMAT

In 1978, Henry Widdowson gave us a compact general formula for teaching language as communication:

> Since our aim is to get the learner to cope with discourse in one way or another, it would seem reasonable to suggest that *instances of discourse should serve as the point of reference for all the exercises which are devised.* I would

like to propose that teaching units and the teaching tasks they specify should be organized as moves from one instance of discourse to another. The first of these [EWS: might, for example, consist of a] reading passage. . . . The second instance of discourse is created by the learners themselves by reference to the first [instance]. *All of the exercises which intervene between the two [are] justified by their effectiveness as stages in the learner's progress from the first instance of discourse to the second.*" [emphasis added].[24]

The Bridge format[25] described below is only a vehicle for developing terminology. It is not intended either to surpass or to supersede other formats. A bridge has three phases:

The DO Phase

In using a bridge, this is chronologically the phase we come to last. Metaphorically, it is therefore the far side of the bridge. In designing a bridge, however, we should ordinarily deal with it first. In the DO phase, learners use language in the process of accomplishing something that is outside of language. The pedagogical aim is to help move words, sounds, structures, and the like into permanent memory. Ideally, therefore, the DO phase of a bridge is communication-oriented and imagination triggering. What is accomplished in it should be:

- □ *Relevant.* It should be relevant to the learners' interests and expected needs. For example, simulating the process of checking credentials would be relevant for security guards but not for high school students. In the other direction, relating to one's host family during a summer homestay abroad would be relevant for some high school students but not for security guards.

- □ *Rewarding.* That is to say, the activity should lead to something that learners wanted. But if the role of purpose in memory structure is really central, then a relevant reward (solving a mystery, showing quickness and accuracy in currency conversion, or the like) should be more effective than more general rewards (such as a "Correct!" response from the teacher, a piece of candy, or extra academic credit). And if the emotional content of a bridge has been pleasant or stimulating, the bridge—its meanings together with its words and structures—is more likely to get replayed in learners' minds.

- □ *Rich.* The place of richness and complexity was mentioned in Chapter 7. Imaginative involvement contributes to richness of nonverbal imagery. For example, planning what to take along and what to leave at home when "traveling light" is richer than playing "Concentration" or "Anagrams" with the same vocabulary; in turn, playing "Concentration" or "Anagrams" is richer than simple alphabetization.

Richness, reward, and relevance may be found in various combinations. Currency conversion may be highly relevant and on occasion rewarding, but it is not very rich. Planning for a kind of trip one never expects to take can be rich and interpersonally rewarding without being relevant.

The most obvious, and in some training programs the most important, of these objectives are professional. Surveying the topography of the far side of a bridge is the chief purpose of needs assessments.[26] But even in the most professionally-oriented program, important sources of personal involvement are to be found in meeting students' needs for long-muscle activity, fun, social interaction, competition, cooperation, or feeling of competence in some nonacademic area.

The OBSERVATION Phase

This is normally the first phase in using a bridge, but the second phase in designing one. In this phase, learners have an opportunity to read, or to hear and possibly also to see, how competent speakers of the language go about handling the same sort of task that they themselves will be undertaking later in the DO phase. The length of the sample discourse, as well as its clarity, degree of authenticity, and other characteristics, will depend both on the level and ability of the learners and on the goals of the teacher.

With regard to memory, whatever meanings and forms are focused on here enter holding memory and become available for use in the DO phase. But material that is not needed for resolving uncertainty about the general messages being conveyed is unlikely to be focused on. Nuances of meaning and form are particularly likely to be overlooked here, especially if they are unfamiliar.

The best-known kind of observable model is the dialog for memorization. However, there are many others, for example, a TPR session, a reading, a field trip, or movies. The most obvious kinds of observation are listening and reading. But the value of these can be enhanced by arranging for what is observed to provide answers to questions in the students' minds; or by arranging for students to generate some of the forms or some of the meanings (or both). In Chapter 5 we saw that psychological research seems to indicate there may be a "generation effect" that helps get meanings or forms into holding memory, though not into permanent memory.

The SPAN Phase

This is the middle phase in using a bridge, but the last phase in designing it. Here, learners engage in activities in which meanings are explored and forms are observed for their own sake. This adds to the content of holding memory additional material that the DO phase will be able to move farther into permanent memory. Such activities may include old standbys (e.g., flash cards, massive "mimicry," comprehension questions, grammar drills) as well as more sophisticated techniques (e.g., experience charts, preference ranking, swapping personal experiences on some topic).

Metaphorically, then, observation followed by span activities with no DO phase is a bridge with a footing on the near side of the river, and with a nice span, but with no footing on the other side of the river. Observation followed directly by a DO activity is two footings with no connector, so that passage from one side is available only to the hardy few, who will probably arrive with very muddy feet. Drills that are neither preceded by observed discourse nor followed by doing something are loose pontoons.

Obviously one could suggest many components other than OBSERVATION, SPANNING, and DOING. An example is ELICITATION, or talking about a subject with students to let them contribute and thus activate what they already know about it, before OBSERVING a sample of discourse on it.[27] On the other hand, it is possible to see ELICITATION as an optional satellite to OBSERVATION.[28]

□ SAMPLES OF THE BRIDGE FORMAT

Bridges come in all shapes and sizes. They can last for several consecutive class hours, but they can also occupy only a page in a textbook, and last just a few minutes. Here are two examples taken from first drafts of a project in which I once participated.

A Culvert

Early in the unit from which this example is taken, students met a conversation about work hazards. This was good OBSERVATION material. The top of the next page was occupied by a picture of a work site showing many hazardous situations: frayed electrical cord, a blocked exit, and so on. Most of the bottom half contained a reading that mentioned various hazards, including those shown in the picture. On the last line of the page, students were instructed to underline the hazards in the reading, and then to draw lines from the sentences to the pictures. So far, this is just SPAN construction, practice in matching up linguistic forms with their meanings. There is no accompanying DO activity.

One fairly quick way to add some DO and complete the bridge without increasing the linguistic requirements would be to ask students to draw up a list, putting first the situation that they consider most dangerous, and rank-ordering the rest; then to compare their lists and discuss any discrepancies among them. Making judgments, and knowing how one's judgments compare with the judgments of peers, are skills that contribute both toward survival and toward standing within a work group. They are therefore DO activities. This is true even when the content itself is frankly simplified and artificial, as in this example.

A Larger Bridge

In a second example of bridge completion, students had met:

- □ A short dialog in which a worker was injured on the job (OBSERVA-TION);
- □ Captioned pictures showing other kinds of injuries, with practice in matching captions and pictures (SPAN);
- □ A second short dialog in which the accident is reported (OBSERVA-TION); and
- □ A thinly disguised drill requiring the simple substitution of various injuries in a slot in a sentence (SPAN).

This says to the students, in effect:

- □ "Here's a sample of language you might need for DOing something—someday."
- □ "And here's some practice in the kinds of changes you may need to make in the sample in order to DO what you need to do—someday."

We can convert these activities into parts of a bridge by changing "someday" to "right now":

- □ After the OBSERVATION and SPAN activities, the instructor begins the DO phase by telling about a real accident known to him/her. Where? When? Who? What happened? Injuries?
- □ Students then take turns telling about accidents known to them. The instructor acts the part of an interested listener, giving brief exclamations and paraphrases usual in that role.
- □ After the students have told their stories, the instructor retells them in his or her own words, asking for confirmation or correction of the facts. Students are in the dual role of authorities on facts, and listeners to a further sample of their target language.
- □ Students answer questions about, or even retell, each other's stories.
- □ Students "phone" their safety officer (played by the instructor) to report the accidents they have told about.

Adding Spans

The audiolingual French course I once took was just a collection of OBSERVE and SPAN materials, with no significant DO phases. In one recent series of workshops on this Bridge format, by contrast, most groups of teachers tended to create excellent OBSERVATION materials and appropriate DO activities to follow them, but to skip the SPAN phase. For example, students might be given an interview in which Carla, a gifted language learner, was explaining what did and did not work for her, and then be asked to talk about themselves as language learners.[29] No doubt students could draw on material that such an observation may have bought into their holding memory. But that material would consist largely of:

- ☐ words, structures, and meanings already within the individual learner's range of understanding;
- ☐ *and which* the student had needed to notice in order to make sense of the model as he or she observed it;
- ☐ *plus* assorted words, structures, and meanings (correct or not) that the model might have brought into holding memory;
- ☐ *but not* any correct words, structures, or meanings that either were unfamiliar or had proved to be unnecessary for understanding the message.

If the subsequent "rich and complex" activity of the DO phase does indeed tend to push the contents of holding memory toward a more permanent status in non-electrical storage, then the above set of conditions may open the way for what is sometimes called the "fossilization" of incorrect forms.

A few SPAN activities that might be useful here include:

☐ Discussion

1. If you had read only lines 1–2 of Carla's account, what would you think about her feelings? Only line 14? Only 18–19?
2. After reading the entire interview, how do you think Carla likes her German class? Which of her statements make you think this?

> [This activity should (a) allow extra time and attention for key parts of the text; (b) allow and require learners to make and compare judgments about the text, and not just "comprehend" it.]

☐ Elicitation   Language learners are quite different from one another. Suggest some other ways in which various learners might complete these sentences:

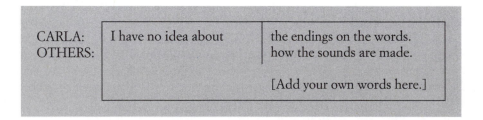

| CARLA:
OTHERS: | I have no idea about | the endings on the words.
how the sounds are made.

[Add your own words here.] |

CARLA: OTHERS:	There's something	terrifying pleasant	about	memorizing. drilling.
		[Add your own words here.]		

[This activity should: (a) lead learners to focus once more on Carla's words and meanings; (b) allow and require them to generate words and associated meanings that are tied in with their own experiences— their own permanent memories; (c) provide for social interchange among learners.]

□   ## Vocabulary Recall

1. Exactly what did Carla say?

   If I _____ a country, I speak.

   I say what comes out according to the _____.

   I felt I spoke much better than I _____ do speak.
   etc.

2. What words or phrases could be used in these blanks other than the ones Carla actually used?

   [This activity should: (a) cause learners to focus on exact forms; (b) lead them to generate forms from their own existing permanent memory resources; (c) allow these forms to be verified or corrected by the teacher.]

□   ## Structured Conversations (using material from the above elicitation)

1. A: There's something (terrifying) about (memorizing).
   B: Oh, you (don't) like to (memorize)!
      I (don't) like to memorize (either/too)!

2. A: I have no idea about (the endings on the words)!
   B: For me, (the endings on the words) | is | a mystery, too!
      | are | very interesting.

   [Because the person in Role B must respond in one way or another depending on what the person in Role A has said, this kind of practice is actually a simple, controlled form of communication. At the same time, however, it is sufficiently simple and controlled so that some focus can be retained for the grammatical aspects.]

□ SUMMARY OF THE BRIDGE FORMAT

There are, then, characteristic questions that we will ask about each phase of a bridge:

- About the DO phase: How relevant will this activity be to my students' needs and interests? How rich is it? What rewards does it offer?
- About the OBSERVATION phase: How will this sample of discourse contribute to performance in the DO phase? How clear and accessible will its language be for my students?
- About the SPAN phase: What contributions will each activity make toward putting appropriate words, structures, and meanings into holding memory?

■ ■ ■ *Some Answers I Reached*

Chapter 10 outlines three different general views of method. The first, which appeared also in the original edition, emphasizes distinctions between "self-started" and "reflective" ("echoic") performance, and between "defensive" and "receptive" learning.

The second general view is based on a relatively recent summary of the principles of the communicative approach. Key elements are the maximization of meaningful use of the new language; a relaxed policy toward correction of minor errors; reliance on exposure more than on explanation for the clarification of new structures; tying in with the needs and interests of individual learners; transferring as much responsibility as possible, and as soon as possible, from teacher to learners; and the role of the teacher as one who makes learning easier, but who does not *cause* it to happen.

The third general view is couched in terms, not of principles, but of a format for teaching. It draws more directly on the memory chapters, and particularly on the distinction between the "holding" and "permanent" ends of the continuum that we call "long-term memory." The difference is a matter of degree, depending largely on the richness and complexity of the networks in which material has been stored. Richness and complexity are in turn affected by what the learner has done with the material since first meeting it.

The chapters on meaning emphasize that some of the key elements in these "rich and complex networks" come not from pages or from pictures or from hopping to the door when told to do so, but from the learner's reactions to these outward things, experiencing them as meeting or as frustrating his or her own needs for performing important acts, or for having fun, or for preserving self-image, for example.

These ideas are pulled together in a simple format for organizing lessons. Based on an idea from Henry Widdowson, the format consists of an OBSERVE phase (learners encounter a sample of native speakers accomplishing some interesting task), a SPAN phase (learners engage in activities that focus their attention on details of the sample), and a DO phase (learners use the language in accomplishing a similar task).

■ ■ ■ *Further Questions*

▫ How might one use a single piece of material (e.g., a videotape or a newspaper ad) in the manner of two or more of the three phases of the Bridge format?

▫ Under what conditions, if any, would it be appropriate to have students attempt a DO activity before meeting the OBSERVE phase of a bridge?

Notes

1. This meaning for "reflective" is unrelated to meanings found in Ho (1995) and in Felder and Henriques (1995).

2. Wardhaugh 1971:19.

3. Titone 1970:47.

4. Jakobovits 1970:19f.

5. Mehan 1972:7.

6. Rivers 1972.

7. Prabhu 1992:229.

8. Clément, Dörnyei & Noels 1994:423.

9. Prabhu 1992:234.

10. Much of this description of "defensive" learning is based on Curran (1966; 1972; 1968:349). Compare Bruner (1967:129f.).

11. Clément, Dörnyei & Noels 1994:424.

12. Rivers 1964:70.

13. Gardner & Lambert 1972.

14. Elliott 1970:53.

15. Newmark 1966:77–83.

16. Larson & Smalley 1972:3.

17. O'Malley & Chamot 1990.

18. Oxford 1990.

19. Wenden & Rubin 1987; Wenden 1991.

20. Holec 1981.

21. Mitchell 1994:38f.

22. Hallgarten (1988) gives a similar list of areas for the development of learner autonomy.

23. Nunan (1988:23) notes that adult learners particularly are less interested in mastering something just because it may be useful "someday" (what I have called "stockpiling"), and more responsive to acquiring skills that may be put to immediate use.

24. Widdowson 1978:145f.

25. Widdowson himself did not use the term "bridge" in his description.

26. Two extended examples may be found in Stevick (1977: Appendix Q; 1984:90f.).

27. Carrell, Pharis & Liberto 1989:654; Stevick 1984.

28. One reviewer pointed out that this Bridge format is reminiscent of Paulston's well-known recommendation that students first practice a new point mechanically, then practice it meaningfully, and finally use it in actual communication. I see four differences: (1) The opening OBSERVE phase does not necessarily involve practice, mechanical or otherwise. (2) The SPAN phase can contain both mechanical and meaningful practice. (3) In itself, the DO phase resembles the communicative part of Paulston's formula. But too many of us, certainly including me, who used the formula tended to plan the steps in the order listed. We decided how to present and drill the new point, and only later rummaged around for some context in which it could be used, at least in some minimal sense, communicatively. By contrast, the Bridge formula plans the spans after the other two phases have been at least roughed out. (4) The activity that makes up the DO phase should be more than minimally communicative; it should also be "relevant, rewarding and rich."

29. This illustration is taken from a workshop I have given for several groups of language teachers, based on Stevick (1989: Chapter 3).

Chapter 11

Six Methods

Questions I Asked Myself:
- ☐ How do the concepts found in Chapters 1–10 apply to some frequently cited methods?
- ☐ How can we interpret the results that typically come from these methods?

INTRODUCTION

C. S. Lewis believed "it is a very silly idea that in reading a book you must never 'skip'. All sensible people skip freely . . ."[1] I agree with Lewis. I do hope, however, that of all chapters, readers will not skip this one. The first ten have been prologue to it, and the last chapter will put it into a broader perspective, but more than any of them, Chapter 11 unites the three themes of memory, meaning, and method.

ON VARIOUS METHODS

The six methods with which I will illustrate the place of memory and meaning in method are Grammar-Translation, the Reading Method, Audiolingualism, the Silent Way, Community Language Learning, and the Natural Approach. I have had substantial firsthand experience with all but the last. We will look at these methods in the same order in which I happened to encounter them.[2] Along the way, we will also notice how concepts from Chapter 10 do or do not figure in them. Then I will offer a few tentative suggestions for optimizing them without abandoning them.

GRAMMAR-TRANSLATION

Most venerable among the host of language-teaching methods is Grammar-Translation. The following comments are largely autobiographical, drawn from years in superficially successful study of high school Latin.

What Happened

Each chapter in the first-year book began with a list of Latin words to memorize with their English equivalents. This was followed by rules and paradigms for one or more new points of grammar. The culmination of the lesson consisted in translating lists of unrelated sentences, first from Latin into English, and then in the opposite direction. Later lessons in the book contained connected texts describing places and things that few of us would have chosen to read about even in English. Our activities in the last 3 years of the program consisted of deciphering Caesar, Cicero, and Vergil a few lines a day, pausing now and then for a little parsing. This was supplemented by tests of our ability to reproduce paradigms. Here was a method notoriously reflective or echoic (p. 194) in its demands on the learner, which led to overwhelmingly defensive rather than receptive learning.[3]

What the Method Required of the Learner

In Chapter 4 I speculated that ability with any particular type of activity consists partly in being able to hold onto whatever types of data that activity requires. In Grammar-Translation, we needed to:

- □ Remember exactly *where* individual endings had been met, *when these facts were pointed out to us*: whether on nouns, verbs, or other parts of speech; or after the certain prepositions such as *ad,* or *per*; or on a word that was the direct object (whatever that means!) of a transitive (whatever that means!) verb; or in agreement (whatever that means!) with a noun of which gender (whatever that means!). Thus we amassed information about the "operating characteristics" (p. 11) of various grammatical items.
- □ Attach this collection of *where*'s to a grammatical label (in this example, "the accusative case"), and to a particular location within the printed paradigm (in this example, fourth line from the top).
- □ Remember which other *what*'s could also be used in this same set of *where*'s: the full range of accusative endings (*-um-, -am, -ēs,* and so on).

Grammar-Translation and Mitchell's Principles of the Communicative Approach

Meaningful use of language is notoriously minimal in Grammar-Translation. Indeed, Rowlinson sees this method, which came into prominence during the Age of Reason in the 17th and 18th centuries, as a special case of that era's emphasis on thought and logic rather than on doing. He tells us that this shift of emphasis was personified in the career of Comenius, whose early works with use of pictures and the senses in general were precursors of some modern methods, but who by the end of his life was proposing "the derivation of language by the learner from a pre-learned set of rules of grammar."[4]

Grammar-Translation obviously fails Mitchell's other five criteria for the communicative approach as well. Error correction was the name of the game; there was little but analysis and explanation available to profit from; no interests of the learner were taken into account except academic recognition, and no needs except the needs to pay attention, be careful, and work hard; the learner was responsible only for getting the right answers; and the language learning process was only a product of the process of language teaching.

Observing, Spanning and Doing

For me at least, 4 years of Latin by Grammar-Translation were 4 years of SPAN-building—4 years of loose pontoons. Even reading Caesar and the other authors was not so much OBSERVATION of competent users of the language as it was wrestling with black marks on pages. And a DO activity, to have any value, would have had to tie in with our own existing or anticipated use of the language. The latter would have included reading the classics in the original, easier comprehension of technical terminology in law school or medical school, ability (as one recent book advertises itself) to impress friends in later years with one's erudition, or at least to avoid misspelling Latin phrases *ad nauseum*.[5] For most of us, none of these was really present in our course. Happily, classical languages need not be taught by Grammar-Translation, and some Latin instruction these days is quite up to date and exciting.[6]

Optimizing Grammar-Translation without Abandoning It

I very much doubt that there exists a type of learner for whom Grammar-Translation would be the best way to study any language, even a dead one such as Latin. But even this method might be improved by providing OBSERVATION content fairly early that would allow for differences of interpretation or opinion that could be expressed in Latin as simple DO activities.

Postscript

The conclusions I reached during these 4 years were very Utopian, and not at all Arcadian. In spite of all this, I loved my study of Latin. Why? Partly because the talents it demanded and rewarded were ones I happened to have. Partly also, I believe, because it was fun to watch my own mind doing parlor tricks, much as a diver enjoys the feel of a cleanly executed dive. And partly, no doubt, because it fed a generalized and chronic xenophilia.[7]

□ THE READING METHOD

The Reading Method aimed to help students achieve as much control of a new language as possible in the days when access to samples of native speech was for most students limited to relatively expensive, primitive, and perishable 78 rpm phonograph records.[8] It was the basis for the excellent freshman German course I had in college.

What Happened

The initial weeks of our German course contained a fairly heavy concentration of information about the pronunciation and structure of German. Almost immediately, however, we began the first of 10 graded readers, each of which must have been between 3,000 and 5,000 words in length. The first *(Allerlei)* contained brief paragraphs on a number of topics, all basically unconnected with each other. The second, titled *Erzählungen und Anekdoten*, consisted of several pieces of simple fiction. In the rest of the series, I believe each reader contained only a single story.

The first time a word appeared, it was glossed in a footnote. We were assured by our teachers that the readers had been carefully constructed in such a way that once a new word had been introduced, it would recur a certain number of times in the next so-and-so-many pages. What we noticed, however, was only that the readers were interesting, even entertaining, and that they were hard enough to be challenging but not so hard as to be discouraging. The readers provided us with a context in which we could both apply what we were being told about grammar *and* engage in simple conversation-like activities with our teacher. After these first 10 booklets, we went on to increasingly longer pieces of fiction. (I recently noticed that at least one of these booklets, *Emil und die Detektive*, is still very much in use.) Most of our reading was rapid, with focus on overall meaning, but each week we also did some reading with focus on details of meaning and on linguistic form. In my experience of it, the Reading Method in its early stages was about as echoic (p. 194) in its demands as Grammar-Translation, and like that method led to largely defensive learning, though without being as tiresome and onerous.

What the Method Required of the Learner

Like Grammar-Translation, this version of the Reading Method required us to retain in holding memory the nature, nomenclature, and at least the written forms of various grammatical categories. It did not, however, require us to apply this information out of context. Also unlike Grammar-Translation, this course did not require us to keep producing mental images of some uncontexted *agricolae* as they allegedly labored in otherwise-undescribed *agrīs*, and so on. Not only was everything in context, but the contexts were better suited to postadolescent interests and attention span than a description of the Roman Forum, or Cicero's thoughts on the topic of friendship. In short, the method "triggered" imagination more than it "required" it. (p. 201)

Not least, the oral practice in this course required us to *use* sentences in the language, and not just to *cite* them or *recite* them. Our production of German at these times was intelligible, but often far from perfect. In the eyes of the designers of the course, "thoroughness apples to mastery, not to the practice stage."[9] A degree of inaccuracy acceptable during the process was not acceptable in the product. The goal was eventual elimination of our errors,[10] and this was to be accomplished not merely by additional reading, but by judicious and well-timed corrections of a fairly conventional sort.[11] "Fossilization" was not acceptable.

The Reading Method and Mitchell's Principles of the Communicative Approach

Although from a purely linguistic point of view Cicero's treatment of *Friendship* is at least as "meaningful" as *Emil and the Detectives*, most readers will create less meaning *in* it and extract less meaning *from* it. The Reading Method's selection of material therefore brings it closer than Grammar-Translation to meeting Mitchell's first criterion. The deleterious effect of too much error correction in the first phases is recognized, but the eventual elimination of errors remains a goal for the later phases. Explanation is regarded as a valuable tool, but still as only a supplement to exposure to comprehensible input. The nonlinguistic needs and interests of the learner are to some extent taken into account in the selection or creation of the reading materials. In the Reading Method as described by Bond, advanced students read books of their own choosing, at their own pace. In the early phases, the teacher is a teacher, but later becomes more of a facilitator.[12]

Observing, Spanning and Doing

The presentation of phonetic and grammatical information at the beginning of the course was a kind of SPAN activity. With a little effort on our part, most of this information made its way into holding memory, where for a time it remained available for explicating what we found in our readings. Presumably every time a piece of this information from holding memory proved useful in this way, it moved a bit further toward permanence.

The readings themselves, being stories, gave us countless delightful opportunities to OBSERVE German speakers doing a bit of this and a bit of that. Whenever necessary, we switched from this OBSERVATION back to the grammar outline. We did not, however, use any form of what today would be called "grammar drill."

About the only thing we ever DID was answer questions that checked on our comprehension.

Optimizing the Reading Method without Abandoning It

The simplest way to have improved the course as I experienced it would have been to have had the teacher's questions call not only for information but also for judgments, opinions, and other individual reactions[13]—a wider variety of purposes. Then the teacher's responses to our answers would have been able to include some emotion—enthusiasm, doubt, or amusement as well as the usual information about correctness.[14] Such interaction would have expanded the area of personal meanings, and would have allowed us to function sometimes in the Adult or Natural Child ego states, instead of always in the Adapted Child state. (p. 165) Moreover, it would have made our class time occasionally "self-started" instead of always "echoic." (p. 194)

Also helpful, though more demanding, would have been simple DO activities related to something we had OBSERVED the characters in a story doing, on the order of what was described in the "culverts" section of Chapter 10.

☐ AUDIOLINGUALISM

In 1958, when I was in Brazil promoting what was coming to be called Audiolingualism, I found that the method everyone seemed to slip into most naturally—what in computer jargon today would be called the "default" method—was Grammar-Translation. More recent contacts indicate that Audiolingualism itself may have become the new default method in some parts of the world.

The originators of this method observed that language is in all cultures encountered at least through sound waves (hence "audio") produced by motions of the tongue (hence "lingual") and other articulators, and that the same was true of language as experienced by all children during the first few years of their lives. They concluded that language must therefore *be* something physical: "a system of oral symbols," as they liked to put it. They went on to reason that the production of language was in turn nothing but the enactment of a set of muscular skills, to be mastered through muscular practice. This was all part of a generally behaviorist, materialist, antimentalist orientation.

What Happened

The basic procedures of Audiolingualism are too well known to require detailed description: learning pronunciation through being corrected in one's attempts at "mimicry"; repeating basic dialogs after the teacher to the point of memorization, and beyond memorization to "overlearning"; gaining control of grammar by means of cued multiple modifications of sentences from the dialog ("drills"); a few carefully structured activities in which learners were led gingerly into a little use of the language in the absence of direct cues; and so on. This was often done in a relatively mechanical fashion. Overall, then, Audiolingualism was based on Utopian assumptions and led students toward the Utopian set of conclusions.

What the Method Required of the Learner

In order to learn a language well through the Audiolingual Method, a student needed a range of qualities somewhat different from those needed in other methods:

□ It placed great value on the ability to pick up nuances of sound beyond what was covered in the notes on pronunciation. A learner's ability to accomplish this may be partially due to what kinds of data his or her brain stores best, (p. 102) and partially to matters related to the expression of loyalties. (p. 129)

□ It demanded willingness to work for long periods of time in order to achieve exact and fluent control of invariant texts. There was no recognition of memory as a process of construction rather than of simple retrieval. (p. 57)

□ It also demanded willingness to limit what one said mostly to whatever ideas and wordings had been provided by the textbook—things whose meaningfulness and truth existed only within the context of the basic dialog. It was thus very "echoic". (p. 194)

□ This led to what for me was the crucial requirement of Audiolingualism: the ability on very short notice to form one's own mental images corresponding not only to the dialogs, but also to the uncontexted sentences of the drills. Only in this way could the massive mechanical practice of the method lead to repeated pairings of the phonetic substance and structural patterning with meanings. This kind of pairing is surely the sine qua non of any style of language learning.

□ It placed relatively light demands on the learner's ability to perceive and name grammatical categories, so important in Grammar-Translation and to a smaller extent in the Reading Method.

Audiolingualism and Mitchell's Principles of the Communicative Approach

Although eventual usability of what had been learned was a long-term goal of Audiolingualism and was therefore taken into account in the writing of the basic dialogs, and although some talented practitioners like Rassias and Barrueta (p. 167) provided lots of day-to-day highly meaningful practice, most Audiolingual instruction was more concerned with making students *able* to communicate than with their actually *communicating*. "Accuracy before fluency" was a common battle-cry. And explanation was thought of as a necessary precursor to intensive drills, at least in the courses I had anything to do with. So Audiolingualism met none of Mitchell's first three criteria.

Similarly, learner interests were taken into account only in the writing of the dialogs, and the learner's overriding need was thought to be for a set of new habits. Learner responsibility was minimal. Control by the teacher was seen as a necessary good (indeed, teacher-proof methods and materials were a goal of course designers and textbook writers). Altogether, then, Audiolingualism was only minimally consistent with modern communicative approaches.

Observing, Spanning and Doing

I found three features of the Audiolingual Method particularly attractive. One was that the dialogs consisted of people doing things, and that 100% of the sentences were ones I might someday be able to use either as they stood or in a slightly adapted form. I considered this a high-quality opportunity for OBSERVATION.

To me, the other attractive features of Audiolingualism were its SPAN activities. One of these was use of structure drills as a means of internalizing grammar. The other was memorization of short sample texts. I had independently hit on both of these during my second-year German course, and had found them most helpful—even enjoyable. Overall, then, the method fitted very well my own set of abilities, and its theory accounted for the successful aspects of my own experiences. I therefore concluded that Audiolingualism was *the* method for everyone, if only they would stop fretting and trust themselves to it.[15]

The great weakness I see in most of the Audiolingual courses I met was the absence of DO activities that would trigger (p. 201) or even permit the students' imagination in areas related to their real interests and prospective needs.

Optimizing Audiolingualism without Abandoning It

Some teachers (two of whom I have already mentioned by name) have brought great emotional vitality to the initial presentation of each unit (OBSERVATION) and triggered their students' imagination in the DO activities that ended it, in this way achieving superior results. In an otherwise very mechanically taught Audiolingual course I once worked with, one hour out of six was set aside to let students ask for sentences or short exchanges they thought might someday be useful to them personally. This learner-guided OBSERVATION also led to desirable outcomes. All of these expedients served to reduce the effect of Audiolingualism's most dangerous assumption: that once the meaning of a form was in some sense "known"—retrievable even with effort from somewhere in long-term memory—then every future repetition of that form would be accompanied by repetition and strengthening of the form–meaning nexus.[16]

□   THE SILENT WAY

One original contributor to the field of language learning was the late Caleb Gattegno. I believe we have much to learn from his "Science of Education," whether or not we decide to adopt it as our principal or only way of working with students. I have elsewhere set forth my understanding of Gattegno's thought[17] and my observations of it in practice.[18] Here, I shall present only enough of a summary to provide a basis for comments comparable to those made on the other methods discussed in this chapter.

The most conspicuous tenet of Gattegno's "Science of Education" is that learning is the result of internal work—or it *is* that internal work—done and doable only by the learner, and that teaching should therefore be subordinated to learning. The role of the teacher is to constantly study and learn the learner—to be "with" the learner—and from that vantage point to provide one after another a series of minimal, elegantly designed challenges ("impacts") that will impel the learner to do within him-/herself an appropriate next bit of learning. This requires the teacher to work from the Adult ego state, rather than the Parent state in which my teachers by the Grammar-Translation, Reading, and Audiolingual methods seemed to spend most of their time. In such a role the teacher frequently has no need for speaking, which is why the methodology, as distinct from the underlying philosophy, is usually called "the Silent Way."

In designing challenges, the teacher takes into account:

□   The *independence* of the learner. The learner brings to the encounter a vast and unique array of preexisting inner resources: knowledge and skills on various levels.

□   The *autonomy* of the learner. The learner is able to choose among various ways of deploying those inner resources.

□   The *responsibility* of the learner. The learner must work out for him-/herself how to reshape and add to those resources in such a way that they will lead to satisfying interactions with the outside world.

What Happens

Rather than trying to sketch Silent Way methodology in this brief space, I will describe one very specific technique, contrasting it with how other approaches might handle the same task. The task is to teach a group of literate English speakers the names of four colors in Turkish. Readers who are interested in more details are referred to the writings of Gattegno and his intellectual heirs.

The most traditional way, consistent with Grammar-Translation, would be to include in the textbook something like the following:

| beyaz | white | yeşil | green |
| mavi | blue | sarı | yellow |

The phonetic values of the letters would have been displayed in a "Pronunciation Key" somewhere in the front matter of the book.

Strict Audiolingual teaching of this same material would have exemplified the formula "Hearing before Speaking, Speaking before Reading, Reading before Writing." Students would first hear a word ("How can they hope to produce it correctly without a model?") and try to repeat it exactly as they had heard it (This was what in those days we liked to call "mimicry.") The teacher would point out any discrepancies he/she was aware of ("After all, the students' ears have not yet been trained!" In general, the discrepancies teachers were able to notice were features distinctive in the new language, but not nuances.) and offer a new model. Where necessary, modeling might be supplemented by explicit hints ("The first vowel of *mavi* is extra long."). Once pronunciation was acceptable, students might be directed to open their books and produce the same sounds while looking at the corresponding printed forms. (This was the beginning of reading.) The sometimes-spoken admonition to the student was "Don't worry about the how or the why. Just keep producing after me, and trust me to shape your behavior by my confirming or disconfirming reactions to what you have produced!"

A technique more consistent with the Silent Way is the following:

□ The teacher begins by writing on the board all four Turkish words. Since the students already control a number of letter-sound correspondences that also work in Turkish, this feature illustrates the principle of independence.

□ At first the Turkish words are shown without their English equivalents. Since the learners are the ones who are going to be doing the work of learning, they need to focus (as Gattegno would have said, "pinpointedly") on only one aspect of the new material at a time.

□ The teacher then simply sits down and waits. One unspoken message here, illustrating the principle of autonomy, is "You are able to choose among alternatives as to when to speak and what to try!" Another is "How you act now will determine what—even whether—you learn!" Here we see the principle of responsibility.

□ In response to a learner's effort, the teacher indicates nonverbally either that the learner's version needs no further work, or that it does. In the latter case, the gesture is a hint to the learner about where to search in some way (the principle of autonomy again) among his/her pre-existing resources (the principle of independence) in order to produce a new attempt which will need no further work (the principle of responsibility).

I have used the above technique in a number of teacher-training demonstrations over the years. Linguistically it has always worked quite well. What has been of greater interest to me, however, it has never failed to be eye-opening for many of those present. The most striking bit of the demonstration has to do with the vowel of the stressed second syllable of *sarı*. This is a sound that simply does not occur in any stressed syllables of English or of languages commonly studied in English-speaking society, so that these learners were unlikely to have pulled it from memory. Yet I have never failed to elicit it, and rather quickly, in any of these demonstrations. I interpret this result as a bit of vindication for the importance attached to independence and autonomy in the Silent Way.

What the Method Requires of the Learner

The twin requirements of the Silent Way are that the learner focus on her/his own internal resources and processes, and that she/he do with a minimum of the kinds of teacher direction and confirmation found in other methods. From this point of view, the more the teacher talks and explains, the less internal work the learner is likely to do. This principle holds true whether the teacher is talking and explaining in the usual way, or is offering (imposing?) input through texts, films, videos, or simulations. If learning is compared to working with a computer, a blank or nearly blank screen gives me opportunity and challenge; a screen full of directions, menus, and other paraphernalia make me feel I have to divert my energy away from learning, and use it to resist the input so as to keep it from overwhelming me.[19]

In effect, then, the Silent Way pushes learners to operate in the relatively demanding Adult ego state rather than in the more familiar Dependent Child state. It allows, requires, and verifies many levels of "generating," comparable to Rabinowitz's subjects working with fragmentary stimuli such as "AL_O__L." These requirements account for much of the stress, even anger, that some students display in the early stages of studying a language using this method. But if the experience is to be Education (in Gattegno's sense) and not merely a bit of language acquisition, then negative emotion is acceptable in the short run, and in the long run usually evaporates.

The Silent Way and Mitchell's Principles of the Communicative Approach

In fairness to Gattegno, we must remember that he intended his Science of Education to be employed throughout all of learning, indeed throughout living in general. The learner need to which he therefore addressed his life's thought and labor was the need to evolve to an existence one level beyond where most people are now, and to become a person self-directed and responsible, detecting and correcting one's own errors, in a universe of ever fuller and more vital meaning. This answers very well the criteria embodied in Mitchell's list of principles.

Here, however, I will consider the Silent Way as it has most often met the public eye, as a technology for introductory study of languages. In this setting, almost everything the learner does is meaningful, but meaning is commonly limited to configurations of rods, or to a series of simple but lively monochrome drawings. Errors are valued as indicators of "where more work needs to be done," so in calling them to the learner's attention the teacher is actually doing him or her a favor, rather than imposing a burden or a threat. Any explicit analysis is always about what has just been done, rather than about what is to come next. Content vocabulary is kept at a minimum so as not to dilute concentration on how the language works. As a result, the learner's conscious, superficial needs cannot be catered to. Although the end goal is an independent, autonomous, and responsible human, the teacher in the courses I have participated in and the demonstrations I have observed generally maintained very tight moment-to-moment control. "Subordination of teaching to learning" means only that the teacher should be controlled by what he or she sees the learner doing, and not that the teacher should follow the learner's uninformed whims about what to do next. Here, then, is another method which, for all its (in my view) unique strengths, certainly does not fit Mitchell's description of the communicative approach. My two 20-hour experiences as a learner (one of them conducted by Dr. Gattegno) also proved highly reflective in the demands placed on learners, and produced—at least in me—a degree of defensive learning I had not encountered elsewhere. Perhaps if I had continued beyond the end of the workshops, this reaction would have abated.

Observing, Spanning and Doing

The Silent Way eschews such popular types of OBSERVABLE discourse as relevant or lively dialogs and readings. Instead, it concentrates initially on what other methodologists would call developing mastery of basic phonology and structure within a very limited vocabulary. From this point of view, it is wall-to-wall SPANNING—another set of loose pontoons.

From another point of view, however, what the Silent Way has done is shift the principal field of OBSERVATION away from discourse and toward the learner's own internal resources and processes. Similarly the most important DOING is at least for a while confined to that same inner field. The emphases on independence and autonomy cause the learner to do almost constant "generating," (p. 115) and, as we saw in earlier chapters, the generation effect helps to make what has been generated more available for storage in holding memory as potential SPAN material. The emphasis on responsibility in turn helps to shape what is retained in holding memory. This is true both for the words and the structures of language, and for the resources and ways of using resources in the learning process itself.

Optimizing the Silent Way without Abandoning It

I would have two suggestions for anyone interested in using the Silent Way. The first has to do with the second step in the technique I outlined above, the step in which the teacher sits down and waits. This kind of teacher behavior has been very rare in the Silent Way training I have either undergone or observed. More commonly, the teacher has emitted a steady, sometimes rapid stream of small tasks or challenges or "impacts" to which learners were to respond. I agree that *most of the time* this may be the best way to use the method. But I think there is also value in periodically handing the initiative over to one learner at a time.

My second suggestion is that some attention might be given to designing tasks that would recognize learner independence, allow learner autonomy, and require learner responsibility in relation to samples of interesting and useful discourse, and that such tasks might be introduced occasionally almost from the beginning.[20]

□ COMMUNITY LANGUAGE LEARNING

Another original contribution to language teaching methodology came from the late Charles A. Curran. A clinical psychologist by trade, Curran developed a system called Community Language Learning (CLL) as a by-product of his training of future counselors and psychotherapists. As with the Silent Way, one does not have to totally embrace this method in order to profit from the insights it embodies and the results it can achieve.

CLL is the linguistic application of a more general approach to education called Counseling-Learning. The central ideas of Counseling-Learning can be summarized in four statements:

- □ The essence of learning lies in identifying, accepting, and internalizing new *distinctions* in a wide range of areas: in pronunciation and grammar, of course, but also in lexical differentiations, cultural interaction, even in how one goes about the learning task.

- □ One can distinguish two items only when one is able to *retain* both of them, *retrieve* them when needed, and *repeat* them mentally. (This fits with what was said in the memory chapters about the pervasive role of comparison.)

- □ But (as we saw above) retention and retrieval of an item are greatly helped by the quality of *attention* the learner had given to it earlier, and attention is enhanced as the learner *asserts* her-/himself more fully into the learning activity.

- □ Readiness to assert oneself into any situation depends in turn on the learner's level of *security* in that situation.

These principles, derived from Curran's style of counseling, are expressed in Counseling-Learning theory in the opposite order, using the acronym SARD: Security enables Assertion and Attention, which lead to Retention and Retrieval, which are indispensable for Differentiation. Readers interested in more details of Counseling-Learning theory should consult Curran's own works.[21] My own understanding of the theory and practice have been set forth elsewhere.[22]

What Happens

Although precise techniques vary from class to class and from day to day, a general outline consists of four phases:

- □ An *accumulation* phase. Here, learners sit in a circle and engage in a free conversation. Utterances may originate either in the new language or in the native language. In the latter case, the teacher (called in Counseling-Learning the "knower") supplies the equivalent in the new language, and the learner repeats it. In the interest of promoting the learners' sense of security, the knower remains unobtrusively outside the circle, and corrects only the potentially most disastrous errors. The new-language parts of these proceedings are recorded on tape. The recording then becomes the source for activities in the remaining phases.

  In this phase, learners are generating—and investing their attention in—at least the meanings that are being expressed. Whenever a student originates an utterance in the new language, he or she is also generating forms. Some learners will from time to time be able to note discrepancies between forms originated by themselves or other learners, and what has come from the mouth of the knower.

- □ An *analysis* phase. In this phase, the conversation is played back, and the knower transcribes it onto a chalkboard or preferably a flip chart. The slowdown this entails works to the advantage of the learners, for it allows them to hear the newly accumulated spoken corpus several times, and also lets them observe the corresponding written forms at their own pace while the knower is busy writing. Once the transcription is complete, learners look it over in silence for a few moments. Then the knower points to one part of the transcript at a time, silently inviting the learners to guess its meaning or function. Compared with teacher-paced explanation, this procedure fosters security by never putting any one learner on the spot, and by moving at a more deliberate rate. Here again, learners have an opportunity to notice discrepancies between the actual form and what they had thought the form was.

- □ An *assimilation* phase. After learners have understood what the text means, and have had a glimpse of how it is put together, they still need to get its parts better established in long-term memory. To this end they work and rework the new material in any of a large number of ways. Vocabulary, for example, is often written on small cards and turned into a game of "Concentration." For all their variety, however, the numerous techniques of the assimilation phase share certain characteristics: cooperative, nonconfrontational, with plenty of learner initiative.

- □ An *appraisal* phase. Learners are invited to talk about what has been going on within their own learning. Where appropriate, they may incidentally refer to what the knower-leader has been doing. The knower gives SUNny responses: supportive, understanding, and nondefensive. This phase has the dual functions of providing useful feedback to the knower-leader, and of helping the learners to examine and modify their own attitudes and behavior. The method intends that learners learn new differentiations not only in language, but also in their own personal functioning.

  It is from this appraisal phase that Counseling-Learning derives its name. The SUNny responses of the knower are intended to foster openness in and among the learners and so to prevent the buildup of anxieties and tensions. This system works very well for many learners. For some, however, the activity is by its very nature and intent offensive and therefore counterproductive. Prabhu has warned that, although personal factors operate powerfully in the classroom and may defeat an otherwise perfectly good procedure, any attempt to provide some general procedure for reconciling conflicts is likely to be unfruitful.[23]

CLL is thus quite unlike the Silent Way in the area of personal meanings. The latter aims for the early establishment of an Adult–Adult nexus between teacher and learner, (p. 166) and sees no necessary conflict between defensive feelings and receptive learning. (p. 195) CLL, at least in its early stages, cultivates a Nurturing Parent–Natural Child nexus, and sees defensive feelings as inimical to receptive learning. In practice as well as in theory, I have found that it elicits self-starting rather than echoing, and that it succeeds in reducing defensiveness and promoting receptivity.

What the Method Requires of the Learner

Because its tone is supportive rather than confrontational, and because of the wide range of learning styles catered to by the varied activities of the analysis and assimilation phases, most learners find CLL to be a freeing and relatively undemanding method. On the other hand, learners must be (or become!) willing to forgo three features of much conventional instruction: the brisk pace; the pattern of responding individually to the teacher's questions or other cues and receiving immediate confirmation or correction; and a preexisting, well-organized syllabus. Absence of these features in CLL—to many learners a welcome blessing—can produce intense anxiety and frustration in others.

Community Language Learning and Mitchell's Principles of the Communicative Approach

In CLL, the sentences and the meanings are generated entirely by the learners. Thus the language samples have full and immediate meanings, even though the same sentences placed in a textbook might seem disjointed and uninteresting. In the early stages, errors are corrected only if they interfere with communication; the stage at which the knower begins to offer corrections of other errors is by definition the stage at which the learner has become mature enough to ask for that kind of help. Explanation too is given only on request, and individual explanations are kept very brief. The knower makes available to the learners his or her knowledge of human functioning as well as of the language, but remains just that: a knower and facilitator, not a teacher. The entire method, especially the appraisal phase, ensures that learners will learn responsibility by carrying it. Here at last, then, we have found a method that fits all six of Mitchell's principles.

Observing, Spanning and Doing

In the basic procedure I have sketched above, learners DO nothing but converse among themselves, and OBSERVE no native-speaker behavior except how the knower translates the sentences of their conversation into the new language. Using learner-generated conversations may enhance the immediate relevance of the content, but often at a cost to long-term usefulness. Many of the other activities, such as "Concentration," are simply SPAN work.

Optimizing Community Language Learning without Abandoning It

On the other hand, the CLL teachers I have known have been good at creating appropriate DO activities to build on what turned up in the conversations. This should certainly be encouraged.

The practice of letting the conversations originate out of the completely free improvisations of the learners presumably originated in the experiential training of psychological counselors. Perhaps for the purposes of language study a greater degree of focus and continuity could be obtained by having the community of learners select ahead of time some general topics or situations, and then applying the basic procedure to what has been agreed on. It should even be possible to apply SARD-like techniques to a preexisting, organized textbook.[24]

□ THE NATURAL APPROACH

In the early 1980s, Krashen and Terrell developed what they called the Natural Approach. This model took into account seven observations about how a child comes to control its first language:

1. The child hears a great deal of language, and simultaneously observes what objects and actions precede, accompany, or follow it.

2. At first, the child does not produce any language.

3. Gradually the child begins to notice recurring forms, recurring meanings, and recurring relationships between form and meanings. (According to what I said in Chapter 3, this presumably results in corresponding modifications to the networks of long-term memory.) Just which data, and how many data, get processed in this way depends on the state of an "affective filter."[25]

4. This builds a mass of information against which the child will later on be able to compare its own output.

5. As the child begins to attempt production, it compares its own intended meanings with the reactions obtained from other people. It also compares the forms it produces with what has been put together in Steps 1–4. Any discrepancies serve to modify the networks that were responsible for shaping the forms, and any agreements serve to strengthen those same networks. When other people offer explicit corrections of forms, those corrections are registered primarily as in Steps 1–4. The above steps

describe a process that Krashen calls "acquisition." In his view, acquired competence is the sole source of whatever ability the student has to produce language rapidly and automatically.

6. Eventually, the acquired pronunciation, vocabulary, grammar, and other aspects of the child's language become indistinguishable from the same aspects of the speech of the immediately surrounding community—they display the same "regularities". (p. 35) *Quod erat desideratum.*

7. But certain features of this immediately surrounding speech community (e.g., "for him and me") may turn out to differ from the corresponding features of a more prestigious, more powerful part of the same overall speech community (e.g., "for he and I").[26] Under these circumstances, other people may offer explicit rules (p. 35) for modification of what has been acquired. Control of these explicit rules requires a process called "learning," which Krashen believes is entirely separate from "acquisition." The use of learned knowledge is a "Worktable activity" that eats into a speaker's limited resources of time and attention.

What Happens

These observations are paralleled by features of the Natural Approach:

1. In the first stages of instruction, the teacher produces a great deal of language, always in a meaningful context.

2. At first, the student remains silent. (This silent period may last much longer for some students than for others.)

3–4. A first principle of the Natural Approach is that acquisition takes place through comprehensible input, that is, through the understanding of messages that contain manageable amounts of hitherto unfamiliar material.

5–6. A student's production receives direct correction only when it has actually or potentially interfered with communication.

7. Explicit rules and corrections are viewed as neither necessary nor sufficient for shaping acquired competence. Explicit rules therefore receive little or no attention. The same is true of drills, which are the enacted counterparts of rules.

The Natural Approach may incorporate techniques from any of a number of communication-based methods. In the early stages, for example, it may draw comprehensible input from Total Physical Response activities, and in later stages from the kind of extensive reading that gave the Reading Method its name.

What the Method Requires of the Learner

With its flexibility and its emphasis on relaxed, enjoyable focus on meaning, the Natural Approach is relatively gentle in its demands on students. Some students with traditional backgrounds may, however, become restive at the absence of nice, clear rules and drills. The approach therefore allows for inclusion of occasional activities of these kinds, but only as a means of allaying anxiety and reducing resistance to the method as a whole. Students may also become impatient if they feel they are not learning anything because they haven't yet begun to produce their own speech.

The Natural Approach and Mitchell's Principles of the Communicative Approach

I am less sure how the Natural Approach stacks up against Mitchell's principles than I am about the other five methods, partly because of my lack of direct experience with it, and partly because it is deliberately eclectic in the technologies it employs. Its emphasis on interesting comprehensible input ensures that its meaningfulness quotient will remain relatively high. Correction and explanation are both kept at a minimum, since neither is thought to lead to significant acquisition. The Natural Approach thus clearly satisfies Mitchell's first three criteria.

If input is to remain interesting as well as comprehensible, it cannot afford to stray too far from the learners' interests—Mitchell's fourth principle. The degree to which learner responsibility and control are developed is less clear, but depends partly on which technology has been selected. Overall, however, the Natural Approach seems to qualify as "communicative" in Mitchell's sense.

Observing, Spanning and Doing

The Natural Approach allows for a wide range of excellent OBSERVING and DOING activities, ranging from a single sentence ("Walk backward between Rona and Roy.") to the reading and critical discussion of entire novels. On the other hand, SPAN activities appear to be almost entirely omitted.

A crucial question about the Natural Approach is just what is being "observed." I said earlier that material not needed for resolving uncertainty about the general messages being conveyed is unlikely to be focused on, and that nuances both of meaning and of form are particularly likely to be overlooked here, especially if they are unfamiliar. For example, the utterance *"And all the children above average" would in practice mean the same as Garrison Keillor's "And all the children are above average." The student therefore does not need to notice the copula *are* in order to understand the message, nor would a Natural Approach teacher correct an omission of it in the student's production.

In Krashen's terms, such a student would simply "acquire" the English copula late. Others, however, have questioned whether that student may in fact ever "acquire" the copula at all.[27] The same question can be asked about any method in which communication is emphasized to the near-exclusion of overt focus on form. Krashen and Terrell appear to believe that the answer is simply more comprehensible input. I doubt it, for reasons that will be outlined at the end of this chapter in some thoughts on feedback.

Optimizing the Natural Approach without Abandoning It

If indeed the ultimate goal of language study is to shape networks that will embody the needed connections between meanings and forms, and if indeed we acquire what we focus on, then it seems that one role of the teacher is to arrange for forms and their corresponding meanings to be on the Worktable at the same time.[28] Perhaps somewhere between the high-quality OBSERVE and DO activities of the Natural Approach, there might be room for unapologetically integrating into the course a few simple SPAN activities such as rules and drills that incorporate content from recent OBSERVE activities. An experiment reported by VanPatten and Cadierno[29] indicates that there may be an advantage in SPAN activities that require students to demonstrate *comprehension* of items that contain the new grammar, rather than only by activities that require them to *produce* the forms being studied.

AN ASIDE ON FEEDBACK

I would like to close this chapter with a few remarks on the subject of feedback—remarks that will apply to methods in general. In the chapters on memory we found that working memory (metaphorically, the "Worktable") presents an opportunity to compare what has just come in through the senses with related material produced from long-term nonelectrical storage (popularly, "long-term memory"). We saw further that long-term memory is capable of sending to working memory not just one, but two or more replies, and that these replies too may be compared with one another.

I also said that the networks of long-term memory are constantly being shaped and reshaped by experience. This means that any particular feature of a learner's speech (e.g., precise placement of the tongue tip somewhere near the teeth; difference between the pronunciations of *seat* and *sheet*; use or omission of English 3 sg. *-s*; use or omission of English plural *-s*; choice between *do a mistake* and *make a mistake*; choice between *hear* and *understand*) may change over time, or it may remain stable. The difference between change and stability depends on what feedback the learner receives. Let us further assume[30]:

□ Feedback may be of at least two kinds: cognitive ("How satisfactorily did I get my message across?") or affective ("What kind of feeling did I come away with?").

□ Feedback may come from either of two sources: external (other people) or internal (the coterminous pathways of long-term memory [p. 65] and the Worktable).

□ External cognitive feedback shapes whatever features of form are message bearing (difference between the pronunciations of *seat* and *sheet*; use or omission of English plural -s; choice between *hear* and *understand*). It may be either positive ("Apparently my message got across all right.") or negative ("All or part of my message seems to have been lost or garbled.").

□ External affective feedback works primarily on the need for acceptance. (p. 9) It influences willingness to keep on trying to communicate in spite of occasional negative feedback of the external cognitive variety. It may be either positive (attention, apparent enjoyment, etc.) or negative (indifference, annoyance, etc.).

□ Internal cognitive feedback contributes to mental planning of prospective utterances, as well as to self-correction of what has just been said. It may be either positive (An intended message M_1 brings some form F from long-term memory. F in turn brings from long-term memory an expected effect M_2 consistent with M_1.), or negative (M_2 is not consistent with M_1.). Sharwood Smith suggests that the teacher may try to "enhance" input by designing it so that such discrepancies are more likely to be "worrying" and therefore to get "registered."[31]

□ Internal affective feedback works primarily on the need for identification with one group and for nonidentification with other groups. It shapes whatever features of form are not message bearing (e.g., precise placement of tongue tip somewhere near the teeth; use or omission of an inflectional ending; choice between *do a mistake* and *make a mistake*). It may be either positive (A detail is identical to how long-term memory indicates the surrounding community would say it.) or negative (There is a discrepancy.).

Each of these two kinds of internal feedback requires the learner to make comparisons. The extent to which these comparisons are actually made and registered on the Worktable varies according to at least two factors. One is the degree of expertise.[32] Another is probably related to integrative and instrumental motivations.

A child learning its first language in a homogeneous surrounding community would receive:

□ *mixed external cognitive feedback*, which would shape message-carrying features in the direction of those found in the surrounding community.

□ *overwhelmingly positive external affective feedback*, which would ensure that the process continued.

□ therefore increasingly *reliable internal cognitive feedback*, which would produce appropriate planning and self-correction of utterances.

□ *mixed internal affective feedback*, which would bring the non-message-bearing features into conformity with the surrounding community.

Summary: a new native speaker.

Someone learning a new language in an accuracy-oriented course would receive:

□ *mixed external cognitive feedback*, which would shape message-carrying features in the direction of those found in the surrounding community.

□ *frequently negative external affective feedback,* which would limit the extent of this shaping process.

□ therefore *a relatively slow-growing supply of internal cognitive feedback*, resulting in performance that in turn would lead toward negative cognitive and affective external feedback from the teacher.

□ *internal affective feedback* based largely on the norms of a peer group made up of other nonnatives, which would leave any unfamiliar non-message-bearing features largely untouched.

Summary: a graduate who controls many, even all, of the message-bearing features of the new language, but who speaks neither idiomatically, comfortably, nor fluently. This is true of the Grammar Translation and Audiolingual methods, of the most familiar procedures of the Silent Way, and possible of the Reading Method as well.

Someone learning a new language in an exclusively communication-oriented course would receive:

□ *mixed external cognitive feedback*, which would shape message-carrying features in the direction of those found in the surrounding community.

□ *overwhelmingly positive external affective feedback*, which would ensure that the process continued.

□ therefore *increasingly reliable internal cognitive feedback*, which would produce appropriate planning and self-correction of the message-bearing features of utterances.

□ *internal affective feedback* based largely on the norms of a peer group made up of other nonnatives, which would leave any unfamiliar non-message bearing features largely untouched.

Summary: a graduate who controls many, even all, of the message-bearing features of the new language, and who speaks comfortably and fluently but not natively. This seems to be the case for the Natural Approach, and for at least the early stages of Community Language Learning. Krashen and Terrell say that "[w]e acquire when we focus on *what* is being said, rather than on *how* it is being said" [emphasis added].[33] Perhaps "acquire" should not be treated as an intransitive verb here. Perhaps the statement should be modified to read, "When we focus on *meaning*, we acquire *control of meaning*."

■ ■ ■ *Some Answers I Reached*

The chapter considers six methods: Grammar-Translation, the Reading Method, Audiolingualism, the Silent Way, Community Language Learning, and the Natural Approach. Sets of concepts like working/holding/permanent memory, rich/impoverished networks, Utopian/Arcadian conclusions, ego states, echoic/self-started performance, defensive/receptive learning, and the requiring/stimulating of imagination appear to be useful in describing and comparing these methods.

The types of organized study represented by these methods differ from what happens in first language acquisition with regard to the absence of a native-speaking peer group, and sometimes also with regard to the presence of frequent negative affective feedback. These differences have corresponding effects on the final product.

■ ■ ■ *Further Questions*

□ What would comparable descriptions of various kinds of computer-assisted instruction look like? What about competency-based courses? Immersion training? Other methods?

Notes

1. Lewis 1952:142.

2. For a detailed and insightful description and analysis of a number of other methods, see the works by Diller cited in the references.

3. Let no one suppose that any of the four skills were neglected under Grammar-Translation! The "Helps and Hints" for Lesson 3 of an elementary college textbook advised the reader: "Try pronouncing the Latin word after the teacher, giving the translation. Then reverse the order. Write the Latin words in one column and the English in another, and cover the columns alternately, giving the translations of the uncovered columns. Try it up and down, and also skipping about. Always think of derivatives to help you. This gives you practice in *hearing, seeing, speaking,* and *writing* Latin." (Janney 1958:9).

4. Rowlinson 1994:39.

5. Here is a succinct statement of motivation as seen by the Grammar-Translation Method: "An elementary knowledge of Latin will make you secure in your use of English and will ensure you against many common slips and errors. Furthermore, you will receive a training in accuracy, application, memory, and reasoning which will help you to think straight in school and in later life. Best of all, Latin will help you to enjoy the companionship of cultured people because you too will share their heritage." (Janney 1958:xv) This quotation is from a used textbook I found in a yard sale. Inside the front cover, the owner had written *"Cave magistrum!" "Latina mortua est!"* and *"Dic de Latina nil nisi malum!"* (Beware the teacher! Latin is dead! Say nothing good about Latin!) Amateur psychoanalysts are invited to interpret these lines, together with the line at the very top of that page: *Sine auxilio hunc laborem feci"* (I did this work without help). They may also wish to take into account that a brief hectographed quiz paper folded between the pages of the book, based on material near the end of the book, had received a straight A.

6. Donald Freeman, private communication.

7. An excellent thumbnail description of Grammar-Translation is found in H. D. Brown (1987:74ff.). A more extended recent treatment is Chapter 2 of Larsen-Freeman 1986.

8. For a historical summary, see Bond (1953).

9. Bond 1953:114.

10. Bond 1953:115.

11. Bond 1953:111.

12. "Gwen" (in Stevick 1989) is explicit on this subject in her own study.

13. Stevick 1986: Option 23.

14. Stevick 1986: Option 12.

15. Thus exemplifying the Converse of Oakley's Thesis (Chapter 12).

16. Chapter 4 of Larsen-Freeman 1986 is a readable exposition of Grammar-Translation. A briefer account is provided at the end of Chapter 4 of H. D. Brown 1987.

17. Stevick 1990: Chapter 6.

18. Stevick 1980: Chapters 3–6.

19. Bernhardt 1995:30.

20. H. D. Brown's (1987) account of the Silent Way is very brief. To the best of my knowledge, his description is generally accurate. There are, however, a few points where it may be misleading: (1) In spite of what I thought when I wrote Chapter 9 of the first edition of this book, most of the Silent Way teachers I have since observed or learned language from are very slow to, as Brown puts it, "get out of the way while students work out solutions" to problems they have encountered. (2) In the strictest version of the method, the teacher often does not provide even one single-word stimulus as a model. (3) I'm not sure what Brown means by saying that some of the printed charts "introduce pronunciation models." (4) The standard charts of the Silent Way do not include grammatical paradigms. (5) Overall, Brown's suggestions as a language teacher are understandably aimed at *using* the method to achieve a specified linguistic *product* as quickly and efficiently as possible. This inevitably tends to obscure Gattegno's more fundamental concern with the general "education of awareness."

Chapter 5 of Larsen-Freeman 1986 is a fuller description of the Silent Way in action. My own developing understanding of the thinking behind this demanding but fascinating method is set out in Chapters 3 and 4 of Stevick 1980 and in Chapter 6 of Stevick 1990.

21. Curran 1972, 1976.

22. Stevick 1980: Chapters 7–17; Stevick 1990: Chapter 5.

23. Prabhu 1992:230f.

24. H. D. Brown's summary of CLL (1987:117ff.) is as usual generally accurate, but it does contain three or four small but important omissions. He is understandably more concerned with the language-teaching side of the method than with the human-development side. I generally agree with the recommendations at the end of his summary. But I have not in practice found the exact accuracy of the knower's translation to be as much of a problem as Brown seems to think it is, and a well-conducted CLL course definitely does not lead to "days and weeks of floundering in ignorance." For a fuller treatment of CLL, see Larsen-Freeman (1986: Chapter 7). Detailed accounts of some of my own experiences with the method are in Stevick 1980. Both there and in Chapter 5 of Stevick 1990, I offered extended explanations of my understanding of the thinking that underlay it.

25. For an interpretation of what this term may stand for, see pages 100, 106 and 226.

26. I am aware that "for him and me" is the form traditionally taught as correct. But "for he and I" is heard everywhere these days, even from prestigious personalities on television, so in a descriptive sense it must be considered the new correct form. (*Ohne mich*, however!)

27. An even simpler point is the distinction between *its* and *it's* in written English. I once was acquainted with a native speaker of English, holder of an advanced degree and an expert writer, who had persistent trouble in choosing between these two forms, even though the act of writing should have allowed plenty of time for application of the simple rules governing the choice.

28. VanPatten and Cadierno (1993:226f.) express this principle more fully.

29. VanPatten & Cadierno 1993.

30. This side comment is an elaboration of ideas suggested by Vigil and Oller in 1976. In an article that appeared just as this book was going to press, Pulvermüller and Schumann assume that there are two conditions that must be met in order for language acquisition to take place: The learner must be (1) motivated to learn the language, and (2) neurologically equipped to handle phonological and syntactic information. This distinction is apparently related to Vigil and Oller's distinction between affective and cognitive feedback. One difference between the two treatments is, however, that Pulvermüller and Schumann provide a detailed account of the neurological basis for the distinction. Another is that Pulvermüller and Schumann emphasize that the message-bearing functions of phonology and syntax (what they call the "grammar" of the language) are not treated the same as the message-bearing functions of semantics and pragmatics (688).

31. Smith 1993:168.

32. Leather & James 1991:316.

33. Krashen & Terrell (1983:19).

Chapter 12

Tradition, Diversity and Oakley's Thesis

Questions I Asked Myself:

☐ How shall I decide among competing methods and styles of language teaching?

☐ What factors are likely to influence my decisions?

INTRODUCTION

Teaching means choosing. For example, in Chapter 8 we considered several sets of sometimes sharply contrasting conclusions that our students may derive from their time with us. These conclusions have to do with the nature of language and of themselves as learners and users of a new language; with the appropriateness of working in one or another "ego state"; with the usefulness or unsuitability of making their own input to the process; and with whether or not they need to defend themselves with one hand while learning with the other. We as teachers may *choose* to encourage one or another conclusion in each of these sets. Later, in Chapter 11, we looked at a few of the methods among which we *choose*. Now in this final chapter, I would like to reflect briefly on what such high-level choices may mean to the one who is making them.

DIVERSITY AND TRADITION

The history of formal language study has seen constant interplay between diversity and tradition. Diversity has, of course, long been a hallmark of our profession, whether on the level of overall approaches, or of full-scale methods, or of individual techniques.[1] In 1969, Kelly[2] remarked that

> [l]anguage teaching has shared neither the honesty nor the self-knowledge of the fine arts. Whereas artists are willing to seek inspiration from the past, teachers, being cursed with the assumption that their discoveries are necessarily an improvement on what went on before, are reluctant to learn from history.

Chapter 11 sampled methodological diversity. Now let us turn and look at tradition.

TRADITION

"Tradition" is a word that comes from Latin, and its literal meaning there was simply that of "handing something over" from one person to another. Actually, though, this is the same Latin word that, via Old French, gave us our word "traitor"—which certainly is an unfavorable meaning. These days, I suppose there are two phrases in which we most often find the word "tradition." One of these phrases—also with an unfavorable meaning—is "the dead hand of tradition." The other phrase, which is often but not always intended as favorable, is "traditional values."

So the connotations of the word "tradition" are at best mixed. Yet it stands for something that we couldn't live—or at least we couldn't be human—without. A culture without tradition would be chaos, and an intellect without tradition would constantly be reinventing not only the wheel but also the flat tire.

□ A POETIC ILLUSTRATION

Here is a very beautiful but also very instructive picture of tradition. I found it in a brief poem by a young Kiowa named Rudy Bantista. The title of his poem is *My Father and My Son*.

> I was young
> my father said I was to dance
> and I danced
> He said I was to sing
> and I sang with beauty
> Then he told me I must hate
> My hate became fierce
> My father said to me
> > First I was strong
> > Now you are strong
> > How will you raise your son
> I say
> > Now you are young
> > You have danced
> > You have sung
> > And your hate is fierce
> > How will you raise your son.

I don't know what readers will find in these few lines. Perhaps we can take the references to dancing as representative of all the nonverbal side of the poet's culture. Then the references to singing can stand for the verbal side, and the references to hating for the emotional side of life as it's shared with one's group. At least that is one possible interpretation.

But right along with these three themes, or perhaps I should say running at right angles to these three themes, we have very clearly what seems to me to be the central theme of the poem, and that is continuity. And continuity shows up in at least two ways. One way is in consciousness. One might almost say that at least in this human life, I *am* my memories of the past, plus my awareness of the present, plus my expectations for the future.

□ INVESTMENT

The other way in which continuity shows up is in commitment—or in commitments. One of the points I remember best from my time with Charles A. Curran and the Counseling-Learning people is their analogy between living and investing. Just as an investor has a limited amount of money to put into stocks or real estate or whatever, so each of us has a limited amount of time, ability, and energy. Peirce develops this economic metaphor in terms of cultural capital, which can be invested with the goal of acquiring greater "symbolic" resources (e.g., language, education, friendship), or "material" resources (e.g., capital goods, real estate, money), or both.[3]

Now, investments, once made, can of course be changed. But they do require choices among things that are mutually exclusive: it is impossible to invest the same thousand dollars at the same time in General Motors and in the Marriott Corporation, for example. That is what Curran and his friends meant by "values." A person's values are derived both from personal experiences and from the surrounding culture.[4] And once the choice has been made, changing it can be difficult, it can be expensive, and in the meantime the choice has brought either gain or loss, perhaps even wealth or bankruptcy. So it is quite understandable that we tend to have a fairly strong emotional commitment to our investments.

In the same way, the young father in the poem is asking from his son three things in regard to the cultural investments that he (the father) has made. One thing he is asking for—and here is that word again—is *continuity*: he asks for affirmation that his own memories, and the values that he has internalized, represent something that is lasting, something that is *permanent*. Here, he is looking to the past. But he is also asking for confirmation that in his son's eyes the commitments he had made in his life had been *right*. Here he is looking at the present. And finally, he is asking for *confidence*: for reassurance that his own actions, actions based on his memories and on his commitments, will continue to get from his son the same sort of reactions that he has come to expect. Here, his focus is on the future.

This is a poem in which I always find not only pleasure, but also a certain amount of challenge. But what does all this have to do with the learning and teaching of languages? What all this has to do with the learning and teaching of languages is that in this setting too, we find things being put together, and things being passed on to others, on the basis of what has worked for oneself, what one has invested oneself in, in the past; and the implied expectation—even the implied demand—that others should affirm the value of those same investments, and should continue the same thing we have handed over to them, the same tradition. So the next question is, "What tradition or traditions do we find in the field of language study?"

I think we can shed some light on this question if we take a few minutes to look at the stories of four actual and quite different language learners, and at what worked and didn't work for them, and particularly, look at the reactions of a number of language teachers *to* those stories.

OAKLEY'S THESIS: A SOURCE OF DIVERSITY

At one period in my career, I had the opportunity to interview seven people, each of whom had in some way been exceptionally successful as an adult learner of foreign languages. A few years later, I used transcripts of those interviews with my students in classes on language learning in two different settings, as well as with a number of workshops in the United States and abroad, and eventually they became the basis for a book.[5] Over the years, the reaction to these interviews has been very positive, apparently for two reasons: (1) The seven gifted learners are quite different—sometimes dramatically different—from one another. (2) The interviews are long enough and full enough so that readers have the feeling that they have come to know the seven gifted learners almost personally.

And so, a few years later still, I decided to ask my then-current batch of students to answer two pairs of questions about the first four of these seven learners. The first pair of questions was, "Which of these four people do you personally, as a language learner, find it easiest to identify with, and why?" The second pair was, "Which of the four do you find it most difficult to identify with, and why?" The replies of that group and of their successors the following year can, I think, cast some light on where language teachers are coming from, on what has been handed on to them, and on what they may be likely to try to hand on to their students.

Which brings us to Oakley's Thesis. Oakley's Thesis, or rather its converse, is a colorful wording of what may be one of the most important principles in the history of the language teaching profession down through the ages. The thesis itself, in its original statement, was "Anything you can do, I can do better," and its classic restatement was "I can do anything better than you." The Converse of Oakley's Thesis, and it is the Converse that we are interested in here, is "Anything I can do, you can do too, although probably not as well," or perhaps "Whatever I can't do or enjoy, you won't be any good at either, so forget about it!" Some research indicates that students learn best from teachers whose styles are consistent with their own.[6] It may also be true that teachers teach best in styles they can relate to intuitively, and that they teach much less well in styles that deep-down just don't make sense to them as learners.

And that is why I asked my students for their reactions to the interviews with Ann, Bert, Carla, and Derek. These two groups, totaling about 50 people, consisted almost entirely of practicing teachers, many of them with a significant history of time in the classroom, and most of them with significant experience of learning and using one or more foreign languages. To the extent that these 50 are representative of the profession as a whole, their reactions may suggest to us both some prospects and some caveats with regard to the various methodologies of language teaching.

Here is a brief summary of the data that my respondents were working with.[7] Readers may want to keep in mind the same questions that I asked my students: "Which person is easiest, and which is hardest, to identify with as a learner, and why?" Readers may either answer the questions for themselves, or try to predict the rather clear results that I obtained from my questions.

□ ANN

The first of the four gifted learners was Ann, a dignified, well-educated woman married to a senior military officer. She was studying Norwegian. Some of the facts that readers learned about Ann were:

1. She was good with sounds—both at reproducing sounds and at identifying regional and foreign accents. In order to remember how certain words were to be pronounced in Norwegian, she sometimes made up her own phonetic symbols rather than using the phonemic transcription that was provided in her textbook.

2. Once in a small hotel in India, Ann was subjected to what she called a "torrent of sound" in a totally unknown language. Instead of simply giving up, as many people might have done, she was unflustered, and coolly went about sorting out recurring bits of sound and meaning.

3. Ann was convinced that she had a knack for communicating with small babies, and even with the zebras and rhinoceroses in the zoo.

4. A few dozen hours into the study of Norwegian, Ann happened to overhear a conversation between two native speakers of that language, and understood essentially all that they said. (The accuracy of her understanding was later verified by a third party.) Ann's success here was evidently due to rapid and skillful top-down processing, plus her knowledge of a few common words.

5. During our interview, Ann happened to overhear a comparable conversation between two speakers of a totally unrelated language. She again had a very strong sense of understanding everything. In this case, her understanding was entirely wrong, but it had clearly been reached by the same top-down processing that she had used in the earlier conversation.

6. Ann's only failure in language study had been in a second-year college course where she had been required to memorize long lists of uncontexted vocabulary every night.

□ BERT

Bert, the second learner, was a middle-grade official in his 30s. He talked about his earlier experiences with the study of Chinese, a language in which he had become exceptionally proficient.

1. He had studied Chinese for a year in college some years before he went to Taiwan.

2. In the first part of his program in Taiwan, most of Bert's time was spent sitting across the table from his tutor, 30 hours a week, repeating words and lists of sentences, and being corrected. He called this "the natural way" of learning a second language.

3. Bert believed that for mastering grammar, the best method was intensive drills that would "burn the patterns into the brain."

4. Later in his training, Bert was given the same series of textbooks that Chinese-speaking children used in their schools. He took the books home, studied them, left them at home, and then came to class and discussed them with his tutor.

5. Still later, Bert spent a lot of time in activities that required paraphrasing from Chinese into Chinese, but little or no time in anything that involved translation between English and Chinese. He felt that this accounted for much of his practical proficiency in speaking.

6. Bert was concerned to get the segmental phonemes and the tones of Chinese words right. He was not, however, interested in getting the nuances of pronunciation right so as to avoid having a foreign accent. "After all," he reasoned, "my skin is white and my nose is big, so nobody is going to take me for a Chinese anyway."

□ CARLA

The third interviewee, Carla, was a secretary in her late 20s. She had picked up Portuguese in Brazil and German in Germany, both to the S-2+ level,[8] with virtually no formal instruction. At the time of our interview, Carla was taking further training in German. Some of the facts that readers learned about Carla were:

1. The oral testers in both Portuguese and German reported that although Carla's language was only at the S-2+ level, her overall way of communicating left them almost feeling that they were dealing with a native speaker.

2. Carla had had a brief and happy experience in self-initiated learning of Japanese from a fellow worker in a factory.

3. Carla's view of how she had succeeded in Portuguese and German was that she simply "threw herself into" life as it was being lived by speakers of the languages, and just began saying whatever came to her, without thinking or analyzing.

4. Carla was having considerable difficulty and discomfort in her present German course, both linguistically and emotionally. This was a traditional

audiolingual course that was built around mastery of dialogs and drills, and that insisted on correct endings for verbs, nouns, and noun modifiers. The fact that Carla was already able to express her thoughts effortlessly and fairly correctly in her own German had no value. She was required to learn to express the thoughts in the textbook, in the exact words of the textbook.

5. For Carla, the very idea of thinking about "why" she should use one ending and not another was intimidating, and yet she repeatedly expressed regret that she had not been taught in this way from the beginning.

□ DEREK

The last of the four was Derek, a fairly senior official about 50 years old. He had been highly successful overseas with both German and Russian. The language he was studying at the time of the interview was Finnish, which has tremendously complex paradigms both for nouns and for verbs. About Derek, readers seemed to remember:

1. He claimed to have derived great benefit from writing the paradigms out numerous times, not just copying them mechanically, but trying to arrange them in more and more economical, systematic, illuminating ways. Once he was satisfied with a formulation, Derek put the paradigm aside and seldom or never looked at it again.

2. Derek volunteered the information that he placed great value on drills, and that he rated teachers according to how "limp and exhausted" they left him at the end of a drill session.

3. Derek had accumulated for himself and made use of a stockpile of little words and phrases that held conversations together, or bought time, or indicated transitions between successive parts of the discourse—the kind of thing that Nattinger and DeCarrico call "lexical phrases."[9]

4. Derek emphasized the importance of having the meaning of forms vividly in mind while he was practicing them. To this end, he had invented for himself an imaginary brother to talk about during conversation practice—a rather flamboyant brother who did all sorts of things that Derek himself would never have done.

5. In German and in Russian, Derek's pronunciation was good enough so that he was sometimes mistaken for a child of native speakers.

RESULTS OF THE FIRST QUESTIONNAIRE

The answers to the *Who?* questions are very brief and also very clear-cut. The learner far and away most identified with was Derek, at 63% of the vote, with Carla, Ann, and Bert as a distant second, third, and fourth, respectively. And the one least identified with was Carla, at 52%, followed by Ann, Derek, and Bert. Derek was also the learner who received the largest total number of comments (105), followed by Carla (62), Ann (55), and Bert (21).

The really interesting question of course is not Who? but Why? That is to say, of the facts that readers had retained about the four learners, which did they respond to, and how did they respond to them? Without trying to answer these questions in detail, here is a summary of the six findings that came out most clearly:

1. Derek's homemade charts of the noun and verb morphology drew 41 comments—twice as many as its nearest competitor. Of those 41 comments, 36 (88%) were favorable. That is, the teacher-respondents to the questionnaire were saying that messing around with charts was an activity in which they felt that they as learners could identify with Derek.

2. Two other topics in the comments on Derek were closely related to the charts. These were his need to see structure in what he was doing, and his belief in the value of mechanical drills. The favorable comments on these topics were respectively 86% and 82% of the total.

3. A closely related topic, found in the Carla comments, was the fact that she went ahead and spoke before she had developed any idea of the structure of Portuguese or German. Ninety-four percent of the comments on this topic cited it as a reason why the respondents could *not* identify with Carla.

4. Carla's statement that she just "threw herself into" the life of the country was frequently quoted by respondents. That, plus their references to her fear*less*ness and their own fear*ful*ness about making mistakes, accounted for a total of 21 comments, 81% of which said that this was a way in which they were *not* like Carla.

5. The value of mechanical drills was mentioned a total of 16 times in the comments on Bert and Derek. Of these, 11 (69%) were favorable.

6. Finally, 25 comments on Ann, Bert, and Derek touched on the value of near-native accuracy in pronunciation. Of these, 20 (80%) either identified with Ann or Derek for trying to have a good accent, or they disapproved of Bert for not caring about one. (One respondent even said she would like to punch him in his big nose!)

These, then, were the most conspicuous results that showed up when I tabulated the results from my assignment. I hardly need point out that although I used something that could be called a questionnaire, and although my results are expressed in terms of numbers, this was not a piece of scientific research, but only an informal exploration. For that reason, it cannot give us any answers or even suggest any answers. I do think, however, that it can suggest an uncomfortable question.

For just suppose that these 50 respondents are at least fairly representative of public school FL and ESL teachers at least in the United States. What kind of composite image do we get from the six findings that I've just reported?

To me, this composite is of a person who very much needs structure—who is active and creative within that structure, but who still demands it. The extreme manifestations of structure in a language class are of course tables of forms, and mechanical drills, both of which received overwhelming support from these teachers when they were thinking of themselves as learners. In fact, they are quite uncomfortable without the social support of the classroom (as contrasted with what Carla would have called "throwing themselves into" everyday life among foreigners), and without the linguistic support of knowing how the language works before they try to speak it.

Even their attitude toward foreign accents contributes to this image. Thirty or forty years ago, pronunciation was seen as the indispensable basis for all else in language study. Nowadays, it receives little or no overt attention in most language courses.[10] Some methodologists seem to believe that pronunciation will take care of itself in the course of general exposure to the language; others assume that for most people nothing can really be done about pronunciation after the age of puberty anyway; still others see concern for accurate reproduction of the standard pronunciation of prestigious monolinguals as elitist, as a relic of colonialism, and as a means by which a ruling oligarchy expresses and perpetuates its own power.[11] If this is the case, then the clear trend among the teacher-respondents to my little questionnaire seems to be very conformist. What does this suggest in the light of the Converse of Oakley's Thesis?

THE SECOND QUESTIONNAIRE

The results of that unscientific survey led me to try another one. I have also done this second survey with several groups of language teachers, first at the Mediterranean Institute in Barcelona in 1990. I began by giving very brief examples of seven fairly common ways of presenting or studying a point of grammar. (The point I chose to illustrate was prepositions at the end of English sentences.) Ranging from what I would consider the least traditional to what I would consider the most traditional, the seven ways were:

1. Comprehensible input: letting students hear or read connected, meaningful material that contains numerous examples of the point being aimed at.
2. Organized communication: similar to #1, but involving the students in two-way exchanges focused on meaning.
3. Contexted drill: conventional drills, but using content derived from recent meaning-oriented activities.
4. Uncontexted drill: conventional drills with no reference to any meaningful text or experience.
5. Tables, diagrams, and paradigms.
6. Explicit descriptions.
7. Traditional rules.

Here are examples of these seven ways of promoting the absorption of grammar, with apologies to C. L. Dodgson:

Sample of comprehensible input: One time, Alice had a dream. She was in a little boat with another person. First she was rowing, and then she was reaching for some things. But it was a strange dream. The little boat she was in had been a shop until a minute before. The person she was with was actually a sheep. The oars she was rowing with were needles. And what she was reaching for were beautiful rushes, but she never got any.

Sample of organized communication: One time, Alice had a dream. She was in a little boat with another person. First she was rowing, and then she was reaching for some things. But it was a strange dream. For instance:

- □ The boat she was in—What do you think it had been?
- □ The person she was with—Guess what that person actually was!
- □ The oars she was rowing with—What do you suppose they were?
- □ The things she was reaching for—Guess what they were!

After students have guessed, they hear the rest of the description and answer questions:

- □ What had the shop become? (The boat Alice was in.)
- □ What was/were the sheep? the needles? the rushes?

Sample of contexted drill:

      Cue: Alice was in a boat.
Response: What was the boat she was in?
      Cue: She was with a person.
Response: Who was the person she was with?
      Cue: She was rowing with something.
Response: What was she rowing with?
      Cue: She was reaching for something.
Response: What was she reaching for?

Sample of uncontexted drill:

This cup is full of something.
    What is it full of?
You look happy about something.
    What are you happy about?
She's in one of the classrooms.
    Which classroom is she in?
We drove past a stop sign.
    Which stop sign did you drive past?

Table organized so as to highlight what the learner needs to notice.					
	Alice	was	IN		a boat.
The boat	Alice	was	IN		had been a shop.
	She	was reaching	FOR	some things.	
The things	she	was reaching	FOR		were rushes.
			etc.		

Sample of explicit description:

- □ Each of the sentences in the above diagram contains a preposition *(in, with, for)*.
- □ In the first sentence of each pair, a noun comes after the preposition.
- □ In the second sentence of the pair, the same noun comes at the beginning.
- □ The preposition stays where it was in the first sentence.

Sample of traditional-style rule:
"In a relative clause, the preposition that governs the antecedent of the relative pronoun may remain in its original position following the verb."

I then gave the teachers in the group a 4-point scale, and asked them two questions. The first question was, "If you were beginning the study of an entirely new language, how would you as a learner regard each of these seven activities: as a blessing, as useful, as not very useful, or as a blight?" The second question was, "How would you predict that the majority of the other teachers in this group will regard each item?" That is to say, I was interested not only in how the respondents themselves felt. I was also interested in any discrepancy between an individual and how that individual *thought* the profession *as a whole* felt.

Of course, some of the results were unsurprising. Most conspicuously, there was unanimous support for comprehensible input, and only a few people thought uncontexted drill would be an actual blessing. But there were also some results that I had not expected. In particular, there was overwhelming support for contexted drill. We also found that uncontexted drill and traditional rules seemed less of a blight than we might have anticipated. In fact, there was a large difference *between how the respondents themselves felt* about uncontexted drill and traditional rules, *and how they thought their colleagues would feel.* In both instances, their own tastes and preferences were *more traditional* than they estimated their colleagues' tastes and preferences would be.

THOUGHTS ABOUT THE QUESTIONNAIRES

The apparent concern of the teachers in both of my little informal surveys, when they think of themselves as learners, for structure and paradigms and drills raises questions for methods such as the Natural Approach and Total Physical Response, which deemphasize the overt and serious study of grammar. It also raises questions for methods such as the Silent Way and Community Language Learning, which do not have a clearly specified and organized, explicit syllabus. In the overall strategy of communicative language teaching outlines by Brumfit[12] (1979), there are four basic steps: (1) the teacher selects some practical task; (2) the students try to do that task; (3) the teacher presents whatever new language turns out to be needed; and finally (4) the students practice the new language—if necessary. Here again, I suspect my composite teacher-as-learner will feel a bit uneasy with Brumfit's outline. Whitley notes that after 20 years, communicative teaching is not widely understood, and that most teachers seem to show "a continuing reliance on earlier or idiosyncratic approaches, and even a determined preference for them."[13] To the extent that this observation is accurate, it could of course be due partly to difficulties or defects inherent in the communicative approach itself. But one may wonder also about the role of teachers' own past experiences and personal investments.

On the other hand, an overall teaching strategy that seems to fit the composite image I have sketched here is the five-step outline of Hector Hammerly[14]: (1) *identify* a new item, to find out how it sounds and looks; (2) *reproduce* the new item, either overtly or covertly; (3) *understand* what the item does, and how it relates to other items; (4) *manipulate* the new item, first in a mechanical way and then meaningfully; (5) *apply* the new item, putting it into real or realistic use. Note that I am not recommending or rejecting any of the approaches I have mentioned here, but only pointing out their apparent relationship to a composite image derived from the responses of a hundred or so teachers to my questionnaires. Hammerly's outline is certainly more "traditional" than Brumfit's is, as most people would use that word these days. It is certainly much more consistent with the experiences and commitments of teachers in their experiences as learners, and Oakley's Thesis is simply a statement of how those experiences and those commitments turn into tradition, into something that is handed on to learners or junior colleagues, and something that the learners or junior colleagues are expected to perpetuate.

Even the challenges to a given tradition may come from a comparable source: from personal experience and personal values. If I have recently been through an exciting demonstration course in which I myself learned an amazing amount of some new language, and if the basic principles behind that course seem to be more consistent with my values than are the traditions with which I am familiar, then I may become quite zealous not only in promoting the new method, but in urging the overthrow of any and all past tyrannies. I may even begin to feel moral outrage against defenders of the status quo, and they against me. We may both fail to keep the commendable balance shown by one writer at the end of her report on the recent happy experience of a class she had worked with: "Finally, a caveat: *cooperative learning* is not a panacea. It cannot and should not be used to replace all other types of teaching and learning, but it can effectively be implemented in conjunction with *expository teaching* and the practice of *focusing on individual writing and reading skills.*"[15] I have italicized the places in this sentence where I would recommend that any teacher with a new enthusiasm consider substituting other lexical items.

N. S. Prabhu's interpretation is of interest in this regard. In a subtle and lucid examination of classroom dynamics, he speaks not of tradition and diversity, but of routines and efforts to change or replace routines. From one point of view, he says, a language lesson is simply another social routine, and for practical purposes routines are necessary as a source of predictability and security. Any particular routine is the result not only of a pedagogical plan, but also of the interaction among the teacher's own needs and those of the students. One such need on the part of the teacher is to preserve his or her personal, largely unconscious working theory of language study, either to vindicate it or at least to protect it from too sudden change. That "theory" is, so to speak, the net result of all previous training and experience, including specific experiences as a learner and including personal values derived from life experiences in general. The teacher's conscious access to his or her own theory may be more or less ready, and more or less complete. To the extent that theory and its sources are readily and fully accessible to conscious inspection, the teacher's need for security in the familiar may be partially replaced by the excitement of exploring the new. Any attempt by external experts or educational authorities to introduce a new teaching practice is doomed to dilution, distortion, or outright failure unless teachers are able to understand the theory behind it, and to incorporate that theory into their own.[16] As Peirce might put it, the leader of a training workshop is urging teachers to "reinvest" in the new method with the prospect of greater material rewards in the form of improved student proficiency. But the prospective investors may still be wary of sustaining a loss of some of their symbolic resources.[17]

DEALING WITH DIVERSITY AND TRADITION

Within this very human enterprise of learning and teaching languages, there are, always have been, and always will be "diversities" between what has worked for one person and what has worked for another. There is nothing we can do about that reality. (These diversities may be partly due to one's genes [heredity], and partly due to one's previous experiences [environment].)

It follows that there are and always have been and always will be diversities in the investments different people have made. There is nothing we can do about that, either.

And so different people will respond to, and will try to perpetuate, different pedagogical "traditions." Again, there is nothing to be done about that.

But it is also true that there is and generally has been a certain amount of moral outrage felt by proponents and defenders of conflicting traditions. Maybe that is something that we can do something about. Maybe that is something that doesn't always have to be.

Because just as our choice of techniques and methods depends on what has worked for us in the past, and on the personal investments that flow from those experiences, so these choices and these investments are related to— are an expression of—our deeper values. And if these relationships—if these values—are not clearly recognized, then they can give rise to reactions that are expressed not in logical propositions, but in epithets. And then the aspects of one method that its adherents describe as "responsible" may be described by adherents of another method as "dull." Other pairs of terms are "orderly"/"lock-step," "thorough"/"compulsive," "accurate"/"conformist," and "discipline"/"drudgery." The first descriptor in each pair is earnest; the second is an expression of that "moral outrage" that I mentioned earlier. Or those who prefer yet a third method may say that certain of its features "encourage spontaneity," while those who don't like that same method complain that those same features just "create confusion." Additional pairs of epithets from this point of view might be "excitement"/"self-indulgence," "exploration"/"dilettantism," "concern for security"/"coddling," "intuition"/ "mysticism," and "flexible"/"fumbling." Again, note the contrast between earnestness and moral outrage.

And here, unfortunately, is where values and investments—precisely because they and their sources are dimly recognized if they are recognized at all—here is where "diversity" can be both distracting and destructive. If what we want to generate is light and not heat, if we intend to make choices that are informed and not just intuitive or ideological, then we need to expend no little effort first in identifying our own values, and only then devising or rejecting, adopting or adapting our beloved "traditions."

MY OWN POSITION

Having said that, let me now abandon the attempt to be even-handed, and let me say plainly what I regret to find, whom I fear, and what I hope for. I regret to find a method ignoring the primacy of comprehension over production, both in its time of development and in its scope. I even more regret to see a method emphasizing form plus superficial meaning over genuine meaning expressed through form, or cognitive abilities to the exclusion of affective needs. I regret to find a method that does not recognize the ability of students, even as adults, to learn directly through communication, without explicit point-by-point teaching; but I also regret to find a method that ignores their ability to profit from formal study. I regret it if a method seems so concerned with accuracy in production that it stifles meaningful production; but I also regret a method that is so concerned with spontaneity that it is does not aim toward eventual conformity with acceptable norms.

My fears are directed not at features of methods, but at people. To begin with, I fear outside experts from whatever field who seek or who even accept some sort of intellectual hegemony over mere language teaching practitioners. In my view, language teaching may well be interested in and apply insights from many fields, but it is not itself applied psychology or applied linguistics or applied computer science or applied anything else.

I fear any teacher who emphasizes copying over creating. I fear the Annie Oakley whose early success by any method—Grammar-Translation or Natural Approach or anything in between—leads him or her (Annie Oakleys can be of either gender) to "squat sequestered in the fastness" of that particular brand of pedantry, but I particularly fear the Annie Oakley for whom that success was as an industrious, conforming Adapted Child paired with a teacher's Controlling Parent, secure only within a structure provided by someone else, avoiding risk and suppressing any stray spontaneity or initiative. Most of all, I suppose, I fear whoever, by Grammar-Translation or Natural Approach or anything in between, focuses more on teaching language than on teaching people.

What, then, do I hope to find? First of all, I know that the kind of teaching I have called for makes heavy demands on the teacher—demands on time and skill, of course, but also on flexibility and commitment. So I hope that in the future we will all find a growing public appreciation not only for the value of our product, but also for the special intricacy and delicacy of the process that we are responsible for guiding.

SUMMARY: WHAT I HOPE FOR IN A CLASSROOM

In Chapter 11, we have looked at a few of the many methods that are available to a language teacher. As the years go by, I find myself less concerned with *which* method has been chosen for a particular class, and more interested in *how* it is being used. I am particularly aware of what I see when I look at students and teacher.

Students

1. I hope to find the students involved in whatever they are doing, contributing to it and getting satisfaction from it on many levels of personality.

1. That is to say, I hope *not* to find them concentrating on merely coming up with correct responses (even in a structure drill), or on grinding out correct sentences or free conversations just for the sake of grinding out correct sentences or free conversations.

2. I hope to find the students comfortable and relaxed, even in the midst of intense intellectual activity or vigorous argument.

2. (a) This does *not* mean that they are loafing on the job. In fact, students who are really comfortable with what they are doing are less likely to loaf. (b) This also means that the students are not apprehensive that they will be punished if they fail to live up to the teacher's expectations.

3. I hope to find that the students are listening to one another, and not just to the teacher. I also hope that they will be getting help and correction from one another, and not just from the teacher.

3. This means that the students are *not* like separate lamps plugged into a single power supply, in such a way that the power used by one diminishes the voltage available to the rest.

Teacher

4. The teacher is in general control of what is going on.

4. This does *not* mean that everything the students do comes as a direct response to a specific cue from the teacher.

5. The teacher allows/encourages/requires originality from students, whether in individual sentences, or in larger units of activity, or in choice among a range of techniques.

5. This does *not* mean anarchy or chaos.

6. One of the first things I notice is whether the teacher seems relaxed and matter-of-fact in voice and in manner, giving information about the appropriateness or correctness of what the students do, rather than criticizing or praising them.

6. The teacher does *not,* either by word or by unspoken message, say to students, "Now always remember . . . ," "You shouldn't have forgotten . . . ," "You are a good/poor student," or "Now try to do this so that I may judge you on it."

These six points imply that the function of "originator," so often a monopoly of the teacher, is shared, though not to such a degree as to make the students insecure. The same is true for the function of "evaluator." Teacher and students are aware of what is going on cognitively, but also on other levels. No one, on the other hand, is haunted by what he or someone else thinks *ought* to be going on. There is evidence both of self-confidence, and of confidence in the other people in the room. And all of these things may happen, or fail to happen, with any of the methods I have described. So, of the three subjects of this book, Memory is a by-product of Meaning, and Method should be the servant of Meaning, and Meaning depends on what happens inside and between people.

■ ■ ■ Some Answers I Reached

On the highest level, language teachers may choose to make one or another set of assumptions about language, and about their students as learners. These assumptions are likely to be reflected not only in the details of classroom procedures, but also in the conclusions that the learners draw about language and about themselves.

A related high-level choice is between commitment to familiar procedures and power relationships, and the willingness to explore the untried, that is, between tradition and diversity. In our field, tradition and diversity are in constant tension with each other. If this tension is to lead to creativity rather than only to conflict, we need to make this choice with our eyes wide open. To the extent that such choices are based on observation and reasoning, they lead to verifiable (or falsifiable) predictions, and to valuable discussion. But to the extent that they are based on unrecognized intuitions whose origins lie in the half-forgotten past life and learning experiences of the person making them, they may give rise not to illuminating debate, but to heated controversy. A certain amount of forbearance and self-examination can help here.

■ ■ ■ Further Questions

- □ To what extent are one's high-level choices about language teaching related to what one knows of wider trends within the culture of the moment?
- □ To what extent are they influenced by the general profile of one's personality?

Notes

1. Anthony 1963.
2. L. G. Kelly 1969.

3. Peirce 1995:17.

4. For a historical sketch of how values in language teaching are often taken from broader cultural trends, see Rowlinson (1994).

5. *Success with Foreign Languages* (1989).

6. Hartnett 1985; Felder and Henriques 1995.

7. The transcripts my students had read are from Stevick 1989.

8. At this level, a learner can use the language confidently and effectively in a wide range of situations, but still lacks control of some conspicuous features of the grammar.

9. Nattinger & DeCarrico 1992.

10. Recent years have brought a number of publications on pronunciation, either discussing it or trying to help learners with it. Adam Brown (1991) supplies a collection of readings on the subject. But Virginia Samuda (1993:757), guest editor of a series of book notices on pronunciation materials, remarks that [d]espite the best efforts of well-known pronunciation specialists such as Joan Morley, Judy Gilbert and Rita Wong, the teaching of pronunciation can probably claim the dubious title of 'most likely to fall between the cracks.'"

Equipping teachers with basic information about pronunciation is a related but separate undertaking. Adrian Underhill (1994) has taken a refreshing approach to this task by designing his textbook around discovery activities that enable users to find out the basic facts for themselves through working with and observing their own pronunciation.

11. Loveday 1982.

12. Brumfit 1979:183.

13. Whitley 1993.

14. Hammerly 1985:90.

15. Szostek 1994:259. This author is assistant principal of a secondary school.

16. Prabhu 1992.

17. Peirce 1995:17.

Afterword

Like the writer of Ecclesiastes, I have tried in this book to pass along what I have learned from my many days "under the sun." Let me now, like him, offer a brief summary of "the end of the matter": some differences between what I would have said in those early, simple days with my new M.A., and what I would say now:

1. *Then:* Method is important because it determines how learners are exposed to the forms of the language together with the corresponding meanings.

   Now: Method is important because it helps to shape what goes on between the people in the classroom. This in turn helps to shape what goes on inside those same people, and the meanings they respond to.

2. *Then:* The meanings relevant to language teaching are principally linguistic: the referents of the words, structures, and utterances of the language.

   Now: Alongside linguistic meanings are personal meanings: how the activity relates to each learner's immediate purposes, overall objectives, loyalties, self-image, emotions, and the like.

3. *Then:* Personal meanings are important because they may cause a student to either continue or discontinue work with the language.

   Now: In addition, personal meanings affect the ongoing learning process, and are also part of what gets learned.

4. *Then:* Memory is a warehouse.

   Now: Memory is a set of inner resources for continuously creating responses to what is happening outside one's skin.

5. *Then:* The working of memory is a black box.

   Now: The working of memory is a mystery, but what we do know about it can help us in designing and evaluating classroom procedures.

6. *Then:* Learning means internalizing what has been presented by teacher and textbook.

   Now: Learning means constructing new inner resources, guided partly by what is happening outside one's skin.

7. *Then:* Everyone learns in about the same way, but some people are better at it than others.

   Now: People differ markedly in how they go about constructing and using their inner resources.

8. *Then:* Experiences are stored in memory.
    Now: Information from experiences is stored in networks.

9. *Then:* Short-term memory is a stage on the way from sensory input to long-term memory.
    Now: Working memory is a state into and out of which material constantly moves in the complex traffic between the external world and long-term memory.

10. *Then:* Memory for a particular item is either strong or weak.
    Now: The networks from which the item must be reconstructed are more or less rich and complex.

11. *Then:* A new stimulus from the senses simply activates a corresponding response in memory.
    Now: Activation from a new stimulus spreads through the networks of memory in complex ways.

12. *Then:* Learners should be able to let the teacher bear responsibility for making the choices that guide the study process.
    Now: The teacher should constantly seek opportunities to develop learner independence, autonomy and responsibility.

13. *Then:* The chief end for the learner to pursue is accurate and fluent control of the phonological patterns and structural devices of the language, with vocabulary sufficient for his or her needs.
    Now: The chief end for the learner is his or her own voice (and ear!) in a new speech community.

14. *Then:* "To learn" is the passive form of the very active verb "to teach."
    Now: "To learn" is the main verb. "To teach" is an auxiliary verb.

Ecclesiastes put his conclusions about living into a nutshell:

□ Fear God.
□ And keep God's commandments.

My own additional conclusions about the part of life we call teaching are:

□ Recognize and respect the whole complex person, not only in each student, but in yourself and your colleagues as well.
□ And teach accordingly.

It was also Ecclesiastes who observed that of the making of many books there is no

END

Nikijaliwa, nikijaliwa, nimejaliwa.

REFERENCES

Abbs, Brian & Sexton, Malcolm. 1978. *Challenges.* London: Longman.

Abel, Ernest L. 1971. Marihuana and memory: Acquisition or retrieval? *Science,* 173, 1038–1040.

Ahsen, A. 1981. Imagery approach in the treatment of learning disability. *Journal of Mental Imagery*, 5, 157–196.

Ahsen, A. 1984. ISM: The triple code model for imagery and psychophysiology. *Journal of Mental Imagery*, 8(4), 15–43.

Ahsen, A. 1987. Principles of unvivid experience: The Girdle of Aphrodite. *Journal of Mental Imagery*, 11(2), 1–52.

Allen, Scott W., & Larry L. Jacoby. 1990. Reinstating study context produces unconscious influences of memory. *Memory and Cognition*, 18(3), 270–278.

Allibone, S. Austin. 1876. *Prose quotations from Socrates to Macaulay.* Philadelphia: Lippincott.

Allwright. R. L. 1984. The importance of interaction in classroom language learning. *Applied Linguistics*, 5(2), 156–171.

Anderson, J. R. 1984. Spreading activation. In J. R. Anderson & S. Kosslyn (eds.), *Tutorials in learning and memory,* 61–90. San Francisco: Freeman.

Anthony, E. 1963. Approach Method and Technique. *English Language Teaching,* 17(3), 63–66.

Ard, Josh. 1989. A constructivist perspective on non-native phonology. In Susan M. Gass & Jacquelyn Schachter (eds.), *Linguistic perspectives on second language acquisition*, 243–259. New York: Cambridge University Press.

Asher, J. J. 1965. The strategy of the total physical response: An aapplication to learning Russian. *International Review of Applied Linguistics*, 3, 292–299.

Asher, J. J., JoAnne Kusudo, & R. de la Torre. 1974. Learning a second language through commands: The second field test. *Modern Language Journal*, 58, 24–32.

Atkinson, R. C. 1975. Mnemotechnics in second language learning. *American Psychologist*, 30(8), 821–828.

Atkinson, R. C., & R. M. Shiffrin. 1968. Human memory: A proposed system and its central processes. In K. W. Spence & J. T. Spence (eds.), *The psychology of learning and motivation*, 2:90–122. New York: Academic Press.

Bachman, J. G. 1964. Motivation in a task situation as a function of ability and control over the task. *Journal of Abnormal and Social Psychology*, 69, 272–281.

Baddeley, A., & G. Hitch. 1974. Working Memory. In G. Bower (ed.), *Education Psychology of Learning and Motivation.* London: Academic Press.

Baddeley, A. 1986. *Memory,* 42. Oxford: Clarendon Press.

Bahrick, Harry P. 1984a. Semantic memory content in permastore: Fifty years of memoy for Spanish learned in school. *Journal of Experimental Psychology: General,* 113, 1–29.

Bahrick, Harry P. 1984b. Associations and organization in cognitive psychology: A reply to Neisser. *Journal of Experimental Psychology: General,* 113, 36–37.

Bahrick, Harry P. 1984c. Notice of "Academic memories: The long goodbye," by B. Bower. *Journal of Experimental Psychology: General,* 113:36–37.

Bantista, Rudy. 1971. My father and my son. In T. D. Allen (ed.), *Arrow III*. N.P.: Pacific Grove Press.

Barber, Elizabeth 1980. Language acquisition and applied linguists. *ADFL Bulletin* 12:26–32.

Barnes, Vincent G. 1991. Review of *Doublespeak* by William Lutz. *TESOL Quarterly*, 24(3), 517–518.

Baron, Jonathan, & Anne Kaiser. 1975. Semantic components in children's errors with pronouns. *Journal of Psycholinguistic Research*, 4(4), 303–318.

Bartlett, F. C. 1932. *Remembering: A study in experimental and social psychology*. Cambridge: Cambridge University Press.

Baumbach, Jonathan (ed.). 1970. *Writers as teachers/Teachers as writers*. New York: Holt.

Bedford, David. 1985. Spontaneous playback of the second language. *Foreign Language Annals*, 18, 279–287.

Bégin, Y. 1971. *Evaluative and emotional factors in learning a foreign language*. Montreal: Bellarmin.

Bennis, W. G. 1964. Patterns and vicissitudes in T-group development. In Bradford et al. (eds.), Chapter 9.

Benson, D. F. & N. Geschwind. 1967. Shrinking retrograde amnesia. *Journal of Neurology and Neurosurgical Psychiatry*, 26, 127–135.

Berne, E. 1964. *Games people play*. New York: Grove Press.

Benne, E. 1972. *What do you say after you say hello?* New York: Bantam.

Bernhardt, Bill. 1995. Energy: Input and output. *Questions*, no. 12, 29–31.

Bjork, R. A. 1970. Repetition and rehearsal mechanisms in models for STM. In D. Norman (ed.), *Models of human memory*, 307–330. New York: Academic Press.

Blackmore, Susan. 1987. Where am I?: Perspectives in imagery and the out-of-body experience. *Journal of Mental Imagery*, 11(2), 53–66.

Bley-Vroman, Robert 1989. What is the logical problem of foreign language learning? In Susan M. Gass & Jacquelyn Schachter (eds.), *Linguistic perspectives on second language acquisition*, 41–68. New York: Cambridge University Press.

Block, David. 1990. Seeking new bases for SLA research: Looking to cognitive science. *System*, 18(2), 167–176.

Blubaugh, J. A. 1969. Effects of positive and negative audience feedback on selected variables of speech behavior. *Speech Monographs*, 36, 131–137.

Bogoch, Samuel 1968. *The biochemistry of memory, with an inquiry into the function of the brain mucoids*. Oxford: Oxford University Press.

Bond, Otto F. 1953. *The reading method*. Chicago: University of Chicago Press.

Borden, R. A., & A. C. Busse. 1925. *Speech correction*. New York: Crofts.

Bosco, Fred, & Robert DiPietro. 1971. Instructional strategies: Their psychological and linguistic bases. In R. C. Lugton (ed.), *Toward a cognitive approach to second language acquisition*, 31–52. Philadelphia: Center for Curriculum Development.

Bower, Bruce. 1988. Chaotic connections. *Science News*, 133(4), 58–59.

Bower, G. H., & D. Winzenz. 1970. Comparison of associative learning strategies. *Psychonomic Sciences*, 20, 119–120.

Bowers, Jeffrey S. 1994. Does implicit memory extend to legal and illegal nonwords? *Journal of Experimental Psychology: Learning, Memory, and Cognition*, 20(3), 534–549.

Boxer, Diana, & Lucy Pickering. 1995. Problems in the presentation of speech acts in ELT materials: The case of complaints. *English Language Teaching Journal*, 49(1), 44–58.

Bradford, L. P., J. R. Gibb, & K. D. Benne (eds.). 1964. *T-Group theory and laboratory method.* New York: Wiley.

Bradley, V. A., & M. E. Thompson. 1984. Residual ability to use grapheme–phoneme conversion rules in phonological dyslexia. *Brain and Language,* 22, 292–302.

Bransford, John D. 1979. *Human cognition.* Belmont, CA: Wadsworth.

Brennen, Tim, Thom Baguley, Jim Bright, & Vicki Bruce. 1990. Resolving semantically induced tip-of-the-tongue states for proper nouns. *Memory and Cognition,* 18(4), 339–347.

Brierly, J. B. 1966. Some aspects of the disorders of memory due to brain damage. In Richter (ed.), 25–37.

Brown, Adam (ed.). 1991. *Teaching English pronunciation: A book of readings.* London: Routledge.

Brown, H. Douglas. 1987. *Principles of language learning and teaching: Second edition.* Englewood Cliffs, NJ: Prentice-Hall.

Brown, Marvin. 1968. *Language Center Thai Course.* Bangkok: A. U. A. Language Center.

Brown, Roger, & Richard J. Herrnstein. 1981. Icons and images. In Ned Block (ed.), 1981 *Imagery,* 19–30. Cambridge, MA: MIT Press.

Brumfit, C. J. 1979. "Communicative" language teaching: An educational perspective. In C. J. Brumfit & K. Johnson (eds.), *The communicative approach to language teaching,* 183–191. Oxford: Oxford University Press.

Bruner, Jerome. 1967. *Toward a theory of instruction.* Cambridge, MA: Harvard University Press.

Bryant, David J. 1990. Implicit associative responses influence encoding in memory. *Memory and Cognition,* 18(4), 348–358.

Bub, D., & A. Kertesz. 1982. Deep agraphia. *Brain and Language,* 17, 146–165.

Bugelski, B. R. 1962. Presentation time, total time, and mediation in paired associate learning. *Journal of Experimental Psychology,* 63, 409–412.

Carlson, Richard A., Marc A. Sullivan, & Walter Schneider. 1989. Practice and working memory effects in building procedural skill. *Journal of Experimental Psychology: Learning, Memory, and Cognition,* 15(3), 517–526.

Carrell, Patricia L., Becky G. Pharis, & Joseph C. Liberto. 1989. Metacognitive strategy training for ESL reading. *TESOL Quarterly,* 23(4) 647–678.

Carrier, Mark, & Harold Pashler. 1992. The influence of retrieval on retention. *Memory and Cognition,* 20(6), 633–642.

Carroll, John B. 1966. The contributions of psychological theory and educational research to the teaching of foreign languages. In A. Valdman (ed.), *Trends in language teaching,* 93–106. New York: McGraw-Hill.

Carroll, Susanne. 1989. Second-language acquisition and the computational paradigm. *Language Learning,* 39(4), 535–594.

Carroll, Susanne, & Merrill Swain. 1993. Explicit and implicit negative feedback: An empirical study of the learning of linguistic generalizations. *Studies in Second Language Acquisition,* 15(3), 357–386.

Casey, Edward S. 1976. *Imagining: A phenomenological study.* Bloomington: Indiana University Press.

Celce-Murcia, Marianne. 1993. Review of *Learning strategies in second language acquisition,* by Michael O'Malley & Anna Uhl Chamot. *TESOL Quarterly,* 27(1), 115–118.

Ceraso, J. 1967. The interference theory of forgetting. *Scientific American,* 216, 117–124.

Chafe, W. L. 1973. Language and memory. *Language,* 49, 261–281.

Chastain, Kenneth. 1971. *The development of modern language skills: Theory to practice.* Philadelphia: Center for Curriculum Development.

Chastain, Kenneth. 1975. Affective and ability factors in second language acquisition. *Language Learning,* 25, 153–161.

Church, Barbara A., & Daniel L. Schacter. 1994. Perceptual specificity of auditory priming: Implicit memory for voice intonation and fundamental frequency. *Journal of Experimental Psychology: Learning, Memory, and Cognition,* 20(3), 521–533.

Ciccone, D. S. 1973. Massed and distributed item repetition in verbal discrimination learning. *Journal of Experimental Psychology,* 101, 396–397.

Clark, Herbert H., & Eve V. Clark. 1977. *Psychology and language: An introduction to psycholinguistics.* New York: Harcourt Brace Jovanovich.

Clément, Richard, Zoltan Dörnyei, & Kimberly Noels. 1994. Motivation, self-confidence, and group cohesion in the foreign langauge classroom. *Language Learning,* 44(3), 417–448.

Clifford, B. R., & C. R. Hollin. 1981. Effects of the type of incident and the number of perpetrators on eyewitness memory. *Journal of Applied Psychology,* 66(3), 364–370.

Coggins, Truman E., & Robert L. Carpenter. 1981. The Communicative Intention Inventory: A system for observing and coding children's early intentional communication. *Applied Psycholinguistics,* 2(3), 235–251.

Cohen, Andrew D. 1987. The use of verbal and imagery mnemonics in second-language vocabulary learning. *Studies in Second Language Acquisition,* 9(1), 43–62.

Coles, Robert. 1971. The middle Americans. Boston: Atlantic Press, Little, Brown.

Craik, Fergus I. M. 1973. A levels of analysis view of memory. In P. Pliner et al. (eds.), *Communication and affect: Language and thought,* 45–66. New York: Academic Press.

Craik, Fergus I. M., & R. S. Lockhart. 1972. Levels of processing: A framework for memory research. *Journal of Verbal Learning and Verbal Behavior,* 2, 671–684.

Cubelli, Roberto. 1991. A selective deficit for writing vowels in acquired dysgraphia. *Nature* 353, 258–60.

Curran, Charles A. 1968. *Counseling and psychotherapy.* New York: Sheed and Ward.

Curran, Charles A. 1972. *Counseling-learning: A whole-person model for education.* New York: Grune and Stratton.

Dark, Veronica J. 1990. Switching between memory and perception: Moving attention or memory retrieval? *Memory and Cognition,* 18(2), 119–127.

Darley, C. F., & B. M. Murdock. 1971. Effects of prior free recall testing on final recall and recognition. *Journal of Experimental Psychology,* 91, 66–73.

Davis, James N. 1988. Review of Ruth Garner 1987. *Metacognition and reading comprehension. Language Learning,* 38(4), 615–620.

Deese, J. 1959. Influence of inter-item associative strength upon immediate free recall. *Psychological Reports,* 5, 305–312.

de Guerrero, Maria. 1987. The din phenomenon: Mental rehearsal of the second language. *Foreign Language Annals,* 20, 537–548.

Dickel, M. J. 1983. Principles of encoding mnemonics. *Perceptual and Motor Skills,* 57, 111–118.

Dickel, M. J., & S. Slak. 1983. Imagery vividness and memory for verbal material. *Journal of Mental Imagery,* 7(1), 121–126.

Dickinson, David K. 1984. First impressions: Children's knowledge of words gained from a single exposure. *Applied Psycholinguistics,* 5(4), 359–373.

Diller, K. 1971. *Generative grammar, structural linguistics, and language learning.* Newburyport, MA: Newbury House.

Diller, K. 1978. *The language teaching controversy.* Rowley, MA: Newbury House.

Diller, K (in progress). *Language teaching at the millennium: The perfect method vs. the Garden of Variety.*

Dörnyei, Zoltán. 1990. Conceptualizing motivation in foreign-language learning. *Language Learning,* 40(1), 45–78.

Dulay, H., M. Burt, & S. D. Krashen. 1982. *Language two.* Oxford: Oxford University Press.

Dunlosky, John, & Thomas O. Nelson. 1992. Importance of the kinds of cue for judgments of learning (JOLs) and the delayed JOL effect. *Memory and Cognition,* 20(4), 374–380.

Dunlosky, John, & Thomas O. Nelson. 1994. Does the sensitivity of judgments of learning (JOLs) to the effects of various study activities depend on when the JOLs occur? *Journal of Memory and Language, 33,* 545–565.

Earhard, M. 1970. Individual differences in subjective organization. *Psychonomic Sciences, 18,* 220–221.

Easterbrook, J. A. 1959. The effect of emotion on cue utilization and the organization of behavior. *Psychological Review,* 66(3), 183–201.

Eckman, Fred R. 1985. Some theoretical and pedagogical implications of the Markedness Differential Hypothesis. *Studies in Second Language Acquisition,* 7(3), 289–307.

Ehrman, Madeline E., & Rebecca L. Oxford. 1995. Cognition plus: Correlates of language learning success. *Modern Language Journal,* 79(1), 67–89.

Elliott, George. 1970. Teaching writing. In Baumbach (ed.), 45–59.

Ellis, N. R., D. K. Detterman, D. Runcie, R. B. McCarver, & E. M. Craig. 1971. Amnesic effects in STM. *Journal of Experimental Psychology, 2,* 357–361.

Ellis, Rod. 1986. *Understanding second language acquisition.* Oxford: Oxford University Press.

Felder, Richard M., & Eunice R. Henriques. 1995. Learning and teaching styles in foreign and second language education. *Foreign Language Annals,* 28(1), 21–31.

Fendrich, David W., Alice F. Healy, & Lyle E. Bourne Jr. 1991. Long-term repetition effects for motoric and perceptual procedures. *Journal of Experimental Psychology: Learning, Memory, and Cognition,* 17(1), 137–151.

Ferguson, Erika L., & Mary Hegarty. 1994. Properties of cognitive maps constructed from texts. *Memory and Cognition,* 22(4), 455–473.

Ferrand, Ludovic, Jonathan Grainger, & Juan Segui. 1994. A study of masked form priming in picture and word naming. *Memory and Cognition,* 22(4), 431–441.

Finocchiaro, Mary, & Christopher Brumfit. 1983. *The functional-notional approach: From theory to practice.* Oxford: Oxford University Press.

Fischman, M. G. 1985. Comparison of two methods of teaching the breast stroke to college-age nonswimmers. *Perceptual and Motor Skills,* 61(2), 459–462.

Flowerdew, John. 1990. Problems of speech act theory from an applied perspective. *Language Learning,* 40(1), 79–105.

Fowler, M. J., M. J. Sullivan, & B. R. Ekstrand. 1973. Sleep and memory. *Science, 179,* 302–304.

Fox, Barbara, & Donald K. Routh. 1975. Analyzing spoken language into words, syllables, and phonemes: A developmental study. *Journal of Psycholinguistic Research,* 4(4), 331–342.

Frankel, Irene, & Cliff Meyers. 1991. *Crossroads 1.* New York: Oxford University Press.

Frensch, Peter A., & Caroline S. Miner. 1994. Effects of presentation rate and individual differences in short-term memory capacity on an indirect measure of serial learning. *Memory and Cognition,* 22(1), 95–110.

Freudenstein, Reinhold. 1992. Wählen sie kanal 93! Info Daf, 5(19), 543–550.

Fuster, J. M., & G. E. Alexander. 1971. Neuron activity related to short-term memory. *Science,* 173, 652–654.

Gardiner, John M., & Rosalind I. Java. 1990. Recollective experience in word and nonword recognition. *Memory and Cognition,* 18(1), 23–30.

Gardiner, John M., & Alan J. Parkin. 1990. Attention and recollective experience in recognition memory. *Memory and Cognition,* 18(6), 579–583.

Gardner, Howard, & Thomas Hatch. 1989. Multiple intelligences go to school: Educational implications of the theory of multiple intelligences. *Educational Researcher,* 18(8), 4–10.

Gardner, R. C., & W. E. Lambert. 1972. *Attitudes and motivation in second-language learning.* Rowley, MA.: Newbury House.

Gardner, R. C., & P. F. Tremblay. 1994. On motivation, research agendas, and theoretical frameworks. *Modern Language Journal,* 78, 359–368.

Gartman, L. M., & N. F. Johnson. 1972. Massed versus distributed repetition of homographs: A test of the differential-encoding hypothesis. *Journal of Verbal Learning and Verbal Behavior,* 11, 801–808.

Gathercole, S., & M. Conway. 1988. Exploring long-term modality effects: Vocalization leads to best retention. *Memory and Cognition,* 16(2), 110–119.

Gattegno, Caleb. 1972. *Teaching foreign languages in schools: The Silent Way.* New York: Educational Solutions.

Gattegno, Caleb. 1973. *The universe of babies.* New York: Educational Solutions.

Geen, Russell G. 1974. Effects of evaluation apprehension on memory over intervals of varying length. *Journal of Experimental Psychology,* 102(5), 908–910.

Gehring, Robert E., & Michael P. Toglia. 1989. Recall of pictorial enactments and verbal descriptions with verbal and imagery study strategies. *Journal of Mental Imagery,* 13(2), 83–98.

Gibb, J. R. 1961. Defensive communication. *Journal of Communication,* 11, 141–148.

Gibb, J. R. 1964. Climate for trust formation. In Bradford et al. (eds.), 279–299.

Gibson, Eleanor, & Harry Levin. 1975. *The psychology of reading.* Cambridge, MA: MIT Press.

Giffin, K. 1967. Interpersonal trust in small-group communication. *Quarterly Journal of Speech,* 53, 224–234.

Glanzer, M., & A. Meinzer. 1967. The effects of intralist activity on free recall. *Journal of Verbal Learning and Verbal Behavior.* 6, 928–935.

Glisky, E. L., & J. C. Rabinowitz. 1985. Enhancing the generation effect through repetition of operations. *Memory and Cognition,* 11, 193–205.

Goldstein, Kurt. 1963. *The Organism.* Boston: Beacon Press.

Goodglass, Harold, Jean C. Theurkauf, & Arthur Wingfield. 1984. Naming latencies as evidence for two modes of lexical retrieval. *Applied Psycholinguistics,* 5(2), 135–146.

Granit, Ragnar. 1977. *The purposive brain.* Cambridge, MA: MIT Press.

Green, Celia, & William Leslie. 1987. The imagery of totally hallucinatory or "metachoric" experiences. *Journal of Mental Imagery,* 11(2), 67–74.

Greenburg, Dan. 1965. *How to be a Jewish mother.* Los Angeles: Price, Stern, Sloan.

Gregg, Kevin R. 1989. Second language acquisition theory: The case for a generative perspective. In Gass & Schachter (eds.), 15–40.

Groberg, D. 1972. *Mnemonic Japanese.* Salt Lake City: Interac.

Guiora, A. Z. 1970. Transpositional research in the clinical process. *Comprehensive Psychiatry,* 11(6), 531–538.

Guiora, A. Z. 1972. Construct validity and transpositional research: Toward an empirical study of psychoanalytic concepts. *Comprehensive Psychiatry,* 13, 139–150.

Guiora, A. Z., B. Beit-Hallahmi, Robert C. L. Brannon, & C. Y. Dull. 1972. The effects of experimentally induced ego states on pronunciation of a second language: An exploratory study. *Comprehensive Psychiatry,* 13(5), 421–428.

Guiora, A. Z., Harlan I. Lane, & L. A. Bosworth. 1967. An exploration of some personality variables in authentic pronunciation of a second language. In H. Lane & E. Zale (eds.), *Studies in language and language behavior,* 261–266. Ann Arbor: University of Michigan Press.

Gurowitz, E. M. 1969. *The molecular basis of memory.* Englewood Cliffs, NJ: Prentice-Hall.

Hallgarten, Katherine. 1988. Student autonomy: Learner training and self-directed learning. In Nicholls & Hoadley-Maidment (eds.), 108–121.

Halliday, M.A.K. 1978. *Language as social semiotic: The social interpretation of language and meaning.* London: Edward Arnold.

Halliday, M.A.K. 1993. The act of meaning. In James E. Alatis (ed.), *Language, communication, and social meaning: Proceedings of the 1992 Georgetown University Round Table on Languages and Linguistics,* 7–21. Washington, DC: Georgetown University Press.

Hamilton, Vernon. 1983. *The cognitive structures and processes of human motivation and personality.* Chichester, UK: John Wiley and Sons.

Hammadou, Joann. 1991. Interrelationships among prior knowledge, inference, and language proficiency. *Modern Language Journal,* 75(1), 27–38.

Hammerly, Hector. 1985. *An integrated theory of second language teaching, and its practical consequences.* Blaine, WA: Second Language Publications.

Hanley, Gerard L., & Donna Chinn. 1989. Stress management: An integration of multidimensional arousal and imagery theories with case study. *Journal of Mental Imagery,* 13(2), 107–118.

Harris, Thomas A. 1967. *I'm OK—You're OK.* New York: Harper and Row.

Hartnett, Dayle Davidson. 1985. Cognitive style and second-language learning. In Marianne Celce-Murcia (ed.), *Beyond basics,* 17–34. Rowley, MA: Newbury House.

Hatch, Evelyn, Yasuhiro Shirai, & Cheryl Fantuzzi. 1990. The need for an integrated theory: Connecting modules. *TESOL Quarterly,* 24(4), 697–716.

Hawkes, John. 1970. The Voice Project: An idea for innovation in the teaching of writing. In Baumbach (ed.), 96–105.

Hayakawa, S. I. 1962. Conditions of success in communication. *Bulletin of the Menninger Clinic,* 26(5), 225–236.

Hebb, Donald. 1974. *The organization of behavior.* New York: Wiley.

Hill, Jane H. 1970. Foreign accents, language acquisition, and cerebral dominance revisited. *Language Learning,* 20, 237–248.

Hirshman, Elliott, & Neil Mulligan. 1991. Perceptual interference improves explicit memory but does not enhance data-driven processing. *Journal of Experimental Psychology: Learning, Memory, and Cognition,* 17(3), 507–513.

Ho, Belinda. 1995. Using lesson plans as a means of reflection. *English Language Teaching Journal,* 49(1), 66–71.

Hogan, R. M., & W. Kintsch. 1971. Differential effects of study and test trials on long-term recognition and recall. *Journal of Verbal Learning and Verbal Behavior,* 10, 562–567.

Holec, H. 1981. *Autonomy and foreign language learning.* Oxford, UK: Pergamon Press.

Hollin, C. R. 1984. Arousal and eyewitness memory. *Perceptual and Motor Skills,* 58, 266.

Hosenfeld, Carol. 1992. Review of *Learning strategies in second language acquisition,* by Michael O'Malley & Anna Uhl Chamot. *Modern Language Journal,* 76(2), 235–236.

Höweler, Marijke. 1972. Diversity of word usage as a stress indicator in an interview situation. *Journal of Psycholinguistic Research,* 1(3), 243–248.

Hydén, H., & P. W. Lange. 1968. Protein synthesis in the hippocampal pyramidal cells of rats during a behavioral test. *Science,* 159, 1370–1373.

Ilfeld, F. W., & E. Lindemann. 1971. Professional and community: Pathways toward trust. *American Journal of Psychiatry,* 128, 583–589.

Jacoby, L. L. 1983. Remembering the data: Analyzing interactive processes. *Journal Of Verbal Learning and Verbal Behavior,* 22, 485–508.

Jakobovits, L. A. 1970. Prolegomena to a theory of competence. In R. C. Lugton (ed.), *English as a second language: Current issues,* 1–39. Philadelphia: Center for Curriculum Development.

Jakobovits, L. & B. Gordon. 1974. *The context of foreign language teaching.* Rowley, MA: Newbury House.

Jamieson, D.G., & G. Schmipf. 1980. Self-generated images are more effective mnemonics. Journal of Mental Imagery, 4(2), 25–33.

Janney, Charles, Jr. 1958. *Smith and Thompson's first year Latin.* Boston: Allyn and Bacon.

Jersild, Arthur T. 1955. *When teachers face themselves.* New York: Teachers College Press.

Johnson, George. 1991. *In the palaces of memory.* New York: Knopf.

Johnston, William A., Kevin J. Hawley, & John M. G. Elliott. 1991. Contribution of perceptual fluency to recognition judgments. *Journal of Experimental Psychology: Learning, Memory, and Cognition,* 17(2), 210–223.

Jordan, Charles S. 1984. Psychophysioligy of structural imagery in post-traumatic stress disorder. *Journal of Mental Imagery,* 8(4), 51–66.

Kail, Robert, Catherine A. Hale, Laurence B. Leonard, & Marilyn A. Nippold. 1984. Lexical storage and retrieval in language-impaired children. *Applied Psycholinguistics,* 5(1), 37–49.

Kamano, D. K., & J. E. Drew. 1961. Selectivity in memory of personally significant material. *Journal of General Psychology,* 65, 25–32.

Kasper, Loretta F. 1993. The keyword method and foreign language vocabulary learning: A rationale for its use. *Foreign Language Annals,* 26(2), 244–251.

Keatley, Catharine W., John A. Spinks, & Beatrice de Gelder. 1994. Asymmetrical cross-language priming effects. *Memory and Cognition,* 22(1), 70–84.

Kelly, Louis G. 1969. *Twenty-five centuries of language teaching.* Newburyport, MA: Newbury House.

Kingston, John, & Randy L. Diehl. 1994. Phonetic knowledge. *Language,* 70(3), 419–454.

Kintsch, W., E. J. Crothers, & C. C. Jorgensen. 1971. On the role of semantic processing in short-term retention. *Journal of Experimental Psychology,* 90, 96–101.

Klapp, S. T., E. A. Marshburn, & P. T. Lester. 1983. Short-term memory does not involve the "working memory" of information processing: The demise of a common assumption. *Journal of Experimental Psychology: General,* 112(2), 240–264.

Klatzky, Roberta L. 1984. *Memory and awareness: An information-processing perspective.* New York: W. H. Freeman.

Klein, G. S. 1956. Perception, motives, and personality. In J. L. McCary (ed.), *Psychology of personality*, 173–185. New York: Grove Press.

Kleinberg, J., & H. Kaufman. 1971. Constancy in STM: Bits and chunks. *Journal of Experimental Psychology*, 90, 326–333.

Kleinsmith, L. J., & S. Kaplan. 1963. Paired-associate learning as a function of arousal and interpolated interval. *Journal of Experimental Psychology*, 65, 190–193.

Kliegl, Reinhold, & Ulman Lindenberger. 1993. Modeling intrusions and correct recall in episodic memory: Adult age differences in encoding of list context. *Journal of Experimental Psychology: Learning, Memory, and Cognition*, 19(3), 617–637.

Koch, B. R. 1972. Report on intercultural workshop in Germany. *Communique: Newsletter of Intercultural Communications Programs.*

Kosslyn, Stephen M. 1984. Mental representation. In Stephen M. Kosslyn & John R. Anderson (eds.), *Tutorials in learning and memory*, 91–128. San Francisco: Freeman.

Kozlowski, Lynn T. 1977. Effects of distorted auditory and of rhyming cues on retrieval of tip-of-the-tongue words by poets and nonpoets. *Memory and Cognition*, 5(4), 477–481.

Krashen, Stephen D. 1982. *Principles and practice in second language acquisition.* Oxford, UK: Pergamon Press.

Krashen, Stephen D. 1983. The din in the head, input, and the Second Language Acquisition Device. *Foreign Language Annals*, 16, 41–44.

Krashen, Stephen D. 1993. Some unexpected consequences of the Input Hypothesis. In James E. Alatis (ed.), *Strategic interaction and language acquisition: Theory, practice, and research*, 6–21. Washington, DC: Georgetown University Press.

Krashen, Stephen D., & Tracy Terrell. 1983. *The natural approach.* Oxford, UK: Pergamon/Alemany.

Krumm, H. J. 1973. Interaction analysis and microteaching for the training of modern language teachers. *International Review of Applied Linguistics*, 11, 163–170.

Kunihara, S., & J. J. Asher. 1965. The strategy of the total physical response: An application to learning Japanese. *International Review of Applied Linguistics*, 3, 271–289.

Labov, W. 1966. *The social stratification of English in New York City.* Washington, DC: Center for Applied Linguistics.

Lado, Robert. 1965. Memory span as a factor in second language learning. *International Review of Applied Linguistics*, 3, 123–130.

Lado, Robert, T. V. Higgs, & J. Edgerton. 1971. The relationship of thought and memory in linguistic performance: "Thought" exercises in foreign language teaching. USOE Contract No. OEC-0-70-1626.

LaForge, P. 1971. Community language learning: A pilot study. *Language Learning*, 21, 45–61.

LaForge, P. 1975. *Research profiles with community language learning.* Apple River, IL: Counseling-Learning Institutes.

Lambert, Wallace. 1962. Psychological approaches to the study of languages. In *Seminar in Language and Language Learning: Final Report,* 63–90. Seattle: University of Washington.

Larsen-Freeman, Diane. 1986. *Techniques and principles in language teaching.* New York: Oxford University Press.

Larson, Donald N., & William A. Smalley. 1972. *Becoming bilingual.* New Canaan, CT: Practical Anthropology.

Leather, Jonathan, & Allan James. 1991. The acquisition of second language speech. *Studies in Second Language Acquisition,* 13(3), 305–342.

Lennon, Paul. 1989. Introspection and intentionality in advanced second-language acquisition. *Language Learning,* 39(3), 375–396.

Leow, Ronald P. 1993. To simplify or not to simplify: A look at intake. *Studies in Second Language Acquisition* 15(3), 333–356.

Lesgold, Alan M. 1984. Acquiring expertise. In Stephen M. Kosslyn & John R. Anderson (eds.), *Tutorials in learning and memory,* 31–60. San Francisco: Freeman.

Levertov, Denise. 1970. The untaught teacher. In Baumbach (ed.), 145-191.

Lewis, C. S. 1952. *Mere Christianity.* Westwood, NJ: Barbour.

Lewis, M., & R. Freedle. 1973. Mother–infant dyad: The cradle of meaning. In Pliner et al. (eds.), *Communication and affect: Language and thought,* 127–155. New York: Academic Press.

Libit, E. C., & D. R. Kent. 1970. *The Secondary school level.* In Nelson et al. (eds.), 78–81.

Lipson, A. 1971. Some new strategies for teaching oral skills. In R. C. Lugton (ed.), *Toward a cognitive approach to second language acquisition,* 231–244. Philadelphia: Center for Curriculum Development.

Logan, Gordon D., & Michael A. Stadler. 1991. Mechanisms of performance improvement in consistent mapping memory search: Automaticity or strategy shift? *Journal of Experimental Psychology: Learning, Memory, and Cognition,* 17(3), 478–496.

Logie, Robert H., Kenneth J. Gilhooly, & Valerie Wynn. 1994. Counting on working memory in arithmetic problem solving. *Memory and Cognition,* 22(4), 395–410.

Loomis, J. L. 1959. Communication, the development of trust, and cooperative behavior. *Human Relations,* 12, 309–315.

Lott, A. J., B. E. Lott, & M. L. Walsh. 1970. Learning of paired associates relevant to differentially liked persons. *Journal of Personality and Social Psychology,* 16, 274–283.

Loveday, Leo. 1982. *The sociolinguistics of learning and using a non-native language.* Oxford, UK: Pergamon Press.

Luborsky, L. 1971. Introduction to Rapaport 1971.

Lugton, R. C. (ed.). 1970. *English as a second language: Current issues.* Philadelphia: Center for Curriculum Development.

Lugton, R. C. (ed.). 1971. *Toward a cognitive approach to second language acquisition.* Philadelphia: Center for Curriculum Development.

Luria, A. R. 1968. *The mind of a mnemonist.* New York: Basic Books.

Luria, A. R. 1974. Language and brain: Towards the basic problem of neurolinguistics. *Language and Brain,* 1(1), 1–14.

Lyon, H. C. 1971. *Learning to feel—Feeling to learn.* New York: Merrill.

Martin, E., K. H. Roberts, & A. M. Collins. 1968. Short-term memory for sentences. *Journal of Verbal Learning and Verbal Behavior,* 7, 560–566.

Maslow, Abraham H. 1970. *Motivation and personality.* 2d ed. New York: Harper and Row.

MacCarthy, Peter. 1978. *The teaching of pronunciation.* Cambridge: Cambridge University Press.

MacIntyre, Peter D., & R. C. Gardner. 1989. Anxiety and second-language learning: Toward a theoretical clarification. *Language Learning,* 39(2), 251–275.

MacIntyre, Peter D., & R. C. Gardner. 1991. Investigating language class anxiety using the focused essay technique. *Modern Language Journal*, 75(3), 296–304.

McClain, Lucinda. 1983. Color priming affects Stroop interference. *Perceptual and Motor Skills*, 56, 643–651.

McLaughlin, Barry. 1987. *Theories of second language acquisition*. London: Arnold.

McLaughlin, Barry. 1990. "Conscious" versus "unconscious" learning. *TESOL Quarterly*, 24(4), 617–634.

McNamara, Timothy P. 1994. Theories of priming: 2. Types of primes. *Journal of Experimental Psychology: Learning, Memory, and Cognition*, 20(3), 507–520.

Mehan, H. 1972. Language using abilities. *Language Sciences*, 22, 1–10.

Melton, A. W. 1970. The situation with respect to the spacing of repetitions and memory. *Journal of Verbal Learning and Verbal Behavior*, 9, 596–606.

Metcalfe, Maryse. 1966. Problems of memory in man. In Derek Richter (ed.), *Aspects of learning and memory*, 5–14. New York: Basic Books.

Meyer, D. E., R. W. Schvaneveldt, & M. G. Ruddy. 1974. Functions of graphemic and phonemic codes in visual word recognition. *Memory and Cognition*, 2, 309–321.

Miles, Christopher, Dylan M. Jones, & Clare A. Madden. 1991. Locus of the irrelevant speech effect in short-term memory. *Journal of Experimental Psychology: Learning, Memory, and Cognition*, 17(3), 578–584.

Miles, Matthew. 1964. The T group and the classroom. In Bradford et al. (eds.), 465–477.

Miller, G. A. 1951. *Language and communication*. New York: McGraw-Hill.

Miller, G. A. 1956. The magical number seven, plus or minus two: Some limits on our capacity for processing information. *Psychological Review*, 63, 81–97.

Miller, G. E., J. R. Levin, & M. Pressley. 1980. An adaptation of the keyword method to children's learning of foreign verbs. *Journal of Mental Imagery*, 4(2), 57–61.

Miller, Harry. 1964. *Teaching and learning in adult education*. New York: Maccmillan.

Mitchell, Rosamond. 1994. The communicative approach to language teaching: an introduction. In Swarbrick (ed.), 33–42.

Modigliani, V., & J. G. Seamon. 1974. Transfer of information from short- to long-term memory. *Journal of Experimental Psychology*, 102, 768–772.

Molfese, Dennis L. 1985. Electrophysiological correlates of semantic features. *Journal of Psycholinguistic Research*, 14(3), 289–299.

Morris, C. D., J. D. Bransford, & J. J. Franks. 1977. Levels of processing versus transfer appropriate processing. *Journal of Verbal Learning and Verbal Behavior*, 16, 519–533.

Moskowitz, G. 1968. The effects of training foreign language teachers in interaction analysis. *Foreign Language Annals*, 1, 218–235.

Moskowitz, G. 1971. Interaction analysis—A new modern language for supervisors. *Foreign Language Annals*, 5, 211–221.

Moskowitz, G. 1974. How does your classroom go? *English Teaching Forum*, 12(2), 361.

Moskowitz, G. 1978. *Caring and sharing in the foreign language class*. Rowley, MA: Newbury House.

Mozer, Michael C. 1983. Letter migration in word perception. *Journal of Experimental Psychology: Human Perception and Performance*, 9(4), 531–546.

Murphey, Tim. 1990. The song stuck in my head phenomenon: A melodic din in the LAD? *System*, 18, 53–64.

Murphey, Tim. 1995. Identity and beliefs in language learning. *The Language Teacher*, 19(4), 34–36.

Nairne, James S. 1990. A feature model of immediate memory. *Memory and Cognition*, 18(3), 251–269.

Nattinger, James R., & Jeanette S. DeCarrico. 1992. *Lexical phrases and language teaching.* Oxford: Oxford University Press.

Nayak, Nandini, Nina Hansen, Nancy Krueger, & Barry McLaughlin. 1990. Language-learning strategies in monolingual and multilingual adults. *Language Learning,* 40(2), 221–244.

Neisser, Ulric. 1984. Interpreting Harry Bahrick's discovery: What confers immunity against forgetting? *Journal of Experimental Psychology: General,* 113, 32–35.

Nelson, Gayle, & Thomas Schmid. 1989. ESL reading: Schema theory and standardized texts. *TESOL Quarterly,* 23(3), 539–543.

Nelson, R. J., L. A. Jakobovits, F. del Olmo, D. R. Kent, W. E. Lambert, E. C. Libit, J. W. Torrey, & G. R. Tucker. 1970. Motivation in foreign language learning. In J. A. Tursi (ed.), 31–104.

Nelson, Thomas O. 1971. Savings and forgetting from LTM. *Journal of Verbal Learning and Verbal Behavior,* 10, 568–576.

Newmark, L. How not to interfer with language learning. *International Journal of American Linguistics,* 32, 77–83.

Nicholls, Sandra, & Elizabeth Hoadley-Maidment. 1988. *Current issues in teaching English as a second language to adults.* London: Edward Arnold.

Nida, Eugene A. 1972. Sociopsychological problems in language mastery and retention. In P. Pimsleur & T. Quinn (eds.), *The psychology of second language learning.* Cambridge: Cambridge University Press.

Nunan, David. 1988. *The learner-centered curriculum.* New York: Cambridge University Press.

O'Brien, Edward J., & Jason E. Albrecht. 1991. The role of context in accessing antecedents in text. *Journal of Experimental Psychology: Learning, Memory, and Cognition,* 17(1), 94–102.

Oller, J. W. 1971. Language use and foreign language learning. *International Review of Applied Linguistics,* 9, 161–168.

O'Malley, Michael, & Anna Uhl Chamot. 1990. *Learning strategies in second language acquisition.* New York: Cambridge University Press.

Osborn, Anne G., J. P. Bunker, L. M. Cooper, G. S. Frank, & E. R. Hilgard. 1967. Effects of thiopental sedation on learning and memory. *Science,* 157, 574–576.

Ott, C. E., D. C. Butler, R. S. Blake, & J. P. Ball. 1973. The effect of interactive-image elaboration on the acquisition of foreign language vocabulary. *Language Learning,* 23, 197–206.

Oxford, Rebecca. 1990. *Language learning strategies: What every teacher should know.* New York: Newbury House.

Oxford, Rebecca, & Jill Shearin. 1994. Language learning motivation: Expanding the theoretical framework. *Modern Language Journal,* 78(1), 12–28.

Paolino, R. M., & H. M. Levy. 1971. Amnesia produced by spreadiing depression and ECS: Evidence for time-dependent memory-trace localization. *Science,* 172, 746–749.

Parkin, Alan J., Thomas K. Reid, & Riccardo Russo. 1990. On the differential nature of implicit and explicit memory. *Memory and Cognition,* 18(5), 507–514.

Parr, Patricia, & Stephen D. Krashen. 1986. Involuntary rehearsal of second language in beginning and advanced performers. *System,* 14(3), 275–278.

Peirce, Bonny Norton. 1995. Social identity, investment, and language learning. *TESOL Quarterly,* 20(1), 9–31.

Pennycook, Alastair. 1990. Critical pedagogy and second language education. *System,* 18(3), 303–314.

Perecman, Ellen. 1984. Spontaneous translation in aphasia. *Brain and Language*, 23, 43–63.

Perrig, W., & P. Perrig. 1988. Mood and memory: Mood-congruity effects in absence of mood. *Memory and Cognition*, 16(2), 102–109.

Peters, Ann M., & Lise Menn. 1993. False starts and fillers: Ways to learn grammatical morphemes. *Language*, 69(4), 742–777.

Peterson, L. R., & M. J. Peterson. 1959. Short-term retention of individual items. *Journal of Experimental Psychology*, 58, 193–198.

Pinkus, A. L., & K. R. Laughery. 1970. Recoding and grouping processes in STM: Effects of subject-paced presentation. *Journal of Experimental Psychology*, 85, 335–341.

Poffel, S., & H. J. Cross. 1985. Neurolinguistic programming: A test of the eye-movement hypothesis. *Perceptual and Motor Skills*, 61, 1262.

Postman, Leo, G. Keppel, & R. Zacks. 1968. Studies of learning to learn: The effects of practice on response integration. *Journal of Verbal Learning and Verbal Behavior*, 7, 776–784.

Prabhu, N. S. 1992. The dynamics of the language lesson. *TESOL Quarterly*, 26(2), 225–241.

Prator, Clifford H. 1971. Adding a second language. In R. C. Lugton (ed.), *Toward a cognitive approach to second language acquisition*, 137–152. Philadelphia: Center for Curriculum Development.

Pulvermüller, Friedemann, & John H. Schumann. 1994. Neurobiological mechanisms of language acquisition. *Language Learning*, 44(4), 681–734.

Quartermain, D., B. S. McEwen, & E. C. Azmitia Jr. 1970. Amnesia produced by ECS or cycloheximide: Conditions for recovery. *Science*, 169, 683–686.

Rabinowitz, Jan. 1990. Effects of repetition of mental operations on memory for occurrence and origin. *Memory and Cognition*, 118(1), 72–82.

Rapaport, D. A. 1971. *Emotions and memory* 5th ed. New York: International Universities Press.

Rappold, Virginia A., & Shahin Hashtroudi. 1991. Does organization improve priming? *Journal of Experimental Psychology: Learning, Memory, and Cognition*, 17(1), 103–114.

Rappoport, D. A., & H. F. Daginawala. 1968. Changes in RNA of brain induced by olfaction in catfish. *Journal of Neurochemistry*, 15, 991–1011.

Reason, John. 1984. Absent-mindedness and cognitive control. In J. E. Harris, & P. E. Morris (eds.), *Everyday memory, actions, and absent-mindedness*, 113–132. New York: Academic Press.

Reason, John, & D. Lucas. 1984. Cognitive diaries. In J. E. Harris, & P. E. Morris (eds.), *Everyday memory, actions, and absent-mindedness*, 53–70. New York: Academic Press.

Richards, Jack C., & Theodore S. Rodgers. 1986. *Approaches and methods in language teaching: A description and analysis.* New York: Cambridge University Press.

Richter, Derek. 1966. Biochemical aspects of memory. In Derek Richter (ed.), *Aspects of learning and memory*, 73–99. New York: Basic Books.

Rivers, Wilga M. 1964. *The psychologist and the foreign language teacher.* Chicago: University of Chicago Press.

Rivers, Wilga M. 1968. *Teaching foreign language skills.* Chicago: University of Chicago Press.

Rivers, Wilga M. 1972. *Speaking in many tongues.* Rowley, MA: Newbury House.

Roediger, H. L., III, & T. A. Blaxton. 1987. Effects of varying modality, surface features, and retention interval on priming in word fragment completion. *Memory and Cognition*, 15, 379–388.

Rowlinson, William. 1994. The historical ball and chain. In Swarbrick (ed.), 7–17.

Rugg, M. D. 1995. Memory and consciousness: A selective review of issues and data. *Neuropsychologia* 33(9), 1131–1142.

Rumelhart, David E. 1980. Schemata: The building blocks of cognition. In Rand J. Spiro, Bertram C. Bruce, & William F. Brewer (eds.), *Theoretical issues in reading comprehension*, 33–58. Hillsdale, NJ: Erlbaum.

Russell, W. R., & F. Newcombe 1966. Contributions from clinical neurology. In D. Richter (ed.) *Aspects of learning and memory*, 15–24. New York: Basic Books.

Sacks, Oliver. 1985. *The man who mistook his wife for a hat, and other clinical tales.* New York: Summit.

Sadow, Stephen A. 1994. "Concoctions": Intrinsic motivation, creative thinking, frame theory, and structured interactions in the language class. *Foreign Language Annals*, 27(2), 241–249.

Salas, Jesus, Hans de Groot, & Nicholas P. Spanos. 1989. Neurolinguistic programming and hypnotic responding: An empirical evaluation. *Journal of Mental Imagery*, 13(11), 79–90.

Salomon, Gavriel. 1983. The differential investment of mental effort in learning from different sources. *Educational Psychologist*, 18(1), 42–50.

Salthouse, Timothy A., Debora R. D. Mitchell, Eric Skovronek, & Renee L. Babcock. 1989. Effects of adult age and working memory on reasoning and spatial abilities. *Journal of Experimental Psychology: Learning, Memory, and Cognition*, 15(3), 507–516.

Sampson, G. 1987. Review of *Parallel distributed processing*, by David E. Rumelhart et al. *Language*, 63(4), 871–886.

Samuda, Virginia. (Ed.). 1993. Book notices on the teaching of pronunciation. *TESOL Quarterly*, 27(4), 757–776.

Santee, J. L., & H. E. Egeth. 1980. Interference in letter identification: A test of feature-specific inhibition. *Perception and Psychophysics*, 27(4), 321–330.

Schafer, Roy. 1958. Regression in the service of the ego. In Gardner Lindzey (ed.), *Assessment of human motives*, 120–129. New York: Holt, Rinehart and Winston.

Schank, Roger. 1982. *Dynamic memory: A theory of remembering in computers and people.* Cambridge: Cambridge University Press.

Schmidt, Richard. 1992: Psychological mechanisms underlying second language fluency. *Studies in Second Language Acquisition*, 14(4), 357–385.

Schmitt, Norbert 1995. The word on words: an interview with Paul Nation. *The Language Teacher,* 19(2), 5–7.

Schooler, Jonathan W., Rachel Ann Foster, & Elizabeth F. Loftus. 1988. Some deleterious consequences of the act of recollection. *Memory and Cognition*, 16(3), 243–251.

Scovel, Thomas. 1988. *A time to speak: A psycholinguistic inquiry into the critical period for human speech.* New York: Newbury House.

Schumann, John H. 1994. Where is cognition? Emotion and cognition in second language acquisition. *Studies in Second Language Acquisition*, 16(2), 231–242.

Seely, Contee, & Elizabeth Romijn. 1995. *TPR is more than commands—at all levels.* Berkeley, CA: Command Performance Language Institute.

Seliger, Herbert W. 1984. Processing universals in second language acquisition. In Fred R. Eckman, Lawrence H. Bell, & Diane Nelson (eds.), *Universals of second language acquisition*, 36–47. Rowley, MA: Newbury House.

Seliger, Herbert W., S. D. Krashen, & Peter Ladefoged. 1975. Maturational constraints in the acquisition of second language accent. *Language Sciences*, 36, 20–22.

Sharwood Smith, Michael. 1981. Consciousness-raising and the second language learner. *Applied Linguistics*, 2(2), 159–168.

Sharwood Smith, Michael. 1986. Comprehension versus acquisition: Two ways of processing input. *Applied Linguistics*, 7(3), 237–256.

Sharwood Smith, Michael. 1993. Input enhancement and instructed SLA: Theoretical bases. *Studies in Second Language Acquisition*, 15(2), 165–180.

Sheer, D. E. 1970. Electophysiological correlates of memory conolidation. In Ungar, G. (ed.) 1970 Molecular Mechanisms in Memory and Learning. Plenum Press, 177–211.

Shiffrin, R. M. 1970. Memory search. In D. Norman (ed.), *Models of human memory*, 375–447. New York: Academic Press.

Shiffrin, R. M., & W. Schneider. 1977. Controlled and automatic human information processing: 2. Perceptual learning, automatic attention, and a general theory. *Psychological Review*, 84, 127–190.

Silberman, C. 1970. *Crisis in the classroom.* New York: Random House.

Simon, H. A. 1974. How big is a "chunk"? *Science*, 183, 482–488.

Singer, J. L., & K. S. Pope. 1978. The use of imagery and fantasy techniques in psychotherapy. In J. L. Singer, & K. S. Pope (eds.), *The power of human imagination*, 3–34. New York: Plenum Press.

Smith, Edward E., & Steven A. Sloman. 1994. Similarity- versus rule-based categorization. *Memory and Cognition*, 22(4), 377–386.

Smith, Gregory J. 1985. Effects of limited-bandwidth noise on the recall of words presented orally. *Perceptual and Motor Skills*, 61, 636–638.

Smith, Marilyn Chapnik. 1991. On the recuitment of semantic information for word fragment completion: Evidence from bilingual priming. *Journal of Experimental Psychology: Learning, Memory, and Cognition*, 17(2), 234–244.

Snyder, D. M. 1982. An exploration of mood and learning. *Perceptual and Motor Skills*, 55, 727–733.

Soares, Carlos. 1984. Left-hemisphere language lateralization in bilinguals: Use of the concurrent activities paradigm. *Brain and Language*, 23, 86–96.

Sperling, G. 1960. The information available in brief visual presentations. *Psychological Monographs,* 74, 1–29.

Spolsky, Bernard. 1988. Bridging the gap: A general theory of second language learning. *TESOL Quarterly*, 22(3), 377–406.

Spolsky, Bernard. 1989. *Conditions for second language learning.* Oxford: Oxford University Press.

Stanovich, K. E., & R. F. West, 1983. On priming by a sentence context. *Journal of Experimental Psychology: General*, 112(1), 1–36.

Stern, C., & W. Stern. 1907. *Die Kindersprache.* Leipzig: Barth.

Stevick, Earl W. 1971. *Adapting and writing language lessons.* Washington, DC: Superintendent of Documents.

Stevick, Earl W. 1980. *Teaching languages: A way and ways.* Rowley, MA: Newbury House.

Stevick, Earl W. 1986. *Images and options in the language classroom.* New York: Cambridge University Press.

Stevick, Earl W. 1989. *Success with foreign languages.* Hemel Hempstead, UK: Prentice-Hall.

Stevick, Earl W. 1990a. Research on what? Some terminology. *Modern Language Journal*, 74(2), 143–153.

Stevick, Earl W. 1990b. *Humanism in language teaching.* Oxford: Oxford University Press.

Straight, H. Stephen. 1977. Consciousness as a workspace. Paper presented at the Third Annual Meeting of the Society for Philosophy and Psychology, 18–20 March 1977, at the University of Pittsburgh.

Straight, H. Stephen. 1978. Consciousness as anti-habit. In K. D. Irani, Louis Horowitz, & Gerald Myers (eds.), *Pathology and consciousness*, 1–4. New York: Haven.

Straight, H. Stephen. 1979. A redefinition of the relationship between psycholinguistics and linguistics? *International Journal of Psycholinguistics*, 6, 57–60.

Straight, H. Stephen. 1980. Structural commonalities between comprehension and production. *Revue de Phonétique Appliquée,* 55–56, 313–316.

Straight, H. Stephen. 1993. Persistent fallacies in psycholinguistic metatheory and how to overcome them. In Ron Harré, & Roy Harris (eds.), *Linguistics and philosophy*, 199–216. Oxford, UK: Pergamon Press.

Straight, H. Stephen. 1994. Some psycholinguistic arguments in favor of the Binghamton LxC model for languages across the curriculum. In H. S. Straight (ed.), *Languages Across the Curriculum: Translation Perspectives VII*, 35–46. Binghamton, NY: Center for Research in Translation.

Strasheim, Lorraine A. 1971. "Creativity" lies trippingly on the tongue. *Modern Language Journal*, 55, 339–345.

Strobel, Gabrielle. 1993. Papers presented at the 1993 annual meeting of the Society for Neuroscience. *Science News,* November 27, 1993, 367.

Sutherland, Marcia E., Jules P. Harrell, & Claudia Isaacs. 1987. The stability of individual differences in imagery ability. *Journal of Mental Imagery*, 11(1), 97–104.

Swarbrick, Ann (ed.). 1994. *Teaching modern languages.* New York: Routledge.

Szostek, Carolyn. 1994. Assessing the effects of cooperative learning in an honors foreign language classroom. *Foreign Language Annals,* 27(2), 252–261.

Taft, R. 1954. Selective recall and memory distortion of favorable and unfavorable material. *Journal of Abnormal and Social Psychology*, 49, 23–28.

Tarone, Elaine. 1983. On the variability of interlanguage systems. *Applied Linguistics*, 4(2), 142–164.

Tart, Charles T. 1987. The world simulation process in waking and dreaming: A systems analysis of structure. *Journal of Mental Imagery*, 1(2), 145–158.

Taylor, L. L., J. C. Catford, A. Z. Guiora, & H. Lane. 1971. Psychological variables and the ability to pronounce a second language. *Language and Speech*, 14, 145–157.

Thomas, Robert, & Jeffery Allen. 1991. Pattern analysis: An alternative approach to interpreting serial recall data in studies of hypermnesia. *Perceptual and Motor Skills*, 72, 193–194.

Thompson, Irene. 1987. Memory in language learning. In Anita Wenden, & Joan Rubin (eds.), *Learner strategies in language learning,* 43–56. Englewood Cliffs, NJ: Prentice-Hall.

Thompson, R. F. 1986. The neurobiology of learning and memory. *Science*, 233, 941–947.

Tiger, Lionel. 1969. *Men in groups.* New York: Random House.

Titone, Renzo. 1970. A psycholinguistic model of grammar learning and foreign language teaching. In R. C. Lugton (ed.), *ESL: Current issues*, 41–62. Philadelphia: Center for Curriculum Development.

Toffler, Alvin. 1970. *Future shock.* New York: Random House.

Treisman, A., & H. Schmidt. 1982. Illusory conjunctions in the perception of objects. *Cognitive Psychology,* 14, 107–141.

Tulving, Endel. 1962. The effect of alphabetical structuring on memorizing unrelated words. *Canadian Journal of Psychology*, 16, 185–191.

Tulving, Endel. 1969. Retrograde amnesia in free recall. *Science*, 89–90.

Tulving, Endel. 1972. Episodic and semantic memory. In E. Tulving & W. Donaldson (eds.), *Organization and memory*, 381–403. New York: Academic Press.

Tursi, J. A. (ed.). 1970. *Foreign languages and the new student*. Northeast Conference on the Teaching of Foreign Languages.

Underhill, Adrian. 1994. Sound foundations: Living phonology. Oxford, UK: Heinemann.

Underwood, Benton J. 1969. Some correlates of item repetition in free-recall learning. *Journal of Verbal Learning and Verbal Behavior*, 8, 83–94.

Underwood, Benton J. 1970. A breakdown of the total-time law in free-recall learning. *Journal of Verbal Learning and Verbal Behavior*, 9, 573–580.

VanPatten, Bill, & Teresa Cadierno. 1993. Explicit instruction and input processing. *Studies in Second Language Acquisition*, 15(2), 225–244.

Vigil, N., & J. Oller. 1976. Rule fossilization: A tentative model. *Language Learning*, 26(2), 281–296.

Wall, Harriet M., & Ann Routowicz. 1987. Use of self-generated and others' cues in immediate and delayed recall. *Perceptual and Motor Skills*, 64, 1019–1022.

Wardhaugh, R. 1971. Teaching English to speakers of other languages: The state of the art. In R. C. Lugton (ed.), *Toward a cognitive approach to second language acquisition*, 7–29. Philadelphia: Center for Curriculum Development.

Warren, Robert E. 1972. Stimulus encoding and memory. *Journal of Experimental Psychology*, 94(1), 90–100.

Wayland, Sarah C., Arthur Wingfield, & Harold D. Goodglass. 1989. Recognition of isolated words: The dynamics of cohort reduction. *Applied Psycholinguistics*, 10, 475–487.

Weinstein, Claire E., & Richard E. Mayer. 1986. The teaching of learning strategies. In Merlin C. Wittrock (ed.), *Handbook of research on teaching: Third edition*, 315–327. New York: Collier Macmillan.

Weldon, Mary Susan. 1991. Mechanisms underlying priming on perceptual tests. *Journal of Experimental Psychology: Learning, Memory, and Cognition*, 17(3), 526–541.

Wenden, Anita. 1991. *Learner strategies for learner autonomy*. Hemel Hempstead, UK: Prentice-Hall.

Wenden, Anita, & Joan Rubin. 1987. *Learner strategies in language learning*. Hemel Hempstead, UK: Prentice-Hall.

Werbos, Paul J. 1988: Paper at IEEE International Conference on Neural Networks, San Diego. Reported by Bruce Bower, *Science News* 134(6), August 6, 1988.

Whissell, Cynthia. 1991. An heuristic for the study of the effects of emotion on memory. *Perceptual and Motor Skills*, 72, 3–10.

Whitley, M. S. 1993. Communicative language teaching: An incomplete revolution. *Foreign Language Annals*, 26, 137–154.

Widdowson, Henry G. 1978. *Teaching languages as communication*. Oxford: Oxford University Press.

Widdowson, Henry G. 1989. Knowledge of language and ability for use. *Applied Linguistics*, 10(2), 128–137.

Wilson, V., & B. Wattenmaker. 1973. *Relevant, enjoyable, and live communication in foreign language*. Unpublished manuscript.

Wixted, John T., & Doug Rohrer. 1994. Analyzing the dynamics of free recall: An integrative review of the empirical literature. *Psychonomic Bulletin and Review*, 1(1), 89–106.

Wolf, Thomas. 1976. A cognitive model of musical sight-reading. *Journal of Psycholinguistic Research*, 5(2), 143–172.

Wolters, Albert M. 1985. *Creation regained.* Grand Rapids, MI: Eerdman.

Woytak, Lidia. 1992. Interview with Rohrer. *Dialog on Language Instruction*, 8(1–2), 1–28.

Zacks, R., L. Hasher, H. Sanft, & K. Rose. 1983. Encoding effort and recall: A cautionary note. *Journal of Experimental Psychology: Learning, Memory, and Cognition,* 9(4), 747–756.

Zaleznik, A., & D. Moment. 1964. *The dynamics of interpersonal behavior.* New York: Wiley.

Zuengler, Jane. 1989. Identity and IL development and use. *Applied Linguistics*, 10(1) 80–95.

Zurif, E. B., & A. Caramazza. 1974. Semantic feature representation for normal and aphasic patients. *Brain and Language*, 1(2) 167–187.

INDEX

Abel, E. L., 126
Abstractions, 14, 22, 53, 97, 100
of linguistic meaning, 15
Academic motivations, 8
Accents in native language, 151, 152
Accuracy, 81, 92, 94, 120, 121, 142, 143, 145,
    146, 151, 152, 153, 154, 164, 215–7,
    230, 232, 242, 243, 249, 254
"Acquisition" in Krashen's sense, 87, 108,
    227, 231
ACT* model of spreading activation, 33, 34
Activation, 54, 72, 82, 83, 148
Activity within networks, 57
Adapted Child (ego state), 165, 167, 168,
    170, 216, 249
Adult (ego state), 166, 167, 168, 171, 172,
    173, 180, 184, 216, 219, 221, 225
Affect, 6, 30, 50, 52, 73, 78, 103, 131, 145,
    181, 230, 231, 232, 234, 249
Affective filter, 7, 30, 100, 106, 226
Afterimages, 50
Agricultural metaphor, 196
Ahsen, Akhter, 9, 20, 49, 50, 55, 73
Aims, alternative sets of, 164
Allen, Scott W., & Larry L. Jacoby, 46, 127
Allwright, R. L., 173
Alternative pathways (see also coterminous
    pathways), 66, 69
Amnesia, 61
Analytical view of pronunciation, 142, 143
Anderson, J. R., 44, 45, 74
Anglo-Saxon, 5
"Ann", 237, 239, 241, 242
Anomie, 8
Anthony, Ed, 251
Anxiety, 30, 98, 100, 124, 142, 176, 177, 225
    "facilitating", 134
    "debilitating", 134
    communicative, 99, 100
    FL class, 100
    general, 99
    state, 99
    trait, 99
Aphasia, 6, 7
Apparitions, 85
Approach, design, and procedure, 161
Arcadian conclusions by the learner, 159,
    251

Arcadian technique, 163
Ard, J., 22, 158
Arousal, 98, 133, 134
Articulatory loop, 28
Asher, J. J., 132, 138
Associative priming, 76
Atkinson, R. C., & R. M. Shiffrin, 127
Attention, 52, 89, 91, 94, 111, 169, 223, 224,
    227
Attention hypothesis about dinning, 89
Auden, W. H., 173
Audience sensitivity, 99
Audiolingualism, 108, 162, 181, 216, 220,
    231
Authority Structures, 180
Automatic processing, 63
Autonoetic consciousness, 46
Autonomy, 160, 219, 220, 221, 222, 254

Bachman, J. G., 188
Bahrick, Harry, 44
Barber, Elizabeth, 86, 104
Barnes, Vincent G., 19
Baron, Johathan, & Anne Kaiser, 21
Barrueta, Marilyn, 167, 217
Bartlett, F. C., 16
Bedford, David, 104
Behavioral changes, 48
Bennis, W., 188
Benson, D. F., & N. Geschwind, 125
Berne, E., 173, 174, 188
Bernhardt, Bill, 233
"Bert", 237, 239, 241, 242
Biochemical aspects of memory, 25
Bjork, R. A. 126
Blackmore, Susan, 104
Bley-Vroman, R., 21, 22
Block, Ned, 18
Blubaugh, J. A., 158
Bob Hope, 17
Bogoch, Samuel, 6, 19
Bond, Otto, 126, 233
Borden, R. A., & A. C. Busse, 188
Bower, G. H., & D. Winzenz, 126
Boxer, Diana, & Lucy Pickering, 21
Bradford, L. P., J. R. Gibb, & K. D. Benne,
    188
Bradley, V. A., & M. E. Thomson, 77

Bransford, John D., 22, 42, 46, 49, 72, 74, 126
Brennen, Tim et al., 44, 105
Bridges, 109, 201ff.
Brierly, J. B., 6, 19, 125
Brown, Adam, 252
Brown, H. D., 7, 74, 106, 125, 233, 234
Brown, M., 173
Brown, Roger, & Richard J. Herrnstein, 73, 75
Brumfit, C. J. 246, 252
Bruner, Jerome, 9, 20, 134, 138, 209
Bryant, David J., 46, 74
Bub, D., and A. Kertesz, 77
Bugelski, B. R., 127

Capacity limitations, 29, 31, 44, 45, 58
Rogers, C., 188
"Carla," 21, 173, 205, 206, 207, 240, 241, 242, 243
Carlson, Richard A., Marc A. Sullivan, & Walter Schneider, 43, 45
Carrell, Patricia, Becky G. Pharis & Joseph C. Liberto, 22, 210
Carrier, Mark, & Harold Pashler, 104
Carroll, John B., 43
Carroll, Susanne, 77
Carroll, Susanne, & Merrill Swain, 76
Casey, Edward S., 18, 19, 42, 43, 73
Celce-Murcia, Marianne, 45
Ceraso, J., 126
Chafe, W., 44, 125
Chastain, Kenneth, 189
Chess, 11, 32
Child (ego state), 165, 166, 167, 168, 170, 171, 172, 221
Choosing, 39, 58, 64, 66, 80, 83, 91, 101, 114, 118, 122, 124, 143, 170, 171, 172, 183, 200, 215, 221, 226, 230, 231, 235, 248, 251
Choosing the teacher's aims, 172
Chunking, 31, 44
Chunks versus segments, 31
Church, Barbara A., & Daniel Schacter, 45, 75
Ciccone, D. S., 125
Clark, H., & E. Clark, 18, 22
Clément, Richard, Zoltan Dörnyei, & Kimberly Noels, 10, 21, 209
Clifford, B. R., & C. R. Hollin, 106
Coggins, Truman E., & Robert L. Carpenter, 20
Cognitive depth, 116

Cognitive information, 10
Cognitive operations, memory for, 11, 12
Cohen, Andrew, 21, 22
Colton, Caleb, 18
Commitment, 121, 132
Communication, 8, 93, 128, 130, 131, 136, 137, 156, 202, 217, 225, 227
Communication-oriented activity, 201
Communicative anxiety, 99, 100
Communicative approach, 199, 208
Community, 175, 186, 226
Community Language Learning, 135, 181, 223, 231, 234, 246
Comparing, 29, 39, 66, 67, 69, 78, 81, 83, 85, 91, 92, 93, 97, 101, 112, 118, 122, 169, 170, 171, 172, 223, 226, 230, 231
Comparison of working memory and long-term memory, 29
Comprehensible input, 227, 228
Comprehension, 60
Concentrated learning versus diffused learning, 107, 108
Concept-driven, 63
Conceptual networks, 53, 61
Conceptual priming, 59, 60
Conceptual structures, 7
Concreteness versus abstractness, 13
Conforming, 160, 161, 163, 166
Connectionism, 69, 77, 83
Conscious processing, 63
Consciousness-raising, 126
Construction in memory, 57, 85, 217, 254
Context, 61, 116, 215, 217, 227, 239, 243, 244, 245
Continuity, 237
"Control" versus "initiative", 173, 228
Controlling Parent (ego state), 166, 167, 168, 170, 249
Controlling Parent_Adapted Child nexus, 168
Cooperation, 165
Coping—see defending, 134
Correction of errors, 215, 216, 225, 227, 228
Corrective maintenance, 80
Coterminous pathways (variety of alternative pathways, which see), 65, 66, 67, 69, 77, 79, 81, 83, 85, 93, 97, 118, 119, 124, 149, 150, 200, 229, 230
Counseling-Learning, 223, 224, 237
"Counseling response", 184
Craik, Fergus I. M., 116, 126, 129
Craik, F., & R. S., Lockhart, 126

Crowding, 112, 113, 118, 169
Cubelli, Roberto, 44
Cued recall, 39, 41, 169
Curran, Charles A., 44, 124, 127, 134, 135, 138, 174, 176, 184, 188, 189, 209, 223, 233, 237

Dark, V., 44
Darley, C. F., & B. M. Murdock, 126, 174
Data-driven, 63
Davis, James N., 21
Dealienation, 199
Decision on familiarity, 38, 39
Declarative versus procedural, 32, 45
    knowledge, 35
    memory, 32, 42, 44
Deese, J., 127
Defending versus coping, 134
Defensiveness,
    learning, 196, 214
    reactions, 154, 197, 225, 235
Defensive versus receptive learning, 196, 212
de Guerrero, Maria, 104, 105
Delayed speech feedback, 56
Depth, 116, 128, 129, 134, 136, 137, 155, 185, 196, 197, 198
Depth of Processing, 116, 121
"Derek," 126, 241, 242
Dickel, M. J., & S. Slak, 73, 127
Dickinson, David K., 21
Differences among learners, 92, 94, 102, 103, 148, 150, 168, 213, 217, 225, 227, 253
Diffused learning, 109
Diller, Karl, 174
Dinning, 86, 87, 88, 104
Distributed practice, 112, 113, 169
Diversity, 235
DO activities in Bridge format, 203, 204, 205, 206, 208, 209, 210, 213, 216, 218, 226, 229
DO Phase, 202
Dörnyei, Zoltan, 20, 187
Dreaming, 85
Drills, 88, 130, 168, 217, 218, 227, 240, 241, 242, 243, 244, 245, 246
Dual coding model, 48, 77
Dulay, H., M. Burt & S. D. Krashen, 106, 125
Dunlosky, John, & Thomas O. Nelson, 44, 103, 104
Dyslexia, 66

Earhard, M., 126
Easterbrook, J. A., 106
Echoic activities, 214, 216, 217, 225
Echoic memory, 24
Eckman, Fred, 21
"Ed," 21
Ego boundaries, 157
Ego defenses, 197
"Ego states" of Transactional Analysis, 165, 216, 231
    in language study, 167, 235
Ego-involvement, 133
Ehrman, Madeline, 157
Ehrman, M., & R. Oxford, 134, 138, 157
Eidetic image, 50, 73
Electrical aspects of learning and memory, 24, 25, 26, 29, 30, 41, 64, 81, 109, 110, 111
Elliott, George, 189, 209
Ellis, Rod, 5, 19, 138
Emotion, 6, 7, 10, 17, 52, 94, 98, 99, 100, 111, 128, 129, 131, 132, 133, 134, 135, 141, 144, 145, 146, 154, 161, 165, 166, 176, 179, 182, 185, 198, 201, 202, 216, 218, 221, 237, 240, 253
    as organizing principle for memory, 135
Empathy, 144, 145, 146, 169
Encoding time, 79
Episodic memory or knowledge, 18, 37, 38, 42, 46, 63, 111, 123
Error correction (see Correction of errors)
Errors, 38, 85, 103, 155, 170, 200, 208, 215, 221, 224, 225, 232
Execution time, 79
Expectations, 51
Explicit (intentional) learning, 39, 44
Explicit memory, 39, 42, 46, 47, 111, 121

Fact-fict information, 129, 131
"Fear" versus "anxiety", 176
Feedback, 62, 232
    cognitive or affective, 230
    external or internal, 230
    positive or negative, 230
Felder, Richard M., & Eunice R. Henriques, 19, 209, 252
Fendrich, David W., Alice F. Healey & Lyle E. Bourne, 21, 47, 76, 103
Ferrand, Ludovic et al., 103
Files (metaphor for long-term memory), 30, 41, 57
Finocchiaro, Mary, 10
Finocchiaro, M., & C. J. Brumfit, 20

Fischman, M. G., 22
Five senses, 5, 17, 197
FL class anxiety, 100
Flaggenheisch Incident, 74, 96, 106, 108
Flashcards, 79, 84
Flowerdew, John, 21
Fluency, 152
Focus, 228
Foreign accent, 142, 145, 150, 151, 156
Forgetting, 26, 43, 74
Form is not a single entity, 55, 92
Form-meaning linkages, 49
Form-oriented activity, 201
Formants as abstractions, 14
Fossilization, 215, 228
Fowler, M. J., et al., 125
Fox, Barbara, & Donald K. Routh, 21
Fraenum fork, 182
Frankel, Irene, & Cliff Meyers, 173
Fraternal-permissive authority structure,
    181
"Fred," 127
Free recall, 39, 40, 114, 125, 170
Freedom, 160
Freeman, Donald, 232
"Freida," 21, 103, 158
Frensch, Peter A., & Caroline S. Miner, 44,
    45, 47
Freudenstein, Reinhold, 20
Fricator, 182
Functional language teaching materials, 20
Functions, 10
Fuster, J. M., & G. E. Alexander, 42

"Games" (Transactional Analysis), 167,
    176, 179, 198
Gardiner, John M., & Rosalind I. Java, 21,
    45, 46, 47, 76
Gardiner, John M. & Alan J. Parkin, 46
Gardner, Howard, & Thomas Hatch, 106
Gardner, R. C., & Wallace Lambert, 209
Gardner, R. C., and P. F. Tremblay, 20
Gartman, L. M., & N. F. Johnson, 126
Gathercole, S., & M. Conway, 127
Gattegno, Caleb, 45, 166, 173, 219
Geen, Russell G., 138
Gehring, Robert E., & Michael P. Toglia, 73
Generation by the mind, 11, 13, 50, 51, 60,
    63, 66, 75, 84, 85, 88, 103, 115, 118,
    120, 121, 123, 125, 203, 221, 224–6
  acoustic information, 121
Generation effect, 119, 121, 122, 123, 181
Gibb, J. R., 188, 189
Gibson, E., & H. Levin, 21, 22

Giffin, K., 188
Gilbert, Judy, 252
Glanzer, M., & A. Meinzer, 126
Glisky, E. L., & J. Rabinowitz, 127
Goldstein, Kurt, 174
Goodglass, Harold, Jean C. Theurkauf, &
    Arthur Wingfield, 75
Grammar-Translation, 180, 211, 231, 232,
    233
Granit, R., 17
Green, Celia, & William Leslie, 104
Gregg, Kevin R., 18, 43, 45
Groberg, D., 127
Guiora, A. Z., 143, 144, 145, 146, 157
Gurowitz, E. M., 42, 43
"Gwen," 233

Hagboldt, Peter, 126
Hallgarten, Katherine, 210
Halliday, M.A.K., 18
Hamilton, Vernon, 19, 74, 105, 106
Hammadou, Joann, 173
Hammerly, Hector, 246, 252
Hanley, Gerald L., & Donna Chinn, 73
Harris, T. A., 105, 173
Hartnett, Dayle Davidson, 252
Hatch, Evelyn, Yasuhiro Shirai, & Cheryl
    Fantuzzi, 17, 18, 42, 77, 104
Hawkes, John, 189
Hayakawa, S. I., 187
Hebb's principle, 53
Hierarchy, 9
Hierarchy of needs, 185, 186
Hill, Jane H., 157
Hirshman, Elliott, and Neil Mulligan, 104
Ho, Belinda, 209
Hogan, R. M., & W. Kintsch, 127
Holding memory, 27, 29, 41, 42, 43, 57, 65,
    102, 108, 109, 111, 112, 113, 114, 119,
    124, 132, 171, 201, 203, 206, 208, 214,
    215, 222
Holec, H., 209
Holistic view of pronunciation, 142, 143
Hollin, C. R., 106
Hosenfeld, Carol, 18
Höweler, M., 158
Human Computer™, 163
"Humanistic", 172
Hydén, H., 42
Hydén, H., & P. W. Lange, 42
Hypermnesia, 135, 136, 138

I + 1, 87
Iconic memory, 24

Identification, 37, 38, 39, 40, 45, 65, 117, 121
Ilfeld, F. W., & E. Lindeman, 188
Image, 40, 49, 51, 52, 57, 73, 84, 85, 95, 100, 118, 120, 123, 130, 169, 214, 217
  stabilization of, 85
Imagination, 19, 23, 43, 52, 62, 201, 202, 215, 218
Imagination image, 50
Implicit (incidental) learning, 39
Implicit knowledge, 35
Implicit learning, 44
Implicit memory, 39, 42, 46, 47
Implicit tasks, 39
Independence, 165, 219, 220, 221, 222, 254
Infantilisation, 136
Initiative, 164
Initiative by learners, 218
Inner criteria, 119
Inner resources, 219, 221, 253
Insincerity, 19
Integrative versus instrumental motivation, 10, 181, 198
Intelligences, 102
Intentions, 7
Interactional Analysis, 180
Interest, importance of, 87
Interests, 218
Interpersonal meaning, 159
Intrinsic motivation, 9
Involuntary auditory playback, 86
Involuntary visual playback, 90
ISM model, 49, 51, 73

Jacoby, Larry, 76
Jakobovits, L., 209
Jakobovits, L., & B. Gordon, 188
Janney, Charles, Jr., 232
Jersild, Arthur, 187, 188
Johnson, George, 43, 72, 74
Johnston, William A. et al., 45
Jordan, Charles S., 73
Judgments of learning, 80

Kamano, D. K., & J. E. Drew, 138
Kant, Immanuel, 22
Kasper, Loretta F., 127
Keatley, Catherine W., John A. Spinks, & Beatrice de Gelder, 46, 77, 74
Kelly, L. G., 251
Keyword method, 122, 123
Kinds of data stored in memory, 146
Kinesthetic, 19

Kingston, John, & Randy L. Diehl, 44
Kintsch, W. E., et al., 126
Klatzky, Roberta, 44, 45, 46, 76
Klein, G. S., 7, 19
Kleinberg, J., & H. Kaufman, 44
Kleinsmith, L. J., & S. Kaplan, 138
Kliegl, Reinhold, & Ulman Lindenberger, 18, 46
Koch, B. R., 189
Kosslyn, S., 45
Kozlowski, L., 105
Krashen, Stephen D., 47, 86, 87, 88, 89, 90, 94, 104, 105, 106, 108, 145, 153, 157, 226, 227, 228, 231
Krashen, S. D., & T. Terrell, 21, 105, 125
Krumm, H. J., 188
Kunihara, S., & J. J. Asher, 138

Labov, William, 157
LAD hypothesis about dinning, 88, 90
Lado, R., 43, 44
LaForge, P., 188
Langer, Ellen, 76
Language, 12
Language acquisition device, 87, 104
Language data and the network concept, 55
Language ego, 144
Larsen-Freeman, Diane, 233, 234
Larson, Donald N., & William A. Smalley, 209
Lathophobic aphasia, 170
Lathophobic apraxia, 174
Learner-centered teaching, 181
Learning, 4, 8, 13, 17, 45, 84, 107
"Learning" in Krashen's sense, 87, 108, 227
Leather, Jonathan, & Allan James, 158, 234
Leftovers from living and learning, 48, 57, 63
Lennon, P., 20
Leow, R. P., 76
Lesgold, Alan M., 45
Levertov, Denise, 189
Lewis, C. S., 211
Life motivations, 8, 9
Light bulb, 21
Linguistic information, kinds of, 13
Lipson, A., 138
Locke, John, 18
Logan, Gordon D., and Michael A. Stadler, 77
Logie, Robert H. et al., 43, 44

Long-term memory, 24, 26, 27, 41, 57, 62, 81, 115, 124, 169, 200, 224, 226, 229, 230
Looming, 14
Loomis, J. L., 189
Lott, A. J., B. E. Lott & M. L. Walsh, 138
Loveday, Leo, 173, 252
Loyalties, 129, 143, 151, 156, 198, 217, 230, 253
Lozanov, Georgi, 135, 137
Luborsky, L., 138
Luria, A. R., 105, 117, 127
Lyon, H. C., 187, 188

MacCarthy, Peter, 157
MacIntyre, Peter D., & R. C. Gardner, 106, 157
Managing memory, 108
Martin, E. et al., 127
Maslow, Abraham, 8, 9, 20, 143, 186, 188
Massed practice, 112, 169
Maternal-expressive authority structure, 181
Maturity and therapy of limits, 182
McClain, L., 76
McLaughlin, Barry, 18, 43, 106
McNamara, Timothy P., 76
Meaning, 3, 4, 51, 79, 141, 194
Meaningful learning versus rote learning, 125
Meanings, 131, 138, 156, 253
Meanings for the teacher, 175, 253
Mehan, H., 209
Melton, A. W., 125, 126
Memorization, 108, 115, 216, 218
Memorizing rules, 88
Memory, 3, 4, 115, 194
    as a dynamic process, 111
    as construction, 94, 95, 96, 97, 149, 150, 217
    as stages, 62
Memory image, 50
Memory is always in transition, 58, 61, 64
Mental pictures, 49
Mental videotapes, 163
Metacognition, 12
Metacognitive monitoring, 80
Metacognitive strategies, 199
Metcalfe, Maryse, 43, 125
Meyer, D. E., R. W. Schvaneveldt, & M. G. Ruddy, 76
Micro-momentary expressions, 144
Miles, Matthew, 187, 188

Miles, Christopher et al., 44, 76
Miller, George A., 44, 125, 188
Mind, 4
Minimal pairs, 125
Mitchell, Rosamond, 209
Mitchell's Principles of the Communicative Approach, 199, 212, 215, 217, 221, 225, 228
Mnemonics, 122, 123, 169
Mnemonist, 117
Modification of networks, 79, 92, 93, 94, 107, 108, 109, 111, 112, 125, 130, 134, 148, 150, 156, 169, 200, 218, 226, 229, 230, 231, 253
Modigliani, V., & J. G. Seamon, 126
Molfese, Dennis L., 21, 44
Monitoring, 47, 94, 153
"Mood", 7
Moral outrage, 247, 248
Morley, Joan, 252
Morris, C. D., J. D. Bransford & J. J. Franks, 126
Moskowitz, G., 188, 189
Motives/motivation, 7, 19, 20, 84, 156, 198
    complexity in the teacher, 177
Mozer, Michael C., 75
Multisensory images, 49, 132
Murphey, Tim, 9, 20, 105, 158
Mutual independence of the affective and the lexical/grammatical, 6
Mystery, 3

Nairne, J., 43, 44, 75
Nation, I.S.P., 79
Nattinger, James R., & Jeanette M. DeCarrico, 241, 252
Natural Approach, 226, 231, 246
Natural Child (ego state), 165, 167, 168, 216
Needs, 8, 124, 142, 169, 200, 218
Neisser, Ulric, 16, 18, 22, 43
Nelson, Thomas O., 126, 189
Nelson, Gayle, & Thomas Schmid, 22
Networks, 13, 52–54, 56, 57, 61, 64, 69, 82, 83, 88, 96, 123, 124, 169, 200, 201, 229, 254
Neurochemical changes, 48
Neurolinguistic Programming, 102
Nida, Eugene A., 158
Nodes, 53, 54
Nonelectrical storage, 25, 26, 29, 41, 57, 81, 109, 206, 229

Noticing, 29, 64, 66, 67, 92, 93, 114, 118, 122, 169, 170, 171, 172, 221, 222, 224, 226, 230, 231
Nouns, 5
Nunan, David, 173, 188, 210
Nurturing Parent (ego state), 166, 167
Nurturing Parent_Natural Child nexus, 225

Oakley's Thesis, 238, 246
O'Brien, Edward J., & Jason E. Albrecht, 74, 77
O'Malley, M., & A. U. Chamot, 45, 209
Oakley's Thesis., 234
OBSERVATION activities in Bridge format, 203, 204, 205, 208, 209, 210, 216, 218, 228
Observing, Spanning, and Doing, 213, 218, 215, 222, 225, 228
"OK/NOT-OK", 167, 176
Oller, John, 126
Operating characteristics, 10, 11, 35, 212
Oral Approach, 193
Orwell, George, 19
Osborn, Anne G. et al., 126
Ott, C. E. et al., 127
Outlook, 3, 4, 20, 30, 71, 91, 211, 237, 253f.
Out-of-body experience, 84
Output from the networks, 61
Overchoice, 143
Oxford, Rebecca, 46, 209
Oxford, R., & J. Shearin, 10, 21

Pacing, 113, 130
Paired Associates, 41
Paivio, Alan, 49, 77
"Pallid, fragmented, indefinitely localized, and brief," 50, 51, 90, 120, 130
Paolino, R. M., & H. M. Levy, 42
Parent (ego state), 165, 166, 167, 170, 171, 172, 173, 176, 219
Parkin, Alan J., Thomas K. Reid & Riccardo Russo, 46, 47, 126
Parr, Patricia, & S. D. Krashen, 104, 105
Paternal-assertive authority structure, 180
Pattern completion, 39
Pedagogical versus experimental tasks, 80, 84
Pedantry, 18
Peirce, Bonny Norton, 155, 158, 252
Perceiving, 74
Perceptual fluency, 37, 40, 45
Perceptual memory, 37
Perceptual priming, 37, 60

Perecman, E., 77
Permanent memory, 27, 42, 57, 102, 108, 109, 112, 113, 114, 124, 132, 171, 201, 202, 203, 231
Permeability of ego boundaries, 144
Personal significance, 132
Personal theories of language study, 247
Peters, Ann M., and Lise Menn, 21
Peterson, L. R., & M. J. Peterson, 43
Phonemic distinctions, 142
Phonological representations, 146
Physical changes in the nervous system, 72
Physical needs, 132
Physiological changes, 51
Pinkus, A. L., & K. R. Laughery, 126
Poffel, S., & H. J. Cross, 106
Postman L. et al., 126
Power, 156, 159, 160, 163, 165, 175, 218, 222, 223, 225, 227, 228, 235
Power structures, 175
Prabhu, N. S., 209, 225, 234, 247, 252
Practice, 148
Preventive maintenance, 80
Primacy effect, 110, 115
Primary memory, 44, 75, 116
Priming, 59, 63, 76
  associative, 76
  conceptual, 59, 60
  perceptual, 37, 60
  repetition, 76
  semantic, 76
Procedural versus declarative, 38, 45
  knowledge, 33
  memory, 42
Procedures, 33
Processual neutrality, 56, 92
Production, 38, 64
Productions, 33
Pronunciation, 119, 125, 142, 156, 240, 241, 242, 243, 252
Propositional knowledge, 33
Psychodynamic meanings of pronunciation, 142
Pulvermüller, Friedemann, & John H. Schumann, 6, 7, 19, 74, 104, 158, 234
Purpose, 4, 7, 8, 9, 10, 11, 52, 141, 144, 146, 151, 169, 172, 200, 201, 202, 216, 253

Quartermain, D. et al., 42

Rabinowitz, J., 11, 21, 127
Range in speaking, 154

Rapaport, D. A., 135, 138
Rapid complex simulation, 84, 85, 86, 93
Rappold, Virginia A., & Shahin
    Hashtroudi, 76, 126, 127
Rappoport, D. A., & H. F. Daginawala, 43
Rassias, John, 32, 167, 217
Rational-procedural authority structure, 182
Reading Method, 112, 213, 227, 231
Realities, 177, 178, 182, 183, 185, 186
Reality-testing, 182, 183
Reason, John, 106
Reason, J., & D. Lucas, 105
Reasoning, 100, 101
Recall, 36, 37, 38, 96
Recency effect, 26, 110
Receptive learning, 196, 197
Receptivity, 225
Recognition, 36, 37, 38, 39, 41, 45, 65, 96
Recollective experience, 37, 46
Record of cognitive operations, 121
Reflective versus echoic
    learning, 212, 222
    performance by the learner, 195 f.
Regression in service of the ego, 136, 145
Regularities, 35, 36, 71
Rehearsal, 64, 108
Reification, 5, 18, 26, 27, 43, 71, 87, 166
Reinforcement (Skinnerian), 79, 169
Repetition, 108
Repetition effect, 79
Repetition priming, 76
Representations, 42, 80
Response preparation, 79
Responsibility, 164, 165, 200, 218, 219, 220,
    222, 225, 228, 254
Retrieval, 58, 82
Richness and complexity, 55, 116, 124, 128,
    155, 164, 201, 202, 208
Richards, J., & T. Rodgers, 161, 173
Richter, D., 7, 19, 43
Riddle of the Right Method, 193
Rivers, Wilga, 157, 170, 189, 209
Roediger, H. L., III, & T. A. Blaxton, 127
Rogers, C., 7, 176
Rohrer, Josef, 46
Rote learning—see meaningful learning,
    125
Rowlinson, William, 252
Rules, 35, 36, 68, 70, 71, 94, 124, 220, 227,
    245
Rumelhart, David E., 22
Russell, W. R., & F. Newcombe, 125

Sacks, Oliver, 6, 19
Sadow, S., 17, 20, 22
Salas, Jesus et al., 106
Salience, 125
Salomon, Gavriel, 74, 76
Salthouse, Timothy A., Debora R. D.
    Mitchell, Eric Skovronek & Renee L.
    Babcock, 18, 43, 74
Sampson, Geoffrey, 77
Samuda, Virginia, 252
Santee, J. L., & H. E. Egeth, 21
SARD acronym, 223, 226
Schafer, Roy, 138, 157
Schank, Roger, 7, 19, 46
Schemas, 16, 63
    not hierarchical, 17
Schmidt, Richard, 44, 45, 47, 74, 77, 158
Schmitt, Norbert, 103
Schooler, Jonathan W. et al., 127
Schumann, John, 6, 19, 73
"Science of Education," (Gattegno), 219,
    221
Scovel, Tom, 45, 72, 157
Scratch pads, 28
Security, 8, 124, 167, 168, 183, 223, 224
Segments, 44
Self-actualization, 20
Self-concept, 145, 153, 156, 176, 177, 208,
    253
Self-investment, 134, 135, 237, 247, 248
Self-started performance by the learner,
    195, 196, 216, 225
Seliger, Herbert et al., 138, 157
Semantic memory, 37, 38, 42, 63
Semantic priming, 76
Sensory input, 254
Sensory persistence, 24, 201
Sensory retention, 41
Sensory material, features of, 57
Sharwood Smith, Michael, 20, 45, 126, 127,
    234
Sheer, D. E., 43
Sheikh, A., 50
Shiffrin, R. M., 126.
Shiffrin, R. M., & W. Schneider, 44, 76
Shoe-tying, 32
Shoemaker, Virginia, 158
Short-term memory, 24, 26, 28, 41, 62, 110,
    111, 113, 169, 254
Silberman, C., 187
Silent Way, 32, 119, 218, 225, 231, 234, 246
Simon, H. A., 21

Simulation by the mind, 85
Simultaneous interpreters, 32, 109, 131
Singer, J. L., & K. S. Pope, 73, 75
Size of items in memory, 13
Sleep, 111, 125
Slips of the tongue, 99
Smith, G. J., 75
Smith, M.C., 126
Smith, Edward E., & Steven A. Sloman, 74, 77
Snyder, D. M., 7, 19
Soares, C., 75
Social aspects of learning and memory, 9, 172, 243
  of feedback, 230   of motivation, 232
  of pronunciation, 143
Social identity, 156
Social meanings, 130, 161
Social needs, 132, 143, 171
Social pressures, 160, 163
Social significance of subtleties, 142
Somatic response, 49, 51
Spacing, 112
SPAN activities in Bridge format, 79, 203, 204, 205, 206, 208, 209, 210, 213, 215, 218, 222, 226, 228, 229
Speaking as a source of stress, 141
Speech acts, 21
Sperling, G., 42
Spolsky, Bernard, 14, 21
Spreading activation, 54, 57, 58, 60, 64, 72, 76, 96, 99, 106, 123, 148, 150, 254
Stability, 185
Stabilization of images, 85
State anxiety, 100
State of consciousness, 85
Stern, C., and W. Stern, 104
Stochastic, 69
Stockpiling, 79, 210
Straight, H. Stephen, 43, 74, 75, 76, 86, 104, 105, 158, 174
Strategies, 27, 29, 44, 58, 69, 77, 199
Stream of consciousness, 30, 58
Stress, 98, 99, 100, 141
Structure, need for, 242
Subjective organizing, 114, 115
Subphonemic distinctions, 147
Subvocal rehearsal, 28
Suggestive barriers to learning, 136
Suggestology, 136
Suggestopedia, 135, 138
SUNny responses, 224

Sutherland, Marcia E. et al., 19
Synesthesia, 117
Szostek, Carolyn, 252

Taft, R., 138
Tarone, Elaine, 45, 61, 76
Tart, Charles T., 104
Tasks experimental and pedagogical, 39
Taylor, L. L. et al., 157, 158
Terra Incognita, 193
Thomas, Robert, & Jeffery Allen, 138
Thompson, Irene, 127
Tiger, L., 157
Time, 13, 31, 40, 52, 64, 65, 66, 72, 74, 80, 81, 82, 84, 94, 109, 110, 111, 112, 113, 114, 119, 123, 124, 130, 134, 200, 227
Tip-of-the-tongue, 97, 106, 149
  grammatical information, 98
  meanings, 98
Titone, R., 209
Toffler, A., 157
Total Physical Response, 131, 203, 227, 246
Tradition, 235, 236
Transactional Analysis, 165, 169, 171, 176, 184, 198
Transfer-appropriate processing, 117, 121
Treisman, A., & H. Schmidt, 75
Trust, 175, 183, 185, 186
  conditions for building, 184
Tulving, E., 46, 125, 126, 138
Tulving, E., & D. Schacter, 74, 76
Tursi, J. A., 189
Two-way traffic, 29, 30, 58, 60, 61, 63, 64, 65, 67, 68, 72, 81, 93, 94, 97, 98, 99, 111, 229, 254
Type 1 and Type 2 processing, 116
Type-token ratio, 155

Underwood, B., 125, 126
Universals, 22
Utopian, 217
  conclusions by the learner, 160, 251
  technique, 162

Values, 237, 246, 248
VanPatten, Bill, 76
VanPatten, Bill, & Teresa Cadierno, 76, 234
Various societics, 9
Verbal memory, 49
Vigil, N., and J. Oller, 234
Visual images, 50
Visual memory, 49

Visualization, 115, 130
Vividness, 50, 115, 124
Voice (and ear!) in a new speech community, 185, 254

Wall, Harriet M., & Ann Routowicz, 127
Wardhaugh, Ron, 209
Warren, R. E., 74, 76
Wayland, Sarah C., Arthur Wingfield, and Harold D. Goodglass, 74, 76
Weinstein, Claire E., & Richard E. Mayer, 7, 19, 75
Weldon, M. S., 76
Wenden, Anita, 209
Wenden, Anita, & Joan Rubin, 127, 209
What I hope for in a classroom, 249
Whissell, C., 19
Whitley, M. S., 252
Widdowson, Henry, 77, 201, 210
Willingness to speak, 153, 155, 167

Willingness to use the language, 153
Wilson, Virginia, & Beverly Wattenmaker, 189
Wolf, T., 16, 22
Wolters, Albert M., 18
Wong, Rita, 252
Working memory, 26, 27, 28, 29, 41, 43, 58, 81, 82, 109, 201, 229, 254
Working memory contrasted with short-term memory, 57, 58, 65
Worktable (metaphor for working memory), 27, 28, 29, 31, 41, 54, 57, 75, 94, 110, 114, 229, 230
"Worse than average" illusion, 95, 96
Woytak, Lidia, 46

Zacks, R. L. et al., 127
Zaleznik, A., & D. Moment, 188
Zurif, E. B., & A. Caramazza, 6, 19